WHISTLEBLOWING NATION

EDITED BY KAETEN MISTRY
AND HANNAH GURMAN

WHISTLEBLOWING
NATION

The History of National Security Disclosures
and the Cult of State Secrecy

Columbia University Press / New York

Columbia University Press
Publishers Since 1893
New York   Chichester, West Sussex
cup.columbia.edu
Copyright © 2020 Columbia University Press
All rights reserved

Library of Congress Cataloging-in-Publication Data
Names: Mistry, Kaeten, 1980– editor. | Gurman, Hannah, editor.
Title: Whistleblowing nation : the history of national security disclosures and
the cult of state secrecy / edited by Kaeten Mistry and Hannah Gurman.
Description: New York : Columbia University Press, 2020. |
Includes bibliographical references and index.
Identifiers: LCCN 2019032907 (print) | LCCN 2019032908 (ebook) |
ISBN 9780231194167 (cloth) | ISBN 9780231194174 (paperback) |
ISBN 9780231550680 (ebook)
Subjects: LCSH: Whistle blowing—United States—History. |
Official secrets—United States—History. | Leaks (Disclosure of information)—
United States—History.
Classification: LCC JK468.W54 W46 2020 (print) | LCC JK468.W54 (ebook) |
DDC 353.4/60973—dc23
LC record available at https://lccn.loc.gov/2019032907
LC ebook record available at https://lccn.loc.gov/2019032908

Cover design: Milenda Nan Ok Lee

CONTENTS

CONTENTS

CONTENTS

ACKNOWLEDGMENTS

THIS VOLUME IS one part of a collaborative research project on the history of U.S. national security whistleblowing. Working on the project has been the most rewarding intellectual and personal experience. We are grateful to the people and organizations who enabled the journey and made it so enjoyable.

First, we would like to thank the UK's Arts and Humanities Research Council (AHRC) for its generous financial backing (grant AH/P00461X/1). At a time of tremendous financial strains on the humanities, this research simply could not have been completed without the AHRC's support. Thanks also to the University of East Anglia and New York University's Gallatin School of Individualized Study for providing additional assistance for the project.

We have been extremely lucky to work with so many wonderful people on this volume. It has been a stroke of good fortune to collaborate with a stellar group of scholars. Their intelligence, creativity, and commitment have given life to the book and, equally, provided companionship and good cheer on the way. This volume is a product of several dynamic and stimulating exchanges over the last few years. In many respects it is a coauthored book. The bulk of the chapters first emerged at a 2018 workshop at NYU Gallatin, where we discussed one another's essay drafts and collectively explored the broader questions examined in these pages. Those conversations over two days were pivotal in giving shape to the book and highlighting the stakes of our research. They were also tremendous fun. Thanks to all the contributors, to Chase Madar, Anders Stephanson, and Hugh Wilford for incisive commentaries, and to Gallatin for generously hosting the event.

Several colleagues and friends have assisted us since the earliest phase of the project, providing feedback, discussing ideas, contributing to events, inviting us to give talks, offering help, and providing constructive criticism and encouragement. Lloyd Gardner, Richard Immerman, Sam Lebovic, Bevan Sewell, and Kim Phillips-Fein read umpteen drafts of proposals, bids, and chapters. We suspect Lloyd and Richard ended up contributing chapters in the hope that our queries and requests for help would slow down. They didn't, but we're delighted to have included two excellent pieces by the two kindest, most generous, and most humble historians in the business. Marilyn Young was a great source of advice and support not only on this project but on our work and careers overall. Her wit and wisdom are sorely missed. We also thank Dean Susanne Wofford, Nathaniel Sikand-Youngs, David Milne, Nick Grant, Emma Long, Mario Del Pero, David Mead, Andrew Preston, John Prados, Becky Amato, DaShante Smith, Rachel Plutzer, Theresa Anderson, Mike Koncewicz, Laura Potts, Jay Sexton, Ben Wizner, Anna Myers, the staff at NYU London, and colleagues at UEA and NYU New York.

Jenny Kijowski did a marvelous job designing our project website (https://wp.nyu.edu/whistleblowing/) and was always there to help us Luddites out whenever we had questions or problems. Aaron Cedolia, KC Trommer, and their team designed a fantastic logo and created elegant posters and programs for events, often on short notice. Polly Harrison, Linda Wheeler Reiss, and Gisela Humphreys guided us through the labyrinthine world of grant budgets and spreadsheets and bravely navigated the wild transatlantic exchange-rate fluctuations. We are grateful to all of them.

A particularly satisfying part of the project has been the opportunity to discuss key questions, themes, findings, and problems with a variety of audiences. Thanks to the scholars and participants at the Society for Historians of American Foreign Relations conferences in Philadelphia and San Diego, the annual British and European Associations of American Studies gathering in London, and the Historians of the Twentieth Century United States conference in Dublin, the Trowbridge Center at the University of Illinois, and the Center for Ethics and the Rule of Law at the University of Pennsylvania. We are grateful to public audiences at talks at the 2nd Air Division Library in Norwich and the Kinder Institute on Constitutional Democracy at the University of Missouri. And thanks to all the participants of the public symposium at NYU, which was kindly cosponsored by the Tamiment Library and Gallatin's Urban Democracy Lab, and the final project conference in London. These events included a wonderful mix of scholars, journalists, NGOs, whistleblowers, and members of the public. Particular thanks to Anna Myers, Tom Devine, Ewen MacAskill, Tom Drake, John Kiriakou, Edward Snowden, and all the presenters.

At Columbia University Press, Stephen Wesley has been our editor extraordinaire. He supported and guided the project from start to finish with passion, precision, and professionalism. His sound judgment and editorial talents improved many aspects of this book, especially our introduction, joint chapter, and conclusion. Equally impressive was Stephen's disclosure on where to find moonshine. It was, fortunately, authorized and legal. Thanks as well to Christian Winting for editorial assistance, Michael Haskell for guiding the book through production, and Robert Fellman for superb copy editing.

Our families provided unconditional love and support throughout the project. They kept us going. We thank them for their patience during our absences, our many transatlantic Skype sessions, and for their companionship along the way. One of the greatest joys working on the project has been getting to know each other's families and sharing updates on the highs and lows of daily life. We dedicate this book to Sofia, Sammy, the latest arrival to the Gurmalban clan, Sara, and Joe.

INTRODUCTION

KAETEN MISTRY AND HANNAH GURMAN

T HE TWENTY-FIRST CENTURY ushered in a new age of national security whistleblowing. When Edward Snowden, a National Security Agency (NSA) contractor, made startling disclosures about the U.S. government's warrantless global surveillance programs in June 2013, he emerged as the most famous—although not the first—high-profile whistleblower of the era. Snowden followed in the footsteps of Thomas Drake (who revealed waste, fraud, and abuse in the NSA), Chelsea Manning (who divulged military and diplomatic cables on the wars in Iraq and Afghanistan), Stephen Kim (who disclosed North Korea's nuclear capacities in protest of official U.S. policy), and John Kiriakou (who exposed CIA torture of al-Qaeda detainees), among others. Alarmed by the reincarnation of the World War I–era Espionage Act to prosecute dissenting government officials, the documentary filmmaker Robert Greenwald and others warned of a "war on whistleblowers." The struggle has continued into the Donald Trump administration, with the conviction of Reality Winner for exposing evidence about Russian interference in the 2016 U.S. presidential election, the arrest of Daniel Hale for disclosing further details of the secretive U.S. drone program, and the dramatic revelations by whistleblowers in the national security establishment of Trump's dealings with the president of Ukraine.[1]

The response to Snowden's revelations proved that attitudes toward national security whistleblowing are ambiguous and paradoxical. The U.S. national security establishment immediately condemned him and brought charges carrying a possible sentence of decades in prison. Barack Obama said, "If any individual who objects to government policy can take it in their own hands to publicly disclose classified information, then we will never be able to keep our people safe or conduct foreign policy." Bemoaning the "avalanche of unauthorized disclosures," the president said, "Our nation's defense depends in part on the fidelity of those entrusted with our nation's secrets."

While he condemned the messenger, Obama simultaneously heralded the democratic dialogue the message instigated. Announcing reforms for the embattled NSA, he insisted that "important decisions about how to protect ourselves and sustain our leadership in the world" had to be reconciled with "the civil liberties and privacy protections our ideals and our Constitution require." How could the nation balance security and civil liberty in the wake of Snowden's revelations? "One thing I'm certain of," said Obama, "this debate will make us stronger."[2]

The phenomenon of national security whistleblowing has a long, revealing genealogy in the United States. Snowden's act and Obama's resolute denunciation have replayed themselves in every generation since the early twentieth century, and a pattern has emerged. An insider discloses privileged national security information, often to the press, in the name of the public interest. The U.S. government condemns the act as an "unauthorized disclosure" that undermines American security and leadership and moves to prosecute. In the public debate, the whistleblower is celebrated as a patriot or condemned as a traitor. Eventually, questions about the legitimacy of the disclosure and the character of the whistleblower overtake public consideration of the contents of the revelation. The pattern is well established. It plays out with virtually every new case of whistleblowing.

The most famous historical episode remains Daniel Ellsberg. Ellsberg was a strategic analyst with the RAND Corporation and a former Pentagon official who contributed to an internal Defense Department study about U.S. decision making in the Vietnam War. In 1971, he disseminated this report, the top-secret Pentagon Papers, to the *New York Times*. Ellsberg avoided prosecution because of the shenanigans of the White House "plumbers," created to curb similar "leaks," and became a touchstone for modern whistleblowers.

When we focus on recent events and canonical cases, we forget earlier and equally consequential moments of whistleblowing. Over eighty years before Snowden, a cryptologist named Herbert O. Yardley published secret details of the first U.S. cryptanalysis agency in a book that celebrated American codebreaking and lamented the group's disbandment in peacetime. The Franklin D. Roosevelt administration censored Yardley (after prosecution was deemed infeasible) and revised the espionage statutes to prohibit government employees from disseminating information gleaned from code.

Testifying before Congress in 1968, an executive at the Air Force named A. Ernest Fitzgerald revealed gross overspending in avionics and defense to a congressional subcommittee, for which the Nixon administration fired him. Fitzgerald's reputation was only rehabilitated amid efforts to enact limited whistleblower protections in a post-Nixonian political age.

In 1975, in an effort to curb CIA interventionism abroad, Philip Agee exposed U.S. covert action by detailing Agency "tradecraft" and revealing the identity of officers and agents through information in the public domain. Agee lived in exile, but the Carter and Reagan administrations revoked his passport, censored his writing, and cited his case to enact the 1982 Intelligence Identities Protection Act.[3]

Whether famous or forgotten, celebrated or neglected, such episodes and the developments around them have shaped the modern face of whistleblowing, the tools of state retaliation, and the response in the public consciousness.

* * *

This book presents the first comprehensive history of U.S. national security whistleblowing. With a wide historical lens, it looks beyond the reductive characterization of whistleblowers as heroes or traitors and rejects the notion of a simple choice between civil liberty and security. It eschews a biographical, case-by-case approach and the binary framing adopted by much social science and legal scholarship on the issue. Instead, it charts the evolving and intertwined histories of national security whistleblowing and the national security state since the early twentieth century. While the specific labels were popularized in later decades, the origins of both can be traced to the start of the century. Whistleblowing is, of course, not unique to the United States. But the scale and frequency with which it occurs is. The developments we examine exist within distinctly American political, legal, and cultural contexts that shaped the phenomenon in the modern era.

Whistleblowing remains highly contentious terrain. As chapter 1 reveals, there is little consensus on how to define and identify a national security whistleblower. The term carries sharply contrasting meanings in political, legal, civic, and cultural contexts. While the state insists that any revelation constitutes an "unauthorized disclosure," popular narratives emphasize the importance of transparency as a salve to the ills of democracy. The ongoing divide encourages isolated political and social debates on the subject that reinforce existing frameworks. There is a pressing need for a multidisciplinary history that explores how we arrived at this impasse and how it has served as a barrier to a fuller understanding of the phenomenon and its significance.

Although there is no settled definition, national security whistleblowing is distinguished by several key characteristics: a revelation of privileged (not necessarily "secret") information by a state insider seeking to challenge the status quo, a form of dissent that invokes public interest and the need to break the rules of the system if necessary, an individual whose identification authenticates the information being exposed, routine state retaliation, and civic and political contests over the legitimacy and significance of the revelation and whistleblower.

National security whistleblowing is far from homogenous. It encompasses a range of ideological and political positions, motives, and objectives. While it resembles whistleblowing in the corporate and state sectors, it involves "national defense" information—classified but also unclassified information—which historically has placed it in a different category. It is also often conflated with "leaks," but there are important distinctions between the two. Leaking is typically anonymous, highly political, and rarely punished. Blurring the line between whistleblowing and leaking—often a political move intended to stigmatize both—occludes important distinctions. Leaking is frequently sanctioned by the very officials that condemn whistleblowers.

The following pages offer a conceptual, chronological, and thematic account of national security whistleblowing in the *longue durée*. It uses an expansive and multidisciplinary approach that draws on political, legal, cultural, social, and diplomatic history alongside research on state power, social movements, and dissent, as well as personal experience. Examining the emergence and evolution of whistleblowing, it analyzes the concerns of whistleblowers from waste, corruption, and flawed decision making to covert wars and the surveillance state. It traces the networks and structures that have enabled disclosures and the state reflex to criminalize them indiscriminately. The book also traces how efforts to prosecute whistleblowers tapped broader constitutional nerves, stirring resistance by Congress, the press, and the public. In Hollywood movies, documentaries, magazines, and novels, the whistleblower became a significant cultural icon.

Informing broader developments in modern American politics, law, culture, and society, whistleblowing has shaped the rise of the national security state, the classification regime, and understandings of First Amendment rights. It has provided the public with unprecedented insights into the cult of state secrecy and shed light on the overt and covert dimensions of American power, from involvement in World War I to the Cold War to the Vietnam War to armed conflicts in Iraq and Afghanistan in the twenty-first century, from secret codebreaking at the turn of the twentieth century to covert operations in the Global South to the modern surveillance state.

Years after Snowden's revelations, the whistleblower remains the subject of intense political struggle. On the campaign trail, Donald Trump raged that "Snowden is a traitor and a disgrace" and suggested he "should be executed." Mike Pompeo, who would become CIA director and secretary of state, said Snowden deserved the death penalty.[4] Under Trump,

Reality Winner became the first successful prosecution via the Espionage Act. In September 2019, reports of an intelligence community whistleblower who revealed the contents of Trump's phone call with the leader of Ukraine dramatically kickstarted impeachment proceedings. President Trump retaliated with threats of violent punishment: "You know what we used to do in the old days when we were smart? . . . With spies and treason? We used to handle it a little differently than we do now."[5] The historic war against whistleblowers continues to escalate. Yet this will not stop whistleblowing. Despite efforts since World War I to curb the phenomenon, the next disclosure is a matter of *when*, not *if*.

NOTES

1. Robert Greenwald, dir., *War on Whistleblowers: Free Press and the National Security State*, (Culver City, CA: Brave New Films, 2013); John Hudson, "Obama's War on Whistle-Blowers," *Atlantic*, May 24, 2011, https://www.theatlantic.com/politics/archive/2011/05/obamas-war-whistle-blowers/351051/; Harry Litman and Molly Knobler, "Trump's War on Leaks Is Really a War on Whistleblowers," CNN, August 9, 2017, https://edition.cnn.com/2017/08/09/opinions/whistleblowers-opinion-litman-knobler/index.html; Amy Goodman, "Trump Steps Up War on Whistleblowers with Arrest of Veteran," *Truthout*, May 10, 2019, https://truthout.org/video/trump-steps-up-war-on-whistleblowers-with-arrest-of-veteran/.

2. "Transcript of President Obama's Jan. 17 Speech on NSA Reforms," *Washington Post*, January 17, 2014, https://www.washingtonpost.com/politics/full-text-of-president-obamas-jan-17-speech-on-nsa-reforms/2014/01/17/fa33590a-7f8c-11e3-95564a4bf7bcbd84_story.html.

3. Malcolm Gladwell, "Daniel Ellsberg, Edward Snowden, and the Modern Whistle-Blower," *New Yorker*, December 19 and 26, 2016; Kaeten Mistry, "Embarrassing Indiscretions: The Origins and Culture of U.S. National Security Whistleblowing," in *The Culture of Intelligence: Germany, Britain, France, and the USA*, ed. Andreas Gestrich et al. (Oxford: Oxford University Press, forthcoming); Kaeten Mistry, "A Transnational Protest Against the National Security State: Whistleblowing, Philip Agee, and Networks of Dissent," *Journal of American History* 106, no. 2 (September 2019): 362–89; Hannah Gurman, "National Security Whistleblowing: The Creation of a Legal Paradox," paper for the Navigating Law and Ethics at the Crossroads of Journalism and National Security conference, University of Pennsylvania Center for Ethics and the Rule of Law, November 9–10, 2017.

4. Donald J. Trump (@realDonaldTrump), Twitter, May 30, 2014, https://twitter.com /realdonaldtrump/status/472447734860218369, and October 30, 2013, https://twitter.com /realDonaldTrump/status/395683702757662721; "Trump's CIA Pick Rep. Mike Pompeo Thinks Snowden Deserves Death Penalty," C-Span, November 18, 2016, https://www. c-span.org/video/?c4631588/trumps-cia-pick-rep-mike-pompeo-thinks-snowden -deserves-death-penalty.

5. Maggie Haberman and Katie Rogers, "Trump Attacks Whistle-Blower's Sources and Alludes to Punishment for Spies," *New York Times*, September 26, 2019, https://www .nytimes.com/2019/09/26/us/politics/trump-whistle-blower-spy.html. The Ukraine-whistleblowing issue was unfolding as this book went to press.

1

THE PARADOX OF NATIONAL SECURITY WHISTLEBLOWING

Locating and Framing a History of the Phenomenon

HANNAH GURMAN AND KAETEN MISTRY

T HERE IS A central paradox to national security whistleblowing: It is a
phenomenon widely recognized yet systemically denied.

In public and civic discourse, whistleblowing is treated as a central feature of democracy, a remedy to the ills of excessive government
secrecy, corruption, and abuses of power. Whistleblowers are often
enshrined in the tradition of civil disobedience, heroes acting for the greater
good. The government, meanwhile, unequivocally rejects this premise and
insists that any public revelation of national security information is an
"unauthorized disclosure" that threatens the security of the nation. The legal
and legislative frameworks stem from the executive position, shaping the
norms and discourses within the state. National security whistleblowing is
not officially recognized but is nonetheless invoked as an existential threat.[1]

Curiously, there is no history of the phenomenon. While whistleblowing in the corporate sector has a vast literature, there has yet to be a systematic historical analysis of national security disclosures. In part, this
absence is rooted in the highly divisive nature of the topic and disagree-
ment over the concept. Scholars face methodological hurdles and difficulties in addressing a subject on which there is essentially no historiography. Whistleblowing, as both a term and act, is rarely found in archives or
discussed at academic events. Several critical episodes also unfolded before

the notion of whistleblowing gained widespread appeal in the 1970s; before then, those who revealed government secrets were not considered whistleblowers and did not identify themselves as such. Terms like "leaker" and labels like "unauthorized disclosure" conflate distinct situations. The terrain is contested, and the terms are fuzzy, posing challenges to locating and framing national security whistleblowing. Yet the history of the phenomenon is instructive and too important to ignore.

The history shows a deeper pattern that has characterized and shaped whistleblowing since the early twentieth century. An individual with access to privileged information and government programs unveils the secretive—not necessarily "secret"—world of the state in the name of the public interest. This disclosure provokes indiscriminate state retaliation, regardless of motive, ideology, or objective. Questions of legitimacy and the significance of the exposure are debated in the civic and public realms while the state persecutes the whistleblower. The cycle repeats in every generation. Embedded within this dynamic are critical yet unexamined facets of U.S. global power, mechanisms of state secrecy, executive authority, and prospects for civil liberty, including First Amendment rights, freedom of the press, democratic accountability, and the public's right to know.

This chapter addresses the key questions involved in tracing the history of whistleblowing: What is it, and how is it distinct from other forms of disclosure? When and where did the concept originate, and how did it develop over time? Who determines the benefits and costs of exposure? What is its relationship to the national security state and the expanding secrecy regime? Why and how have whistleblowers been retaliated against? How effective have legal protections been? Why does the very definition and framework of whistleblowing continue to be contested to this day?

In this historicization of whistleblowing, we highlight the uniqueness of the official secrecy apparatus in the United States and its development over the twentieth century in response to the exposure of national defense information. In so doing, we introduce national security whistleblowing as a critical phenomenon of historic and contemporary significance.

This book does not look to flatten the discussion by advancing a single thesis. However, it does offer a critical historical perspective that challenges the state's attempts to deny the existence of national security whistleblowing and civil society's efforts to idealize it. In lieu of such normative perspectives, the following chapters show how state secrecy has evolved in perennial tension with avowed principles of U.S. democracy. They underscore the historical limits of truth and revelation as a substitute for wider political struggle.

But tracing the history of whistleblowing need not be an exercise in fatalism. For those seeking alternative ways forward, the historical perspective is essential. It reminds us that the frameworks we operate under were not born but made. Over the last century, whistleblowers, politicians, advocacy groups, intellectuals, writers, and filmmakers have collectively wrestled with the scope, meaning, and legacy of whistleblowing. They have forged and challenged the central paradox of this phenomenon. The history of national security whistleblowing involves contingency and improvisation and has critical consequences for the present and future.

THE HISTORY OF THE CONCEPT
OF WHISTLEBLOWING

Whistleblowing is a modern idea that emerged in America during the twentieth century. Although themes and ideas commonly associated with it, such as dissent and protest, have a longer history—and while the term has been applied to some who lived centuries ago—whistleblowing as a concept and practice developed in response to the exponential growth and increasingly unchecked power of corporations and the state. It is, of course, not unique to the United States. But it grew in the context of American political, legal, and social events, and the term entered popular usage in the 1970s.

The whistleblowing metaphor draws on the whistle as an image of regulation and fairness. Used for thousands of years as musical instruments and toys, whistles became tools and symbols for the implementation of rules in Victorian England. Designed in the early 1870s by the British inventor

Joseph Hudson, the brass whistle, also known as the "Acme" whistle, originated as a novelty. In 1883, Hudson's newly designed, louder pea whistle won a competition held by the Metropolitan Police Service to improve communication among bobbies on the beat as they maintained law and order on the streets of London. In 1884, the first sports whistle, the "Acme Thunderer," was used to referee a football match, thereafter becoming a regular feature of sporting events.[2] In sports and policing, the shrill blast of the whistle commanded attention, signaling a pause in which to ascertain and remedy the breaking of rules.

In P. G. Wodehouse's comical Jeeves and Wooster series, the wise servant tells the story of the grammarian who "blew the whistle" on his buffoonish master's "spelling and dictation." In Raymond Chandler's 1953 hardboiled detective novel *The Long Goodbye*, a tough cop threatens to arrest the gumshoe detective for accessory to murder. "Come on, Marlowe," he says, "I'm blowing the whistle on you."[3] Early uses of the metaphor by politicians were of a piece with these cultural invocations. Perpetuating the anticommunist zeal of the early Cold War period, in 1963 Senator Strom Thurmond, an arch-conservative, praised Otto Otepka, who had disclosed confidential files on suspected State Department liberal "dissidents," and defended this act of "whistle-blowing."[4] But whistleblowing was still inchoate as a political and civic act.

The turning point came in the early 1970s. As cracks in the American postwar order and Cold War consensus grew wider, whistleblowing began to crystallize into a more left-leaning philosophy and movement for legal reform. Beginning as a challenge to unchecked corporate power, it quickly spread to encompass government wrongdoing.

A thirty-six-year-old lawyer named Ralph Nader played a crucial role in popularizing the whistleblowing metaphor as a noble civic action. In the wake of his best-selling 1965 book *Unsafe at Any Speed*, which prompted the creation of federal safety standards for automobiles, Nader decided that making corporations and governments accountable to the public required the cooperation of people working in those organizations. While many insiders were troubled by the wrongs they witnessed or participated in, few were willing to speak out. Nader and his gaggle of likeminded young lawyers and law students, known as "Nader's Raiders," sought to inspire a culture where professionals developed a sense of vocational duty to the public that transcended loyalty to bosses. Drawing on traditions of civil disobedience, Nader called it an "ethic of whistleblowing."[5]

In January 1971, Nader's newly created group, the Clearinghouse for Professional Responsibility, hosted a conference on professional responsibility at the Mayflower Hotel in Washington. In his keynote address, Nader spoke in heroic terms about the "act of a man or woman who, believing that the public interest overrides the interest of the organization he serves, publicly 'blows the whistle' if the organization is involved in corrupt, illegal, fraudulent, or harmful activity."[6] Whereas the referee blows a whistle to enforce the rules of a particular sport and the police officer blows a whistle to enforce the laws of the state, Nader's whistleblower protected a broader and more abstract entity, the "public interest."

The conference proceedings were published as a seminal 1972 treatise, *Whistle Blowing*, which Nader coedited with Peter Petkas and Kate Blackwell. In the same year, the editors of the *Washington Monthly*—a new periodical that provided a forum for state officials willing to speak out and expose government corruption—published *Blowing the Whistle*, in praise of dissenters working in the public interest to further the right to know.[7]

The emerging philosophy of whistleblowing built upon the Progressive legal tradition of the early twentieth century, when reform-minded lawyers like Louis Brandeis framed justice as a struggle between ordinary individuals—the "public"—and corporate monopolies, the "interests." Inheritors of Enlightenment liberalism, Brandeis and other public-interest lawyers believed in the role of rational thought in politics, the promise of the public sphere as a site of democratic debate, and the centrality of law in protecting basic freedoms. Nader was tapping this tradition, rooted in staunch defense of free speech and greater transparency. "Sunlight is said to be the best of disinfectants," Brandeis famously declared, "electric light the most efficient policeman."[8]

Over half a century later, the new public-interest lawyers took up the mantle from their Progressive Era peers.[9] They played a key role in the emerging "right to know" movement, popularized by Rachel Carson's *Silent Spring*, a 1962 exposé of the public health and environmental harms caused by chemical corporations.[10] "A well informed citizenry is the lifeblood of democracy," Nader wrote, "and in all arenas of government, information, particularly timely information, is the currency of power." The movement lobbied for citizen access to government information, partially achieved through the 1966 Freedom of Information Act (FOIA).[11]

The new public-interest lawyers reflected the dramatic changes taking place in politics and political thought during the 1960s. But unlike their Progressive forbears, who regarded the state as a protector of the people, they were more suspicious of the state, which they associated with violence, capitalist collusion, and threats to individual freedom. Herbert Marcuse, an intellectual icon of the New Left, warned that the institutions of modern society threatened to entrench "the power of the whole over the individual.[12] "The organization," Nader said, "has emerged and spread its invisible chains" to cement the "tyranny of organizations."[13] But in contrast to the New Left, which distrusted the law as an instrument of the powerful, the new public-interest lawyers regarded law as a tool of reform and embraced the ethics of professionalism. As insiders, professionals were uniquely privy to the ills of the system; the key was to reorient professional ethics to serve the public. A whistleblower, according to Nader, was "anyone in any organization who draws a line in his own mind where responsibility to society transcends responsibility to his organization."[14]

Although it drew on the ideas of the European New Left as well as on Marxist critiques of the ruling class's domination over workers, this philosophy of whistleblowing was distinctly American, steeped in the ideology of classical liberalism and personal freedom and conditioned by the Cold War. Targeting the "organization" as the central threat, *Whistle Blowing* evoked 1950s critiques of homogeneity and workplace convention that stifled creativity, youth, and individuality in postwar American society, including the best-selling books *The Organization Man*, by William H. Whyte, and *Growing Up Absurd*, by Paul Goodman, as well as Sloan Wilson's novel *The Man in the Gray Flannel Suit*. Whistleblowing advocates also drew on earlier critiques of totalitarian bureaucracy; Nader contrasted whistleblowers to Nazis who "just followed orders."[15]

Muckraking journalism, which had contributed to significant social and political reform during the Progressive Era, reemerged in the 1960s in the form of investigative reporting that challenged the consensual state-press culture of the early Cold War. The work of Seymour Hersh, Bob Woodward, and Carl Bernstein in the *New York Times* and *Washington Post*—which relied on anonymous leaks—grabbed the headlines, although a host of smaller magazines and underground media also fostered whistleblowing. Magazines like *Ramparts* and the *Village Voice*, with links to the New Left and 1960s counterculture, drew on insiders to expose CIA covert operations at home and abroad.[16] The *Washington Monthly*, less hostile to the state but eager for a vigilant fourth estate that kept government honest, began publishing in 1969.

Whistleblowing had entered the popular lexicon and was increasingly prominent in public and political discourse. There remained some debate, specifically around who qualified as a whistleblower and the ethics and politics of the act, but the principle of calling out wrongdoing and wrongdoers had gained momentum—with tangible political consequences.

THE NATIONAL SECURITY AND SECRECY REGIMES

The paradigm of whistleblowing opened significant possibilities for checking concentrated power and ensuring accountability. But uncertainty remained around public-interest whistleblowing that involved the exposure of national security abuses, corruption, and possible crimes. Moreover, the principle confronted a national security state whose prerogative to control information and maintain secrets had significantly expanded since the beginning of the twentieth century. Although the term "national security" became widespread only during World War II and the formal national security state wasn't created until 1947, the concept of national defense, like whistleblowing, has a longer genealogy.[17]

Secrecy is as old as the state, and according to Max Weber it is a particular feature of the bureaucratic state. But the legal regime of secrecy is a modern creation. There were almost no federal laws pertaining to "defense information" before the twentieth century. The only statutes regulating secrets concerned treason, unlawful entry to military bases, and theft of government property.[18]

The First Amendment to the Constitution precluded an Official Secrets Act—as was common in many countries—but a piecemeal and ad hoc system of maintaining national security information nonetheless emerged. It originated with the American rise to global power at the turn of the century, especially the acquisition of Caribbean and Pacific territories and colonies, construction of military bases, and formation of a modern diplomatic service. These developments raised new concerns about the vulnerability of defense information in far-flung locations, especially military installations in Panama and the Philippines, that locals might easily gain access to. The Defense Secrets Act of 1911 was the first statute to criminalize the exposure of state secrets.[19]

The imperative to protect secrets accelerated during World War I. In 1915, President Woodrow Wilson called on Congress to pass new legislation, warning that foreign enemies and disloyal individuals within the nation "have sought to pry into every confidential transaction of the Government in order to serve interests alien to our own." An article in the *North American Review*, an influential magazine run by Wilson's close associate George Harvey, called for the classification of all government documents, including sensitive information in industrial sectors related to national defense, and strict punishments for public disclosure.[20] The push for sweeping presidential power met vehement criticism in Congress and in the press, who saw it as an affront to the First Amendment. Although Congress rejected the president's claim to unilateral control of the circulation of "information relating to the public defense," two months after the United States declared war against Germany, it passed the Espionage Act. The July 1917 legislation made it a criminal offense for anyone with lawful or unlawful possession of "any document, writing, code book, signal book, sketch, photograph, photographic negative, blue print, plan, map, model, instrument, appliance, or note relating to the national defense" to "willfully communicate or transmit" this information to "anyone not entitled to receive it."[21]

Over the next century, the Espionage Act became the primary legal instrument to prosecute individuals who publicly disclosed national security information. Yet from the outset, it was a flawed piece of legislation and widely criticized. Several members of Congress identified it as a threat to free speech and civil liberties. Senator Albert Cummins, a Republican, called specific attention to the problematic phrase "relating to the national defense." In times of war, he noted, virtually every aspect of life can be related to the national defense. Newspapers also warned of the threat to press freedom. The term "willful communication" potentially encompassed every act of information exchange, including publication and speech.[22] As legal scholars later concluded, lawmakers lacked a "precise understanding" of the "meaning of basic terms" related to the espionage statutes as they approved them. This led to a curious situation wherein the disclosure of national security information was criminally sanctioned without a clear explanation of what information actually fell under this scope or how access to it was regulated. In short, it was illegal to expose secrets, but there was no definition of what a secret was or who could handle it.[23]

It took over thirty years to gain some clarity on these questions. The modern U.S. classification system emerged in the early 1950s through executive orders. Earlier mechanisms were ad hoc military efforts pertaining to narrow operational matters and wartime attempts at establishing information-handling practices. By 1953, the Harry Truman and Dwight Eisenhower administrations had extended the classification system to all executive-branch agencies, establishing three categories of secrecy—confidential, secret, and top secret—and standardizing handling processes. Furthermore, the new system threatened prosecution through the espionage statutes to deter noncompliance or disclosure.[24]

A culture of overclassification took root. In the zero-sum Cold War, a competition marked by espionage scandals and hysteria, it was simply easier to classify vast swaths of documents than carefully evaluate what information should not circulate in the public sphere. Agencies censored at source with little oversight and few incentives *not* to classify information. With no instructions for considering issues of public interest and no sanctions for excessive classification, everything from sensitive to trivial was swept up.

The epidemic of overclassification aroused concerns. The 1955 Defense Department Committee on Classified Information (the Coolidge Committee) noted that the Pentagon had found a way to "classify the unclassifiable." The 1957 bipartisan Commission on Government Security (the Wright Commission) warned against "the dangers to national security that arise out of over-classification of information which retard scientific and technological progress." Forty years later, the bipartisan Commission on Protecting and Reducing Government Secrecy (the Moynihan Commission) critiqued the development of secrecy as a mode of regulation. While there would be further attempts to reform the classification system in the post–Cold War era, the head of the Information System Security Office (ISSO) conceded in 1993 that he had no idea how many classified documents there were: "It's a huge mountain. Perhaps billions." Since the inauguration of the classification system, the number of classified documents has grown exponentially. The high-water mark came in 2012, when 95 million documents were classified that year alone.[25]

Alongside this classification, the state secrecy regime emerged and expanded without much civic or political protest. Because it did not explicitly infringe on First Amendment rights, specifically freedom of speech and freedom of the press, the essential compromise struck during the approval of the Espionage Act continued to hold: the state could maintain secrets, and the press could publish any information that it obtained.[26] Thus the burden and risk to disclose national security information fell unequivocally on one figure: the government employee.

STATE RETALIATION

Rank-and-file government officials had disclosed national security information to the public and press since the early twentieth century. Besides triggering indiscriminate state retaliation via the Espionage Act, these early episodes also motivated the revision of criminal statutes. And they shifted the U.S. government's persecution of whistleblowers as the phenomenon gained widespread attention.

The popular image of the whistleblower as a liberal, antiwar protester crystallized in the early 1970s around Daniel Ellsberg, the former U.S. military official and RAND analyst who passed the top-secret Pentagon Papers study of U.S. intervention in Vietnam to the *New York Times* and other newspapers. In reality, many factors influenced Ellsberg's decision, which had similarly been the case for previous insiders exposing national security information.[27] These earlier cases demonstrated a range of ideological positions and motives that were not necessarily adversarial to the substance of U.S. policy. They also reveal the entrenched, habitual nature of executive retaliation toward whistleblowers.

Forty years before Ellsberg, Herbert O. Yardley penned an exposé of the first U.S. cryptanalysis agency in peacetime. A disgruntled former head of a now defunct agency, motivated in part by personal and financial gain, Yardley had retained translated ciphers to write a cryptanalysis primer that criticized the conduct of U.S. foreign relations. When he attempted to publish a follow-up work—and with prosecution reluctantly deemed impractical—Congress and the Franklin D. Roosevelt administration censored Yardley and criminalized publication of information gathered from code or intercepted communications.[28] Six years after the creation of the modern classification system, John Nickerson was the first American charged with transgressing it, after he disclosed details of an Army ballistic missile program in 1957. As Sam Lebovic discusses (chapter 2), Nickerson's motives were also a complex mix of turf war, desire for personal gain, and exposure of decision-making inefficiencies. As the case increasingly generated press headlines, the Army dropped the Espionage Act charge out of fear that further classified evidence would be revealed during the trial, with Nickerson eventually pleading guilty to lesser charges of mishandling classified information.[29]

By the 1960s, government officials making unauthorized disclosures, even to Congress, faced dismissal. Otto Otepka, the deputy director of the

State Department's security office who provided classified information to a Senate subcommittee on internal security, was fired by Secretary of State Dean Rusk in 1963. An arch anticommunist who refused to waive security clearances for John F. Kennedy administration officials, Otepka became a martyr for the Right much as Ellsberg later would for the Left.[30] Five years later, A. Ernest Fitzgerald, an Air Force employee, revealed a $2 billion cost overrun on a C5A military cargo plane by testifying to the Congress Joint Economic Committee. Fitzgerald had identified inefficiency and waste but was accused of exposing classified information and fired, with Richard Nixon caught on tape issuing an order to "get rid of that son of a bitch." Fitzgerald was eventually reinstated and, as we shall see, later refashioned as a model whistleblower.[31]

More immediately, Fitzgerald's case featured in Nader's whistleblowing conference and book. But both the conference and the book evaded the critical issue of blowing the whistle on national security transgressions.[32] Ellsberg's spectacular exposure in 1971 could have clarified the issue because it resulted in two high-profile legal cases. In the first, the Supreme Court reaffirmed the ability of the press to publish classified information.[33] The second, against Ellsberg and his collaborator Tony Russo, was vital for prosecuting whistleblowers through the Espionage Act but famously ended in a mistrial in 1973 after revelations that the Nixon administration had ordered the wiretapping of Ellsberg's phone and the president's henchmen had broken into the office of his psychiatrist. Although a poll of jurors reported at least half would have acquitted Ellsberg, the mistrial left unresolved the fate of national security whistleblowing.[34]

Ellsberg's case continued a curious trend of the state's having never successfully prosecuted an individual for unauthorized disclosure via the espionage statutes in open court. As a new generation of anti-imperial whistleblowers emerged during the 1970s—which Kaeten Mistry and Jeremy Varon examine in their chapters—the state changed disciplinary tactics, increasingly relying on prior restraint of government employees. In response to revelatory books by former CIA officials—specifically Victor Marchetti, Philip Agee, and Frank Snepp—the U.S. government won crucial legal victories that clamped down on whistleblowers through censorship, the surrender of publishing profits, and exposure of covert operations personnel. Even though most of the 1970s generation did not reveal classified information—fundamentally, they questioned the underlying purpose of national security and its machinations—the courts and Congress supported the executive in curbing all forms of disclosure related to the national defense. Key rulings saw executive-branch secrecy agreements (otherwise known as nondisclosure agreements) effectively stifle the First Amendment rights of national security personnel, with any public writing or speech to be submitted for prepublication review. This process was soon rolled out across the executive branch and, as Richard Immerman details, has been blighted by censorship and ineptitude.

Paradoxically, as the state moved aggressively against national security disclosures, the philosophy of whistleblowing began to receive greater political and civic attention. Yet there was little in the way of protection for national security whistleblowers. Even though the new public-interest lawyers and an emerging whistleblower-advocacy community, including the Government Accountability Project (GAP, formed in 1977), highlighted the problems of the national security establishment, their lobbying did not affect the secrecy regime. The state continued to deny the premise of national security whistleblowing, and when the first federal whistleblower-protection laws were created by Congress and the executive, revelations involving national security information were deliberately excluded.

CODIFYING WHISTLEBLOWING: PROTECTION LAWS AND INTERNAL CHANNELS

From the mid-1970s, the act of whistleblowing moved from the marginal realm of legal advocacy to the center stage of national politics. Public attention to state wrongdoing had been galvanized by crises at home and abroad, epitomized by Watergate and Vietnam, with political leaders pressed to confront the issue. Their response was to define executive-branch whistle-blowing narrowly in relation to fraud, waste, and egregious crime. The codification sought to improve the functioning of the state rather than question the underlying tenets of national security policy or the culture of secrecy. It was designed to encourage whistleblowers as organizational defenders and to discourage those making disclosures in the public interest.

The unraveling details of the Nixon administration's crimes and the president's departure from office conditioned the political debate, with Democrats and Republicans on the 1976 campaign trail portraying whistleblowers during the Nixon years as America's unsung heroes. On election eve, Jimmy Carter called Fitzgerald a "dedicated civil servant," vowing "to seek strong legislation to protect our employees from harassment and dismissal if they find out and report waste or dishonesty by their superiors or others."[35] In Congress, a bipartisan cohort of young legislators—including Democrat Patrick Leahy and Republican Charles Grassley—began to advocate on behalf of whistleblowers. "Employees in reporting illegal acts are not trying to destroy [government], they're trying to save it," commented Leahy. "They're public servants in the truest, best sense." Congress passed the first laws to protect federal government whistleblowers as part of the 1978 Civil Service Reform Act. The legislation prohibited reprisals against employees who reported violations of laws or rules and regulations, managerial abuses of authority, and dangers to the public welfare. One of the tasks of the newly created Office of Special Counsel (OSC) was to manage complaints of retaliation against whistleblowers. Crucially, the law did not cover public disclosures of classified information, thus excluding protection for employees of the U.S. foreign policy, military, and intelligence establishments.[36]

Like his predecessor, Ronald Reagan styled himself as a protector of whistleblowers. But his administration narrowed the issue further while strengthening the national security establishment. As the Reagan administration relaunched an ideological, belligerent, and militaristic Cold War, boosting military spending and "unleashing" CIA covert operations, it expanded the secrecy regime and mechanisms of retaliation against national security whistleblowers. Executive Order 12356 (1982) reversed many of the Carter-era reforms of the classification system, even reclassifying "information previously declassified and disclosed." In response to whistleblowers like Agee, the 1982 Intelligence Identities Protection Act made it a federal crime to reveal the identity of covert intelligence personnel, even if the information was already in the public sphere. Nondisclosure agreements became mandatory for all federal employees requiring access to classified materials, which not only prohibited the disclosure of classified information but also "classifiable" information. Any violation would be "enforceable in a civil action."[37]

It was increasingly clear that codification of whistleblowing offered limited protection for federal employees while making it especially precarious for national security officials. The OSC was a "toothless terrier on valium," in the words of one critic, lamenting that the office served mainly as a tool for agencies to retaliate against whistleblowers.[38] In 1987, responding to these criticisms, senators Carl Levin and Grassley cosponsored new protection legislation. During hearings on the bill, Tom Devine, the legal director of GAP, declared that the executive branch had effectively "gagged" national security employees. These policies were nonetheless upheld when the Supreme Court ruled in 1988 that, in matters of national security, the judiciary must demonstrate the "utmost deference" to the executive branch. The Whistleblower Protection Act of 1989 maintained the narrow definition of whistleblowing and aversion to challenging executive power. Emphasizing the protection of individuals who "serve the public interest by assisting in the elimination of fraud, waste, abuse, and unnecessary Government expenditures," the act did not apply to anyone disclosing information related to national security.[39]

Despite the significant expansion of legal strictures in the final decades of the twentieth century, unauthorized disclosures of privileged information continued to plague the national security establishment. In 1985, Samuel Loring Morison was charged and imprisoned for passing to a British defense magazine classified satellite images that revealed the scope of Soviet warship power. Critics commented on the chilling effect the prosecution would have on would-be whistleblowers.[40] Advocacy groups stepped up their calls for the legal protection of national security whistleblowers. The attempted government fix was the establishment of internal channels, operated by the inspector general (IG) in each executive agency, where grievances and concerns could be raised. Yet this internal government watchdog was less about promoting whistleblowing than creating a mechanism to shield important revelations from the public. Furthermore, not only did they fail to protect whistleblowers; they also, in several instances, fueled retaliation against them.

The State Department's effort to manage dissent since the mid-1960s served as one of the inspirations for internal reporting channels. As Foreign Service officers grew increasingly disillusioned by the Vietnam War, reformist administrators echoed the ideas of new management theories, which argued that morale and loyalty were best achieved by giving employees a voice in decision making. In 1971, the State Department established an official "Dissent Channel," through which the rank and file could submit dissenting policy views directly to the secretary of state without fear of retaliation. "The right of dissent is very important," explained one senior official, "But we want to keep it in the house." Over the next several decades, hundreds of messages were submitted through the Dissent Channel. While few authors experienced retaliation, none had a significant impact on the policies they protested, with one critic arguing that the Dissent Channel was "merely a management tool for letting the system vent bottled-up pressures."[41]

Containing and diffusing dissent underpinned the mechanisms for national security insider channels from the late 1980s. After an uphill legislative battle, featuring testimonies from Navy Reserve and Army National Guard whistleblowers, Congress passed the Military Whistleblower Protection Act in 1988. This legislation allowed members of the armed services to disclose information related to waste, fraud, and abuse to the Department of Defense's IG or Congress.[42] Ten years later, the Intelligence Community Whistleblower Protection Act was introduced, which allowed officials to disclose information of "urgent concern" to the Department of Justice's IG, who would determine whether to pass it on to Congress.[43] As the 2019 whistleblowers who exposed the details of Trump's phone call with Ukraine's president showed, the in-house reporting mechanism ensures complaints can remain within the executive branch. The revelations by the Ukraine whistleblowers made it to Congress and the public only because congressional Democrats decided to break with the long bipartisan consensus on whistleblowing in their efforts to impeach Trump.[44]

The guidelines for internal reporting define whistleblowing in very narrow terms and, while formally shielding employees, offer extremely limited protection against retaliation. The acting IG of the Defense Department went so far as to note in 2006 that it was a "misnomer" to call them whistleblower-protection statutes.[45]

As the dictates of national security amid a "Global War on Terror" dominated in the early twenty-first century, there was little dissent and thus scant attention to internal channels or whistleblower protection. This changed when Chelsea Manning disclosed thousands of classified documents about the Iraq and Afghanistan wars to WikiLeaks in 2010. In response, Barack Obama reinforced the paradox of national security whistleblowing, simultaneously denying its existence and insisting it was a threat. While suggesting the responsible option was for whistleblowers to use internal channels and promising to enhance protections, the administration sought to deter individuals from going public by introducing the "Insider Threat" program, encouraging federal employees to monitor coworkers to guard against those "who may use their authorized access to compromise classified information" through unauthorized disclosures. Obama's much-heralded Presidential Policy Directive 19, "Protecting Whistleblowers with Access to Classified Information," again covered an extremely narrow scope of "protected disclosures" that remained in-house and related to "waste, fraud, and abuse." Advocates argued the program failed to live up to its lofty promises, and congressional researchers noted that "none of these measures protect against retaliation or potential criminal liability arising from disclosures to media sources."[46]

In the wake of Edward Snowden's disclosures about National Security Agency (NSA) surveillance, Obama insisted, "I signed an executive order well before Mr. Snowden leaked this information that provided whistleblower protection to the intelligence community, for the first time. So there were other avenues available for somebody whose conscience was stirred and thought that they needed to question government actions."[47] The president's position, echoed by many public officials, epitomized the irony of internal channels. Snowden might have legally been recognized as a whistleblower by using one, but he would then not have shared information with the public, thereby perpetuating the secrecy he sought to challenge and undermining the fundamental spirit of whistleblowing as an act of public interest.

The experiences of individuals who used these channels highlighted the hollowness of their promises. In 2002, Thomas Drake, a senior NSA executive, contributed to a report denouncing the illegality and fiscal inefficiency of the "Trailblazer Project," a massive NSA surveillance program. The report was submitted to the Defense Department's IG. Drake also initiated contact with a reporter from the *Baltimore Sun*, who published a series of articles in 2006 about Trailblazer. In the following four years, the FBI raided Drake's home, and the government sought to prosecute him under the Espionage Act for the retention of classified information. Following an intense media campaign, including a profile on *60 Minutes*, the charges were dropped on the eve of trial. But in addition to ruining his career, the ordeal left Drake buried in legal debt.[48] Instead of protecting Drake, internal channels were used to retaliate against him. The IG's general counsel gave information to the FBI and destroyed documents supporting Drake's defense. When John Crane, the assistant IG of the Defense Department, attempted to advocate on behalf of Drake and other whistleblowers, he too was fired.[49]

The problem was systemic. A subsequent investigation found that in 2015, the Pentagon's IG investigated nine allegations of reprisal against Defense Department employees and fifty-two against contractors, amounting to just 9 percent of the claims it received. None of the investigations concluded in favor of the claimants. One-quarter of all IG employees and one-third of all reprisal investigators said they feared retaliation, revealing a culture of fear and intimidation within the oversight system.[50] In 2017, the Trump administration put an abrupt end to an equally damning investigation conducted by the intelligence community's IG and suppressed the final report.[51] There remains ambiguity over responsibility for private contractors, who are a core feature of the modern national security state, since the law considers them differently to state employees with respect to whistleblowing channels.[52]

Despite these internal channels, the post-9/11 era has been marked by a new boom in public disclosures, with whistleblowers exposing the unprecedented scope of U.S. wars and the pervasive culture of surveillance carried out and overseen by the gargantuan national security state. As with previous generations, motives and ideologies vary in exposing privileged information in the public interest. Manning disclosed cables detailing the reality of the Global War on Terror, Jeffrey Sterling discussed a botched CIA covert plot to disrupt Iran's nuclear program with the journalist James Risen as the drumbeat for war with Iran grew louder, Stephen Kim disclosed North Korea's nuclear capacities in protest of Obama's policies as too soft, John Kiriakou confirmed the CIA torture of al-Qaeda detainees to the press, and Reality Winner exposed evidence about Russian interference in the 2016 U.S. election. Amid archetypal arguments over whether they should be categorized as national security whistleblowers and judgments about their supposed motives, the indisputable link among these episodes was state reprisal: all were prosecuted under the Espionage Act or the Intelligence Identities Protection Act.

The early twenty-first century has, like the 1970s, marked a new age of national security whistleblowing. State retaliation has morphed and expanded, even targeting journalists that collaborate with whistleblowers and insiders, as Lloyd Gardner examines in his chapter. The government's internal channels have proven to be ineffective. Kiriakou stated he "wouldn't have gotten anywhere" by using them. Moreover, retribution against individuals has not gone unnoticed. Indeed, it has even encouraged further episodes. Snowden explained that his decision to go to the press rather than use internal channels was a direct response to Drake's ordeal: "If there had been no Thomas Drake, there would be no Edward Snowden."[53]

CONTESTED DEFINITION, FRAMEWORKS, AND DISCONNECTED LITERATURES

The contemporary wave of disclosures has resurrected familiar questions of labels and definitions. What is national security whistleblowing, and who is a whistleblower? What are their motives? The term has been used to describe everyone from Drake, Manning, and Snowden to intelligence leaders under Obama, former FBI director James Comey, the "deep state," and a Trump administration official who penned an anonymous *New York Times* op-ed. The charged political environment, particularly around the 2016 election and the Trump presidency, has seen an uptick in references to whistleblowing and leaking. Even the Ukraine whistleblowers, who followed the state-sanctioned pathway for reporting national security abuse, fueled partisan clashes around motives, espionage, and whether these cases involved whistleblowing at all.[54] In this flurry, labels and concepts have been blurred and misappropriated, stirring confusion and losing relevance.

While there may not be a settled description across academic, journalistic, civic, legal, or political discourse, national security whistleblowing goes beyond politically defined internal channels and matters of waste and fraud. In accounting for the broader phenomenon, we should consider its essential attributes and the evolution of themes, episodes, and frameworks over a century.

National security whistleblowing is distinguished by five key characteristics. First, an insider discloses privileged information—related to national defense but not necessarily classified—in the name of the public interest, breaking the rules of a system to dissent from the status quo. Second, the individual's identity authenticates the information contained in the revelation. Third, the state indiscriminately retaliates by condemning the "unauthorized" nature of an act that undermines security. Fourth, the individual is prosecuted or otherwise punished. And fifth, questions about the character and actions of the whistleblower overtake discussion of the content of the revelation.

Whistleblowing is distinct from leaking, which is overwhelmingly anonymous, highly political, and, although formally forbidden, rarely—if ever—punished. Leaking is a mainstay of the relationship between the press and the state. It creates a symbiotic relationship in which the state (often through a senior official) can float trial policy balloons, gain leverage for bureaucratic turf wars, present issues in a favorable light, and garner public support. At the same time, the press gains access to inside information, of a kind that has been increasingly hard to obtain over the course of the last century, in the knowledge that they are free to publish. The term *pleak*—a portmanteau of "plant" and "leak" coined by David Pozen and further examined by Matt Jones in his chapter—encapsulates the essence of this dynamic and the central role it plays in the regular workings of the state.[55]

Senior officials popularly characterized as whistleblowers are better understood as leakers. Mark Felt, associate director of the FBI, long known only as "Deep Throat," anonymously divulged the details of Watergate to Woodward and Bernstein not to express dissent but to retaliate against Nixon for choosing a bureaucratic rival to head the FBI. Felt revealed his identity in 2005 at the age of ninety-two, three years before his death. The anonymous official proclaiming to belong to the "resistance inside the Trump administration" did not alert the public to a problem per se in the *New York Times* op-ed but instead offered assurances that there is a vigilant state containing a rogue president.[56] Neither of these leaks was prosecuted. Conversely, every public-interest whistleblower in the post-9/11 era has been identified and prosecuted for their revelations. In 2017, Attorney General Jeff Sessions railed against a "dramatic growth in the number of unauthorized disclosures" and vowed to crack down on a widespread "culture of leaking." While he boasted of a threefold rise in criminal referrals to the Justice Department for "unauthorized disclosures of classified information," the only conviction during his tenure was Winner, a twenty-six-year-old NSA contractor who disclosed an internal report about Russia's attempt to hack U.S. election infrastructure.[57]

The legal term "unauthorized disclosure" is routinely invoked to criminalize whistleblowing, fixing the debate firmly in the realm of national security. It is not about public interest or wrongdoing but the harm done to the state's ability to defend the nation, with prosecution via the espionage statutes fueling notions of disloyalty. It emphasizes the person disclosing secret information, not the contents of the material, why they are deemed secret, or the appropriateness of the classification. It makes the act illegitimate, not the activities revealed. The national security imprimatur isolates this branch of whistleblowing from other, acceptable forms of exposure, such as protecting free markets.[58]

While there is overlap in concepts and although producing a taxonomy that links them together has understandable appeal, whistleblowing is distinct from leaking, and the term "unauthorized disclosure" is reductive and unhelpful to exploring the phenomenon. A precise, universally accepted definition of national security whistleblowing may never materialize, but events over the past century clearly outline key characteristics. These features—privileged information, public interest, identified source, and retaliation—are critical in any debate. Nonetheless, even when looking to question narrow state definitions, scholars and commentators regularly obscure the historical context and the role of ideology in their attempts to delineate between acceptable and unacceptable whistleblowing. These efforts say less about the actual phenomenon or its past than they do about establishment and liberal concerns over perceived threats to and, moreover, faith in the liberal-capitalist system.[59]

Our historical approach also challenges the dominant paradigm of whistleblowers as either heroes or villains. This binary evokes deeply political and emotional responses. Whistleblowers are held up as either martyrs or traitors. Not only does this flatten complex individuals into simple caricatures; it also reproduces the binary worldview of the national security state, especially in the intelligence establishment, where any challenge to norms verges on treason. Whistleblowers are often tarred with the same brush as defectors, snitches, and spies—labels from the black-and-white world of espionage. This hero-villain dichotomy creates an analogous duality of political vision in which whistleblowing poses either an existential threat to national security or a promise of salvation. In national security and civil-libertarian discourses, fantasies and nightmares of disclosure become substitutes for political struggle. As Tim Melley shows, fiction is a key site where this plays out. Not every disclosure poses an existential security threat, nor does "sunlight" purify the body politic or truth always set us free.[60]

A close consideration of the *longue durée* reveals that the motives behind national security whistleblowing are far from homogenous. They are dependent, change over time, and emerge from a variety of ideological and personal roots. Whistleblowers have different goals in their revelations, as do the networks supporting them, and they go on to lead different kinds of lives.

Whistleblowers invariably begin their careers as believers in America's global mission. They hold a broadly conservative and patriotic outlook. While there is a common transformation from insider to dissenter, involving degrees of disillusionment, this is not the same as a clear political conversion. Some move away from conservative ideology and question the beliefs and apparatus of national security (e.g., Ellsberg, Agee, Manning, Kiriakou, Snowden); others continue to adhere to the American mission and work toward enhancing its policies and methods (e.g., Yardley, Nickerson, Fitzgerald, Kim). Some develop into advocates and activists; others continue government service.[61] Not all are individuals of conscience, nor, as several chapters here demonstrate, are their disclosures championed by the press or a political movement. Generalizations of whistleblowers as left wing or right wing, radical or moderate, selfish or idealistic all fall apart under closer historical scrutiny.

Of course, there are key elements of the phenomenon that remain fuzzy and contestable, particularly the moral and ethical claims of national security whistleblowing. The "public interest" is inherently subjective, politically contested, and historically constructed. Whistleblowers motivated by an ethic of a broader good are acting on a *perception* of the public good, which could also be said of those prosecuting them. Issues of ego and personal attention cannot be discounted.[62] All of this reinforces that there is no such thing as an archetypal whistleblower.

To date, discussions of national security whistleblowing have been fragmentary, spread over and divided by several disciplines. The largest body of work about whistleblowing relates to tackling illegality and abuse in the corporate world and public sector, especially health care and social services.

Drawing on Nader's original concept and rooted in social science methodologies, this literature focuses on processes and on providing practical guides to blowing the whistle. One prominent assessment challenges the heroic narrative through a bleak conclusion on the personal fate of individuals making disclosures in the public interest.[63] This substantial literature outlines patterns and methods for whistleblowers and the possibilities and limits of change, but the tradition of state retaliation means it is of limited use in considering national security whistleblowing.

Political science scholarship seeks to assess the relationship among democracy, secrecy, and disclosures. With an eye toward informing policy, this normative body of work tends to take the paradigms and terms employed by the state for granted.[64] Embedded in this line of inquiry are questions about whether whistleblowers succeed in catalyzing specific changes or affecting national policy as part of efforts to improve governance and establish better oversight. National security whistleblowing did indeed influence policies and programs, laws and legislation, and congressional efforts to reform the national security state. But the chapters in these pages also go beyond a strict political framework to challenge, in the words of the historian Nick Cullather, "the imaginary balance" between security and liberty.[65] They underscore how the phenomenon is part of broader debates within Western democracies around government transparency and accountability. And they explore why representations in film, media, and popular culture are critical, especially in providing a medium for the public to negotiate responses to whistleblowing and create sociopolitical meaning out of vast, often complex revelations. As Lida Maxwell (celebrity), Tim Melley (popular culture), and Hannah Gurman (personality) examine, the *image* of the whistleblower is central to the phenomenon and its continued influence outside the institutional realms of politics and security.

Legal scholarship has approached the issue through select episodes, high-level constitutional theory, and landmark court cases and legislation. In drawing attention to the complex and cumbersome nature of the legal system with regard to unauthorized disclosures, many reinforce the status quo by insisting on the government's authority to hold secrets and prosecute, the need to amend existing statutes, and current protection under the

First Amendment.[66] A recent trend in "national security law" has drawn greater attention to the scant protection offered to whistleblowers and advocated for more robust First Amendment protection from prosecution. Stephen Vladeck, one of the leading voices in the subfield, questions the justification for a separate corpus of national security law, characterizing this body as "inherently paradoxical" because of its basis in the exceptional circumstances of the post-9/11 period, raising concerns that "the exceptions will normalize into the rule."[67] While the wave of whistleblowing episodes in the twenty-first century has produced valuable critiques of the current legal system, it has also given rise to advocacy groups that perpetuate the notion that insiders can make disclosures in the public interest without necessarily breaking the law.[68] Normative strains of legal scholarship and advocacy thus continue to naturalize the current legal regime rather than highlight problems and the historical contingencies that gave rise to them.

Historians of the United States, foreign relations, and intelligence have only recently turned to the topic. Most commonly there are passing references to individual whistleblowers, primarily Ellsberg with respect to Vietnam, which ignore the phenomenon itself. The most detailed work has focused on distinct periods. In examining the Obama administration's use of the Espionage Act, Lloyd Gardner's *War on Leakers* draws some parallels to the 1920s and 1970s. Intelligence scholars have offered brief sketches of select whistleblowers in the context of CIA retaliation during the 1970s.[69]

Attempts to sketch a longer genealogy to the Revolutionary era have presented both exposure and state punishment as American as apple pie. "Whistleblower rights and protection in the United States are as old as the republic itself," claimed a recent account of how whistleblowing has held elites to account. Yet the few examples from the eighteenth and nineteenth centuries that are offered in support of this claim—including Benjamin Franklin's revelations of private correspondence during the Revolutionary War and the passage of the False Claims Act against private "relators" defrauding the government during the Civil War—are selective and patchy, as is the notion of the state's natural and eternal right to penalize individuals for disclosures.[70] Moreover, these examples ignore the distinctly modern nature of bureaucratic secrecy and revelation. The systematic and organized face of national security, the classification regime, and the struggle to expose information were twentieth-century developments. National security whistleblowing is a modern phenomenon.

Journalists and pundits provide the sole assessments of modern-day whistleblowing, and most of these texts are narrowly focused, biographical, and structured entirely by the hero-traitor paradigm.[71] Some are unapologetically partisan, if not ideological, in echoing the state line that any disclosure is harmful to national security and aids enemies while attacking individual whistleblowers. "Ever since September 11, the country has been at war," noted the conservative commentator Gabriel Schoenfeld, extolling the necessity for secrecy as "one of the most critical tools of national defense." Schoenfeld also claimed the *New York Times* should be prosecuted under the Espionage Act for reporting on NSA warrantless surveillance.[72] In complicating the hero-traitor binary, this book does not romanticize or demonize disclosure for its own sake, nor does it pass judgment on whistleblower cases. It does, however, explore underexamined or forgotten episodes, themes, and individuals to address the genuine challenge of dissent in the arena of national security. The state may not be a singular or all-powerful entity. But, over the last century, it has achieved an increasingly unlimited and unchecked ability to define, control, and police information related to the national defense.

* * *

This book offers an interdisciplinary history of national security whistleblowing. It moves the debate away from narrow social science or security frames to core issues of U.S. political, legal, social, and cultural history. It is based on original research by scholars who approach the topic from distinct perspectives and with diverse methodologies. It uses new analytical and thematic lenses, incorporates original archival material, synthesizes a vast range of secondary resources, and draws on unique personal experience in government and activism. Rather than attempt a singular voice, the contributions offer a range of interpretations, including on the definition and scope of whistleblowing.

The arc of the volume is broadly chronological. While it spans more than a century, it does not rehearse every episode or adjudicate each case of whistleblowing over this period. Instead, there is particular focus on pivotal eras—especially the long 1970s and post-9/11 eras—that have shaped the phenomenon, allowing the reader to follow the developments as they unfolded. It begins with the interwar and postwar era, when the legal and institutional infrastructure of national security was built, providing a scaffolding for the culture of secrecy that took root in the post–World War II years. While the early decades of the Cold War saw relatively few instances of whistleblowing, the phenomenon spiked in the 1970s amid the political upheaval around Watergate, disillusionment over the Vietnam War, and broader cultural shifts that fueled dissent within the national security establishment and public demands for greater transparency. Several chapters in the volume focus on this critical period, not only examining the famed episode involving Ellsberg through novel legal and gender perspectives but also exploring other important individuals and developments in this era. The 1970s "boom" subsided in the 1980s as the revitalization of the Cold War fueled a crackdown on whistleblowing and the rolling back of earlier reforms. Whistleblowing spiked once again in the twenty-first century in the context of fresh controversies over foreign wars and domestic political schisms. The latter chapters analyze recent whistleblowing developments, fueled by reactions to the post-9/11 Global War on Terror, the rise of the surveillance state, and technological advances that facilitated the disclosure of massive amounts of digital information.

While each chapter considers a particular era, it is also structured around a set of core themes over a longer time. Several chapters in the volume analyze the legal dimensions of whistleblowing (Lebovic, Kraut, Mistry), and others illuminate cultural representations of the phenomenon (Maxwell, Varon, Melley). Some analyze the role of the press (Lebovic, Gurman, Gardner); others, the response of the state (Mistry, Immerman). And some explore the social impact of whistleblowing (Varon, Pozen). Highlighting how these themes bridge particular eras, Maxwell's chapter, on the politics of celebrity and masculinity in the 1970s, speaks to the politics of gender and whistleblowing in the post-9/11 era; Jones's work on technology and contested authenticities ties 1980s policy debates to modern surveillance powers; and Gurman's consideration of journalistic culture in the 1980s reaches back to the early Cold War and forward to present political contests over the credibility of establishment media. The two short pieces concluding the volume—Pozen's coda and our conclusion—reflect on the theory and stakes of national security whistleblowing and how its history continues to shape the phenomenon to this day.

Together, the chapters participate in a sustained interdisciplinary dialogue that encapsulates the multiple dimensions of whistleblowing and their evolution over time. In short, the chronological trajectory and thematic arcs underpin a collective exploration of the multiple facets of national security whistleblowing in the modern era.

NOTES

1. All references to whistleblowing herein relate to national security whistleblowing rather than the broader term incorporating a range of private and public sectors. Unless otherwise stated, citations throughout the volume refer to national security whistleblowing.

2. Avner Strauss, "J. Hudson & Co. New Historical Research," Whistle Museum, http://www.whistlemuseum.com/2016/11/19/j-hudson-co-new-historical-research-and-the-1882-to-1885-the-unknown-police-whistles-asylums-fire-brigades-prison-and-parks-whistles-by-j-hudson-co/; "Acme Whistles Since 1870," J. Hudson & Co. ACME Specialist Whistles, https://www.acmewhistles.co.uk/since-1870.

3. P. G. Wodehouse, *Right Ho, Jeeves* (New York: Overlook, 1934), 207; Raymond Chandler, *The Long Goodbye* (New York: Houghton Mifflin, 1954), 36.

4. "Plot to Get Otepka," 109 Congressional Record, no. 159, S17821 (October 7, 1963); Eric Paul Roorda, "McCarthyite in Camelot: The 'Loss' of Cuba, Homophobia, and the Otto Otepka Scandal in the Kennedy State Department," *Diplomatic History* 31, no. 4 (September 2007): 744.

5. John Morris, "New Nader Group Seeking Tipsters," *New York Times*, January 27, 1971.

6. Ralph Nader, Peter Petkas, and Kate Blackwell, eds., *Whistle Blowing* (New York: Grossman, 1972), vii.

7. Charles Peters and Taylor Branch, *Blowing the Whistle: Dissent in the Public Interest* (New York: Praeger, 1972).

8. Brandeis wrote a series of articles exposing the corrupt practices of investment firms for *Harper's Weekly* in 1914, which were later collected in book form: Louis Brandeis, *Other People's Money and How the Bankers Use It* (New York: Frederick A. Stokes, 1932), 92.

9. "The New Public Interest Lawyers," *Yale Law Journal* 79, no. 6 (May 1970): 1069–1152.

10. See Michael Schudson, *The Rise of the Right to Know: Politics and the Culture of Transparency, 1945–1975* (Cambridge, MA: Harvard University Press, 2015).

11. Ralph Nader, "Freedom from Information: The Act and the Agencies," *Harvard Civil Rights–Civil Liberties Law Review* 5, no. 1 (January 1970): 1. Although Nader supported the principles guiding the Freedom of Information Act, he was also an early critic of the law's significant loopholes, which allowed for the routine denial of FOIA requests.

12. Herbert Marcuse, cited in "The New Public Interest Lawyers," 1071.

13. Nader, Petkas, and Blackwell, *Whistle Blowing*, 3, 11.

14. Julius Duscha, "Stop! In the Public Interest!" *New York Times*, March 21, 1971.

15. William H. Whyte, *The Organization Man* (New York: Simon and Schuster, 1956); Paul Goodman, *Growing Up Absurd: Problems of Youth in the Organized Society* (New York: Vintage, 1960); Sloan Wilson, *The Man in the Gray Flannel Suit* (New York: Simon and Schuster, 1955); see also James Burnham, *The Managerial Revolution* (New York: John Day, 1941); Nader, Petkas, and Blackwell, *Whistle Blowing*, 10.

16. Peter Richardson, *A Bomb in Every Issue: How the Short, Unruly Life of "Ramparts" Magazine Changed America* (New York: New Press, 2009); John McMillian, *Smoking Typewriters: The Sixties Underground Press and the Rise of Alternative Media in America* (New York: Oxford University Press, 2011); Kaeten Mistry, "Narrating Covert Action: The CIA, Historiography, and the Cold War," in *Intelligence Studies in Britain and the US: Historiography Since 1945*, ed. Christopher Murphy and Christopher Moran (Edinburgh: Edinburgh University Press, 2013), 117–18.

17. Andrew Preston, "Monsters Everywhere: A Genealogy of National Security," *Diplomatic History* 38, no. 3 (June 2014): 477–500; Melvyn P. Leffler, "The American Conception of National Security and the Beginnings of the Cold War, 1945–1948," *American Historical Review* 89, no. 2 (April 1984): 346–81; Michael J. Hogan, *A Cross of Iron: Harry S. Truman and the Origins of the National Security State, 1945–1954* (New York: Cambridge University Press, 1998).

18. H. H. Gerth and C. Wright Mills, eds., *From Max Weber: Essays in Sociology* (New York: Oxford University Press, 1946), 233–34; Harold Edgar and Benno C. Schmidt Jr., "The Espionage Statutes and Publication of Defense Information," *Columbia Law Review* 73, no. 5 (May 1973): 940.

19. Disclosure of National-Defense Secrets, Report no. 1250, United States Senate, 61st Cong., 2nd sess., February 27, 1911.

20. John Satchfield, "The Peril of Espionage," *North American Review* 203, no. 727 (June 1916): 830–40.

21. Espionage Act of 1917, 18 U.S.C. §§ 793–98; Sam Lebovic, *Free Speech and Unfree News: The Paradox of Press Freedom in America* (Cambridge, MA: Harvard University Press, 2016), 128.

22. Edgar and Schmidt, "The Espionage Statutes," 957, 993, 998–1002.

23. Edgar and Schmidt, "The Espionage Statutes," 1077; Lebovic, *Free Speech and Unfree News*, 128–29; Stephen I. Vladeck, "Inchoate Liability and the Espionage Act: The

Statutory Framework and the Freedom of the Press," *Harvard Law & Policy Review* 1 (2007): 219–37; Stephen I. Vladeck, "Prosecuting Leaks Under US Law," in *Whistleblowers, Leaks, and the Media: The First Amendment and National Security*, ed. Paul Rosenzweig et al. (Chicago: American Bar Association, 2015), 29–42.

24. Christine Wells, "National Security Information and the Freedom of Information Act," *Administrative Law Review* 56, no. 4 (Fall 2004): 1200; "Keeping Secrets: Congress, the Courts, and National Security Information," *Harvard Law Review* 103, no. 4 (1990): 907; Lebovic, *Free Speech and Unfree News*, 126–27, 166–67; Executive Orders 10290 (September 24, 1951) and 10501 (November 5, 1953), American Presidency Project, http://www .presidency.ucsb.edu/ws/?pid=78426 and http://www.presidency.ucsb.edu/ws/index.php ?pid=485.

25. "Keeping Secrets," 908; "Report of the Commission on Government Security, June 21, 1957," https://archive.org/details/reportofcommissi1957unit/page/n7; Wells, "National Security Information," 1201; Lebovic, *Free Speech and Unfree News*, 169–70; "Report of the Commission on Protecting and Reducing Government Secrecy," 103rd Congress (Washington, DC: U.S. Government Printing Office, 1997); Daniel Patrick Moynihan, *Secrecy: The American Experience* (New Haven, CT: Yale University Press, 1998); Tim Weiner, "President Moves to Release Classified U.S. Documents," *New York Times*, May 5, 1993; Information Security Oversight Committee (NARA), "2015 Report to President," 6–7, https://www.archives .gov/files/isoo/reports/2015-annual-report.pdf. The 95 million figure relates to Derivative Classification, which "is the act of incorporating, paraphrasing, restating, or generating in new form information that is already classified." The amount of classified information has been falling since 2012, with the figure at 49.4 million in 2017. ISSO, "2017 Report to President," 2, 44, https://www.archives.gov/files/isoo/reports/2017-annual-report.pdf. On the perpetuation of the secrecy regime despite calls for greater transparency, see Alasdair Roberts, *Blacked Out: Government Secrecy in the Information Age* (Cambridge: Cambridge University Press, 2006); Jason Ross Arnold, *Secrecy in the Sunshine Era: The Promises and Failures of U.S. Open Government Laws* (Lawrence: University Press of Kansas, 2014).

26. In addition to his chapter herein, see Lebovic, *Free Speech and Unfree News*.

27. There was also a mixed response to Ellsberg at the time, and some recent scholarship has been highly critical. See Judith Ehrlich and Rick Goldsmith, dirs., *The Most Dangerous Man in America: Daniel Ellsberg and the Pentagon Papers* (New York: First Run Features, 2009); Bruce Kuklick, *Blind Oracles: Intellectuals and War from Kennan to Kissinger* (Princeton, NJ: Princeton University Press, 2006), 168–81; Tom Wells, *Wild Man: The Life and Times of Daniel Ellsberg* (New York: Palgrave Macmillan, 2001).

28. Kaeten Mistry, "Embarrassing Indiscretions: The Origins and Culture of U.S. National Security Whistleblowing," in *The Culture of Intelligence: Germany, Britain, France, and the USA*, ed. Andreas Gestrich et al. (Oxford: Oxford University Press, forthcoming).

29. Ian MacDougall, "The Leak Prosecution That Lost the Space Race," *Atlantic*, August 15, 2016; Sam Lebovic, "The Forgotten 1957 Trial That Explains Our Country's Bizarre Whistleblower Laws," *Politico*, March 27, 2016.

THE PARADOX OF NATIONAL SECURITY WHISTLEBLOWING

30. "Otepka Dropped as Security Aide; Held Guilty of Passing Data—Congressmen Protest," *New York Times*, November 6, 1963; Taylor Branch, "The Odd Couple: Ellsberg and Otepka," *Washington Monthly*, October 1971, 50–60.

31. Molly Moore, "A. Ernest Fitzgerald, Analyst Who Knows the Price of Exposing Cost Overruns," *Washington Post*, February 23, 1987; "Tapes Show Nixon Role in Firing of Ernest Fitzgerald," *Washington Post*, March 7, 1979; Branch, "The Odd Couple."

32. Nader, Petkas, and Blackwell, *Whistle Blowing*, 39–54, 126–134. Several whistleblowers featured at the conference worked in the national security state, but the only case of alleged disclosure of classified information involved Christopher Pyle, an Army intelligence officer who authored a January 1970 article in the *Washington Monthly* exposing a domestic surveillance program that gathered information on 25 million Americans, from civil rights and antiwar activists to former presidential candidate Adlai Stevenson. Pyle subsequently collaborated with a Senate Judiciary Subcommittee on Constitutional Rights investigation of the program. In June 1972, the Supreme Court ruled the judiciary did not have the authority to overrule executive-branch surveillance programs unless actual injury could be proved. Jeffrey Vagle, "*Laird v. Tatum* and Article III Standing in Surveillance Cases," *Penn Law: Legal Scholarship Repository* (2016): 1055–66.

33. New York Times Co. v. United States, 403 U.S. 713 (1971).

34. Martin Arnold, "Pentagon Papers Charges Are Dismissed; Judge Byrne Frees Ellsberg and Russo, Assails 'Improper Government Conduct,'" *New York Times*, May 11, 1972.

35. Civil Service Reform Act of 1978 and Reorganization Plan No. 2 of 1978, Hearings Before the Committee on Governmental Affairs, United States Senate, June 1978, Appendix, 317.

36. "Udall-Leahy-Simon News Conference on their bill to protect whistleblowers," October 20, 1977, Box 124, Simon Lazarus' Civil Service Reform Files, Records of the Domestic Policy Staff, Jimmy Carter Library (Atlanta GA); Civil Service Reform Act, 5 U.S.C. § 1101 (1978).

37. Executive Order 12356, April 2, 1982, https://www.archives.gov/federal-register /codification/executive-order/12356.html; NSDD 84 "Safeguarding National Security Information," March 11, 1983, https://reaganlibrary.archives.gov/archives/reference /Scanned NSDDS/NSDD84.pdf; Gerald Schroeder, "FOIA Update: Guest Article: An Overview of Executive Order 12356," *FOIA Update* 3, no. 3 (1982), https://www.justice .gov/oip/blog/foia-update-guest-article-overview-executive-order-12356; Classified Information Non-Disclosure Agreement (SF-189), Department of Defense, July 1985, 29, 36, https://babel.hathitrust.org/cgi/pt?id=uc1.31210023598897.

38. Whistleblower Protection Act of 1987, Hearings Before Subcommittee on Federal Services, Post Office, and Civil Service of the Committee on Governmental Affairs, U.S. Senate, 100th Cong., 1st Session, July 20 and 31, 1987, 70.

39. Department of the Navy v. Egan, 484 U.S. 518 (1988); S.20 Whistleblower Protection Act of 1989, https://www.congress.gov/bill/101st-congress/senate-bill/20/text.

40. Morison's case involved a range of ideological and career motives, but he was nonetheless pardoned by Bill Clinton in 2001. Jennifer K. Elsea, "Criminal Prohibitions on the

Publication of Classified Defense Information," *Congressional Research Service Report*, June 24, 2013, 24–25.

41. Hannah Gurman, *The Dissent Papers: The Voices of Diplomats in the Cold War and Beyond* (New York: Columbia University Press, 2012), 190.

42. Military Whistleblower Protection Act 10 U.S.C. § 1034, https://www.gpo.gov/fdsys /granule/USCODE-2010-title10/USCODE-2010-title10-subtitleA-partII-chap53 -sec1034/content-detail.html.

43. Intelligence Community Whistleblower Protection Act, P.L. 105-272, §701–2, 112 Stat. 2396, 2413 (1998).

44. Hannah Gurman and Kaeten Mistry, "The Ukraine Whistleblowers and the Breakdown of the Bipartisan War on Public Interest Whistleblowing," *Foreign Policy in Focus*, October 17, 2019, https://fpif.org/the-ukraine-whistleblowers-and-the-rise-of-partisan -whistleblowing/.

45. Statement of Mr. Thomas F. Gimble, Acting Inspector General, Department of Defense, House Committee on Government Reform on National Whistleblower Protection, February 14, 2006, https://fas.org/irp/congress/2006_hr/021406gimble.pdf.

46. Executive Order 13587, October 7, 2011, https://obamawhitehouse.archives.gov/the-press -office/2011/10/07/executive-order-13587-structural-reforms-improve-security-classified -net; PPD-19, October 10, 2012, https://fas.org/irp/offdocs/ppd/ppd-19.pdf; Obama to Heads of Executive Departments and Agencies, "National Insider Threat Policy and Minimum Standards for Executive Branch Insider Threat Programs," November 21, 2012, https://fas.org/sgp/obama/insider.pdf; Charles Clark, "National Security Whistleblowers Need More Protections, Advocates Say," *Government Executive*, November 11, 2015, http://www.govexec.com/management/2015/11/national-security-whistleblowers-need -more-protections-advocates-say/123613/; Rodney M. Perry, "Intelligence Whistleblower Protection," *Congressional Research Service Report*, October 23, 2014, 2.

47. Bob Fredericks, "Obama Doesn't Share Holder's View of Snowden," *New York Post*, May 31, 2016.

48. *Frontline*, "United States of Secrets," PBS, May 13, 2014, https://www.pbs.org/wgbh /frontline/film/united-states-of-secrets/; Siobhan Gorman, "Management Shortcomings Seen at NSA," *Baltimore Sun*, May 6, 2006; Siobhan Gorman, "NSA Rejected System That Sifted Phone Data Legally," *Baltimore Sun*, May 18, 2006; *60 Minutes*, "U.S. v. Drake," CBS, May 22, 2011.

49. Mark Hertsgaard, "How the Pentagon Punished NSA Whistleblowers," *Guardian*, May 22, 2016.

50. Ewan MacAskill and Spencer Ackerman, "Future of National Security Whistleblowing at Stake in US Inquiry," *Guardian*, May 23, 2016; "Pentagon Whistleblower's Disclosures Put a Lie to Obama, Clinton Claims About Snowden," *Democracy Now*, May 23, 2016, http:// www.democracynow.org/2016/5/23/pentagon_whistleblowers_disclosures_put_a_lie.

51. Kevin Poulsen, "U.S. Intelligence Shuts Down Damning Report on Whistleblower Retaliation," *Daily Beast*, February 11, 2018, https://www.thedailybeast.com/us -intelligence-shut-downs-damning-report-on-whistleblower-retaliation.

52. Christine Noonan, "Being Green and In-between: Federal Contractors and Whistle-blowing in the National Security State," paper delivered at Exposing Secrets: The Past, Present and Future of U.S. National Security Whistleblowing and Government Secrecy conference, London, January 18, 2019.

53. PEN America, "Secret Sources: Whistleblowers, National Security, and Free Expression," November 10, 2015, 13, https://pen.org/research-resources/secret-sources/; A. J. Plus, "Edward Snowden on the Man Who Inspired His Work," *Al Jazeera America*, August 5, 2015, http://america.aljazeera.com/articles/2015/8/5/exclusive-edward-snowden-on-the-man-who-inspired-his-work.html.

54. Garrett Graff, "How a Former US Spy Chief Became Trump's Fiercest Critic," *Wired*, May 30, 2018, https://www.wired.com/story/how-a-former-us-spy-chief-became-trumps-fiercest-critic/; Jack Goldsmith, "The 'Deep State' Is Real. But Are Its Leaks Against Trump Justified?" *Guardian*, April 22, 2018, https://www.theguardian.com/commentisfree/2018/apr/22/leaks-trump-deep-state-fbi-cia-michael-flynn; Eric Columbus, "Comey's a Whistleblower, Not a Leaker," *Politico*, June 12, 2017, https://www.politico.com/magazine/story/2017/06/12/comey-leak-memo-susan-collins-trump-whistleblower-215248; "White House Whistleblower: Gutsy Saint or Cowardly Rat?" *Federal News Network*, September 7, 2018, https://federalnewsnetwork.com/mike-causey-federal-report/2018/09/white-house-whistleblower-gutsy-saint-or-cowardly-rat/; Hannah Gurman and Kaeten Mistry, "The Ukraine Whistleblowers and the Breakdown of the Bipartisan War on Public Interest Whistleblowing."

55. David Pozen, "The Leaky Leviathan: Why the Government Condemns and Condones Unlawful Disclosures of Information," *Harvard Law Review* 127 (2013): 565–73.

56. David Von Drehle, "FBI's No. 2 Was 'Deep Throat': Mark Felt Ends 30-Year Mystery of *The Post's* Source," *Washington Post*, June 1, 2005; Max Holland, *Leak: Why Mark Felt Became Deep Throat* (Lawrence: University Press of Kansas, 2012); "I Am Part of the Resistance Inside the Trump Administration," *New York Times,* September 5, 2019.

57. "Attorney General Jeff Sessions Delivers Remarks at Briefing on Leaks of Classified Materials Threatening National Security," August 4, 2017, https://www.justice.gov/opa/pr/attorney-general-jeff-sessions-delivers-remarks-briefing-leaks-classified-materials; "NSA Leaker Reality Winner Sentenced to More Than Five Years in Prison," CNN, August 23, 2018, https://www.cnn.com/2018/08/23/politics/reality-winner-nsa-leaker-sentenced/index.html.

58. For instance, see the Office of the Whistleblower, based in the Securities and Exchange Commission, which has comprehensive protection and a Congress-approved reward fund for whistleblowers exposing threats to investors and capital free markets: https://www.sec.gov/whistleblower.

59. Michael Walzer, "Just and Unjust Leaks: When to Spill Secrets," *Foreign Affairs* 97, no. 2 (March/April 2018): 48–59; Peter Feaver, "Too Many Leaks," and Allison Stanger, "No Ordinary Times," in "The Secret Sharers: Leaking and Whistle-Blowing in the Trump Era," *Foreign Affairs* 97, no. 6 (November/December 2018): 199–206; Malcolm Gladwell,

"Daniel Ellsberg, Edward Snowden, and the Modern Whistle-Blower," *New Yorker*, December 19 and 26, 2016.

60. Consider the Assange-esque figure of Andreas Wolf, the leader of the Sunlight Project, in Jonathan Franzen, *Purity* (New York: Farrar, Straus and Giroux, 2015).

61. See Kaeten Mistry, "Embarrassing Indiscretions" and "A Transnational Protest Against the National Security State: Whistleblowing, Philip Agee, and Networks of Dissent," *Journal of American History* 106, no. 2 (September 2019): 362–89.

62. On the ethics of whistleblowing, see C. Fred Alford, *Whistleblowers: Broken Lives and Organizational Power* (Ithaca, NY: Cornell University Press, 2001), 63–96. For philosophy and debates about the "public interest" and "common good," see John Dewey, *The Public and Its Problems* (New York: Holt, 1927); Carl J. Friedrich, *The Public Interest* (New York: Atherton, 1962); Felix E. Oppenheim, "Self-Interest and Public Interest," *Political Theory* 3, no. 3 (August 1975): 259–76; Marcus Raskin, *The Common Good: Its Politics, Policies, and Philosophy* (New York: Routledge, 1986); Carol W. Lewis, "In Pursuit of the Public Interest," *Public Administration Review* 66, no. 5 (September/October 2006): 694–701; Claus Offe, "Whose Good Is the Common Good?" *Philosophy and Social Criticism* 38, no. 7 (September 2012): 665–84.

63. Alford, *Whistleblowers*, 1–3; Geoffrey Hunt, ed., *Whistleblowing in the Social Services: Public Accountability and Professional Practice* (London: Arnold, 1998); Roberta Ann Johnson, *Whistleblowing: When It Works—and Why* (Boulder, CO: Lynne Rienner, 2003); Stephen Martin Kohn, *The Whistleblower's Handbook: A Step-by-Step Guide to Doing What's Right and Protecting Yourself* (Guildford, CT: Lyons, 2011); Frederick D. Lipman, *Whistleblowers: Incentives, Disincentives, and Protection Strategies* (Hoboken, NJ: Wiley, 2011); Marcia P. Miceli et al., eds., *Whistle-Blowing in Organizations* (New York: Routledge, 2008); Tom Devine and Tarek F. Maassarani, *The Corporate Whistleblower's Survival Guide* (San Francisco: Berrett-Koehler, 2011); Tim Schwartz, *A Public Service: Whistleblowing, Disclosure, and Anonymity* (New York: OR, 2019).

64. Rahul Sagar, *Secrets and Leaks: The Dilemma of State Secrecy* (Princeton, NJ: Princeton University Press, 2013); Genevieve Lester, *When Should State Secrets Stay Secret? Accountability, Democratic Governance, and Intelligence* (New York: Cambridge University Press, 2015); Michael Colaresi, *Democracy Declassified: The Secrecy Dilemma in National Security* (New York: Oxford University Press, 2014).

65. Nick Cullather, "Security and Liberty: The Imaginary Balance," in *The Snowden Reader*, ed. David P. Fiddler (Bloomington: Indiana University Press, 2015), 19–25.

66. Geoffrey R. Stone, *Top Secret: When Our Government Keeps Us in the Dark* (Lanham, MD: Rowman & Littlefield, 2007), 1–17; Laura White, "The Need for Governmental Secrecy: Why the US Government Must Be Able to Withhold Information in the Interest of National Security," *Virginia Journal of International Law* 43 (2002): 1071–110; Mark D. Young, "National Insecurity: The Impacts of Illegal Disclosures of National Security Information," *I/S: A Journal of Law and Policy for the Informational Society* 10 (2014): 367–406; Andrew M. Szilagyi, "Blowing Its Cover: How the Intelligence Identities

Protection Act Has Masqueraded as an Effective Law and Why It Must be Amended,"
William & Mary Law Review 51 (2010): 2269–312; Mary-Rose Papandrea, "Leaker Trai-
tor Whistleblower Spy: National Security Leaks and the First Amendment," *Boston
University Law Review* 94 (2014): 449–554.

67. Stephen I. Vladeck, "Is 'National Security Law' Inherently Paradoxical?" *American Uni-
versity National Security Law Brief* 1, no. 1 (2011): 14, 17; Stephen I. Vladeck, "The Espio-
nage Act and National Security Whistleblowing After Garcetti," *American University
Law Review* 57 (2008): 1531–46; Heidi Kitrosser, "Free Speech Aboard the Leaky Ship of
State: Calibrating First Amendment Protections for Leakers of Classified Information,"
Journal of National Security Law and Policy 6 (2013): 409–46.

68. John N. Tye and Mark S. Zaid, "Robert Mueller's Last Resort," *New York Times*, April 25,
2018. See Whistleblower and Source Protection Program at Expose Facts (https://whisper
.exposefacts.org/) and Whistleblower Aid (https://whistlebloweraid.org/). The latter is
representing the Ukraine whistleblowers.

69. Lloyd C. Gardner, *The War on Leakers: National Security and American Democracy, from
Eugene V. Debs to Edward Snowden* (New York: New Press, 2016); John Prados, *The
Family Jewels: The CIA, Secrecy, and Presidential Power* (Austin: University of Texas
Press, 2013), 236–56; Christopher Moran, *Company Confessions: Secrets, Memoirs, and
the CIA* (London: Biteback, 2015), 103–41; David S. McCarthy, *Selling the CIA: Public
Relations and the Culture of Secrecy* (Lawrence: University Press of Kansas, 2018),
11–56.

70. Allison Stanger, *Whistleblowers: Honesty in America from Washington to Trump* (New
Haven, CT: Yale University Press, 2019), 1; Tom Mueller, *Crisis of Conscience: Whistle-
blowing in an Age of Fraud* (New York: Random House, 2019); GAP, "A Timeline of
U.S. Whistleblowers," https://www.whistleblower.org/timeline-us-whistleblowers; Ste-
phen M. Kohn, "The Whistleblowers of 1777," *New York Times*, June 12, 2011; Gabriel
Schoenfeld, *Necessary Secrets: National Security, the Media, and the Rule of Law* (New York:
Norton, 2010), 54–82; Stephen Knott, "America Was Founded on Secrets and Lies," *Foreign Policy*, February 15, 2016.

71. Glenn Greenwald, *No Place to Hide: Edward Snowden, the NSA, and the Surveillance State*
(New York: Metropolitan, 2014); Luke Harding, *The Snowden Files: The Inside Story of the
World's Most Wanted Man* (London: Vintage, 2014); Chase Madar, *The Passion of Bradley
Manning: The Story of the Suspect Behind the Largest Breach in US History* (New York: OR,
2012); Mark Hertsgaard, *Bravehearts: Whistleblowing in the Age of Snowden* (New York:
Skyhorse, 2016); Allison Stanger, "Why America Needs Whistle-blowers: They Are Not
Partisans but Stewards of Our Constitutional Democracy," *New York Times*, October 6,
2019, https://www.nytimes.com/2019/10/06/opinion/trump-whistleblower.html.

72. Schoenfeld, *Necessary Secrets*, 21–22; Schoenfeld, "Has the *New York Times* Violated
the Espionage Act?" *Commentary*, March 2006, https://www.commentarymagazine
.com/articles/has-the-new-york-times-violated-the-espionage-act/; Zachary Keck,
"Yes, Edward Snowden Is a Traitor," *The Diplomat*, December 21, 2013, https://

thediplomat.com/2013/12/yes-edward-snowden-is-a-traitor/; David French, "Trans-genderism Doesn't Excuse Treason," *National Review*, August 10, 2017, https://www.nationalreview.com/2017/08/chelsea-manning-traitor-not-transgender-hero/; Edward Jay Epstein, *How America Lost Its Secrets: Edward Snowden, the Man and the Theft* (New York: Knopf, 2017).

2

FROM CENSORSHIP
TO CLASSIFICATION

The Evolution of the Espionage Act

SAM LEBOVIC

C OLONEL JOHN NICKERSON didn't intend to become a whistleblower,
and he certainly didn't intend to become the first whistleblower
prosecuted under the Espionage Act. In 1956, the decorated World
War II veteran was supervising the U.S. Army's intermediate ballistic missile program at the Redstone Artillery Range and looking forward to a
continuing rise up the military hierarchy. But then, in the midst of one of
the period's interminable interservice disputes, Secretary of Defense Charles
Wilson decided to shut down Nickerson's program, favoring a rival Navy
missile. On Thanksgiving evening, Nickerson went to Washington to
privately protest the decision. When that effort failed, he wrote, anonymously, a twelve-page memo on the two missile systems, arguing that the
Army missile was far more effective than the Navy equivalent and asserting that the decision to discontinue the Army program stemmed from corporate corruption. (The Navy's missile needed parts produced by General
Motors, Secretary Wilson's former employer.) To make his case, Nickerson
revealed the classified results of early tests. He then distributed the memo
to the press. Within weeks, the memo was traced back to Nickerson. In
early 1957, Nickerson was relieved of his duties and charged with perjury,
security violations, and violating the Espionage Act. He faced forty-six
years in prison.[1]

Nickerson was surprised to be charged under the Espionage Act, and for good reason. It wasn't obvious that disclosing information to the press had anything much to do with "espionage"—a term, in the red-baiting 1950s, that carried clear connotations. Leakers, moreover, had never before been charged under the act. In fact, the Nickerson case, though forgotten today, was a significant milestone in the evolution of the Espionage Act—it marked the law's maturation as a tool the national security state could use to police the disclosure of classified information to the press and public.

Since it was passed in 1917, the Espionage Act has had a colorful life. It is a sprawling statute, covering what we might think of as traditional spying alongside a host of other activities. In its latter years, of course, it has become known mostly as a tool used to prosecute leakers. (The 2012 edition of a leading intelligence textbook tellingly discusses the act only once, in the context of leaks.)[2] Historians, meanwhile, primarily know the Espionage Act for its youthful indiscretions, when it was used as a tool of zealous censorship during World War I. Our knowledge of the act's history is therefore lumpy, clustered around distinct poles of activity separated by the best part of a century.[3]

This chapter narrates the history of the first forty years of the Espionage Act, to depict its evolution from a censorship tool used to police antiwar speech during World War I to a classification tool used to police the disclosure of classified information by government employees. In these understudied years, the Espionage Act took on its current form. Focusing on them allows us to see a broader shift in the ways that the U.S. state has managed the flow of information in the American polity—rather than censoring expression in the sphere of circulation, it began to censor information *within* the state. The history of the Espionage Act in these years also reveals three important features of national security secrecy in the modern United States. First, although many scholars follow Weber in seeing secrecy as a timeless attribute of the bureaucratic state, a history of the Espionage Act reveals the considerable improvisation and contingency that attended the political and legal history of the secrecy regime.[4] Second, the history of the Espionage Act reveals how laws of secrecy developed in ways intended to prevent interference with First Amendment rights. Third, these efforts had unintended consequences. They produced badly drawn legislation and a patchwork secrecy regime that developed without a master plan and that was defined and legitimated as much for what it avoided doing as for what it did. The outcome was contradictory and confusing. As two leading legal scholars of the Espionage Act noted in the 1970s, the process produced "legislation [that] is in many respects incomprehensible."[5]

★ ★ ★

The modern American secrecy regime was a product of the twentieth century, not a holdover of undemocratic modes of governance from an earlier time. Throughout the nineteenth century, the American state had sought to protect secrets according to a distinct logic. Rather than secure information at the source, it sought to secure information by regulating the press. For instance, Benjamin Franklin Bache, the prominent publisher and grandson of Benjamin Franklin, was jailed when he published secret diplomatic correspondence in the 1790s. The state saw no difference between his journalism criticizing the state and his publication of leaked secrets; both fell outside the limited protections afforded to press freedom in the early republic. Similarly, during the Civil War, military information was kept secret by regulating the sphere of circulation, not controlling information at the source—newspapers were barred from circulating in military zones, the telegraph was censored, hostile editors were jailed, select periodicals were barred from the mail, and others were forcibly closed by the military.[6]

In the twentieth century, as Americans came to lionize the freedom of their press from government interference, such methods to secure secrets became unacceptable, even as the development of new technologies of war and communication increased state concerns about the possibilities of espionage. The first general military orders to regulate information date to 1869 and were designed to prevent the photography or sketching of military installations. They suggest a newfound concern with the technological reproduction of defense information and were updated several times over the late nineteenth century. In 1911, Congress passed a vague Defense

Secrets Act that made criminal the collection of information about military matters by unauthorized persons.[7]

The outbreak of World War I heightened fears of foreign spies and saboteurs and raised concerns that existing regulations were inadequate to secure state secrets.[8] The Woodrow Wilson administration therefore introduced an expansive Espionage Act to Congress in 1917. The first draft of the law would have authorized the president to ban the circulation of "any information relating to the public defense, or calculated to be, or which might be useful to the enemy." This sweeping censorship provision was met with vehement criticism that it violated First Amendment rights. Newspapers protested, one million citizens signed a petition, and congressmen attacked the section, which was repeatedly identified as "Prussian," an effort to "muzzle the press," and "an absolute overthrow of a free press." Congress removed the offending section from the final act.[9]

In the short term, of course, other provisions in the Espionage Act, focused on preserving the integrity of the draft and respect for the military, would be used by zealous local prosecutors to police the speech of a wide variety of dissenters, particularly once these powers had been expanded with the Sedition Act amendments of 1918. This is the familiar story of the Espionage Act during World War I: among the two thousand individuals prosecuted for war criticism were Charles Schenck, Eugene Debs, Rose Pastor Stokes, the makers of the misguidedly patriotic film *The Spirit of '76*, and so forth. The logic of this sprawl was perhaps captured best in the relatively neglected prosecution of Jacob Frohwerk from Kansas City, who was jailed for a series of critical articles about the war in his small German-language newspaper. The case went to the Supreme Court in the spring of 1919, alongside the cases of Schenck and Debs, and it too was unanimously upheld by the court. The decision revealed the ineffectiveness of congressional efforts to revise the Espionage Act to protect press freedom. Writing for the Supreme Court, Oliver Wendell Holmes turned apparently limited Espionage Act provisions about interfering with the draft into a sweeping justification for press censorship. While Holmes conceded that Frohwerk's publications had not made "any special effort to reach men who were subject to the draft," he argued that it was "impossible to say that it might not have been found that the circulation of the papers was in quarters where a little breath would be enough to kindle a flame." The fact the newspapers circulated had turned apparently limited measures to protect the draft into a general censorship provision.[10]

The civil-libertarian backlash to such decisions, as is well known, would ultimately reverse that sort of judicial logic. Holmes changed his mind about the importance of free speech that summer, and in his famous *Abrams* dissent that fall, the aging justice argued that even radical pamphleteers seeking to disrupt war production deserved to have their speech rights protected from prosecution under the Espionage Act. In the long term, of course, Holmes's championing of what was soon dubbed the "free market of ideas" set the template for the vast expansion of First Amendment rights over the remainder of the century. In the short term, too, there was a retreat from what were soon seen as wartime abuses of the Espionage Act. Between 1919 and 1923, presidents Wilson, Warren Harding, and Calvin Coolidge pardoned those convicted under the act; Franklin D. Roosevelt later granted them amnesty. In 1921, Congress repealed the Sedition Act, restoring the original, more limited Espionage Act prohibitions on interfering with the draft. While these sections remain the law of the land— today they are section 2388 of the U.S. Criminal Code—they remain almost entirely unused.[11]

Other sections of the Espionage Act, however, would turn out to have longer and more active lives. And while congressional revision of the Espionage Act had been ineffective in protecting civil liberties during World War I, Congress' attempted civil libertarianism had serious consequences for the development of the rest of the act, particularly for the numerous measures aimed at regulating the disclosure of government information. Some of these covered classic espionage scenarios, such as the smuggling of secret information to a foreign government. But the act also prohibited a wide range of other activities—collecting information about national defense by entering military installations, failing to surrender government documents under orders, and, most importantly, communicating or possessing information about national defense without authorization. These sections have stayed on the books until the present day, where they can be found as sections 793–798 of the U.S. Criminal Code.

Congressional revisions in 1917 had introduced a foundational incoherence into the meaning of these sections. The basic problem centers on provisions in the act that make it illegal to disclose information "related to the national defense" to those unauthorized to receive it. These provisions had been transferred into the Espionage Act from the Defense Secrets Act, and while they may seem commonsensical, the statute defines neither a process for determining what is "related to the national defense" nor a procedure for authorizing individuals to access it. Early drafts of the Espionage Act had vested both powers in the president, but these were the sections that met with criticism as potential violations of press freedom, and they were struck from the bill. In 1917, in other words, the Espionage Act made it illegal to improperly disclose national security information. But these were orphaned provisions, for they defined neither "information related to the national defense" nor the process for regulating proper access to such information.[12]

These problems would haunt the Espionage Act for the rest of its life. By the interwar years, as the federal government tried and failed to prosecute individuals for publishing defense information, Congress and the courts were forced to confront them head on. In 1933, for instance, Congress revised the Espionage Act to allow it to block the impending publication of a book by Herbert Yardley, the former head of the War Department's Cipher Bureau (known colloquially as the American Black Chamber), who had deciphered code between 1917 and 1929. In 1931, Yardley had published a bestselling memoir-cum-exposé about his work; doing so revealed the ambiguities of Espionage Act controls on the disclosure of information. Yardley's publishers and agent had sought legal advice before publishing the work and had received uncertain responses. The agent's lawyers had "seemed to spread themselves . . . and took on all the august deliberations of Supreme Court judges."[13] The publishers' lawyers were similarly divided. Given the "highly unusual nature of the facts," one firm was "unable to find any authority squarely in point" but advised against publication out of fear that government could either claim a property right in the material or enjoin publication for interfering with government functions—it was telling that the Espionage Act was not even considered as a relevant law.[14] Another, faced with the same lack of certainty, came to the opposite conclusion. Deciding that no statutes "defining treason, sedition, or espionage were being infringed," it recommended publication. Yardley published; the federal government found itself powerless to act.[15]

Now, as Yardley sought to publish a sequel to the earlier volume, moves were afoot to tighten the law by revising the Espionage Act. In April 1933, a bill was introduced to the House intended to make illegal the dissemination of information gleaned from foreign code. The bill's proponents hinted vaguely and melodramatically at an urgent need to restrict leaks of information, Representative Joseph Hooper of Michigan suggesting darkly that "the special circumstances under which the bill comes up here are such that I would not care to take the responsibility of disclosing them." The chairman of the House subcommittee considering the bill agreed: "It is highly essential that leaks from confidential official records and communications not occur and that baseless or damaging reports purporting to be disclosures from such documents not be circulated." Under such urgings, a bill to revise the Espionage Act comfortably passed the House after only brief debate.[16]

But as in 1917, efforts to secure secrecy were met with criticism by the press. The bill was so loosely drawn, it turned out, that it risked rendering criminal the publication of almost any government document—the newspaper trade journal *Editor and Publisher*, for instance, protested that the passage of the bill "serves notice upon journalism, and readers who feel like freemen, that their constitutional liberties hang by slim threads" because the bill "dragged the free press by the heels deliberately mercilessly, in the very spirit of a Hitler, Mussolini or a Stalin."[17] Even Cordell Hull publicly urged that "any provisions that could possibly be construed as to the least affecting the freedom of the press be stricken out of the bill."[18] The bill was subsequently revised. As *Editor and Publisher* explained, with considerable relief, the revised law "applies only to persons who publish such codes by virtue of their employment by the United States. The amended bill will not apply to the medium through which any diplomatic codes are published so by no stretch of the imagination can the measure now be construed as an attempt to muzzle the press in any way." The Senate passed the revised bill without recorded vote.[19]

The significance of these developments was not lost on Hiram Johnson, who explained the result to his fellow senators:

> Immediately upon the bill being passed by the House—and it was passed in such a fashion that no one knew anything about it until it had been passed—the members of the press set up the usual howl of the press about the freedom of the press and how this sort of statute would interfere with them. The result was that, of course, everybody ran to cover and the bill was amended in the twinkling of an eye in order that the press should not be interfered with and the freedom of the press at all hazards should be preserved.[20]

That was all well and good, Johnson explained, but the bill still interfered with the rights of the individual who sought to release information to the press—Yardley, or anyone like him. But that was an interference with speech rights, which raised less public concern. Regulation of the press was controversial and unacceptable, but regulation of the government employee was unremarkable and legitimate. Yardley could not publish his sequel and would require War Department review and approval of all subsequent work.[21]

Similar concessions to press freedom were at play in a second effort to amend the laws of secrecy in the early 1940s. Just before the outbreak of World War II, an effort to prosecute three employees who had stolen and sold information from Civil Services Records had collapsed when it became clear that while there were prohibitions on concealing or mutilating government documents, there were no prohibitions on stealing or disclosing the information within them. In February 1942, inspired by the need to prevent otherwise unpunishable leaks of defense information, Attorney General Francis Biddle sent a bill to "plug the loophole" to congressional leaders. Intended to prevent the disclosure of "confidential" government information, the bill threatened a $5,000 fine or two years of jail time for revealing or communicating such information. But the bill was so broadly written that it didn't distinguish between government employees and journalists, in part because it was aimed at preventing leaks from defense contractors. (Biddle also conceded it was "only a skeleton" of a bill, which he hoped Congress would flesh out.) Predictably, the bill was criticized as an interference with the First Amendment. The White House Correspondents Association and a number of journalists protested, and *Editor and Publisher* called the bill "one of the most iniquitous stabs at freedom of press and speech that had ever come before an American legislature." Senator John A. Danaher declared the proposed law "so wholly obnoxious that I would vote against it practically unseen." Biddle, too, struggled to reconcile his broader civil-libertarian commitments to preserving press freedom with his realization that the bill would probably make newsgathering "more difficult"—he did so by claiming to no one's satisfaction that "the press has never been free to disclose government secrets." The bill died in committee. It was simply not possible to pass legislation that threatened to interfere with the rights of the press.[22]

In all, the interwar years witnessed the rise of two trends that would shape the flow of information to the public for decades to come. On the one hand, the press had become more successful in arguing that democracy required that it be free from all forms of government interference. On the other, a growing national security state was becoming ever more anxious to maintain control over information that it believed needed to be kept secret. As these two increasingly irresistible forces in American life began to clash in the years before World War II, freedom of the press proved to be an immovable object.

Even during the pressures of World War II, this respect for the rights of the press held strong. Just days before Pearl Harbor, when the *Chicago Tribune* published leaked defense plans, FDR's press secretary Stephen Early maintained that the *Tribune* was simply "operating as a free press": its "right to print the news is unchallenged and unquestioned."[23] It was the government's responsibility, Early observed, to secure the secrecy of information it did not want to be published. Once the war broke out, both sides of Early's distinction held. The press remained free to publish as it saw fit. There was no repeat of the World War I–era civil-liberties violations; the Supreme Court even overturned a rare Espionage Act conviction of an anti-Semitic pamphleteer hoping for Nazi victory. Instead, an Office of Censorship, staffed by journalists, developed a system of "voluntary censorship" that encouraged the press to abstain voluntarily from publishing information relating to the national defense if they thought it would harm the war effort. The autonomy of the press was thus protected.[24]

But in keeping with the other half of Early's equation, as the state left the press free to publish according to its own judgments, the state began to increase its efforts to secure information at the source. In a 1940 executive order, FDR conferred presidential recognition on the systems of classification that the armed forces had been developing since 1869; during the war, the release of information from military zones was tightly regulated. In 1942, in what it declared to be a "matter of some urgency," the Office of War Information established a "uniform practice" of classification across the federal government for the first time. The next year, it established a Security Advisory Board, which was soon making unprecedented efforts to ensure that federal employees were maintaining the secrecy of classified information.[25] All of these efforts to control information were defined as compatible with First Amendment rights to press freedom. As Byron Price, the director of the Office of Censorship, explained in 1943, "when it is examined in all of its aspects, [the First Amendment] resolves itself into a guarantee of freedom to express opinion, to petition, to criticize, to protest. The language of the amendment certainly cannot be reasonably stretched to include a guarantee of freedom to be criminally careless with information in wartime."[26] As this ever-broadening distinction between freedom of press and freedom of information was hollowing out the First Amendment, it was simultaneously doing important work to legitimate the emerging regime of state secrecy.

But as two Espionage Act prosecutions revealed during the war, the ambiguities of the legislative apparatus continued to thwart the security state's growing desire for control over information. The first case concerned a *Chicago Tribune* story about the Battle of Midway that revealed, by virtue of the information it contained, that the United States had broken the

Japanese naval code. The story, written by the war correspondent Stanley Johnston, was based on a classified radio dispatch from Admiral Chester Nimitz that Johnston had found on a desk on board the Navy transport *Barnett*. Thanks to the efforts of the Reporters' Committee on Freedom of the Press and the National Security Archive, we have recently learned how keen the FDR administration was to prosecute Johnston and the *Tribune* under the Espionage Act. But the recently declassified internal deliberations of the administration also revealed the uncertain application of the act to the press. Seeking some legal clarity, Attorney General Biddle had turned to the Office of Legal Counsel, which determined that Johnston's actions fell within the scope of the information handling provisions of the Espionage Act—he was guilty of taking information related to the national defense and also, by publishing it, of providing it to people not entitled to receive it. But to be found guilty under the vague provisions of the Espionage Act, it was necessary also to show that Johnston had done so with the "intent or reason to believe" that the information would harm the United States or advantage another nation. Assistant Solicitor General Oscar Cox believed that it was "doubtful" that there was specific intent. (In fact, the FBI was simultaneously conducting background checks to see if the Australian-born Johnston was traitorous, though these turned up little.) Nevertheless, Cox concluded that it was "fairly apparent" that there was "reason to believe" that harm would be caused. Moreover, he thought Johnston's actions were "characterized by real turpitude and disregard of his obligations as a citizen. It is hard to believe that any jury or judge would take a sympathetic view of his case . . . he thoroughly deserves punishment." Cox was sufficiently confident about the affair that he entertained the notion that Johnston's editor and publisher might also be charged. And he argued that a prosecution would "serve the public interest" by discouraging "serious leaks": "the indictment alone would have a salutary effect in preventing disclosures so dangerous to our war effort."[27]

Others within the administration were less certain. Former attorney general William D. Mitchell, who was prosecuting the case for the Department of Justice, concluded, "with regret," that "serious doubts as to the prospects of conviction arise because of defects in the statute." In particular, it had become clear that it would be hard to prove that Johnston had reason to think that the information he found lying on the table was secret. Moreover, by conveying it to his editor, Johnston could claim he had not intended to publish it—instead, he had asked his editor to ascertain whether it could be published. Meanwhile, his editor claimed that he thought the information had come from overheard conversations, and the prohibition on disclosing information to those not entitled to receive it covered only information in "a document, writing . . . or note." Most importantly, putting the matter on trial would require making public the fact that Johnston had disclosed information gleaned from a cracked Japanese code, which meant publicizing the fact that the Japanese code had indeed been broken. As the Japanese, remarkably, had not drawn this conclusion, prosecuting the case risked producing the very harm it was meant to punish. Shortly thereafter, following Mitchell's analysis, Assistant Attorney General Wendell Berge recommended that the prosecution under the Espionage Act be dropped despite the fact that the journalists' behavior had been "despicable."[28]

Still, FDR wanted a prosecution. On August 7, despite that he felt he had a "weak case," Biddle ordered the opening of a grand jury investigation in an effort to indict Johnston and the *Tribune* for violating the Espionage Act.[29] At the last minute, the Navy refused to provide the necessary evidence that the code had been broken, because they were worried about publicizing that fact. In the absence of evidence of a crime, the grand jury failed to indict. The *Chicago Tribune* rushed to claim a victory for the press, but William Mitchell's sphinx-like reaction to the decision revealed the ambivalent and half-hearted manner in which the state had pursued Johnston. As Mitchell delicately put it, the grand jury had concluded "that no violation of the law was disclosed." Privately, he was furious with the Navy— "in letting me go to Chicago . . . and then stopping the disclosure at that stage, they sort of sold me down the river and the Department of Justice as well."[30] The whole affair revealed the ambiguities of the Espionage Act, the still delimited understanding of press freedom, and the rickety nature of the World War II system for securing secrets.

A second Espionage Act prosecution, seemingly little related to the press, raised different problems. Arrested as part of the Duquesne spy ring on the eve of U.S. entry into the war, Edmund Carl Heine was sent to jail for eighteen years for sending information about the American aviation industry to Volkswagen, which was then gearing up to build military aircraft for the Third Reich.[31] Heine appealed, arguing that while he had sent information to Volkswagen, he was not guilty of violating the Espionage Act because he had only sent information that he gleaned from public sources—magazines, books, newspapers, technical catalogues, and so forth. In 1945, the Second Circuit Court of Appeals agreed that this was not espionage and overturned the conviction (the court upheld Heine's conviction for failing to register as an agent of a foreign power). The court's opinion, written by Justice Learned Hand, argued that treating even publicly available information as "information related to the national defense" rendered the Espionage Act overly broad. In a total war, where almost any information could potentially relate to the national defense, such an understanding of the Espionage Act would lead to a "drastic repression of the free exchange of information." In order to preserve First Amendment rights, therefore, Hand ruled that information was only related to the national defense for the purposes of the Espionage Act if it was being kept secret by the state. In a failed effort to appeal the decision to the Supreme Court, the Justice Department argued that this reading of the Espionage Act would simply require the state to keep more secrets.[32]

At the end of the war, moves were thus afoot to clarify the jurisprudence of the Espionage Act by enhancing the laws of secrecy. In May 1944, the Security Advisory Board (SAB) consulted with the Department of Justice to produce a memo documenting the laws relating to information security. Reviewing the history of the Espionage Act and the failed 1933 and 1942 bills to criminalize unauthorized disclosures, the memo concluded that although there was "at present no statute which prohibits the disclosure of general information obtained by government employees in the course of their employment," and although "there is an apparent need for a statute of this type," it would be difficult to draft, for it would have to be "very carefully drawn in order to make it sufficiently definite and certain and in order to escape the possible contention that it would curtail freedom of the press."[33] In July 1944, the War Production Board did draft such a bill to criminalize the leaking of information. Simultaneously, the War Department was doing the same.[34] New pressures to tightly regulate information had been produced by the experience of the war and by the destabilizing influence of First Amendment claims on the statutory and jurisprudential basis of the Espionage Act.

In the end, no legislation was forthcoming. Instead, in the waning stages of the war, the SAB developed a new strategy to control information—after consultation with the Department of Justice, it began to draft orders that would establish a new regime of information classification. And although the rest of the Office of Wartime Information was abolished immediately after the end of World War II, the SAB continued its work through the 1940s as part of the State-War-Navy Coordinating Committee.[35]

In 1947, drafts of these classification orders leaked. Ironically, they would have allowed the classification of information that "would cause serious administrative embarrassment or difficulty." As the American Society of Newspaper Editors protested, such a law would mean that "an effective screen would be thrown about governmental operations behind which many evils could flourish without detection."[36] Arthur Krock declared the measure just one more instance of the "recurrent effort to control the news," such as Biddle's 1942 draft legislation, an effort that had been defeated repeatedly.[37] In the face of criticism, Truman denied knowledge of the draft, the drafters retracted the offensive sections in October, and the whole matter went quiet for a time.[38] (The big winner was Nat Finney, who received a Pulitzer for the stories that broke news of the drafts.)[39]

But in 1951 Harry Truman issued Executive Order 10290, which established the modern classification system. The order fixed the problems the SAB had been concerned about during World War II. It created uniform definitions of secret information as well as standardized practices for handling that information and for authorizing access to information. Most significantly, the order explicitly invoked the information-disclosure provisions of the Espionage Act as the law behind the classification regime—when classified documents circulated outside the executive branch, they needed to be stamped with a notation that clarified the legal meaning of classification: "This material contains information affecting the national defense of the United States within the meaning of the espionage laws, Title 18, U.S.C. Secs. 793 and 794, the transmission or revelation of which in any manner to an unauthorized person is prohibited by law."[40] The classification system, in essence, was a plug-in to the Espionage Act. It tried to fill the destabilizing hole created by congressional revisions in 1917. Thirty years after equivalent provisions had been deleted by Wilson's Congress, the criminal sanctions of the Espionage Act were being deployed to enforce executive decisions about what information could be released to the public. Subsequent administrations have tinkered with EO 10290, but its basic logic and structure remains unchanged.[41]

While there was some initial grumbling among the press about the classification system, the legitimacy of classification was soon consolidated. This was largely because it was understood to focus on the regulation of the government employee, who was barred from disclosing information, not the regulation of the press, which was left free to publish and opine without government interference. As Truman explained in issuing EO 10290, "this order only applies to the officials of the U.S. government." Or, as Press Secretary Joe Short reiterated shortly thereafter, "the recent executive order on classified information does not in any way alter the rights of citizens to publish anything." Thus classification distinguished itself from censorship and solidified the line between the regulation of information and the regulation of speech that had been developing in the interpretation of the Espionage Act through the interwar period. As Joe Short put it in 1951, "classification . . . has no realistic relationship to censorship."[42]

Even those most concerned with state security respected this distinction. In 1950, little-noticed sections of the Internal Security Act made minor revisions to the Espionage Act, intended to require unauthorized citizens to turn in classified documents that came into their possession. In response to newspaper-industry inquiries, Senator McCarran added a clause to the law clarifying that "nothing in this Act shall be construed . . . in any way to limit or infringe upon freedom of the press."[43] In 1956, the Committee on Classified Information, established by the Department of Defense to explore the problem of leaks, concluded that information could not be secured by prosecuting journalists—that not only risked turning journalists into martyrs but also required further publicizing the illegal disclosure. In any case, the former assistant secretary of defense Charles Coolidge pointed out, "the real culprit . . . [is] a member of our department rather than the reporter."[44]

* * *

It was in this context that Nickerson made his ill-fated decision to share missile-development information with members of the press. Lured by the promise of a glimpse inside the Cold War arms race and space program, seventy-five reporters came to Huntsville, Alabama, turning Nickerson's trial into a minor media sensation. Media coverage provided a public lesson in the power the Espionage Act gave to the state to prosecute leaks— many newspaper headlines put the still unfamiliar term "leak" in scare quotes—as well as a portrait of the ambivalences of national security whistleblowing. Nickerson argued that he had disclosed information out of a patriotic desire to ensure that the best weapons systems were developed. "I can't believe this is happening," he declared, "to a man whose only crime is loving the Army too much."[45] But at the same time, he was also clearly acting in his self-interest, calling himself "one of a new-breed of missile-men politicians, engaged in a lone-wolf operation to sell new weapons projects to the government."[46] Ever since, Americans have wanted to judge leakers based on their intent—but as Nickerson revealed, motivations for revealing information are always murky.

The case also revealed the power that the sprawling classification system gave the state to prosecute internal dissent. There was reason to believe that the information Nickerson disclosed should never have been classified in the first place. (The rocket scientist Wernher von Braun, for instance, testified that 90 percent of what was classified by the Army would not have been classified by the Navy.)[47] And, as in later leak prosecutions, the Army quickly dropped the Espionage Act charges for a guilty plea to lesser offenses. Nickerson was stripped of command and relegated to a minor task inspecting construction work in Panama. A few years later, he died in a car crash a forgotten man, exiled from the heart of the Cold War security state for exposing information that was certainly classified but perhaps should not have been.[48] As Willard Bascom noted in a rare letter of protest to the *Washington Post*, the Nickerson affair was a product of an "erratic system that condones the release of information by one source while equivalent information is kept classified by another." "Whether or not there is a 'leak,'" Bascom concluded, "depends more on who leaks it than on the character of the information—and most often, I suspect, the largest leaks are at the top."[49] In the six decades since Nickerson's tangle with the Espionage Act opened the modern epoch of leak prosecutions, that logic has become very familiar.

As Nickerson's trial was unfolding, the Wright Commission on Government Security handed down its eight-hundred-page report on the national security apparatus ("the first complete and detailed study of the subject matter ever undertaken"). The commission was dismayed to find classified information published in "airplane journals, scientific periodicals, and even the daily newspaper." For the security-minded commissioners, this unhappy situation was attributable to the fact that "only disclosures by Government employees have been punishable" whereas "in many instances the chief culprits responsible for any unauthorized publication of classified material are persons quite removed from government service and therefore not amenable to applicable criminal statutes or other civil penalties." While the commission acknowledged that "any statute designed to correct this difficulty must necessarily minimize constitutional objections by maintaining the proper balance [with] the guarantees of the First Amendment," it nevertheless called for the passage of a law criminalizing the unauthorized publication of classified material.[50] In a controversial press conference, Lloyd Wright, chairman of the commission, made clear that this law would apply to the press. "We do not," he declared, "believe that journalists will claim a special immunity over their fellow citizens." If anything, Wright thought it was more urgent for the law to apply to the press because "the breadth of the newsman's information magnifies the peril."[51] Criticism of the proposal was swift and uncompromising. *Editor and Publisher* thought the measure would "hog-tie the nation's press"; Senator Ralph Yarborough declared it "as dangerous as the Sedition Acts of 1798"; the *Dallas Morning News* opined that "just because a tactic works well in a communist or fascist state is no reason to insist that it should be adopted in a free country."[52] The bill died a quick and unceremonious death in committee. Even as Nickerson's prosecution proceeded, regulating the press remained beyond the pale.[53]

The difference between these two events in June 1957 signified the culmination of the Espionage Act's evolution in the forty years since it had been passed in June 1917. The Wright Commission's proposition that the state could prosecute the press to secure secrets had become unthinkable. But Nickerson's prosecution for leaking was not protested by the press or treated as an interference with the First Amendment. The state's right to protect classified information by prosecuting leakers had become legitimized, seen as compatible with American press freedom. In reality, of course, the classification system, enforced by the penalties of the Espionage Act, seriously undermined the practical ability of the press to circulate information to the American public.

Nonetheless, efforts to preserve the formal autonomy of the press from overt censorship had shaped the Espionage Act throughout its life—they stunted the initial drafting of the act, guided subsequent efforts to amend it, and provided the contours of its jurisprudence. The result was a patchwork system that evolved according to little clear deliberation and in the teeth of the considerable confusion generated by the text of the poorly written act. By 1957, the Espionage Act had evolved into a tool that could be used to prosecute anyone disclosing classified national security information.

At the heights of the Cold War, there were few who tried to blow the whistle on matters of national security. It is telling that Nickerson, the first individual to be prosecuted under the Espionage Act for leaking, was a man committed to the U.S. military, providing classified information to the press in order to help the United States better wage the Cold War. Soon, however, a new generation of whistleblowers would emerge whose disclosures would challenge the prerogatives of the security state in more foundational ways. The Espionage Act would be waiting for them.

NOTES

1. Martin Gross, "Would Do It Again," *Boston Globe*, September 12, 1957, 19; Ian MacDougall, "The Leak Prosecution That Lost the Space Race," *Atlantic*, August 15, 2016, https://www.theatlantic.com/politics/archive/2016/08/the-leak-prosecution-that-lost-the-space-race/495659/.
2. Mark M. Lowenthal, *Intelligence: From Secrets to Policy* (Los Angeles: Sage, 2012), 175.
3. A search of *America: History and Life* for "Espionage Act" in October 2017 produced sixty-three hits: fifty concerned World War I; seven concerned leak prosecutions after the Pentagon Papers. Of the remaining six articles, two were about World War II, and there were individual articles about the Rosenberg case and a statistical summary. Peter Galison's "Secrecy in Three Acts," *Social Research* 77 (Fall 2010): 941–74, jumps from the Espionage Act to the Atomic Energy Act to the PATRIOT Act. Daniel Patrick Moynihan's "The Culture of Secrecy," *Public Interest* (Summer 1997): 55–72, focuses on the Cold War era. In Lloyd Gardner's book-length treatment of national security leaks in the twentieth century, the specific history of the Espionage Act from the 1920s to the 1950s is largely absent, on the understandable grounds that "after World War 1 ended, Debs was released and the Espionage Act was largely forgotten about until 1971." While Gardner is certainly correct that the Espionage Act receded from public view between these famous cases, it nevertheless had an interesting, if obscure, history—the subject of this chapter. Lloyd C. Gardner, *The War on Leakers: National Security and American Democracy from Eugene V. Debs to Edward Snowden* (New York: New Press, 2016), 24.
4. H. H. Gerth and C. Wright Mills, eds., *From Max Weber: Essays in Sociology* (New York: Oxford University Press, 1946), 233–35.
5. Harold Edgar and Benno C. Schmidt Jr., "The Espionage Statutes and Publication of Defense Information," *Columbia Law Review* 73 (1973): 934.
6. Jeffrey A. Smith, *Printers and Press Freedom: The Ideology of Early American Journalism* (New York: Oxford University Press, 1988), 156–61; James Tagg, *Benjamin Franklin Bache and the Philadelphia Aurora* (Philadelphia: University of Pennsylvania Press, 1991), 246–47, 342, 366–94; Everette E. Dennis, "Stolen Peace Treaties and the Press: Two Case Studies," *Journalism History* 2 (1975): 6–14; Geoffrey R. Stone, *Perilous Times: Free Speech in Wartime; From the Sedition Act of 1798 to the War on Terrorism* (New York: Norton, 2004), 126; Arvin S. Quist, *Security Classification of Information*, 2002, 1:13, http://www.fas.org/sgp/library/quist; James G. Randall, "The Newspaper Problem in Its Bearing Upon Military Secrecy During the Civil War," *American Historical Review* 23 (1918): 303–23; Harold Holzer, *Lincoln and the Power of the Press: The War for Public Opinion* (New York: Simon and Schuster, 2014).
7. Timothy Ericson, "Building Our Own 'Iron Curtain:' The Emergence of Secrecy in American Government," *American Archivist* 68 (Spring/Summer 2005): 29; Quist, *Security Classification of Information*, 14–18.

8. John B. Stanchfield, "The Peril of Espionage," *North American Review* 203 (June 1916): 830–40; Hannah Gurman, "National-Security Whistleblowing: The Creation of a Legal Paradox," Navigating Law and Ethics at the Crossroads of Journalism and National Security, Center for Ethics and the Rule of Law, University of Pennsylvania, November 9, 2017.

9. Stone, *Perilous Times*, 147; Edgar and Schmidt, "The Espionage Statutes," 947–57.

10. David M. Rabban, *Free Speech in Its Forgotten Years* (Cambridge: Cambridge University Press, 1997), 27–41, 248–98; Stone, *Perilous Times*, 135–234; Christopher Capozzola, *Uncle Sam Wants You: World War I and the Making of the Modern American Citizen* (New York: Oxford University Press, 2008), 144–72; Paul L. Murphy, *World War I and the Origin of Civil Liberties in the United States* (New York: Norton, 1979); Schenck v. United States, 249 U.S. 47 (1919); Frohwerk v. United States, 249 U.S. 204, at 208–9 (1919); Debs v. United States, 249 U.S. 211 (1919).

11. Stone, *Perilous Times*, 230–32.

12. Edgar and Schmidt, "Espionage Statutes," 1001, 1008–9; Harold C. Relyea, "The Evolution of Government Information Security Classification Policy: A Brief Overview (1775–1973)," in *Government Secrecy, Hearings Before the Subcommittee on Intergovernmental Relations of the Committee on Government Operations*, 93d Cong., 2nd sess., 1974, 852.

13. George T. Bye to Laurence Chambers, February 27, 1931, Box 391, James O. Brown Associates Records 1927–1992, Rare Book & Manuscript Library, Columbia University. My thanks to Kaeten Mistry for sharing these records with me.

14. George T. Bye to Laurence Chambers, February 27, 1931; Reynolds and Goodwin to George T. Bye, January 12, 1931, both in Box 391, Brown Associates Records.

15. Kaeten Mistry, "Embarrassing Indiscretions: The Origins and Culture of U.S. National Security Whistleblowing," in *The Culture of Intelligence: Germany, Britain, France, and the USA*, ed. Andreas Gestrich et al. (Oxford: Oxford University Press, forthcoming).

16. George H. Manning, "Press Gag Averted in 'Secrets' Bill," *Editor and Publisher*, April 8, 1933, 7.

17. "Editorial," *Editor and Publisher*, April 8, 1933, 20.

18. "Hull Says Code Bill Cannot Curb Press," *New York Times*, April 25, 1933, 10.

19. "New Bill Eliminates Press Censorship," *Editor and Publisher*, April 15, 1933, 8; Buel W. Patch, "Protection of Official Secrets," *Editorial Research Reports*, February 25, 1948, 133.

20. *Congressional Record*, May 10, 1933, S.3178.

21. "Code Bill Passed by Puzzled Senate," *New York Times*, May 11, 1933, 20.

22. "Editorial," *Editor and Publisher*, February 29, 1942, 22; Patch, "Protection of Official Secrets," 134; "White House Writers Hit Justice Bill," *Editor and Publisher*, February 28, 1942, 3; C. P. Trussell, "Biddle Presents War 'Secrets' Bill," *New York Times*, February 25, 1942, 1.

23. Arthur Sears Henning, "White House Calls Cabinet Aid to Draft Reply," *Chicago Tribune*, December 5, 1941, 1; "A.E.F. 'Plan' Laid to Army and Navy," *New York Times*, December 5, 1941, 3.

24. Sam Lebovic, *Free Speech and Unfree News: The Paradox of Press Freedom in America* (Cambridge, MA: Harvard University Press, 2016), chap. 5; Michael S. Sweeney, *Secrets of Victory: The Office of Censorship and the American Press and Radio in World War II* (Chapel Hill: University of North Carolina Press, 2001).

25. Lebovic, *Free Speech and Unfree News*, 126.

26. *A History of the Office of Censorship*, 2:4, Box 1, Entry 4, Record Group 216: Records of the Office of Censorship, National Archives and Record Administration II, College Park, MD.

27. Dina Goren, "Communication Intelligence and the Freedom of the Press: The Chicago Tribune's Battle of Midway Dispatch and the Breaking of the Japanese Naval Code," *Journal of Contemporary History* 16 (1981): 663–90; Oliver S. Cox, "Criminal Liability for Newspaper Publication of Naval Secrets," June 16, 1942, in *Supplemental Opinions of the Office of Legal Counsel of the US Department of Justice*, ed. Nathan A. Forrester (Washington, 2013), 1:93–101; John Prados, "Secrecy and Leaks: When the U.S. Government Prosecuted the *Chicago Tribune*," National Security Archive Briefing Book, October 25, 2017, https://nsarchive.gwu.edu/briefing-book/intelligence/2017-10-25/secrecy-leaks-when-us-government-prosecuted-chicago-tribune; Elliot Carlson, *Stanley Johnston's Blunder: The Reporter Who Spilled the Secret Behind the U.S. Navy's Victory at Midway* (Annapolis, MD: Naval Institute Press, 2017), 156.

28. William D. Mitchell, "Report on Chicago Tribune Case for the Attorney General and the Secretary of the Navy," July 14, 1942; Memorandum for the Record, William D. Mitchell (DOJ), "TRIBUNE Case," July 15, 1942; Memorandum, Assistant Attorney General Wendell Berge to Attorney General Francis Biddle, July 27, 1942. All cited from https://nsarchive.gwu.edu/briefing-book/intelligence/2017-10-25/secrecy-leaks-when-us-government-prosecuted-chicago-tribune.

29. "News Story Faces Inquiry," *Los Angeles Times*, August 8, 1942, 7.

30. "U.S. Jury Clears *Tribune*," *Chicago Tribune*, August 20, 1942, 1; Goren, "Communication Intelligence and the Freedom of the Press," 666–71; Carlson, *Stanley Johnston's Blunder*.

31. "33 Indicted Here as a Spy Network Operated by Reich," *New York Times*, July 16, 1941; Peter Duffy, *Double Agent: The First Hero of World War II and How the FBI Outwitted and Destroyed a Nazi Spy Ring* (New York: Scribner, 2014); "33 in Spy Ring Get Heavy Sentences," *New York Times*, January 3, 1942.

32. US v. Heine, 151 F.2d 813 (1945); "Ruling Is Refused in Espionage Case," *New York Times*, April 30, 1946, 10.

33. "Laws Applicable to Officers or Employees of the Government Giving Out Information or Copies of Papers or Results of Investigations Which Are of a Confidential Character," n.d., box 2, folder: SAB Memo 7, Entry 12, Record Group 208: Records of the Office of War Information, National Archives and Record Administration II, College Park, MD.

34. Meeting of SAB, July 26, 1944, 2–3, box 1, folder: SAB Minutes 3, Entry 11, RG 208.

35. "United States Commission on Government Security, *Report of the Commission on Government Security*, S.doc.64, at 155 (1957); Harold C. Relyea, "The Evolution of Government

Information Security Classification Policy: A Brief Overview (1775–1973)," in *Government Secrecy, Hearings Before the Subcommittee on Intergovernmental Relations of the Committee on Government Operations*, U.S. Senate, 93rd Congress, 2nd sess., 1974, 855.

36. Patch, "Protection of Official Secrets," 127; see also *Problems of Journalism: Proceedings of the Annual Meeting of the American Society of Newspaper Editors*, 1948, 200.

37. "A Recurrent Effort to Control the News," *New York Times*, October 24, 1947, 22.

38. David R. Davies, *The Postwar Decline of American Newspapers* (Westport, CT: Praeger, 2006), 34; Patch, "Protection of Official Secrets," 127; "Secrecy Modified on U.S. Material," *New York Times*, October 29, 1947, 56.

39. "Pulitzer Prizes Go to 'Streetcar' and Michener's Stories of the Pacific," *New York Times*, May 4, 1948, 1.

40. Harry S. Truman, "Executive Order 10290," September 24, 1951, American Presidency Project, http://www.presidency.ucsb.edu/ws/?pid=78426; Edgar and Schmidt, "The Espionage Statutes," 1052–54.

41. Executive Order 10290; Lebovic, *Free Speech and Unfree News*, 166–70, 236–37.

42. Arthur Krock, "Truman's Press Views Mystify the Capital," *New York Times*, October 7, 1951, 157; "Text of Truman Security Statement and Transcript of Discussion," *New York Times*, October 5, 1951, 12; President's News Conference, October 4, 1951, AP; Joseph Short to Maclean Patterson, November 5, 1951, folder: Executive Order Re Classified Information, 285-M, misc., Box 928, Truman OF, Truman Library, Independence, MO; David Greenberg, "The Tale of the Upside-Down Recipe Cake: Harry Truman, the Press, and Executive Confidentiality in the Cold War Years," in *Civil Liberties and the Legacy of Harry S. Truman*, ed. Richard S. Kirkendall (Kirksville, MO: Truman State University Press, 2013): 101–12.

43. Edgar and Schmidt, "Espionage Statutes," 1026–27.

44. Committee on Classified Information, U.S. Department of Defense, *Report to the Secretary of Defense* (Washington, DC: Government Printing Office, 1957); *Availability of Information from Federal Departments and Agencies, Part 8: Hearings Before a Subcommittee of the Committee on Government Operations*, 85th Cong., 1957, 2044–45.

45. "The Nickerson Case," *New York Times*, June 30, 1957, 134.

46. Gross, "Would Do It Again."

47. "Ex-Nazi Missile Scientists Testify for Colonel Nickerson," *Boston Globe*, June 27, 1957; "Interservice Row Over Missile Case Foreseen," *Los Angeles Times*, February 24, 1957, 36; "Army Rocket Ace to Be Tried for Secret Data Leak," *Boston Globe*, March 5, 1957; Mike Wright, "Huntsville and the Space Program," *Alabama Heritage*, Spring 1998, 32–46.

48. "Army Suspends Nickerson from Rank for One Year," *New York Times*, June 30, 1957; "The Nickerson Case," *New York Times*, June 30, 1957, 134; "Spy Case Dropped, Nickerson Admits Leak on Missiles," *New York Times*, June 26, 1957; "News of a Forgotten Man," *Boston Globe*, December 19, 1957, 22; MacDougall, "The Leak Prosecution That Lost the Space Race"; Leada Gore, "The Mystery, Intrigue, and High Drama That Surrounded the Most High-Profile Court Martial Held at Redstone Arsenal," Al.com, July 22, 2014, http://www.al.com/news/index.ssf/2014/07/the_mystery_intrigue_and_high.html.

49. Letter to the Editor, *Washington Post*, March 16, 1957, A10.

50. *Report of the Commission on Government Security*, xvi, xxiii, 619–20.

51. "Text of Wright's Statement on Journalists and U.S. Security," *New York Times*, July 1, 1957, 14.

52. *Congressional Record*, June 27 1957, A5155; "Editorial," *Editor and Publisher*, June 29, 1957, 6; "Five Bills Support Security Revision," *New York Times*, June 28, 1957, 35; "Betrayal of US Laid to Newsmen," *New York Times*, July 1, 1957; James Reston, "Security v Freedom," *New York Times*, June 25, 1957, 17.

53. William A. Korns, "Secrecy and Security," *Editorial Research Reports*, August 7, 1957, 571.

3

THE DEVIL'S ADVOCATE

Leonard B. Boudin, Civil Liberties, and
the Legal Defense of Whistleblowing

JULIA ROSE KRAUT

"**Y**OU ASK WHY—I ask myself why—I keep going up against the Government. It's really all I know how to do." This quote from Leonard B. Boudin was the last line of a lengthy profile by Paul Wilkes published in the *New York Times* on November 14, 1971. After speaking with Boudin's friends, colleagues, and clients, as well as watching him argue in the courtroom, Wilkes produced a striking account of one of the most renowned civil liberties attorneys in the nation.[1]

Wilkes wrote that Boudin, a fifty-nine-year-old with a pacemaker and cataracts who spoke with a slight lisp and was "one of America's worst-dressed lawyers," had probably argued more civil liberties cases before the Supreme Court than any other legal advocate. An expert on the law who possessed the ability to charm jurists more than juries, Boudin shined as an appellate lawyer, and judges turned to him for guidance and legal precedent during court proceedings. Boudin was a passionate advocate and an effective representative for his clients. He admired his clients' political philosophies and dedication to their beliefs, but, unlike others, he did not identify with them and was careful to keep his own views and politics out of the courtroom. When Wilkes observed Boudin, he was representing a defendant in the "Harrisburg Seven" conspiracy trial. At the time, Boudin was also preparing for another trial, where he would represent the whistle-blower Daniel Ellsberg.[2]

The criminal prosecution of Ellsberg under the Espionage Act of 1917 for his disclosure of the Pentagon Papers, the top-secret military history of U.S. involvement in Vietnam, is often eclipsed in discussions about the Papers by the Supreme Court's landmark decision upholding the right of the press to publish them. It is frequently overlooked that the Justice Department had charged Ellsberg with theft and espionage and that he was indicted by a Los Angeles grand jury before the Supreme Court's decision in 1971. Interest in Ellsberg's prosecution tends to focus on his trial's conclusion. In the wake of the revelation that President Richard M. Nixon's "plumbers" had burglarized the office of Ellsberg's psychiatrist, Dr. Lewis Fielding, in an attempt to find incriminating information to discredit him, the judge in his case declared a mistrial. The efforts to smear Ellsberg in the press and to influence the outcome of his trial backfired. Instead, they led to the dismissal of the charges against Ellsberg and helped pave the way for the eventual end of Nixon's presidency and jail for members of his administration.

The mistrial and Nixon's campaign against Ellsberg also overshadow Boudin's arguments and legal strategy in the case. Boudin viewed Ellsberg's disclosure as a moral action as well as one protected under the First Amendment. His defense focused on the public's right to know and its ownership of the information in the Pentagon Papers, which, he argued, did not relate to national defense but revealed a history of government deception and lies to the American people. For Boudin, this case was not about national security and loyalty but about information control and secrecy. Ellsberg was a scapegoat, selectively prosecuted for disclosing embarrassing information that should not have been classified in the first place. His trial was an opportunity to consider these arguments and whether a whistleblower like Ellsberg should be prosecuted under the Espionage Act.

While the mistrial led to Ellsberg's freedom, it was not a foregone conclusion. The revelation of the Nixon administration's abuse of power and actions to discredit Ellsberg was fortuitous, but the dismissal of the case was also thanks to Boudin's legal tactics, arguments, and experience. One cannot fully understand the Ellsberg episode without an examination of the Nixon administration's aggressive response and of Boudin's defense and his life and career more broadly. The underlying tenets of the government's accusation against Ellsberg—a traitorous radical who was, in Henry Kissinger's words, "the most dangerous man in America"—were also mapped onto his legal advocate. Yet the state's attempt to cast doubt over both the whistleblower and the lawyer representing him ultimately failed.

Although whistleblowing is often considered a solitary act, the wider phenomenon involves various protagonists. This chapter expands the discussion around whistleblowers to examine the work of lawyers as an integral part of the broader network behind whistleblowing. It begins by describing how Boudin became a civil liberties lawyer and how his career prepared him to navigate the twists and turns of Ellsberg's prosecution. The chapter then examines the trial, focusing on why Boudin agreed to represent Ellsberg, analyzing his defense strategy and explaining how it led to the mistrial. Last, it describes the aftermath of the trial, including the disclosure of the Nixon administration's attempts to discredit Ellsberg through his association with Boudin. The chapter concludes with an assessment of Boudin's legacy and the emergence of a new generation of whistleblower attorneys.

LEONARD B. BOUDIN

Leonard Boudin was born on July 20, 1912, in Brooklyn, New York. He was the son of a real estate lawyer and the nephew of a renowned socialist labor lawyer and legal scholar named Louis B. Boudin, both emigrants from Russia. The "B" stood for "Boudinovitch," the original English transliteration of the family's Russian surname. Leonard later incorporated the "B" initial into his own name in homage to his uncle and mentor.[3] As a child, he was a poor student but an avid and excellent chess player. Despite his grades, Boudin was admitted to his father's alma mater, City College, after a "winning" interview with the college president, and then graduated from

St. John's Law School in 1935.[4] He married Jean Roisman, a poet from Philadelphia, in 1937. Her sister Esther was married to the journalist I. F. Stone. Boudin and Roisman moved to Greenwich Village, where they raised two children, Michael and Kathy.

Boudin went to work in his uncle's labor law practice, Boudin, Cohn, and Glickstein, representing radical labor unions, including communist unions in the Congress of Industrial Organizations.[5] It was through his representation of unions and workers who wanted to start unions that Boudin began to view the practice of law as more than just an "intellectual game" like chess; it was also a way to protect individuals against exploitation, to defend the powerless against the powerful.[6] Victor Rabinowitz was another young lawyer who worked at the firm. They became close friends and later law partners.[7] Rabinowitz was an early member of the National Lawyers Guild, founded in 1937, a progressive legal association and alternative to the conservative American Bar Association. Boudin also joined the guild and wrote for its legal journal.[8]

During World War II, Rabinowitz left to start his own labor law firm, which Boudin joined in 1947. This move marked Boudin's shift from a labor union lawyer fighting against the employer to a civil liberties lawyer fighting against the government. Boudin's change in focus and representation was also guided by the times, in particular the government's efforts to suppress communism in the United States in the late 1940s. Rabinowitz and the firm represented the American Communications Association in a First Amendment challenge to a provision in the Taft-Hartley Act of 1947 requiring union leaders to provide an affidavit stating they were not members of or affiliated with the Communist Party. In May 1950, the Supreme Court upheld the provision.[9]

In June 1950, Rabinowitz told Julius Rosenberg the firm could not represent him in his espionage case because it was already representing Judith Coplon.[10] Coplon was an analyst in the Justice Department who had been indicted for espionage and conspiracy for allegedly passing government documents to Valentin Gubitchev, a KGB agent stationed at the United Nations. In 1949, a New York District Court judge appointed Boudin to defend Coplon after she fired her attorney, Archibald Palmer. Boudin learned Coplon had been arrested without a warrant, and he found FBI reports of information that could only have been obtained through wiretaps of conversations between her and Palmer. After Coplon's conviction in trials in New York and Washington, DC, Boudin used this information to appeal her convictions successfully. He argued that her warrantless arrest was unconstitutional, that the materials in her bag should not have been used as evidence against her, and that the wiretap revealed government misconduct and unconstitutional interference with Coplon and Palmer's attorney-client privilege.[11]

The case brought Boudin national attention, demonstrating his focus on protecting civil liberties and his expertise as an appellate lawyer. He used his skills and knowledge of the law to win a case on appeal that was lost at trial, especially when biases or controversy stacked the decks against him and his client. "At that time the prevailing view was that the F.B.I. could do no wrong, and if they wanted to arrest somebody, that person must have done *something* wrong," said Albert Socolov, one of Boudin's associates at the time (he later married Coplon). "Leonard had to get by that bias and show that without a warrant, regardless of their omniscience, they had no right to arrest her."[12] Boudin handled a few other espionage cases after Coplon, but that case was influential in shaping his subsequent legal strategies.

In 1951, the philosopher and civil libertarian Corliss Lamont and 150 others, including I. F. Stone, founded the Emergency Civil Liberties Committee (ECLC) to challenge anticommunist legislation that restricted civil liberties and to provide legal counsel to those facing prosecution or restriction under such legislation. Stone asked Boudin to serve as its staff attorney.[13] While Boudin represented clients called to testify before Senator McCarthy's committee, the cases he handled for the ECLC primarily had to do with the State Department denying or revoking passports based on an American citizen's alleged communist beliefs and affiliations or past or present membership in the Communist Party. Boudin represented a number of clients who sought to obtain passports, including Lamont, the artist Rockwell Kent, and the actor, singer, and activist Paul Robeson.

Boudin soon found he had to represent himself when his own passport was denied. In 1955, the Passport Office informed him that it had evidence that he was a member of the Communist Party and that his representation was at the direction and furtherance of its goals. While Boudin challenged his passport denial in court, he was called to testify before the House Committee on Un-American Activities. Rather than remain silent, Boudin shocked his colleagues, friends, and clients by answering the committee's questions and openly stating he was not and had never been a communist. He explained he did so because his statements were true, and he did not want any assumptions about him or his beliefs to interfere with his legal representation. "I felt I had to answer to clear the air so I could better defend my clients," Boudin said. He also "wanted to show that the Government was lying."[14] As in his Coplon appeal, Boudin sought to expose the government's misconduct and shift the debate away from questions of loyalty and politics and toward the violation of civil liberties.

Boudin's work at the ECLC led to two landmark civil liberties cases and victories in the Supreme Court. In *Kent v. Dulles* (1958), the court struck down the denial of passports based on belief and association as unconstitutional, violating an individual's fundamental right to travel.[15] In *Lamont v. Postmaster General* (1965), the court struck down a federal law permitting the postmaster general to detain a recipient's foreign mail containing "communist propaganda" as violating the First Amendment.[16] Justice William O. Douglas wrote the court's opinion, as he had in *Kent v. Dulles*. Douglas noted that First Amendment protections included the individual's right to receive information (the right to know) as part of the freedoms of speech and press.[17]

Boudin's wife, Jean, a "self-described parlor revolutionary," was a bit more radical than her husband, but she was quick to defend him and the importance of his work. When I. F. Stone once teasingly accused Boudin of being "apolitical," Jean shouted back, "Leonard's activism is in his goddamn law books."[18] On the weekends, the couple hosted a Sunday brunch, which served as a salon featuring a mix of Boudin's clients, legal colleagues, artists, writers, friends, and activists.[19] Boudin's daughter, Kathy, embraced her family's radicalism, and his son, Michael, shared his father's love of the law. Like Boudin, Kathy distrusted the government, but she was skeptical that the rule of law provided sufficient protection in an unequal society.[20] While

Michael pursued a legal career, Kathy became an activist and involved in the anti–Vietnam War movement in the 1960s. She cowrote *The Bust Book: What to Do Until the Lawyer Comes*, a legal primer to assist individuals facing arrest, which was published by the National Lawyers Guild, with Rabinowitz's assistance.[21] Kathy was also a member of the Weatherman faction of the Students for a Democratic Society and helped organize the "Days of Rage" in 1969, where she was arrested for assaulting a policeman. On March 6, 1970, Kathy, while released on bail, and Cathy Wilkerson escaped a premature detonation of a homemade bomb, which killed three of their fellow Weathermen. Kathy fled and remained a fugitive, pursued by the FBI, until her arrest in 1981.[22]

Boudin's law practice continued to shift with the times, and he now began defending antiwar protesters, dissenters, and draft resisters. Boudin won another First Amendment case in the Supreme Court in *Bond v. Floyd* (1966), representing the civil rights activist Julian Bond, who had been elected to the Georgia House of Representatives but was refused a seat because of his political views and opposition to the Vietnam War. The Supreme Court ordered the legislative body to seat Bond.[23] Boudin also represented Dr. Benjamin Spock in his 1968 conspiracy to "counsel, aid, and abet" resistance to the draft trial. Boudin lost at trial, but he won on appeal, overturning Dr. Spock's conviction.[24]

Boudin viewed his clients' demonstrations, criticisms, and violations of the law as not just a First Amendment issue but one of morality. He explained, "Technically, a person can be a criminal but morally right. My position is that the courts cannot only make judgments by statutes, but have to keep in mind the person's moral convictions. The court has to assess the damage done and see if no sentence or a suspended sentence might not be sufficient."[25]

"There is no normality in the executive branch and the very people who proclaim law and order are the most lawless of all," Boudin remarked in his November 1971 *New York Times* profile, as he prepared for Daniel Ellsberg's trial. "The Government was doing illegal wiretaps in the Coplon case in the nineteen-fifties, and I have no reason to doubt they are doing it in the Harrisburg and the Ellsberg cases," he said. "I'm sure my phone has been bugged. And I'm afraid of what's coming up. Lately I've seen a hysterical quality in the Government's response [in these cases] that hasn't been revealed since the McCarthy days."[26]

Boudin's suspicions about wiretapping were correct, and the revelations of wiretapping were critical in contributing to the subsequent mistrial in Ellsberg's case. Boudin's description of the Nixon administration, his comparisons to the McCarthy era, and his reference to Coplon's case revealed an insight and prescience based on his life experiences and legal career. Boudin would draw upon it all in his defense of Ellsberg.

DEFENDING DANIEL ELLSBERG

In his memoir, *Secrets*, Ellsberg recounted a conversation with Boudin in late 1972 about the indictment against him and Anthony Russo, his colleague at the RAND Corporation who had helped Ellsberg copy the Pentagon Papers. They discussed the research Boudin and the legal team had conducted on the Espionage Act and the charges of conspiracy, theft, and unauthorized possession and disclosure. Ellsberg recalled Boudin declaring, "As far as we can tell, Dan, you haven't violated any law." Ellsberg was thrilled and replied, "That's great! So, I'm home free!" Boudin was not so sure. He gave Ellsberg "fifty-fifty" odds at trial. "Well, let's face it, Dan," Boudin said. "Copying seven thousand pages of top secret documents and giving them to the *New York Times* has a bad ring to it."[27]

Ellsberg and Boudin first met in the spring of 1970 in Cambridge, Massachusetts, when Boudin was a visiting professor at Harvard Law School and Ellsberg was a research fellow at the Massachusetts Institute of Technology.[28] Ellsberg needed to talk with a lawyer, and I. F. Stone had suggested Boudin.[29] Ellsberg told Boudin about the Pentagon Papers and his desire to reveal the internal study to the public in order to end the Vietnam War. Boudin told Ellsberg, "It's a First Amendment issue. The people have a right to know."[30] Concerned about Boudin's health and little trial experience, Ellsberg decided to choose another lawyer.[31]

FIGURE 3.1

Daniel Ellsberg (*left*) speaking with his lawyer Leonard Boudin (*right*),
while on trial for disclosing the Pentagon Papers, April 17, 1973.

Source: Photo by Julian Wasser/Getty Images.

A year later, Ellsberg met with another lawyer who was teaching at Harvard Law, James Vorenberg. As Ellsberg recalled, he described his intentions to Vorenberg, who stopped him and said, "You seem to be describing plans to commit a crime. I don't want to hear any more about it. As a lawyer I can't be a party to it."[32] Ellsberg then went back to Boudin, who agreed to represent him. "You know, I'm not a hero or a martyr," Boudin told Ellsberg. "I'm a lawyer. But I've represented people like that. I'll be happy to represent you."[33] Ellsberg was not the first of his clients who had challenged the government, and he would not be the last. Boudin believed Ellsberg's actions were protected under the First Amendment, but he advised Ellsberg carefully. Boudin did not dissuade Ellsberg from acting but instructed him not to release any "current military secrets or secret codes and any other information that endangered national security."[34]

Boudin invited a Harvard Law professor named Charles Nesson to join him in representing Ellsberg.[35] Boudin drew on his experience avoiding FBI surveillance after Kathy became a fugitive, by communicating with Ellsberg through payphones and codenames.[36] Nesson became another point person for Ellsberg once Ellsberg went underground to avoid FBI investigation, after the journalist Sidney Zion publicly identified him as the source of the Pentagon Papers leak to the *New York Times*.[37] Through June 1971, the Justice Department attempted, under the Espionage Act, to enjoin the *New York Times*, *Washington Post*, and subsequent newspapers from publishing the Pentagon Papers.

The Justice Department also convened a federal grand jury in Los Angeles to hear charges against Ellsberg. On June 23, Ellsberg appeared in a televised interview with Walter Cronkite, where Ellsberg did not discuss his role in disseminating the Pentagon Papers but instead talked about the importance of disclosing them to the public and stressed the public's right to know more about the war in Vietnam.[38] With Nesson's assistance, Ellsberg surrendered to the U.S. Attorney in Boston on June 28, and the Los Angeles grand jury indicted Ellsberg for theft of government property and for violating Section 793 of the Espionage Act. The latter prohibits "unauthorized possession of, access to, or control over" documents "relating to the national defense" or information one "has reason to believe could be used to the injury of the United States or to the advantage of any foreign nation" that he or she "willfully communicates, delivers, transmits" to unauthorized recipients.[39]

Two days later, in *New York Times Co. v. United States* (1971), the Supreme Court issued a *per curiam* opinion (6–3) upholding the right of the *New York Times* and the *Washington Post* to publish the Pentagon Papers under the First Amendment and dismissing injunctions sought by the government as an unconstitutional prior restraint. The court's majority found that the Espionage Act did not apply to the press and that the government had not demonstrated that publication of the Pentagon Papers posed a threat to national security.[40] In his concurring opinion, Justice Douglas described the First Amendment's purpose as "to prohibit the widespread practice of governmental suppression of embarrassing information." He believed the

Pentagon Papers case would "go down in history as the most dramatic illustration of that principle."[41]

Livid about the leak of the Pentagon Papers, President Nixon was determined to prosecute "the Goddamn pricks" that had given it to the *New York Times*.[42] Eager to convict Ellsberg but prevent him from becoming a martyr, Nixon believed the best course of action was to "try him in the press."[43] He recalled his leaks of documents during the Alger Hiss investigation, boasting, "I had Hiss convicted before he ever got to the grand jury."[44] The Nixon White House launched a campaign to publicly discredit Ellsberg and his motivations for leaking the Papers. "Get a story out and get one to a reporter who will use it," ordered Nixon. "Give them the facts and we will kill him in the press. Is that clear? And I play it gloves off. Now, Goddamnit, get going on it."[45] Nixon told Special Counsel Charles Colson, "If you can get him [Daniel Ellsberg] tied in with some communist groups, that would be good."[46] The efforts to obtain disparaging information to smear Ellsberg and to stop similar leakers led to the creation of the White House plumbers in July 1971.

Ironically, the plumbers and their activities would not succeed in discrediting Ellsberg or in stopping future leaks but instead would lead to the dismissal of Ellsberg's espionage case, based on governmental misconduct and abuse of power, and eventually to the end of the Nixon administration. Boudin would demonstrate, despite Ellsberg's reservations, that his prior cases and expertise as an appellate lawyer were essential to help guide the case to a mistrial.

In August 1971, the Los Angeles grand jury subpoenaed Anthony Russo to testify. When Russo refused, he was found in contempt of court and spent forty-seven days in jail. On December 30, 1971, the grand jury presented a fifteen-count indictment of Ellsberg and Russo, who were charged with theft, espionage, and conspiracy.[47]

The Ellsberg/Russo trial was held in the U.S. District Court in Los Angeles. Boudin was the lead counsel and, along with Nesson, represented Ellsberg, while Leonard Weinglass represented Russo. Weinglass was a well-known civil rights and liberties attorney who had represented Angela Davis and had joined William Kunstler in defending the "Chicago Seven."[48]

U.S. Attorney David Nissen prosecuted the case, and Judge William Matthew Byrne Jr. presided. According to Peter Schrag, a journalist who covered the trial and published a book describing the proceedings a year later, Byrne was aware of Boudin's reputation and attempted to impress the veteran attorney, while also deferring to him and his legal expertise. Boudin quickly established a rapport with Byrne and used his knowledge of the law, cogent arguments, and charm and confidence to help guide and pressure Byrne to rule in his favor.[49]

Boudin later lamented that the mistrial and dismissal of the Ellsberg case meant that it could not be used as "the vehicle for resolving the crucial questions it raised" regarding theft, the overclassification of government documents, selective prosecution of leakers, and the vagueness and overbreadth of the Espionage Act. Even without additional guidance or motivation from a jury verdict or judge's ruling on appeal, he hoped Congress would decide to clarify and narrow the act to protect whistleblowers. "So long as the law remains unclear in its defense of the individual's right to speak up," Boudin predicted, "governments will likely be tempted to use concepts like 'theft of property' and 'espionage' to embrace communication of embarrassing information to the American people."[50]

In the months before the trial, Byrne had granted the defense's motions requesting the government to produce all material related to the charges against Ellsberg and Russo, including information on classification, specifics on charges of theft (whether of information or documents), and the damage or potential damage it claimed Ellsberg's disclosure had caused.[51] Boudin was disappointed that Byrne did not grant his motion to hold a separate hearing on the discriminatory prosecution of Ellsberg and Russo. The defense had affidavits from journalists and former government officials describing continuous leaks to the press that had occurred without facing prosecution.[52] Boudin believed the selective prosecution of Ellsberg and Russo did not relate to the national defense or aiding a foreign power but rather reflected a "system of information control for partisan purposes" used to punish those who disclosed information embarrassing to the government.[53] Byrne dismissed his argument. The case moved forward with jury selection. Schrag described it as a game of chess between the defense and prosecution, but Boudin was not winning this game. The jury was "weak." Nissen had removed those with "dovish views" who might have been sympathetic to Ellsberg and Russo.[54]

On July 24, 1971, two days before opening statements, Boudin received a stroke of luck. The prosecution disclosed an "interception" of a wiretapped conversation of a member of the defense (most likely of Boudin and some of his other clients).[55] Boudin and Weinglass called for Byrne to stop proceedings and hold a hearing. Boudin argued for dismissal of the indictment given the government's "shocking" and "shameful" behavior.[56] After he examined the intercept, Byrne refused. Boudin seized this opportunity to appeal. He reached out to Justice Douglas, who had jurisdiction over the Ninth Circuit Court of Appeals, which could hear an appeal of Byrne's ruling. Douglas agreed to issue a stay to stop the court proceedings and convene a three-judge panel to hear arguments on whether the wiretap was unconstitutional and interfered with attorney-client privilege, an argument Boudin had made in the Coplon case.[57]

The panel denied Boudin's appeal, so he went to Douglas again in the hope that he would stop the trial. Douglas concluded that Byrne should have held a hearing on whether the wiretap violated the right to counsel under the Sixth Amendment and that the Supreme Court should hear the appeal.[58] The stay remained until November, when the court then refused to hear the appeal. Boudin had lost, but he had delayed the trial for so long that he argued the jury could be corrupted and should be dismissed. Byrne initially refused but relented after Boudin appealed to the Ninth Circuit, which issued an opinion urging Byrne not to be "foolish" and dismiss the jury.[59]

The trial resumed in January 1973. Presumably, Boudin was much more satisfied with the new jury. Byrne had added questions in the selection process asking if potential jurors thought the government withheld too much information from the public or if they held a bias against those who had spoken out against the war.[60] Yet Boudin remained most concerned with the inclusion of theft in the indictment.[61] His strategy was to focus on Ellsberg's disclosure of the information to the public and to Congress. Boudin not only emphasized the public's right to know but also its ownership of the information. Ellsberg had copied and returned the Pentagon Papers to RAND; the issue was the disclosure of the information within them, which belonged to the public.[62] Boudin attacked the government's classification of the Papers as confidential as failing to meet the classification standards in Executive Order 10501, and he argued that the information within them was already in newspapers and thus the public domain.[63] He returned to his selective-prosecution argument, providing testimony of previous occurrences of mishandling and leaks of classified information without prosecution. Boudin also interrogated the classification system, attempting to reveal it was often meaningless or used as a tool to conceal embarrassing information rather than protect national security.[64]

Boudin described the government's approach to the charge under Section 793 of the Espionage Act as wanting "to have its cake and eat it too."[65] According to Boudin, the broadness of documents related to the "national defense" required proof of specific intent to injure the United States or aid a foreign nation. In this case, the government took advantage of the breadth of national defense but did not think it had to prove specific intent.[66] He dismissed Nissen's principal witness's speculation that information in the Papers "could be 'of use' to a foreign nation since it carried the imprimatur of the Defense Department and was marked 'top secret.'"[67] In fact, Boudin and the defense counsel learned of Justice Department reports, written by State and Defense Department officials, that concluded that nine of the twenty volumes of the Papers did not relate to the national defense.[68] Boudin introduced witnesses who described the Papers as a history, containing information that was out of date and embarrassing to the United States militarily but that could not have injured the United States or aided a foreign power.[69] According to Boudin, the Papers revealed a history of government officials' "deception and self-deception" to gain public support for the war, by concealing immoral and illegal conduct violating international law.[70] Ellsberg and Russo testified that in disclosing the Papers, they did not intend to harm the United States but inform the American people of this deception and end the carnage in Vietnam.[71] Boudin argued Ellsberg was morally right, reflecting a code of ethics and a loyalty to the nation instead of to "persons, party, or government department."[72]

However, the jury never got to deliberate. Nixon's vindictiveness and efforts to influence the case to secure Ellsberg's conviction in court, and in the court of public opinion, led to a mistrial. On April 26, 1973, Nissen told Byrne that he had received information from the Watergate prosecutor that the plumbers G. Gordon Liddy and E. Howard Hunt Jr. had burglarized Dr. Fielding's office in order to obtain the psychiatrist's notes and information on Ellsberg. Byrne ordered Nissen to immediately conduct an investigation about the information obtained and if it had been used to prosecute Ellsberg.[73] On April 30, the *Washington Star-News* reported that Byrne had talked with Nixon's counsel and domestic affairs advisor John Ehrlichman. Byrne admitted Ehrlichman had called him to discuss a "future assignment in government," but the judge said he could not consider it until the trial had ended.[74] Boudin conveyed his concerns about judicial ethics and impropriety. Byrne responded by demanding Nissen submit all information about investigations pertaining to the Pentagon Papers, Ellsberg, and Russo. Schrag described how the disclosures in court "became an open pipeline for Watergate news," where Nissen handed over documents to Byrne, who examined them, then handed them to the defense, which then leaked them to the press.[75]

On May 1, Boudin formally requested a dismissal of the trial, and in pressing his argument, mentioned the possibility of once again appealing to the Ninth Circuit. Byrne was nervous to declare a mistrial, asking Boudin to cite the legal precedent to do so. According to Schrag, Boudin told Byrne, "Surely, I need not remind your Honor that precedents are set by judges, and your Honor is such a judge." Boudin cleverly added, "And in the days to come, other judges won't have to ask me whether there is a precedent, because I will be able to refer to your Honor as having established one."[76]

After the disclosure of illegal wiretaps of Ellsberg and of one of the witnesses, Morton Halperin, conducted in late 1969 and early 1970, Byrne would no longer wait to set a precedent. On May 11, he declared a mistrial and dismissed the charges against Ellsberg and Russo. Byrne described the disclosures of governmental misconduct and concluded, "The totality of the circumstances of this case which I have only briefly sketched offend 'a sense of justice.'" He added, "The bizarre events have incurably infected the prosecution of this case."[77]

FIGURE 3.2

Daniel Ellsberg and his wife, Patricia, outside the courthouse after a federal judge dismissed the Pentagon Papers case, May 11, 1973.

Source: Bettmann/Getty Images.

THE DEVIL'S ADVOCATE

On July 19, 1974, a few weeks before Nixon resigned from the presidency, the *New York Times* published a White House memo and background paper on Boudin,[78] which had been released by the House Judiciary Committee.[79] Dated August 24, 1971, a week before the plumbers broke into Dr. Fielding's office, the memo was sent from Ehrlichman to Colson with the background paper prepared by Hunt entitled "DEVIL'S ADVOCATE—The Strange Affinities of Attorney Leonard Boudin." Ehrlichman noted to Colson that the paper "should be useful in connection with the recent request that we get something out on Ellsberg."[80]

The "recent request" Ehrlichman referenced was to fulfill Nixon's desire to publicly discredit Ellsberg in the press and to tie him in with some communist groups. The Hunt memo was prepared for precisely that purpose, and it began by asking why Ellsberg had selected Boudin as his legal counsel. The answer was Boudin's life and career, which it claimed would "provide at least partial insight into Daniel Ellsberg's motivation for revealing so many of the nation's most sensitive secrets to America's citizens—and enemies." Hunt's memo was a mixture of exaggeration, misrepresentation, innuendo, and complete fabrication. According to Hunt, Boudin had a "unique reputation as an articulate and aggressive advocate of ultra-leftist causes" and was a former, "concealed" communist. Hunt labeled the ECLC and National Lawyers Guild as communist-front organizations and included a long list of Boudin's affiliations and clients, including Coplon. He also mentioned Kathy's involvement with the Weathermen and her status as a fugitive. Hunt then described Boudin as possessing the "odor of espionage" and included a blatant lie that Boudin had been in contact with the KGB or may have met with foreign agents to provide information to communist governments or to take orders from them.[81]

Hunt warned that Boudin was a lawyer who defended traitors and spies and that his representation of Ellsberg would have serious consequences. He declared it was clear Ellsberg had hired Boudin in the hopes he would "escape with impunity," as had Coplon. Hunt predicted that upon learning that Ellsberg had retained Boudin as his legal counsel, there would be more leaks and whistleblowers. "Concealed enemies within our government will be vastly encouraged to go even farther than Ellsberg did, secure in the knowledge that someone—perhaps the celebrated Leonard Boudin himself—will direct their legal defense, if in fact it will then even be possible to indict Americans for compromising government documents."[82]

Attempting to use Ellsberg's words against him, Hunt argued if Ellsberg continued to believe and insist "Americans do have a right to know," then he should tell the American public why he has turned to Boudin. Hunt concluded the memo with an unabashed smear of Ellsberg and Boudin. The retention of Boudin as his legal counsel "tarnishes the idealistic image he tries to project, and becomes just one more client of a man and a law firm whose dedication over the years to the interests of our foreign and domestic enemies has remained unwavering and absolute."[83]

Boudin immediately held a press conference at his office, denouncing the Hunt memo as nothing but "inaccuracies and half-truths" and explaining that Colson had contacted Boudin and "apologized to him for attempting to interfere with Dr. Ellsberg's right to counsel." Colson had just started serving his prison sentence after pleading guilty to obstruction of justice for gathering and disseminating damaging information on Ellsberg to discredit him. Boudin released Colson's letter of apology, which also described such interference as having "had become something of a standard practice for the F.B.I. and other Government agencies."[84]

In an affidavit submitted to the Senate Watergate committee, Jerald ter-Horst, the Washington bureau chief of the *Detroit News*, stated he had received the Hunt memo on Boudin but had declined to use it.[85] It is unclear if other newspapers received the memo, but none appears to have used it to smear Boudin or Ellsberg. In fact, a few months after Colson sent the Hunt memo to terHorst, the *New York Times* published Paul Wilkes's flattering, well-sourced profile of Boudin.

Boudin and his colleagues were less shocked by the Hunt memo than they were by the decision of the *New York Times* to reprint it in its entirety and without any qualification or disclaimer. An article by Geoffrey D. Garin, "Spreading the Word on Len Boudin," published in the *Harvard Crimson*, described their dismay. Boudin believed that by publishing the Hunt memo now, the *New York Times* "inadvertently, no doubt—has succeeded where Hunt, John Ehrlichman and Charles Colson have failed: spreading false, irrational, inflamatory [sic] rhetoric about him in the mass-circulation media." Charles Nesson declared the memo was "defaming when it was written, it was defaming when Colson tried to circulate it in the press, and it was still defaming when The Times printed it."[86]

As Boudin told Garin, "It doesn't feel terrible to be the subject of that kind of attack, and I'm not going to be terribly affected by it," but he doubted readers would be sufficiently "sophisticated" to see the lies and red-baiting within the Hunt memo. He was more disappointed by the decision to print it without any consideration for his reputation and privacy. The *New York Times* told Garin the memo reflected Colson's actions, not Boudin's; it was a "matter of public record and we printed it." Garin noted the newspaper had the right to publish, but, like Boudin, he was unsure readers would interpret a document coming from the White House as a "hack job." The *New York Times* had published under an assumption "everyone has realized just how demented Richard Nixon and his government are," Garin wrote, and "that's not a safe assumption for anyone, let alone a newspaper, to make."[87]

Boudin was correct. He was not terribly affected by the Hunt memo, going on to represent various clients and defend civil liberties until his death in 1989.[88] Yet the *New York Times'* decision to publish the memo raised important and unanswered questions regarding the decision of news media to publish internal government documents and how best to present such documents to the public. Furthermore, senior White House officials readily leaked government documents and information to the press to serve their own interests. Yet they prosecuted mid- to low-level figures like Ellsberg, who disclosed documents that embarrassed them and exposed their lies, under the Espionage Act. This disparity between the government's response to disclosures by high-ranking figures and to those by whistleblowers remains relevant today.

In a 1974 essay about the Ellsberg case, which appeared in *Secrecy and Foreign Policy*, Boudin expressed hope that "no Ellsberg in a future and comparable situation need again be put to the financial and psychological ordeal of demonstrating his rights."[89] As for Ellsberg's legacy, Boudin concluded his leak of the Pentagon Papers, as well as "their impact on the American public consciousness, and the collapse of the Government's case against [Ellsberg], may make it less likely . . . that there will in future be so much government lying to the public" or that whistleblowers "who expose official lying when it occurs" will be treated like criminals.[90] Unfortunately, Boudin was wrong. As other chapters in this volume examine, government secrecy and lying continued in the decades after Ellsberg's revelation of the Pentagon Papers and his trial, as have criminal prosecutions of whistleblowers under the Espionage Act.

Yet there is a new generation of lawyers today who, like Boudin, are willing to represent whistleblowers and use their legal expertise. They also draw on personal experiences to help defend those who expose misconduct, illegalities, and abuses of power and believe in accountability and the public's right to know. Some are civil liberties lawyers, like Ben Wizner. Wizner is the director of the American Civil Liberties Union's Speech, Privacy, and Technology Project and has also served as NSA whistleblower Edward Snowden's principal legal advisor.[91] Other lawyers, for example Barry J. Pollack, specialize in criminal defense and investigations and bring their jury trial and appellate advocacy experience to their representation of whistleblowers.[92] Pollack defended Jeffrey Sterling, a former CIA officer, against charges under the Espionage Act for leaking classified information to a journalist, and he has served as one of the lawyers representing WikiLeaks founder Julian Assange.

Recently, former whistleblowers are representing current whistleblowers, creating organizations dedicated to providing legal assistance to whistleblowers. In addition to their expertise, they are using their own personal experiences to help inform their representation as well as to offer empathy and understanding to fellow whistleblowers. John N. Tye, who worked in the State Department until 2014 and blew the whistle on unconstitutional NSA surveillance practices, joined with his attorney Mark S. Zaid, who has represented federal employees and whistleblowers, to create the nonprofit law firm Whistleblower Aid.[93] Their firm explicitly does not represent anyone disclosing classified information to unauthorized recipients but focuses on "making it easier for whistleblowers to expose wrongdoing without breaking the law or incurring criminal liability."[94] Jesselyn Radack is a human rights attorney who started representing whistleblowers after she blew the whistle on government misconduct in the John Walker Lindh case. She later wrote a memoir about her experience, *Traitor: The Whistleblower and the "American Taliban,"* which was praised by Daniel Ellsberg.[95] Radack's clients include Edward Snowden, NSA whistleblower Thomas Drake, CIA whistleblower John Kiriakou, and former government intelligence analyst and drone warfare whistleblower Daniel Hale. She also heads the Whistleblower and Source Protection Program (WHISPeR) at ExposeFacts,[96] which assists journalists in releasing information and helps support and encourage whistleblowers "to disclose information that citizens need to make truly informed decisions in a democracy."[97] These present-day lawyers have different stories and backgrounds but are united in the belief that the law can and should be used to protect national security *and* to protect whistleblowers.

* * *

"I NEVER viewed myself as a revolutionary," Boudin remarked. "Perhaps that's why I came to admire my clients, from Rockwell Kent on down to Ellsberg. They believe in something to such an extent that they are willing to stand up to the government, challenge it, tell it, it is doing wrong."[98] While Boudin may not have viewed himself as a revolutionary, he did spend most of his career "going up against the government," exposing its misconduct, abuse of power, and violations of an individual's right to travel, to speak, to counsel, and to know. Boudin preferred his wife's description of him and adopted it as his own: "My activism is in my goddamn law books."[99] The Nixon administration sought and failed to paint Ellsberg as the devil by characterizing Boudin as the devil's advocate. Instead, Boudin's defense of a whistleblower revealed he was first and foremost a civil liberties and First Amendment advocate who used his legal knowledge, skills, and charm to defend his client and those constitutional protections. "Every civil liberties lawyer wonders what the results would be if he were completely successful," Boudin said, reflecting on his life's work and legal career. "Maybe all these freedoms will screw up the country completely. We don't know because there's never been a country that has had them. But there is no alternative but to try to preserve those rights."[100]

NOTES

I would like to thank Hannah Gurman and Kaeten Mistry for their guidance and thoughtful suggestions and the participants and audience members at the "Debating U.S.

National Security Whistleblowing: Secrets, the State, and Democracy" symposium for their helpful comments and questions.

1. Paul Wilkes, "Leonard Boudin: The Left's Lawyer's Lawyer," *New York Times*, November 14, 1971, SM56.

2. Wilkes, "Leonard Boudin," SM38–40, 42, 46, 50, 55–56.

3. Susan Braudy, *Family Circle: The Boudins and the Aristocracy of the Left* (New York: Knopf, 2003), 3–8.

4. Braudy, *Family Circle*, 8–10, 16.

5. Braudy, *Family Circle*, 18.

6. Wilkes, "Leonard Boudin," SM42.

7. Victor Rabinowitz, *Unrepentant Leftist: A Lawyer's Memoir* (Chicago: University of Illinois Press, 1996), 21.

8. Wilkes, "Leonard Boudin," SM42, 44.

9. American Communications Ass'n v. Douds, 339 U.S. 382 (1950).

10. Rabinowitz, *Unrepentant Leftist*, 159.

11. Rabinowitz, *Unrepentant Leftist*; Braudy, *Family Circle*, 58, 63–66.

12. Wilkes, "Leonard Boudin," SM50, 53.

13. Braudy, *Family Circle*, 78; Boudin was not Stone's first choice. Stone wanted Paul Robeson's passport denial to be the ECLC's first "test case" challenging its constitutionality in the Supreme Court. After the Harvard law professor Victor Brudney declined his offer to represent Robeson, Stone eventually turned to Boudin, who accepted.

14. Wilkes, "Leonard Boudin," SM53.

15. Kent v. Dulles, 357 U.S. 116 (1958).

16. Lamont v. Postmaster General, 381 U.S. 301 (1965).

17. Lamont v. Postmaster General, 305–7.

18. Braudy, *Family Circle*, 53, 56–57.

19. Wilkes, "Leonard Boudin," SM46; Braudy, *Family Circle*, 96–98.

20. Braudy, *Family Circle*, 181.

21. Braudy, *Family Circle*, 180–81.

22. In 1981, Kathy was arrested for her involvement in the Brink's armored truck robbery-murder. Charged with felony murder, Kathy pleaded guilty and served twenty-two years in prison; she was released on parole in 2003. Lisa W. Foderaro, "With a Bouquet and a Wave, Boudin Is Free 22 Years Later," *New York Times*, September 18, 2003, B1.

23. Bond v. Floyd, 385 U.S. 116 (1966).

24. Boudin succeeded on appeal based on the trial judge's errors in instructing the jury. United States v. Spock, 416 F.2d 165 (1st Cir. 1969).

25. Wilkes, "Leonard Boudin," SM42.

26. Wilkes, "Leonard Boudin," SM56.

27. Daniel Ellsberg, *Secrets: A Memoir of Vietnam and the Pentagon Papers* (New York: Viking Penguin Putnam, 2002), 431–32.

28. Braudy, *Family Circle*, 228; Ellsberg, *Secrets*, 383.

29. Braudy, *Family Circle*, 229. This conflicts with Ellsberg's account in his memoir. Ellsberg wrote he briefly met Boudin through the "radical lawyer Peter Weiss." He does not indicate that he talked with Boudin about the Pentagon Papers until a year later, after Vorenberg refused to represent him. He described meeting I. F. Stone for the first time in the Senate cafeteria in January 1971. Ellsberg, *Secrets*, 359, 383–84.

30. Braudy, *Family Circle*, 229.

31. Braudy, *Family Circle*, 229.

32. Ellsberg, *Secrets*, 383.

33. Ellsberg, *Secrets*, 384.

34. Braudy, *Family Circle*, 230.

35. Peter Schrag, *Test of Loyalty: Daniel Ellsberg and the Rituals of Secret Government* (New York: Simon and Schuster, 1974), 168.

36. Braudy, *Family Circle*, 231.

37. Ellsberg, *Secrets*, 393–94.

38. Tom Wells, *Wild Man: The Life and Times of Daniel Ellsberg* (New York: Palgrave, 2001), 436–40; Ellsberg, *Secrets*, 401–2.

39. Ellsberg, *Secrets*, 406–7; Wells, *Wild Man*, 470; 18 U.S.C. ch. 37 "Espionage and Censorship," Section 793 "Gathering, transmitting or losing defense information," subsection (e).

40. New York Times Co. v. United States, 403 U.S. 713 (1971).

41. New York Times Co. v. United States, 403 U.S. 713 (1971) (Douglas J., concurring), 723–24.

42. Nixon phone conversation, June 14, 1971, 7:13 pm, Conversation with John Ehrlichman, WHT 005–068, Nixon Tapes, http:/nixontapeaudio.org/ellsberg/005-068.mp3.

43. Oval Office, June 30, 1971, 2:55–3:07 pm, Conversation: Nixon, John Mitchell, and Henry Kissinger, in *Abuse of Power: The New Nixon Tapes*, ed. Stanley I. Kutler (New York: The Free Press, 1997), 6.

44. Oval Office, July 1, 1971, 8:45–9:52 am, Conversation: Nixon, H. R. Haldeman, and Henry Kissinger, in Kutler, ed., *Abuse of Power*, 9.

45. Kutler, ed., *Abuse of Power*, 9.

46. Nixon phone conversation, June 29, 1971, 2:28–2:32 pm, Conversation with Charles Colson, in Kutler, ed., *Abuse of Power*, 6.

47. Steven V. Roberts, "Ellsberg Indicted Again in Pentagon Case," *New York Times*, December 31, 1971, 1.

48. Bruce Webber, "Leonard I. Weinglass, Lawyer, Dies at 77; Defended Renegades and the Notorious," *New York Times*, March 24, 2011, A18. Weinglass defended Davis against charges of conspiracy, murder, and kidnapping in 1970. The Chicago Seven (formerly the Chicago Eight—Bobby Seale) included Tom Hayden, Abbie Hoffman, David Dellinger, Jerry Rubin, Rennie Davis, Lee Weiner, and John Froines, who were charged with conspiracy, inciting to riot, and other federal crimes for their involvement in the protests in Chicago outside the Democratic National Convention in 1968. Weinglass also represented Kathy Boudin in the Brink's robbery-murder case.

49. Schrag, *Test of Loyalty*, 180.
50. Leonard B. Boudin, "The Ellsberg Case: Citizen Disclosure," in *Secrecy and Foreign Policy*, ed. Thomas M. Franck and Edward Weisband (New York: Oxford University Press, 1974), 311.
51. Schrag, *Test of Loyalty*, 174–77.
52. Schrag, *Test of Loyalty*, 181–88.
53. Boudin, "The Ellsberg Case," 310.
54. Schrag, *Test of Loyalty*, 203–5.
55. Schrag, *Test of Loyalty*, 207–9. Schrag suggested the wiretap was of Boudin and the Chilean Embassy and Cuban mission to the United Nations. Boudin and Rabinowitz represented the Government of Cuba and Government of Chile.
56. Schrag, *Test of Loyalty*, 206–7.
57. Schrag, *Test of Loyalty*, 208–10.
58. Schrag, *Test of Loyalty*, 210–12.
59. Schrag, *Test of Loyalty*, 215–16.
60. Schrag, *Test of Loyalty*, 226–27.
61. Boudin, "The Ellsberg Case," 304.
62. Boudin, "The Ellsberg Case," 304; Boudin, "Defendant Ellsberg's Opening Statement," in Kenneth W. Salter, *The Pentagon Papers Trial* (Berkeley: Editorial Justa Publications, Inc., 1975), 26.
63. Boudin, "Defendant Ellsberg's Opening Statement," 27.
64. Schrag, *Test of Loyalty*, 254–57, 288, 295–96. One of the witnesses was Morton Halperin, a U.S. foreign policy expert who had worked as a consultant at RAND and served on the National Security Council and as deputy assistant secretary of defense for International Security Affairs. According to Schrag, Halperin described that the most widely circulated classified material was assumed inevitably to leak and that anything extremely sensitive was communicated to a few people and by word of mouth. "Top Secret" was not the highest level of classification, and documents marked "sensitive" had been used to limit access to information that embarrassed certain staffers or officials.
65. Boudin, "The Ellsberg Case," 299.
66. Boudin, "The Ellsberg Case," 299. Boudin cited Gorin v. United States, 312 U.S. 19 (1941), to support the specific-intent requirement despite the vagueness of "relating to the national defense" in the Espionage Act.
67. Boudin, "The Ellsberg Case," 300.
68. Boudin, "The Ellsberg Case," 300; Schrag, *Test of Loyalty*, 263–64.
69. Schrag, *Test of Loyalty*, 284–95. According to Schrag, the defense called a number of witnesses to testify that the Pentagon Papers did not "relate to the national defense" and that disclosure did not injure the nation or aid a foreign power, including the Kennedy and Johnson administration advisers McGeorge Bundy, John Kenneth Galbraith, and Arthur M. Schlesinger Jr., who distinguished the Pentagon Papers from documents containing "genuine secrets" and "real intelligence."

70. Boudin, "The Ellsberg Case," 302.

71. Daniel Ellsberg, "Daniel Ellsberg, Sworn, Direct Examination," in Salter, *The Pentagon Papers Trial*, 111–12; Schrag, *Test of Loyalty*, 316–19.

72. Boudin, "Defendant Ellsberg's Opening Statement," 31–32.

73. Schrag, *Test of Loyalty*, 329–30.

74. Schrag, *Test of Loyalty*, 333.

75. Schrag, *Test of Loyalty*, 338.

76. Schrag, *Test of Loyalty*, 341, 344–46.

77. Schrag, *Test of Loyalty*, 355–56.

78. "A Background Paper on Leonard Boudin Prepared for White House by Hunt," *New York Times*, July 19, 1974, 16.

79. Tom Goldstein, "Ellsberg Lawyer Tells of Apology from Colson," *New York Times*, July 20, 1974, 18.

80. "A Background Paper on Leonard Boudin," 16.

81. "A Background Paper on Leonard Boudin," 16.

82. "A Background Paper on Leonard Boudin," 16.

83. "A Background Paper on Leonard Boudin," 16.

84. Goldstein, "Ellsberg Lawyer Tells of Apology from Colson," 18.

85. Goldstein, "Ellsberg Lawyer Tells of Apology from Colson," 18; Wells, *Wild Man*, 485: "Hunt would claim his piece formed the second half of an article terHorst wrote on Ellsberg's defense team in January 1972. While that is a slight exaggeration, the last third of the article did unmistakably bear Hunt's imprint."

86. Geoffrey D. Garin, "Spreading the Word on Len Boudin," *Harvard Crimson*, July 26, 1974, https://www.thecrimson.com/article/1974/7/26/spreading-the-word-on-len-boudin/.

87. Garin, "Spreading the Word on Len Boudin."

88. Nick Ravo, "Leonard Boudin, Civil Liberties Lawyer, Dies at 77," *New York Times*, November 26, 1989, 45.

89. Boudin, "The Ellsberg Case," 311.

90. Boudin, "The Ellsberg Case," 311.

91. Ben Wizner, ACLU, https://www.aclu.org/bio/ben-wizner.

92. Barry J. Pollack, Robbins Russell, https://www.robbinsrussell.com/attorneys/barry-j-pollack/; Ryan Lovelace, "Robbins Russell Sits Out Julian Assange Case as Pollack Gears Up for Defense," *National Law Journal*, April 11, 2019, https://www.law.com/nationallawjournal/2019/04/11/robbins-russell-sits-out-julian-assange-case-as-pollack-gears-up-for-defense/.

93. "Team," Whistleblower Aid, https://whistlebloweraid.org/team/.

94. "Vision," Whistleblower Aid, https://whistlebloweraid.org/vision/.

95. "DOJ Whistleblower Jesselyn Radack Releases Memoir," Government Accountability Project, February 16, 2012, https://www.whistleblower.org/press/doj-whistleblower-jesselyn-radack-releases-memoir/.

96. "WHISPeR," ExposeFacts, https://whisper.exposefacts.org/.

97. "About ExposeFacts," ExposeFacts, https:/exposefacts.org/about-exposefacts/.

98. Wilkes, "Leonard Boudin," SM46.

99. Braudy, *Family Circle*, 57.

100. Wilkes, "Leonard Boudin," SM56.

4

CELEBRITY HERO

Daniel Ellsberg and the Forging of
Whistleblower Masculinity

LIDA MAXWELL

W HILE THE LATE 1960s and early 1970s saw the birth of the term
"whistleblower" and the growth of what we now call whistleblowing in governments and corporations, it was Daniel Ellsberg's disclosure of the Pentagon Papers that forged the concept of the
national security whistleblower: the person who tells the truth about governmental wrongdoing, even at great personal cost. While we now tend to
consider the whistleblower an abstract category, it gained its legal and moral
salience through concrete acts of disclosure in the 1970s, especially Ellsberg's.
Indeed, it was Ellsberg's exposure of the classified report of American
policy makers' deceptions about the Vietnam War, along with the public
reception and media representations of his actions, that did the most to
generate a model of righteous truth telling about governmental abuses, even
when it means breaking the rules: what Hannah Gurman calls the "civil
disobedient whistleblower."[1]

Most accounts of Ellsberg (including his own) tend to portray his actions
in terms of the truths he revealed, over and against a culture of deception
emanating from the White House.[2] Yet when Ellsberg leaked the documents, first to a few members of the Senate (who did not take immediate
action) and then eventually to the press, no one contested the veracity of
their contents. Rather, the question was whether his decision to release

classified documents was legitimate. In other words, while we often take acts of what we now call whistleblowing as an invitation to political judgments about *truth*, attention to Ellsberg's case shows that a different kind of invitation is actually being issued: to political judgment of whether the whistleblower is a legitimate truth *teller*.[3]

This chapter focuses on how Ellsberg and the mainstream press negotiated this problem: that is, the problem of his credibility, not of the truths he revealed. Through an examination of media coverage of Ellsberg, I make two primary claims: first, that an embrace of celebrity status and culture was necessary to establish Ellsberg's credibility as a truth teller but at the same time unsettled that credibility, and, second, that depictions of Ellsberg's heterosexual masculinity shored up the credibility that had been unsettled through his embrace of celebrity. Rather than offer a justification of his motivations, however, they demonstrated his desirability in the register of what Lauren Berlant calls "national fantasy."[4]

While political theorists and philosophers tend to portray whistleblowing as a moral ideal by which the public might judge new acts of truth telling[5] or guide future individual actions,[6] I suggest that whistleblowing is better understood as a historically forged concept that is gendered, raced, and connected with celebrity media savvy.[7] This contingent historical formation of the whistleblower category demonstrates that whistleblowers become politically compelling not only because of the moral principles they supposedly invoke but also because of the identity and character attributes that individuals must embody to be recognized as whistleblowers in the first place. By attending to how Ellsberg influenced the formation of whistleblowing as a category, we may be more attuned to how moral justification may be necessary but not sufficient to assure the public significance of the acts of whistleblowers in particular and truth tellers more generally. In turn, we may be better positioned to see the limitations of invoking the category of the whistleblower in politics. Even when used as a moral or political defense of people like Edward Snowden, it may reference and reinforce an exclusive model of what it means to tell the truth and who counts as a truth teller.

The political limitations of the whistleblower model lie not only in its exclusivity but also in its orientation around celebrity. The figure of the whistleblower as celebrity tends to fuel a politics of fandom that is often depoliticizing even as it gains cultural and political significance; the whistleblower solicits members of the public less as comrades in struggle and more as *fans* of a desirable celebrity (the whistleblower). When citizens relate to whistleblowers as fans, they are interpolated in a deferential, spectatorial mode rather than in the register of collective action. Whistleblowing *may* serve as a spark for political action, and the acts of fandom—such as becoming Snowden's follower on Twitter or writing a fan letter to Ellsberg— may reveal the presence of sentimental affinities and prove satisfying to fans. Yet these latter acts do not on their own constitute political action, nor do they have any necessary connection to concrete political change.

The Ellsberg case played a formative role in shaping this confusion between fandom and political action around whistleblowing. In what follows, I first discuss Hannah Arendt's analysis of Ellsberg's case, which has become a classic text on lying and politics in political theory, alongside Ellsberg's own representation of it. Next, I make the case for seeing Ellsberg as a participant in celebrity culture and the culture of celebrity politics and show how this (probably unavoidable) imbrication stands in tension with his claim to be a heroic truth teller. I will then suggest that Ellsberg and the friendly press made recourse to his heterosexual masculinity as a way to demonstrate his desirability in the register of national fantasy. Finally, I examine the limitations of whistleblower politics and highlight the stakes of these limitations for our reception and understanding of subsequent whistleblowers, especially in the post-9/11 era.

TRUTH AND CELEBRITY

In her germinal essay on the release of the Pentagon Papers, "Lying in Politics," published in the *New York Review of Books* on November 18, 1971, Hannah Arendt suggested that the most illuminating truth revealed by the Papers was government actors' persistent shielding of reality not only from the public but from themselves. While lying has always been a persistent feature of politics, Arendt argued that the Pentagon Papers revealed a new form of lying in post–World War II American government: not the outright lie on behalf of self- or national interest but a deception rooted in an inability to see reality. This inability is in turn related to two features of contemporary politics: the turn to politics as "public relations," or the preoccupation with image over reality, and the faith those Arendt called the political "problem solvers" had in mathematical and logical reasoning to describe and resolve political problems. The public relations men, Arendt said, "lied not so much for their country—certainly not for their country's survival, which was never at stake—as for its 'image,'"[8] while the "problem solvers" (of which Ellsberg was one) lied insofar as they tried "to fit their reality—which, after all, was man-made to begin with and thus could have been otherwise—into their theory, thereby mentally getting rid of its disconcerting *contingency*."[9]

Ellsberg echoed this account of governmental deception—and especially its connection with the preoccupation with image—in interviews he gave at the time and in his memoir, published in 2002. Quoting a Defense Department memo he helped author, Ellsberg noted that even in this critique of an aggressive Vietnam policy, he "took care to tender that word [aggression] not as a compelling, objective judgment or as my own. It expressed how our bombing a country that had made no overt armed attack against us or anyone else would possibly be 'seen' and condemned by *others*. There was no other way to get such a thought into official discussion internally even once and remain employed." Similarly, he described later "research" he did into Viet Cong atrocities committed against Americans as a "'weekly list of outrages.' Now I was selling the policy, though I didn't think of it that way." Ellsberg also described officials using opinion polls to justify mounting a more aggressive war strategy: "Gallup poll shows people are basically behind our commitment," argued the secretary of the army.[10] Following the release of the Pentagon Papers, mainstream news magazines and newspapers also depicted governmental decision making as based in a concern with image and statistics, rather than reality. For example, *Time* magazine quoted Mort Halperin, Ellsberg's colleague at the Defense Department, stating, in regards to the Pentagon Papers, that "it is wrong to read real beliefs into many of the arguments in these memos. They were often believed neither by the person doing the writing nor by the readers."[11]

Arendt lauded the release of the Pentagon Papers not just because they revealed this deception to the public, who had a "right to know," but also because they held out the possibility of challenging this governmental retreat from reality, which was enabled by acts of overclassification that allowed government actors to live in a world of formulas and image without interference from the public. For Arendt, "what caused the disastrous defeat of American policies and armed intervention was indeed no quagmire . . . but the willful, deliberate disregard of all facts, historical, political, geographical, for more than twenty-five years."[12] Ellsberg's truth telling thus worked not simply to give American citizens the capacity to judge their leaders correctly (indeed, Arendt notes that correct information had been available in the press for years)[13] but rather—at least as importantly—to keep governmental actors in touch with reality.

Arendt framed Ellsberg and the press that published his revelations as a fundamental check on the ubiquitous phenomenon of political lying. "So long as the press is free and not corrupt," she wrote, "it has an enormously important function to fulfill and can rightly be called the fourth branch of government." The press' publication of truth is a condition, on Arendt's account, of meaningful public opinion formation: "Whether the First Amendment will suffice to protect this most essential political freedom, the right to unmanipulated factual information without which all freedom of opinion becomes a cruel hoax, is another question."[14] In an earlier essay, "Truth and Politics," published in the *New Yorker* on February 25, 1967, Arendt suggested that acts of truth telling become political acts—instead of nonpolitical expressions of what is—only when the political realm is taken over by deception. While, under "normal circumstances," truth telling tends "toward the acceptance of things as they are," "where everybody lies about everything of importance, the truthteller, whether he knows it or not, has begun to act; he, too, has engaged himself in political business, for, in the unlikely event that he survives, he has made a start toward changing the world."[15] This is a good description of how Arendt and other sympathetic members of the American public viewed Ellsberg, one echoed by Ellsberg himself as well as by the coverage surrounding the release of the Papers. In a June 24, 1971, editorial in the *New York Times*, for example, Arthur Schlesinger Jr. wrote, "who will seriously contend that a democracy is not better off when it knows more of the truth about its leaders? . . . Any government that subordinates truth to the preservation of reputation will end by losing not only truth but reputation as well."[16]

Yet even as Ellsberg, Arendt, and others framed him as a truth teller, in opposition to governmental deception qua image making, Ellsberg's truth telling proceeded—perhaps inevitably—in a similar register of image making, not in terms of national reputation but in terms of *celebrity*. Suspected almost immediately as the source of the disclosure, Ellsberg responded by coordinating his own media rollout. He gave an interview to *Newsweek*, went underground while more of the Papers were published, and then organized an influential interview with Walter Cronkite. Taking the opportunity to seize control of his image in the interview, Ellsberg said that his "knowledge" of what was happening in Vietnam, as a government and RAND insider, "gave [him] a kind of responsibility that others didn't have."[17] These were just the first of many more such magazine and television interviews, from profiles in the *New York Times Magazine* and *Rolling Stone* to an appearance on the *Today Show*.

Ellsberg's celebrification was not only performed but also frequently commented upon in the national media. For example, in a July 5, 1971, cover story in *Time*, "Ellsberg: The Battle Over the Right to Know," the author wrote:

As the affair of the Pentagon papers went into its second incredible week, antiwar partisans seemed to be manipulating basic U.S. institutions— the press, Government, and even, in a sense, the courts—*to stage-manage a dramatic presentation* of their views far beyond the wildest dreams of the most zealous campus radicals. It was surely the slickest counter-Establishment insurgency of recent times. The climax was the sudden appearance on national television of the man who started it all. There was Daniel Ellsberg, once the gifted and aggressive war planner, speaking softly but leveling the harsh charge that Americans bear the major responsibility for as many as 2,000,000 deaths in 25 years of warfare in Indochina.[18]

Another piece, published a week later in the same magazine, observed, "Temporarily free again, *Ellsberg settled into celebrity status*. He used the services of David Hawk, an experienced press aide who was a coordinator of the 1969 Viet Nam Moratorium, to conduct an elaborate press conference. Flanked by a U.S. flag and facing 21 microphones, Ellsberg refused to divulge how he had distributed the secret papers."[19] Casting Ellsberg in celebrity terms, the piece couples a description of this public appearance with a glimpse into his "private" life: "Earlier, away from the pack of reporters that greeted him upon his arraignment, Ellsberg softly kissed his wife in a taxi as they rode toward their second-floor apartment in a Cambridge house."[20] In a December 1971 *New York Times* profile, J. Anthony Lukas quoted Ellsberg's assistant, who scheduled speaking and awards engagements for him: "They [people in 'the Movement'] know he's a superstar, times are bad, and superstars are rare."[21]

These depictions of Ellsberg traffic in the 1960s and 1970s celebrity discourse described by Josh Gamson. Images of celebrities in the 1920s and 1930s were heavily controlled by the industry, and this gave impetus to widespread skepticism of celebrity as nothing *but* image. By midcentury, Gamson argues, celebrity discourse changed to incorporate this skepticism into its own parameters:

> By embracing the notion that celebrity images were artificial products and inviting readers to visit the real self behind those images, popular magazines partially defused the notion that celebrity was really derived from nothing but images. Celebrity profiling parked in exposé gear, offering instructions in the art of distinguishing truth from artifice, the real Dietrich from the fake one.[22]

Here, the pleasure the public receives from consumption of celebrity coverage and culture is not just the pleasure of *image* but also the pleasure of finding the "truth" behind that image, of being the critically minded author-ity who distinguishes between the truth and falsity of the image.

Ellsberg's appearance on the public scene happened in a period that—in Gamson's schema—is a hinge between the historical moment of the audi-ence as critical authority and another mode of celebrity consumption: the audience as cynical enjoyer of image as such. Gamson writes:

> As such stories [about the publicity machine] have become more common . . . the audience has been instructed not simply in viewing the self behind the image (what the star really thinks, wears, does) but in viewing the fabrication process (how the celebrity is being constructed to amuse). Armed with knowledge about the process, the audience doesn't need to believe or disbelieve the hype, just to enjoy it.[23]

Ellsberg emerges as a celebrity truth teller—or whistleblower—in other words, at a moment when the public both demands a glimpse "behind" the image, as a way of making judgments about that image, and is at the same time becoming more cynical (in part as a result of the truth Ellsberg revealed) about the possibility of ever finding something that is *not* purely image. This emergent public is one that Arendt describes as an "audience . . . forced to disregard altogether the distinguishing line between truth and falsehood in order to be able to survive,"[24] or what Harry Frankfurt would later call the "bullshit" society, a society where a concern with truth or fal-sity is displaced by concern over the compellingness of an image.[25]

Ellsberg's self-conscious embrace of this celebrity culture and his attempt to coordinate the media's revelation of him as the source of the leak were not performed to prove the truth of what he revealed. No one questioned the veracity of the Pentagon Papers. No one suggested he had forged or altered them. Rather, Ellsberg's entrance into celebrity culture and the media's eager embrace of him grappled with and negotiated a different ques-tion: whether his decision to release the papers—which were classified—was legitimate. In this context, Ellsberg's embrace of celebrity culture can be read as a survival tactic: it was the only way to prevent the White House from taking control of the narrative of Ellsberg's disclosure, smearing him, and thus diminishing the import of the Pentagon Papers. In fact, Nixon's "plumbers" were already attempting to do just that. "Don't worry about his trial, just get everything out. Try him in the press . . . leak it out," Nixon told his advisers two weeks after the publication of the Pentagon Papers. Organized by H. R. Haldeman, a former advertising executive, "Project Ellsberg" quickly developed into a full-scale media campaign that employed whatever means possible to get and disseminate dirt on Ellsberg. As discovered during Ellsberg's trial, this included breaking into the office of his psychiatrist.[26]

Entering into celebrity culture was, on this reading, *necessary* to establishing Ellsberg's credibility as a whistleblower: not simply that he was revealing the truth but also that he could be trusted to determine that this truth was worth telling and that shielding it from the public diminished the public good. Yet at the same time, entering into celebrity culture also rendered Ellsberg vulnerable to the critique that his motives were suspect: that he had only publicized the papers to attain the fame his act would bring. To put the point sharply, Ellsberg needed to become a celebrity—to become an image, knowable by the mass public—to establish his credibility, but becoming a celebrity also rendered his credibility suspect in a different way.

EGOTISTICAL MARTYR OR DESIRABLE NATION/AL SUBJECT?

Jann Wenner begins his November 8, 1973, *Rolling Stone* profile of Daniel Ellsberg with a description of Ellsberg as narcissistic and self-centered—a description that had become, by that time, fairly commonplace.[27] Wenner writes:

Daniel Ellsberg was perhaps the first highly placed official (at one time the deputy Assistant Secretary of Defense) to have ever left the inner government and then reveal, with Top Secret documents, its closely guarded secret operations. As befits a man who risks his reputation and ruin, to fight a corrupt and unlawful government, he is vain, egocentric and completely convinced of the rightness of his action.[28]

Yet Wenner goes on to suggest that Ellsberg's self-centeredness and moral self-righteousness was *necessary* for him to do what he did, to tell the truth to the public:

> It is a grandiose attitude—one that seems to have especially offended the press. It supposes the power of truth, of the man who speaks it, and the moral example it sets. Ellsberg quotes Madison's statement that "Knowledge will forever govern ignorance and the people who mean to be their own governors must take care to arm themselves with the power that knowledge gives."[29]

If Ellsberg had not seen himself in grandiose terms—as a great man who only needed a great act to perform and a great audience to see it—he would not have performed an act that was in fact important for public life and democracy.

Yet as theorists of celebrity from Gamson to Schickel to Braudy have argued, traditional heroism—the reward of public acclaim for performing a great achievement—is dead. The celebrity—whose fame depends not on "real" achievement (however constructed in the past such "real" achievement might have been) but on a marketable image that bears a confused relation to reality—has taken the place of the hero.[30] Ellsberg's action, however, also partakes of the traditional traits of the hero: the courageous sacrifice of the self on behalf of the collective, a sacrifice (as with the ancient Greek hero) that elevates and displays this courage in actions that often appear superhuman, beyond the capacity of most ordinary individuals.[31] Wenner's depiction of Ellsberg as an egotistical individual whose egotism allowed him to become a hero captures this tension between hero and celebrity nicely. Ellsberg's desire and capacity for celebrity (what Hobbes would have called the pursuit of "vainglory") allowed him to perform an almost superhuman heroic act, yet as the press often noted, in a celebrity society—where the desire for fame is seen as necessary but also threatening to one's character as a celebrity—this same desire also often appeared to threaten the heroic character of this act.

The press acknowledged the threatening character of Ellsberg's celebrity when they depicted him as having a martyr complex. For example, in an early *Newsweek* profile, Ellsberg was depicted as a "messianic crusader" whose "friends" say may be motivated by "a 'martyr complex,' a compulsion to expiate his guilt." Others, said *Newsweek*, "saw his transformation as just 'an ego trip' or an attempt to 'establish himself.'"[32] Of course, *Newsweek* trafficked in this "egotism" when they placed an ad in the *New York Times* for precisely this June 28, 1971, issue, using an image of Ellsberg and quotes from their interview to market their own take on the Pentagon Papers.

Another gloss on the problematic character of Ellsberg's self-centeredness can be found in depictions of him as a zealot, that is, as thinking in moral absolutes, whether those be the absolutes of the hawk or the dove:

> Ellsberg was for a time one of those faceless bureaucrats who sit at the fulcrum of decision making and are privy to the most guarded information. Yet he has a marked capacity for excess. One friend says that this reversal from a pro-war to an unequivocal antiwar position is completely in character. "That's the kind of guy Dan is. He's sensitive and passionate, as well as being immensely intelligent. When he was a hawk, he wanted to be up along the DMZ [Vietnamese Demilitarized Zone] fighting. When he became a dove, he became an active dove."[33]

Ellsberg's desire for celebrity, in other words, is depicted as a byproduct of zealotry: someone who is motivated by extreme passions rather than reason.

If Ellsberg were a zealot or a martyr, his truth telling would be seen as less legitimate—and, in turn, less necessary—because motivated by private passion or interest rather than the public good, which would demand attention to the perspectives and needs of others. These worries about zealotry and narcissism were addressed and negotiated, but not resolved, by a third set of depictions of Ellsberg, namely, as a sexually and nationally desirable man. His self-love becomes explicable by viewing him through the eyes of women who love him not just as himself but as a symbol of the nation and the national good. Viewed through the lens of women's desire for him as a national celebrity, his own love for himself appears understandable because, in loving himself, he is simply loving the nation, as he in fact claims to do in his act of whistleblowing. His masculine/national self-love, evidenced by women's desire for him as a national masculine love object, becomes part of what it means to be a whistleblower. I do not mean to suggest that all women actually loved and desired Ellsberg or that this image of him was believed by all or even most of the public. Rather, I am interested in how this image becomes, via Ellsberg's example, part of the category of the "whistleblower" and guides who is able to be seen as a whistleblower and what kind of politics becomes available when this term is invoked.

In the Wenner interview, Ellsberg acknowledged that he was operating in the register of image, and he addressed his own credibility not only by describing his moral motives but also by referencing his own desirability. Ellsberg noted at several points that he turned to media interviews and profiles as a way to control his public image, in the face of Nixon and his underlings mounting a smear campaign. For example, he says that he "better" accept an invitation to be on the *Today Show* because "things were getting a little heavy. Strom Thurmond and Hugh Scott had just denounced me—and maybe I should make an appearance."[34] What is the image Ellsberg wanted to convey? Ellsberg worried that he sounded "defensive" on the show—since his appearance directly followed Nixon's smear of him to a group of returned Vietnam POWs—but he offered a few depictions of the image he wanted to convey to the public. He says, "In a general way, what I did could be seen—I did see it as such—in very Gandhian terms. It was nonviolent, in fact an act of pure, abstract truth-telling. It's almost a classic Gandhian dream, to suppose that such an act of truth-telling—and taking personal responsibility for it, publicly—is precisely what it took to disturb this government profoundly." Similarly, he says later, "I haven't said anything misleading and I won't." Yet another image Ellsberg offers is that of his sexual desirability, which he suggests may also be appealing to a broad audience. Speaking of Nixon's attempt to smear his character, Ellsberg says,

"The only thing they could actually find on me would be a particular period of what could be called *promiscuity*, the kind of thing you wouldn't go out of your way to tell a jury—even though I hadn't been married at the time—but with a larger audience might make me a cultural hero."[35] Presenting himself as both a morally and politically desirable truth teller and as a sexually desirable man, Ellsberg's comment suggested that he saw these two forms of desirability as at least complementary, if not connected.

The images of Ellsberg in the *Rolling Stone* interview amplify this dual desirability. The image on the cover may at first appear to evoke self-righteousness. His fist aiming upward, shoulders bare, this image of Ellsberg suggests moral righteousness and transparency. It evokes an image of the martyr he is accused of being in the press: the pure truth teller Ellsberg invokes in the interview, the martyr who risks everything for the purity of his act. Yet the apparent moralism of the image is fused with connotations of sexual desirability. If the image seems naggingly familiar, it is because it evokes Michelangelo's *David*.[36] *David* has been read as both a virile, patriotic, unifying symbol of Renaissance Florence—an image of the hero in repose—*and* as a figure of homoerotic desire. Ellsberg is depicted with a clenched fist (the revolutionary fist), rather than David's slingshot, which he is readying for Goliath. The image's resonances with *David* imbue Ellsberg with the double desirability evident in the Renaissance sculpture: patriotic, political heroism *and* indeterminate sexual desirability.

While sexual and political desirability may appear to be separate characteristics, feminist and queer theory has long suggested that, in different ways, what appears to be personal and private is also public and political. I read the representations of Ellsberg's broad sexual desirability—heterosexual promiscuity in his self-portrayal and an image that solicits homoerotic desire—as a way of enlarging his image, of portraying him as desirable to a broad swath of people, of both assuming and soliciting his national desirability. Yet by politicizing and patriotically *nationalizing* his sexual desirability, I also see a narrowing or limiting of that image: that is, the implication that the form of desirability he represents (masculine desirability) is coincident with the desirability of the nation itself. To be someone able to speak for and act on behalf of the nation, one must be sexually desirable in

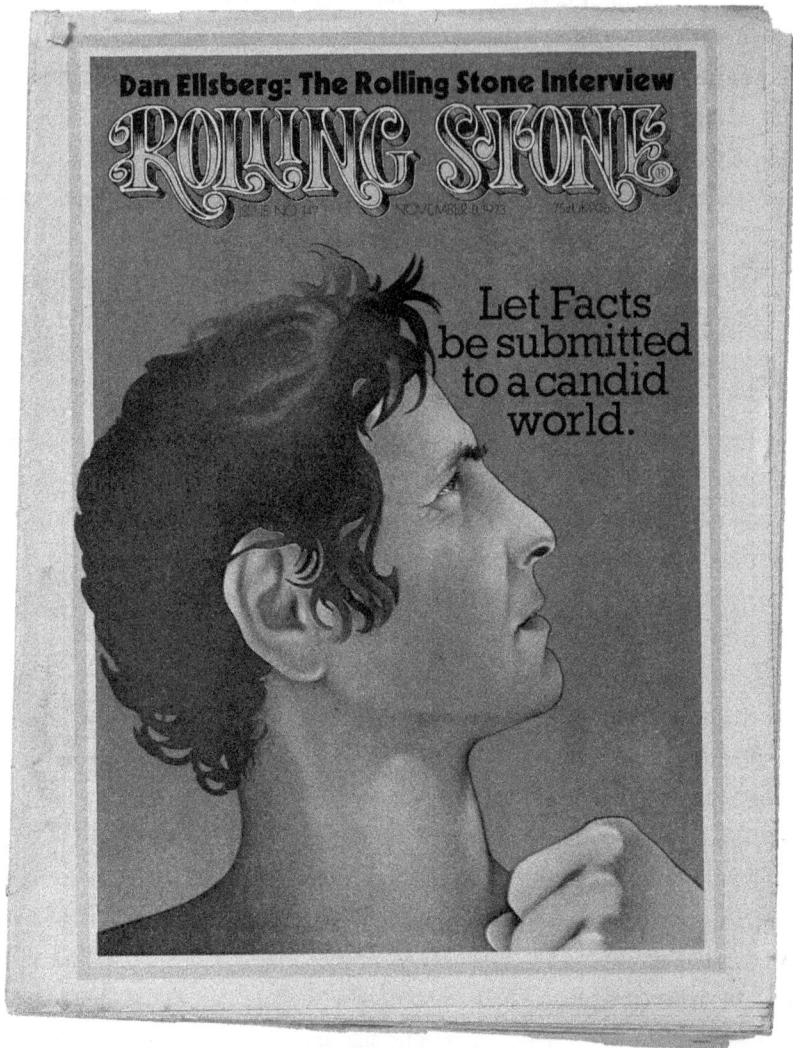

FIGURE 4.1

An image of Daniel Ellsberg graced the cover of the November 8, 1973, issue of *Rolling Stone*, which featured Jann Wenner's interview with Ellsberg.

Source: *Rolling Stone*.

FIGURE 4.2

The image of Ellsberg on the cover of *Rolling Stone* bears a striking resemblance to Michelangelo's *David*.

a particular way, namely, in a masculine way. The fusion of sexual and moral/political desirability expands Ellsberg's desirability to national size but also contracts national desirability to a narrow form of masculine desirability.

By claiming that Ellsberg was depicted (and depicted himself) as a figure of national desirability, I do not mean that he was literally desired by everyone in the nation. Rather, I am suggesting that he became a nationally desirable figure in the sense of "national fantasy." For Berlant, national fantasy flourishes in sites of cultural and intimate life—what she calls "intimate publics"—and offers images of intimate feeling, happiness, and suffering that become sentimental representations of the nation. These images—generated through film, pop culture (from magazines and newspapers to television talk shows to internet celebrity gossip sites), and forms of intimate consumption—render individual suffering meaningful and bearable by staging it as part of a meaningful struggle that others share; at the same time, these images are disconnected from, even if caused by, politics. As Berlant puts it in an account of women's intimate publics, their sentimental depictions of female suffering offer "an alleviation of what is hard to manage in the lived real—social antagonisms, exploitation, compromised intimacies, the attrition of life."[37] Images of national fantasy make suffering meaningful, but they also offer relief from—rather than a spark for engagement in—the political realm.

Depicting Ellsberg as someone who is loved and who loves himself, as someone who is what an American man should be, the media and Ellsberg both solicit the public to adore him as someone whose actions offer them *relief* from political antagonisms by telling the truth about government deception, so that they can return to the pleasures of private, intimate life that Ellsberg also exemplifies. Indeed, while there are some images of Ellsberg in government and military service in the *Rolling Stone* article, there are others taken by Annie Leibovitz, which showcase him as a celebrity and move between images of him alone (which could solicit all kinds of sexual desire, including homoerotic desire) to one taken with Patricia, his very beautiful, younger second wife, with Ellsberg's wedding ring displayed prominently in the photo. With this last photo, Ellsberg is represented as not only being desired by the nation and open-ended others but also as desiring and having a wife. This both amplifies and narrows Ellsberg's national desirability in two ways. First, Ellsberg's marriage to Patricia marks him as fulfilling the national heterosexual love plot (Berlant), in which he shows himself to be a national subject through enacting the sentimental narrative of heterosexual happiness staked out in popular culture as the universal experience of citizens. Second, as Sara Ahmed writes, it shows that one loves and identifies with the nation in part through successfully idealizing and having the appropriate love object:

"the idealization of the loved object can allow the subject to *be itself in or through what it has.*"[38]

Ellsberg thus marks himself as a national subject—someone who loves and desires the nation—through enacting heterosexual happiness. However, he also represents the nation in his act of truth telling. In so doing, he speaks on behalf of the nation, as its true representative (as opposed to the Nixon administration). Thus, when Ellsberg enacts his own desire and love for the nation in his marriage to Patricia, he is at the same time enacting a love for himself *as* the nation. It is here that we can see how recourse to Ellsberg's masculine desirability—and his happy marriage—helps soothe anxieties about his apparent narcissism. That is, recourse to Ellsberg's national/sexual desirability allows us to see that his narcissism is actually just a love for himself as a representative of the nation that we all share—or could share. Self-love or narcissism is appropriate, explicable, and even attractive when the subject loves himself as more than himself, as the national object.

The representation of Ellsberg as both the subject of national love and the object (a sentimental representative or symbol of the nation as such) is at work in portrayals of Patricia as not just Ellsberg's wife but his fan. In a profile of Patricia in the August 30, 1972, "Food, Fashions, Family, Furnishings" section of the *New York Times*, for instance, Judy Kelmesrud depicted Patricia's life primarily in terms of Daniel Ellsberg's actions (and in relation to Patricia's father's reaction to it). Kelmesrud noted that

> although her life since her marriage has revolved mainly around her husband, Mrs. Ellsberg is currently working on a book of her radio interviews for Horizon Press. She has also spoken to peace groups across the country for the Ellsberg defense fund. But mainly, she seems content to bask in her husband's limelight ("I so much believe in what Dan has done"), cook for him, fly around the country with him, hike in the woods with him.

As a couple, Kelmesrud writes, "They look forward to the days when they can settle down in their apartment in Cambridge, Mass., and have two children of their own."[39]

Patricia is even depicted as accepting and adoring Ellsberg's celebrity masculinity, that is, as loving him not just as an individual but as a national celebrity. For example, in the 1971 *New York Times* profile, Lukas portrays Patricia primarily as Ellsberg's accessory as he attends various leftist galas, awards ceremonies, and speaking engagements. Lukas discusses a visit the Ellsbergs made to the Playboy mansion following the "American Peace Awards" (which Lukas describes as the "Academy Awards of Peace"), along with other winners of that award, including John Kerry. Lukas describes the scene:

> After an hour of drinking, some people begin drifting downstairs to the heated pool and cozy bar which looks into the pool's blue waters through a large window. I'm sitting at the bar talking with Patricia and John Kerry when suddenly Dan appears at the window, in one of the Mansion's brown bathing suits, making fish eyes at Patricia. A few minutes later he is followed by Tony Russo and George Wald. I turn back to the bar, *when I hear a little giggle from Patricia.* Turning around, I see two naked women at the window. A tableau of the American peace movement in 1971—Ellsberg, Russo, Wald and four breasts bobbing in their wake. As usual at the Mansion, it's all antiseptic. No real sex, not even any touching. Soon everybody is clothed and upstairs for the buffet supper.[40]

Lukas's description of the scene illustrates the connections between heterosexual promiscuity (or at least its performance) and national/nuclear desire. Patricia's giggle implies that Ellsberg's potential promiscuity—his desirability to others—is part of what makes him desirable to her, as her husband with whom she hopes to have a family. Lukas's description of this scene for a national publication in turn proffers Ellsberg as a celebrity whose desirability is both sexual and national. The occasion for this party and for the adulation of Ellsberg at the Playboy mansion was, after all, his acceptance of an award for his activism. In another moment in the *New York Times* profile, Ellsberg's national/sexual appeal to women is depicted as even exceeding his physical appearance. At a "Federal Employees for Peace" banquet honoring Ellsberg, Lukas notes the presence of a "blind girl from

FIGURE 4.3

Daniel Ellsberg chats with a group of women students after an interview on the University of Maryland campus, October 1, 1976.

Source: Photo by Susan Wood/Getty Images.

Housing and Urban Development and her girlfriend. The friend is describing Ellsberg. 'He's this lovely soft man, with a beautiful half smile.' The blind girl listens intently. 'He's such a mixture of strength and gentleness, and, oh, he's looked at me.' The blind girl's face lights up with a seraphic smile."[41]

In these various depictions of Ellsberg's masculinity and his desirability to women (and there are many more), Ellsberg and his profilers offered a way to understand Ellsberg's moral passion, apparent self-centeredness, and vanity: as an expression of a love for the nation he himself represents. He represented the nation both in his act of truth telling *and* in his fulfillment of the heterosexual love plot. In being potentially desirable to everyone as a truth teller speaking on behalf of the nation, Ellsberg becomes the nation in the register of fantasy. Yet in having that form of desirability fused with and shored up by his heterosexuality, Ellsberg's heterosexual domesticity fills in the content of what national life looks like or should look like. The depictions of Ellsberg offered a vision of national fantasy where the whistleblower tells the truth so that he can leave politics and go back to heterosexual domesticity, the true site of national feeling and desire.

THE LIMITATIONS OF WHISTLEBLOWER POLITICS

The claim laid out here is that Ellsberg's forging of the whistleblower role generated an image of the whistleblower that is gendered and tied to celebrity media savvy—and that demanded a celebrification of the whistleblower that both shored up and unsettled his credibility. The image of the celebrity whistleblower that emerges in media depictions of Ellsberg soothed worries about his credibility by depicting him in the register of national fantasy, where the appeal of his national, masculine desirability smoothed over but did not resolve concerns raised by his celebrity about his justification and motives.

First, while this image of Ellsberg as nationally desirable allowed both Ellsberg and the press to find a narrative and image through which to present him as a sympathetic and legitimate figure, it also inevitably obscured and narrowed Ellsberg's own life, identity, and experience, as well as that of his wife. Ellsberg was raised as a Christian scientist, but his parents were Ashkenazi Jews who had converted to Christian Science when he was eleven. The press rarely raised Ellsberg's Jewishness; a very small mention in the *Rolling Stone* profile of anti-Semitic letters to Ellsberg was a rare public acknowledgment of his Jewish identity. This overwhelming silence surrounding Ellsberg's Jewishness suggests that national desirability demands Ellsberg's (and others') conformity to a dominant national script, where ethnic, racial, gender, and nonheterosexual identities remain out of view, in favor of identification with the white heterosexual love plot. Yet at the same time, Ellsberg's capacity to appear as a symbol of the nation may depend precisely on this self-silencing: that is, in silencing his own Jewishness in favor of his love for the (American) nation and for Patricia, Ellsberg exemplifies what proper national subjects do, how they become worthy of the love of the nation. The homoerotic connotations of the image of Ellsberg on the cover of *Rolling Stone* do similar work. Ellsberg (and the nation) depend for their significance and legitimacy on being desirable in all kinds of ways and by all kinds of people (homosexuals, immigrants, Jewish people, African Americans, etc.), but they track or channel that desirability in a particular way: as a desire for sameness, for the national heterosexual love plot that Ellsberg's image embodies.

Rendering Ellsberg's significance in terms of his national/masculine desirability, the whistleblower model we inherit from his example also generates a particular kind of politics. Specifically, it interpellates those who stand in solidarity with Ellsberg as his (desiring/adoring) fans rather than as his equals in a collective struggle. This has important effects. Asked to desire and adore Ellsberg as a way of affirming his deed, the acts of fandom become confused with political action. The acts of buying a magazine with Ellsberg on the cover, or feeling sympathetically on his behalf while reading a profile of him, or sighing over his romance with Patricia, or writing him a fan letter come to stand in for the difficult work of creating political change—and lead people to believe they are enacting change when all they are doing is consuming media coverage. The celebrity whistleblower model thus leads individuals to overestimate the effect of celebrity consumption while at the same time undervaluing the work of the political movement that makes someone like Ellsberg possible. Ellsberg conceived of the idea of disclosing the Pentagon Papers through his interactions with people in the antiwar movement, and he had a great deal of help in the concrete work of disseminating them.[42] But the broader social movement disappears in celebrity media coverage that sees Ellsberg's masculine appeal and heterosexual domesticity, rather than the nitty-gritty of collective political action, as the locus of national desire and consumption. Even Tony Russo, who took responsibility with Ellsberg at the time for disclosing the Papers and was later on trial alongside him, became largely invisible next to Ellsberg in the coverage. And Ellsberg's wife, who had a complex political perspective[43] and had been an antiwar activist before her husband, too could only appear as a "fan."

If this framing of Ellsberg had costs for our understanding of his actions and the politics it inaugurated, it also has costs in terms of how would-be truth tellers in contemporary politics are understood, as is evident in the differing treatment given to Edward Snowden and Chelsea Manning by the press and public. Like Ellsberg, Snowden coordinated his own press rollout, foregrounding in a Laura Poitras documentary and in a series of Glenn Greenwald articles for the *Guardian* how his actions sprung from moral and political principles and offering his own appearance and image to legitimate his claims.[44] While he does not want to offer much personal information, we learn in the Poitras documentary that he has a girlfriend whom he has shielded from his actions (unlike Patricia Ellsberg) and who later followed him to Moscow. Similarly, in the Oliver Stone biopic, Snowden's girlfriend takes center stage as an influence, and her desire for Snowden serves as a proxy for an audience that the movie suggests should be similarly smitten with him.[45]

Snowden's revelations were taken up immediately by legislators and the public, who called for greater legislative protections for the privacy of Americans. Before President Obama left office, the American Civil Liberties Union mounted an extensive campaign to pardon Snowden, which several celebrities (like Mark Ruffalo) signed onto. While Obama ultimately commuted Manning's sentence (and did not pardon Snowden), Manning's advocates tended to frame that commutation largely as a response to trans* rights claims rather than as legitimating Manning's disclosures.[46] In a recent young-adult book written about Ellsberg, Snowden is cited as the inheritor of Ellsberg's legacy; Manning is not mentioned.[47]

Like Ellsberg, Snowden is represented as a proper national subject whose possible self-love (evident in his media rollout) is rendered explicable and mitigated by his national desirability and his embodiment of the heterosexual love plot. In contrast to the legitimating coverage given to Snowden, Manning's disclosures—which served as the basis for many front-page articles in major newspapers—were for the most part greeted with puzzlement or outright distaste by major newspapers and the American public.[48]

Profiles of Manning highlighted from the outset her gender and sexual non-conformity. While an early profile in the *New York Times* noted that friends wondered whether she had acted out of "delusions of grandeur,"[49] there was no accompanying narrative of her masculinity to assuage worries about her supposed desire for grandiosity. Rather, it appeared perverse. While Manning has taken on a kind of celebrity role surrounding trans issues (as I discuss elsewhere),[50] her information disclosures—which, more than Snowden's, were antiwar and thus could be seen as a more direct inheritor of Ellsberg's legacy—are often seen as illegitimate, sometimes even by her supporters, who often stress how "young" she was when she leaked the documents.[51]

Yet if Ellsberg's forging of the whistleblower category helps us understand the differential treatment given to Snowden and Manning, it may also help explain the ultimate narrowness of the politics inaugurated by Snowden's revelations. While the information disclosure created a national outcry, and although Snowden immediately acquired an immense number of fans (on Twitter and elsewhere), this fandom was largely politically sterile. Apart from some failed legislation in Congress, Snowden's act has not generated a political movement and seemed to have nowhere to go besides further consumption of Snowden, whether through Skyped speeches, movies, or his Twitter feed. While Snowden's image appears to have so much power in the register of celebrity, the inability of celebrity to lead to concrete change may run contra to his and his supporters' intent, generating only a sense of public powerlessness.

If Ellsberg's example forged the category of the whistleblower as a figure of national desire, this has had costs for those individuals taken up, and those not taken up, as its exemplars in the past as well as the present. Ellsberg's example also reveals the limits of the kind of politics the whistleblower inaugurates, namely, one of fandom that bears a largely tangential relation to political action. While it is tempting to continue to invoke this category to defend truth tellers in public, perhaps we would serve ourselves and those truth tellers better by trying to diversify our public lexicon of truth telling. It may be necessary to continue to invoke the whistleblower category as a survival tactic, as a way to render the act of disclosure legible, and potentially legitimate, to a broad audience. Yet perhaps we could also create new categories *alongside* the whistleblower, both to show its limits and to proliferate new ways to understand truth telling in public, ways that may diversify national identity, desire, and political action in response to truth telling.[52]

NOTES

Thanks to the participants in the History of Whistleblowing Workshop in January 2018 for helpful feedback on an early draft. For helpful comments, thanks also to participants in the BU Women's, Gender, and Sexuality Studies Works in Progress series and the Five Colleges Political Theory Workshop—especially to Petrus Liu, Susanne Sreedhar, Cati Connell, Jeremy Menchik, Erin Pineda, Barbara Cruikshank, Angelica Bernal, Ali Aslam, and Elizabeth Markovits. Thanks also to Claire Grossi for research assistance.

1. Hannah Gurman, "National Security Whistleblowing: The Creation of a Legal Paradox," Navigating Law and Ethics at the Crossroads of Journalism and National Security, Center for Ethics and the Rule of Law, University of Pennsylvania, November 9, 2017.
2. For example, see Daniel Ellsberg, *Secrets: A Memoir of Vietnam and the Pentagon Papers* (New York: Penguin, 2002).
3. Thanks to Erin Pineda for this formulation.
4. See, for example, Lauren Berlant, *The Anatomy of National Fantasy: Hawthorne, Utopia, and Everyday Life* (Chicago: University of Chicago Press, 1991); Lauren Berlant, *The Queen of America Goes to Washington City: Essays on Sex and Citizenship* (Durham, NC: Duke University Press, 1997).
5. For example, Myron Glazer and Penina Glazer, *The Whistleblowers* (New York: Basic Books, 1991), argue that the whistleblower is someone who follows rules and regulations (is almost a human extension *of* those regulations) and insists that others follow them—even to the point of having to sacrifice themselves on behalf of fidelity to rules and the authority (the public) who authorizes them. The Glazers date the emergence of whistleblowing as a political phenomenon to the rise of government regulation in the 1950s and 1960s. The increase in whistleblowing as a political activity, they say, was prompted by the "struggle over the new regulations of the private sector in the 1960s and 1970s, widespread disillusionment with government, industry's ability to control technological hazards, and the increasing public cynicism about the integrity of federal officials that grew out of the Vietnam War and the Watergate scandal." These factors, they argue, "created an environment of distrust among employees who witnessed indifference to dangerous and illegal practices condoned by their superiors" (11). Alongside this sense of distrust and increased regulation, the emergence of new public advocacy groups and social movements aimed at government and corporate accountability created an atmosphere where

whistleblowing became possible (4). This is similar to C. Fred Alford's depiction of whistleblowers in *Whistleblowers: Broken Lives and Organizational Power* (Ithaca, NY: Cornell University Press, 2002). Yet where the Glazers want to laud whistleblowing as a form of "ethical resistance," Alford highlights the moral tensions within, and costs of, pursuing this form of whistleblowing.

6. As William Scheuerman writes of Edward Snowden, "his unusually selfless actions seem to demonstrate a morally praiseworthy willingness to sacrifice the private for the public good." William Scheuerman, "Whistleblowing as Civil Disobedience: The Case of Edward Snowden," *Philosophy and Social Criticism* 40, no. 7 (2014): 614. See also David Bromwich, "The Question of Edward Snowden," *New York Review of Books*, December 4, 2014, https://www.nybooks.com/articles/2014/12/04/question-edward-snowden/; Candice Delmas, *The Duty to Resist: When Disobedience Should Be Uncivil* (New York: Oxford University Press, 2018). Delmas argues that whistleblowing is justifiable and can even be morally required because, in holding officials accountable, it strengthens the rule of law and remedies public ignorance by revealing information "in the public interest," a duty that "derives from the duty of justice." On the problems with the privileging of Snowden's example on the Left, see Lida Maxwell, "Chelsea Manning's Integrity," *Jacobin*, October 3, 2016, https://www.jacobinmag.com/2016/10/chelsea-manning-edward-snowden-poitras-citizenfour-greenwald/.

7. Erin Pineda pursues a similar project in "Civil Disobedience and Punishment: (Mis)reading Justification and Strategy from SNCC to Snowden," *History of the Present* 5, no. 1 (2015): 1–30, where she offers an important critique of the assumption that political actors in the civil rights movement accepted punishment for moral (justificatory) reasons rather than for strategic (political) reasons. Pineda shows that the "jail, no bail" strategy of CORE and SNCC activists was not primarily moral but political. Their aim was "to multiply protest across new arenas, to extend and intensify the critique of interlocking networks of unjust institutions, to leverage jail time as a means of building solidarity while disrupting institutional functioning, and, perhaps most creatively, to enact agency and freedom in the midst of domination and incarceration" (10).

8. Hannah Arendt, "Lying in Politics," in *Crises of the Republic* (New York: Houghton Mifflin Harcourt, 1972), 11.

9. Arendt, "Lying in Politics," 12.

10. Ellsberg, *Secrets*, 54, 72, 92.

11. "The Rules of the Game," *Time*, July 5, 1971, 9.

12. Arendt, "Lying in Politics," 32.

13. Arendt, "Lying in Politics," 45.

14. Arendt, "Lying in Politics," 45.

15. Hannah Arendt, "Truth and Politics," in *Between Past and Future* (New York: Penguin, 1969), 251.

16. Arthur Schlesinger Jr., "Truth or Reputation?" *New York Times*, June 24, 1971, 39.

17. "Transcript of Ellsberg Interview on TV," *New York Times*, June 24, 1971, http://www.nytimes.com/1971/06/24/archives/transcript-of-ellsberg-interview-on-tv.html.

18. "Ellsberg: The Battle Over the Right to Know," *Time*, July 5, 1971, 6. My emphasis.
19. "More Pentagon Disclosures," *Time*, July 12, 1971, 12. My emphasis.
20. "More Pentagon Disclosures," 12.
21. J. Anthony Lukas, "After the Pentagon Papers—a Month in the New Life of Daniel Ellsberg," *New York Times Magazine*, December 12, 1971, 104.
22. Josh Gamson, *Claims to Fame: Celebrity in Contemporary America* (Berkeley: University of California Press, 1994), 38.
23. Gamson, *Claims to Fame*, 49.
24. Arendt, "Lying in Politics," 7.
25. Harry Frankfurt, *On Bullshit* (Princeton, NJ: Princeton University Press, 2005).
26. Barry Werth, *31 Days: The Crisis That Gave Us the Government We Have Today* (New York: Nan A. Talese, 2006), 84–87; David Greenberg, *Nixon's Shadow: The History of an Image* (New York: Norton, 2004); "Buchanan Objection Ignored," *Washington Post*, June 19, 1974.
27. These characterizations persist. The relatively recent, highly critical biography of Ellsberg by Tom Wells, *Wild Man: The Life and Times of Daniel Ellsberg* (New York: Palgrave MacMillan, 2001), focuses heavily on Ellsberg's supposed narcissism and self-regard.
28. Jann Wenner, "The Rolling Stone Interview: Dan Ellsberg," *Rolling Stone*, November 8, 1973, 35.
29. Wenner, "The Rolling Stone Interview," 35.
30. On this point, see, for example, Gamson, *Claims to Fame*; Richard Schickel, *Intimate Strangers: The Culture of Celebrity* (New York: Doubleday, 1985); and Leo Braudy, *The Frenzy of Renown* (New York: Oxford University Press, 1986). For a critique of the critical depiction of celebrity as image and a theorization of nineteenth-century celebrity in terms of theatricality, see Sharon Marcus, "Salomé!! Sarah Bernhardt, Oscar Wilde, and the Drama of Celebrity," *PMLA* 4, no. 26 (2011): 999–1021.
31. On the ancient Greek hero, see, for example, Gregor Nagy, *The Ancient Greek Hero in Twenty-Four Hours* (Cambridge, MA: Harvard University Press, 2013).
32. "The Suspect: A Hawk Who Turned Dove," *Newsweek*, June 28, 1971, 16.
33. "Pentagon Papers: The Secret War," *Time*, June 28, 1971, http://www.cnn.com/ALL POLITICS/1996/analysis/back.time/9606/28/index.shtml.
34. Wenner, "Dan Ellsberg," 50.
35. Wenner, "Dan Ellsberg," 50, 54, 50.
36. Thanks to Bonnie Honig for drawing my attention to this similarity.
37. Lauren Berlant, *The Female Complaint* (Durham, NC: Duke University Press, 2008), 5.
38. Sara Ahmed, *The Cultural Politics of Emotion* (New York: Routledge, 2013), 128.
39. Judy Klemesrud, "Daniel Ellsberg's 'Closest Friend': His Wife, Patricia," *New York Times*, August 30, 1972, 24.
40. Lukas, "After the Pentagon Papers," 101.
41. Lukas, "After the Pentagon Papers," 98.
42. Ellsberg makes this claim in *The Most Dangerous Man in America*, dir. Judith Ehrlich and Rick Goldsmith (2009). Recently, Eric Lichtblau detailed some of these other

individuals' stories in "The Untold Story of the Pentagon Papers Co-Conspirators," *New Yorker*, January 29, 2018, https://www.newyorker.com/news/news-desk/the-untold -story-of-the-pentagon-papers-co-conspirators.

43. Only at the very end of Klemesrud's *New York Times* profile is Patricia quoted as saying that she believes "'a great deal of what women's lib is saying is urgent and vital to society. . . . For example, when you read the Pentagon Papers, not one woman's voice is to be heard, it's all men. I believe what they say about the machismo factor, in foreign policy'" (24).

44. See *Citizenfour*, dir. Laura Poitras (2014) and Glenn Greenwald's 2013 series of articles for the *Guardian*: https://www.theguardian.com/us-news/the-nsa-files.

45. *Snowden*, dir. Oliver Stone (2016).

46. On this point, see Lida Maxwell, "Whistleblower, Traitor, Soldier, Queer? The Truth of Chelsea Manning," *Yale Review* 106, no. 1 (2018): 97–107.

47. Steve Sheinkin, *Most Dangerous: Daniel Ellsberg and the Secret History of the Vietnam War* (New York: Roaring Brook, 2015).

48. On this, see Lida Maxwell, "Truth in Public: Chelsea Manning, Gender Identity, and the Politics of Truth-Telling," *Theory and Event* 18 (2015): 1.

49. Ginger Thompson, "Early Struggles of Soldier Charged in Leak Case," *New York Times*, August 8, 2010, http://www.nytimes.com/2010/08/09/us/09manning.html.

50. Maxwell, "Whistleblower, Spy, Soldier, Queer?"

51. For example, see the May 9, 2017, ACLU-sponsored conversation between Chase Strangio and Glenn Greenwald, https://www.youtube.com/watch?v=Ld-cMzvuURc.

52. On "outsider truth-telling" and "transformative truth-teller" as such possible alternative categories, see my *Insurgent Truth: Chelsea Manning and the Politics of Outsider Truth-Telling* (New York: Oxford University Press, 2019).

5

THE RISE AND FALL OF ANTI-IMPERIAL WHISTLEBLOWING IN THE LONG 1970s

KAETEN MISTRY

"I SAW IT first as a problem, next as a stalemate," explained Daniel Ellsberg in his 2002 memoir on U.S. involvement in Vietnam, "then as a moral and political disaster, a crime." When he had come to consider it "a crime," he resolved "to expose and resist it, and to try to end it immediately" by releasing the Pentagon Papers, sacrificing a position at the heart of the U.S. national security establishment and "accept[ing] the prospect of a life behind bars." A criminal offense and custodial sentence were also on Richard Nixon's mind in mid-June 1971, after the *New York Times* published the first stories based on the top-secret report. Eager to prosecute "the goddamn pricks" that gave the classified study to the press, the president wanted to set an example that "unauthorized disclosures" would not be tolerated by putting "the fear of God into other people in this Government." Growing increasingly impatient that the "son-of-a-bitch Ellsberg" was evading U.S. authorities, he exclaimed, "goddamn it, somebody has got to go to jail! . . . that's all there is to it!"[1]

The whistleblower and the president had contrasting views on the public's right to know, but they were curiously on the same page regarding the likely fate of individuals that revealed national security information. Ultimately Ellsberg did not face prison for the disclosure: his trial for violating the Espionage Act was dismissed thanks to the covert schemes of the White

House "plumbers," who had been specifically organized to prevent such "leaks." It was Nixon who fell as details of the plumbers' illegal activities, from a psychiatrist's office in California to the Watergate complex in Washington, engulfed his presidency.[2] Notwithstanding the drama around Ellsberg's case, critical questions for what this meant for national security whistleblowing went unresolved. How would the government respond to other employees making disclosures? Did the press and public have a right to information related to the national defense that the state considered privileged? And could whistleblowers reveal them when acting in the public interest?

Almost half a century after copying the Pentagon Papers, Ellsberg remains a curious poster boy for national security whistleblowing. Embodying the popular understanding of an insider that exposes the excesses of American power, Ellsberg came to symbolize the phenomenon more broadly, becoming not only the most famous whistleblower of his generation but also the source of many historical parallels with contemporaries in the twenty-first century.[3] Despite a number of commonalities with whistleblowers past and present, including his conversion from believer to dissenter, Ellsberg was the exception rather than the rule on several crucial issues, such as revealing classified information, dissemination tactics, and the efficacy of state retaliation. Indeed, his case casts as much shadow as light on the whistleblowing boom during the period from the late 1960s to early 1980s, when a host of disillusioned defense and intelligence officials exposed the theory and practice of U.S. national security. An unprecedented wave of insider accounts that critiqued the machinations of U.S. covert power and cultures of secrecy emerged during this period, generating widespread public and political attention. Whistleblowing exploded, and while Ellsberg was a forerunner, his fate was atypical.

By addressing the political, social, and legal questions that the Ellsberg episode left hanging, this chapter moves beyond the Pentagon Papers to examine the remarkable rise and fall of anti-imperial whistleblowing during the "long 1970s." The period was formative in demonstrating the possibilities, limits, and legacies for government officials making critical disclosures of U.S. national security rituals and policies. The revelations by Perry Fellwock, Victor Marchetti, John Marks, Philip Agee, Frank Snepp, John Stockwell, and Ralph McGehee confirmed key shifts both in the internal culture of the national security establishment and from previous generations of whistleblowers. The whistleblowers tapped an epochal antiestablishment nerve and crisis in American hegemony by shining light on the darkest corners of the national security state, providing stinging details of American aggression and interventionism abroad. Their "anti-imperial" critique chimed with the social and cultural revisionism of the era, which questioned state power, secrecy, and war making. Moreover, their perspective on the expanding power and influence of the U.S. national security apparatus was defined by unique insider knowledge and experiences. This validated the whistleblowers' words as they offered accessible, popular, and powerful arguments against American imperialism.[4]

In exploring this history, several key themes emerge. First, disclosures by the anti-imperial generation both aided and thwarted the whistleblowing phenomenon. On the one hand, the extraordinary concentration of protesting voices, which highlighted past abuses and framed contemporary crises in U.S. politics and foreign affairs, created informal networks that fostered further revelations and contributed to growing dissenting narratives that were broadly leftist-progressive and anti-imperial in nature. On the other hand, the heterogeneity of the generation hampered any movement for change, given its diverging opinions over the public's right to know, transparency, and reform, especially as more radical protest butted up against establishment efforts to rein in executive power and intelligence agencies.[5] In short, the commonalities and differences reflected the broader uncertainty over the politics of disclosures while contributing to cultural shifts in attitudes toward secrecy and foreign relations. This anti-imperial whistleblowing tradition has nonetheless been absent from the scholarly literature on politics and protest in the era, falling between approaches focused on the state and nonstate activism.[6]

Second, the generation posed a curious dilemma for the state, since, unlike Ellsberg's Pentagon Papers, their exposures did not place vast amounts of classified information in the public sphere. In critiquing

American power, the majority drew on firsthand experience and publicly available material. Yet in an era of profound government concern about safeguarding national security information, particularly in preventing the press from publishing details, whistleblowers openly discussing policies and practices—whether classified or not—represented an acute threat. The government's response doubled down on state secrecy through prior restraint of employees and a more stringent classification regime. The clampdown was improvised and hinged on attempts at censorship that effectively suspended First Amendment rights for national security officials and bore the hallmarks of an official secrets act. Landmark legal rulings and legislation placed unprecedented weight on the sanctity of executive-branch secrecy agreements. Third, and related, this history reveals the limits of state retaliation against whistleblowers via the Espionage Act during the twentieth century. Ellsberg was but the latest example of an unsuccessful criminal prosecution for unauthorized disclosure. In confronting the anti-imperial generation, successive U.S. governments preferred to develop new tools to police officials handling national security information rather than prosecute whistleblowers in public courts. The bipartisan response, over successive administrations and all three branches of government, sought to control the flow of information in the public sphere by targeting the state employee. Whistleblowing became more perilous as whistleblowers increasingly became the only source for the public and press to understand what the state was doing in the national security realm.

Finally, if the U.S. government was able to curtail the main challenge posed by the anti-imperial generation, it could not curb the whistleblowing phenomenon itself. State attempts to coerce the definition of whistleblowing were stunted, and efforts to control the words of national security personnel butted up against an ever-expanding bureaucracy producing increasing amounts of classified information. It was a challenge to police the growing numbers of officials and contractors handling more secrets, while the specter of employees acting out of individual conscience and in the public interest continued to haunt the national security state.

BEFORE THE BOOM

National security whistleblowing in the public interest gained traction in the 1970s, but historically it had not been an act that rejected the underlying premises of American power. Motives are notoriously tricky to pinpoint, although a multitude of factors had influenced individuals divulging information before the anti-imperial generation. Nonetheless, the U.S. government had consistently and indiscriminately targeted the state employee. The problem was the government had not successfully prosecuted a case of unauthorized disclosure through the Espionage Act by the time Ellsberg faced trial in 1973. Meanwhile, measures to intimidate whistleblowers—censorship, demotion, and dismissal—only enjoyed mixed results.

Since the early twentieth century, individuals had been motivated to disclose national defense information for a variety of reasons: personal or financial issues, departmental turf wars, and opposition to political decision making and priorities. Herbert Yardley's 1931 exposé of the defunct American Black Chamber argued for continued U.S. cryptanalysis in peacetime and rebuked State Department diplomacy; he also sought personal profit and fame. Over twenty-five years later, John Nickerson's disclosures about an Army ballistic missile program admonished the Eisenhower administration for favoring a rival Air Force program; he was also seeking individual gain.[7] In 1963, Otto Otepka, the vehemently anticommunist deputy director of the State Department's security office, provided classified information to a Senate subcommittee on internal security about suspected Kennedy-era liberal "dissidents," prompting the conservative senator Strom Thurmond to defend his act of "whistle-blowing." Five years later, A. Ernest Fitzgerald, an Air Force employee, revealed a $2 billion cost overrun on a military cargo plane in testimony to the Congress Joint Economic Committee as an example of inefficiency and waste. In short, assorted incentives and objectives were at work in each episode.[8]

The key factor tying these disparate cases together was indiscriminate state retaliation. The U.S. government could not prevent the publication of

Yardley's book but censored its follow-up and enacted new legislation criminalizing the release of government records. Public Law 37 stipulated that anyone "without authorization or competent authority" that sought to "publish or furnish" information gathered from code or intercepted communications could be prosecuted. Part of the United States Statutes at Large—today incorporated in Title 18 of the U.S. Code—it represented the first major revision to the espionage statutes. Nickerson was the first American charged for revealing state secrets, but, with press interest in the case growing and fearful of further revelations in court, the Army dropped the espionage indictment for a lesser charge.[9] By the 1960s, with Espionage Act prosecutions proving problematic, individuals disclosing national security information, even to Congress, were dismissed. Otepka was fired by Secretary of State Dean Rusk, and the Nixon White House instructed the removal of Fitzgerald. The contrasting political contexts of the two cases demonstrated that, for the executive branch, any disclosure of information was unauthorized.[10]

Fitzgerald would, as we will see, later be reinstated and flaunted as a model state whistleblower. More immediately, his case was featured in Ralph Nader's seminal 1971 conference and accompanying book popularizing the concept of whistleblowing. The Report of the Conference on Professional Responsibility introduced the term into the public lexicon to describe individuals serving the public interest over an organizational interest by exposing "corrupt, illegal, fraudulent or harmful activity" and abuses of power. Another publication that hit bookstands in 1972 added momentum to the idea of blowing the whistle in the public interest. The editors of the *Washington Monthly*, a magazine that acted as a forum for state officials willing to speak out, also praised exposures of government corruption in the name of the public's right to know. The definition of whistleblowing was taking shape. Nonetheless, it did not yet address how whistleblowing related to individuals exposing national security abuses and corruption.[11]

That question was largely shaped by a pervasive postwar culture of secrecy. Keeping secrets was deeply embedded in the national security state, underpinned by the modern classification regime. Truman- and Eisenhower-era executive orders established the system of categorizing information in the early 1950s, with federal government agencies each classifying at source, so that national security information could not, in theory, circulate in the public sphere.[12] Furthermore, there was a consensus among government officials that what went on in Washington stayed in Washington. The notion of making disclosures was alien to the culture, with the bureaucracy populated by officials that not only identified with the state and the U.S. Cold War mission but felt part of a civic fraternity. This was buttressed by a consensual state-press relationship that ensured favorable coverage of national security affairs in influential news outlets.[13]

Most national security personnel, particularly those in the intelligence community, signed nondisclosure (aka secrecy) agreements on recruitment. To deter unauthorized disclosures, the secrecy agreement warned of criminal prosecution through the espionage statutes. This was a loose reading of the Espionage Act, but, given that aspiring national security officials did not sign agreements with the intention of disclosing secrets, the legal scaffolding was never questioned during the early Cold War decades.[14] The framing of secrecy contracts emphasized the handling of information, thereby placing the burden on the government employee rather than on the information itself. This was essential to avoid any semblance of an official secrets act, which was common in other countries but precluded by the U.S. Constitution under the First Amendment. The bureaucracy of information control reinforced the significant constitutional authority of the executive over foreign affairs and historic executive-branch privilege, especially in the context of Cold War and espionage anxieties, to enable a very specific form of "authorized" disclosure. As the inaugural National Security Advisor Robert Cutler put it in 1955, "all papers, all considerations, all studies, all intelligence leading to the formulation of national security policy recommendations are the property of the president," and "only he can dispose of them."[15]

Ellsberg's iconoclasm undercut this notion spectacularly. His disclosures gained broad public attention, and he articulated his motives more clearly than previous whistleblowers had, not least through several media appearances. Yet Ellsberg was also squarely in the state's crosshairs. Whether his revelations would have been adjudged legal will, of course, never be known. Critically, there was no precedent for successful state prosecution via the

Espionage Act of individuals revealing national security information. Furthermore, the charge could even open a wider debate about the secrecy regime, namely, that it represented an executive system not rooted in statute. Enforcing executive-branch nondisclosure agreements in court was problematic and potentially raised constitutional questions around freedom-of-speech rights that could leave the government without a law to cite in secrecy agreements with future employees.[16] That whistleblowers in the aftermath of Ellsberg were not targeted through the espionage statutes shows that the U.S. government was cognizant of the limits of the legislation and the need for alternative tools.

THE ANTI-IMPERIAL GENERATION

A defining feature of whistleblowing during the long 1970s was the concentration of former government officials disclosing information and details that fundamentally undermined the theory and practice of U.S. national security. It was in stark contrast to previous cases of whistleblowing, which sought to enhance the instruments and efficiency of American foreign policy. In the footsteps of Ellsberg came Fellwock (aka Winslow Peck), Marchetti, Marks, Agee, Snepp, Stockwell, and McGehee.[17] They represented a new generation of national security official: they had joined in the postwar era to wage Cold War against communism but became disillusioned. Their respective conversions overlapped with the collapsing Cold War consensus in American society, prompting exposures rooted in a progressive vision of public service. In short, these officials not only quit but did not feel bound to the culture of confidentiality prevalent inside the Washington Beltway.

The whistleblowers of this generation offered unprecedented insights into the scale and capabilities of the U.S. national security state, describing its functions and structures as well as providing firsthand accounts of specific operations. Fellwock's interview with the radical left-wing magazine *Ramparts* was one of the first public discussions of the very existence of the

NSA. Agee, Stockwell, and McGehee provided gripping accounts of how the covert Cold War was being waged abroad. Agee's portrayal was so effective that, while angering the CIA, it was later assigned as reading to prospective recruits. As the head of the Agency's clandestine service acknowledged, it was "an excellent reflection of the day-to-day life of an officer."[18] The whistleblowers' revelations explained the way secretive agencies implemented foreign policy through case studies of interventions.

The emerging critical mass provided opportunities to evade state censorship. Informal networks and support structures developed, with individuals assisting one another and learning from one another's experiences to publish and disseminate books. Agee and Snepp traveled to Europe to research in newspaper records, with the former in conversion with Marchetti and the latter assisting Stockwell during the publication process. Fellwock, Agee, and Marchetti were involved in *Counter-Spy*, a magazine linked to Norman Mailer's "Fifth Estate" movement, which encouraged public oversight of U.S. intelligence agencies and routinely exposed CIA and FBI operations. Agee joined with activists to launch the magazine's successor, *Covert Action Information Bulletin*, which Stockwell also promoted.[19] During the preparation of his manuscript, Snepp met secretly with his Random House editor in various New York parks to evade CIA surveillance. The tactic was not only rooted in spy tradecraft but the publisher's earlier experience with *The Invisible Government*, a 1964 book by the journalists David Wise and Thomas Ross that detailed CIA covert operations in the global South. After the Agency clandestinely obtained the manuscript, Wise, Ross, and Random House were threatened with espionage charges but pressed ahead with publication (the book was not written by insiders and didn't include classified information). Alfred A. Knopf also refused to be intimidated when Marks and Marchetti's manuscript, which argued that the CIA's obsession with covert action had sidetracked it from its original task of intelligence collection and analysis, was again secretly obtained by the Agency, which demanded the removal of 339 passages. A legal challenge reduced the number of deletions, and Knopf published the book with blanks for censored passages and boldface type for the reinstated passages, thereby highlighting the often banal and mildly embarrassing things the government had claimed would damage national security, such as officials mispronouncing the name of a country in meetings. That layout tactic was also used in McGehee's 1983 book.[20]

Legal, press, and civil society networks were particularly important as whistleblowers confronted the state backlash. Many turned to the American Civil Liberties Union (ACLU), with the lawyers Melvin Wulf and Mark Lynch representing Marchetti, Agee, McGehee, and Snepp. Morton Halperin, the former National Security Council (NSC) advisor who oversaw the production of the Pentagon Papers, directed several NGO civil liberties projects and testified on behalf of numerous whistleblowers. Leading the ACLU-sponsored Center for National Security Studies, Halperin supported Ellsberg and Marchetti as well as Agee when the latter faced deportation from the United Kingdom and was falsely accused of outing the murdered CIA station chief Richard Welch in Greece. Ramsey Clark, who briefly had a small law practice with Wulf after serving as Lyndon Johnson's attorney general, testified for Agee and endorsed McGehee's book. The Pulitzer Prize–winning *New York Times* legal journalist Anthony Lewis penned forewords for the works by Marks and Marchetti and Snepp. New Left educators like Howard Zinn and Noam Chomsky campaigned prominently at Ellsberg's trial, while Agee and Stockwell collaborated with activists, lawyers, and publishers such as William Schaap, Ellen Ray, and Louis Wolf. Indeed, exposure to progressive-leftist circles, especially Gandhian nonviolence and socialist movements, informed Ellsberg's and Agee's decisions to blow the whistle.[21]

Yet this was no cadre of radical protesters. While whistleblowers dissented from foreign policy orthodoxies, there was no consistency on motive, tactics, or the purpose of disclosing national security information. It was a heterogeneous group challenging U.S. power in diverse ways and with different political worldviews. Agee's more radical critique of U.S. global capitalism differed from Ellsberg's focus on Vietnam and the corruption of the secrecy regime; Snepp provided a relatively conservative critique of the U.S. abandonment of its South Vietnamese allies, as did his friend and colleague Samuel Adams, a CIA analyst who critiqued intelligence estimates in Vietnam. While Marchetti, Agee, and McGehee were determined to expose directly to the public, Ellsberg and Snepp explored internal and congressional channels before taking that route.

Ellsberg and Vietnam cast a curious shadow over the whistleblowing generation. Although several whistleblowers highlighted a personal connection or involvement in the war, it was not the trigger for many to blow the whistle. Covert U.S. meddling in other locales of the global South was the crux for Agee (Latin America), McGehee (Asia), and Stockwell (Africa). Referencing war in Vietnam was likely attributable to the zeitgeist and the demands of commercial publishing. Meanwhile, Fellwock noted that Ellsberg's actions "made me want to talk," whereas Marchetti sought to distinguish his act, stating, "I'm no Ellsberg. I did not walk out with a boxload of stuff. That's not my bag."[22]

The generation was skeptical about the ability and willingness of Congress to rein in intelligence operations, especially CIA clandestine activities, but there also were schisms over the actual change these public-interest exposures could bring. Agee, Marchetti, Marks, and McGehee were the most strident in calling for an end to covert action—which they considered unaccountable, damaging, and a manifestation of American imperial designs—and refocusing on core intelligence gathering and analysis duties.[23] Reform from inside was impossible given the culture of arrogance and lack of commitment, concluded Stockwell. "Only in the forum of public debate, outside the CIA, could effective leverage be had to correct the Agency's wrongs," he argued. "Only an informed American public can bring effective pressure to bear on the CIA." Meanwhile, Snepp's concern lay in producing a meaningful damage assessment, with his book originating as an internal report about Agency failures and political dishonesty during the final phase of formal American involvement in Vietnam. "I'm not a flaming liberal, I'm a pragmatist," he explained. "I don't want to be in the demolition business of destroying the Agency."[24]

The biggest bone of contention regarded activism that hampered ongoing CIA covert operations or unmasked personnel. Furthermore, this illustrated a critical point: exposures did not necessarily divulge classified material. Whistleblowers were offering personal accounts, and much of the information was already in the public domain. Marks detailed how publicly available lists like the Foreign Service Register and Biographic Register could be used to distinguish spies from genuine American diplomatic staff stationed in foreign embassies. *Counter-Spy* enthusiastically embraced the methodology, launching a "Naming Names" column that began by identifying over one hundred CIA station chiefs around the world. The leading advocate was Agee, who explained the objective was to "neutralize" operations by exposing "officers so that their presence in foreign countries becomes untenable."[25] Although Stockwell supported the public's right to know Agency activities, he had "no desire to expose or hurt individuals," adding, "I reject Agee's approach." Snepp also opposed the tactic as endangering careers and lives and even questioned Agee's loyalty and credentials as a whistleblower. Indeed, Snepp repeatedly clashed with other whistleblowers, describing the books by Marchetti and Agee as "an abomination" and needling Stockwell after originally trying to help him secure a publisher.[26]

The heterogeneity of the generation meant it was never a unified movement, let alone a coherent force that could translate critiques of the national security state, especially the lack of accountability and transparency, into radical change or pragmatic reform. Nonetheless, whistleblowing during the long 1970s provided the public with extraordinary details of national security culture and covert operations, contributing to a crucial period when the foundational pillars of postwar U.S. liberal hegemony began to crack.[27] Ellsberg struck a dramatic opening blow, and subsequent whistleblowers chipped away at the notion of benevolence underpinning postwar U.S. foreign relations.

The wave of whistleblowing reassessed past episodes but also cast light on critical contemporary issues relating to America's role in the world. Snepp brought the concept of a "decent interval"—the period between the withdrawal of U.S. troops and communist takeover in Vietnam—into the popular lexicon, while Marks and Marchetti revealed Kissinger's infamous "I don't see why we need to stand by and watch a country go communist due to the irresponsibility of its own people" remark amid plans to overthrow Salvador Allende in Chile. Yet more than choice quotes, whistleblowers confirmed and developed arguments already in the public domain by critics of U.S. wars. Agee, Snepp, McGehee, and Stockwell provided regional political, economic, and social analyses that detailed the damage done by U.S. interventionism. They built on the efforts of authors, journalists, and emerging revisionist historical scholarship. Their perspective had the added value of firsthand knowledge, status, and frontline experience.[28]

In facilitating public discussions of national security, the generation contributed to epochal concerns about the scope of executive power, state secrecy, and war. This brought several whistleblowers into conversation with activists, artists, and organized protest networks. Agency whistleblowers, as Jeremy Varon details, featured prominently in the CIA Off Campus movement; they also spoke abroad and collaborated with citizen groups on resistance to covert activities. McGehee constructed a searchable computer database of books, magazines, congressional reports, and newspaper articles on the CIA as a resource tool for activists, journalists, academics, and policy makers. Whistleblowers also formed organizations, such as the Association for Responsible Dissent and Association of National Security Alumni, to spread their messages more effectively. Stockwell and Agee sought interest from Hollywood, discussing scripts based on their stories with the director Oliver Stone. Such efforts saw mixed results. Stone declined the options, noting the need for "more Hitchcock," but several whistleblowers featured in Allan Francovich's critical documentary *On Company Business*. The organizations, undermined by internal squabbling and uncertain objectives, never properly established themselves. Yet such conversations and interactions continued and bore greater fruit in the twenty-first century, with Stone finding more dramatic material with *Snowden* in 2016 and ex-CIA officials playing a leading role in the emergence of Veteran Intelligence Professionals for Sanity in 2003.[29]

Rather than a targeted movement to reform the system, the anti-imperial whistleblowing generation was part of a broader cultural shift that marked increased skepticism toward government, tangibly revealing the gap between the words and actions of successive U.S. administrations on foreign policy. Peeling back the veil of secrecy, they contributed to calls for accountability and the public's right to know. Whistleblowers had a crucial function in an era where it was harder for the public to get information about the government—the press could publish freely but were increasingly reliant on state news management, and the public's right to information was regulated through the classification system—by helping the flow of information on national security matters in the American polity.[30]

PRIOR RESTRAINT AND CENSORSHIP

When the Supreme Court rejected the Nixon administration's clampdown on the *New York Times* for publishing the Pentagon Papers, the justices also flagged the state's error of framing the response through prior restraint of the press. This had made it a freedom-of-press question, with the burden on the government to prove "grave and irreparable injury." In concurring with the judgment, Byron White noted "that the Government mistakenly chose to proceed by injunction does not mean that it could not successfully proceed in another way," particularly emphasizing how "the Criminal Code contains numerous provisions potentially relevant."[31] While prosecuting the press for violating the espionage statutes was unconstitutional, the state's indictment against Ellsberg for copying and disseminating classified records appeared more straightforward. The shenanigans of the plumbers and the legal strategy of Ellsberg's lawyer, as Julia Kraut explains, ultimately led to a mistrial, but the objective of suppressing the government employee remained. It was nonetheless unclear whether the Espionage Act could be employed to prosecute whistleblowers successfully. White House officials lamented that current statutes required the government to convince a jury that "(i) the accused intended to injure the United States or aid a foreign nation and (ii) the information involved relates to the national defense." Proving the latter often required the release of more classified information, which, in a nod to the Nickerson case, "has led to a decision not to prosecute."[32] Even without the plumbers' ransacking of Ellsberg's psychiatrist's office, there were no guarantees that he would have gone to jail.

The central question was how to control government officials that handled national security information. In the wake of Ellsberg's mistrial, the Nixon White House and CIA shifted from reactive to proactive measures.

Unauthorized disclosures were to be nipped in the bud before they could blossom outside the national security state and therefore need to be fought in the public sphere. Prior restraint of national security officials emerged as the central plank of state retaliation toward whistleblowers through the enforcement of secrecy agreements, backed by landmark legal rulings, and revisions to the espionage statutes. At stake was not so much what individuals were revealing but the fact they were revealing anything at all. In short, any kind of information intended for public consumption was to be curbed.

A crucial precedent was set in censoring Marchetti. In 1971, he published *The Rope Dancer*, a novel about the ills of a fictional "National Intelligence Agency," which was followed by critical press interviews and nonfiction about his experience as an intelligence officer, including "CIA: The President's Loyal Tool" for the *Nation*. Agency anxieties intensified after placing Marchetti under surveillance and discovering he planned to write a book and more articles in popular magazines. Turning to the U.S. district court next to its Langley headquarters, the CIA sought a "permanent injunction against disclosures" by enforcing the secrecy agreement that Marchetti had signed at the start of his career. Granting the injunction, Judge Albert Bryan Jr. noted, "the contract takes the case out of the scope of the First Amendment" and "constitutes a waiver of the defendant's rights thereunder," ordering Marchetti to submit all writing to the CIA before publication. Marchetti appealed the injunction with assistance from the ACLU, but the U.S. court of appeals upheld the decision and, furthermore, rooted the contract issue in existing statutes, noting that the 1947 National Security Act "imposed on the Director of Central Intelligence the responsibility for protecting intelligence sources and methods." Acknowledging "the Government's need for secrecy" and right to protect internal secrets through "a system of prior restraint against disclosure by employees and former employees," Judge Clement Haynsworth concluded the signed secrecy agreement "was not in derogation of Marchetti's constitutional rights." The agreement had been willingly entered and did not impede freedom of speech. The prepublication order was enforced with the CIA to review manuscripts "promptly" and only censor classified information.[33]

FIGURE 5.1

The case of the CIA whistleblower Victor Marchetti established a crucial precedent in the suspension of speech rights for all national security officials.

Source: Photo by Paul Wright/Getty Images.

The courts had ruled that Marchetti's ability to discuss his experiences publicly was an issue of contract law, not constitutional law. An executive-branch secrecy agreement now carried the same weight as a legally binding and enforceable private contract. The ruling effectively suspended First Amendment speech rights for every national security official who had ever signed a secrecy agreement. The decision evaded the question of what was revealed by focusing on the potential for what could be revealed. Indeed, Marchetti had not yet written *The CIA and the Cult of Intelligence* and, as his former boss admitted, had not revealed any intelligence secrets to date. The CIA "is trying to impose a kind of preventive detention in the realm of ideas," commented the *Washington Post.* The episode "tests the reach and the reality of the First Amendment," and "the paramount issue . . . is the right of the people to be informed about matters of public interest."[34]

The magnitude of the ruling was not lost on the government and intelligence community. CIA chief Richard Helms noted, "the Marchetti case concludes the first step in what I consider historic litigation on behalf of the Central Intelligence Agency." The practical impossibility of applying criminal sanctions against unauthorized disclosures had been known for several years, noted the CIA deputy general counsel, but "a workable tool in a court of law, based on a simple contract theory," had now been fashioned that amounted to "a significant victory in a landmark legal case."[35] The Nixon White House immediately attempted to capitalize on the ruling by rolling out the secrecy agreement to the entire national security community and all federal employees with security clearances. The White House counsel explained the "Marchetti principle" could be extended to FBI and NSC officials but that anything beyond that would have to be on a "case-by-case" basis. In subsequent years, officials and staff members associated with major congressional and executive investigations into CIA activities have signed secrecy agreements, including the Rockefeller Commission, Church Committee, Pike Committee, Justice Department, and special prosecutors investigating Watergate.[36]

The Marchetti case laid the legal foundation for creating the CIA Publications Review Board (PRB) in 1976, the first formal prepublication review mechanism in Agency history. All officials, past or present, who had signed a secrecy agreement were required to submit any material intended for a public audience. Whether the mechanism prevents harmful disclosures to national security or shields the Agency from embarrassment has been debated since the PRB's creation. Recounting the frustrations of having his manuscript reviewed, including the reviewers' unwillingness to allow citations even to published congressional records and press reports, McGehee concluded, "Agency officials show no hesitation in trying to censor embarrassing, critical, or merely annoying information. . . . It is obvious that national security has little to do with how the Agency administers the secrecy agreement."[37] While the results of the review process have frequently been criticized, as Richard Immerman reveals in this volume, the history of prepublication review is also one of bureaucratic ignorance and ineptitude.

The state had successfully weaponized secrecy agreements, although there remained the specter of officials refusing to submit writing for prepublication review. When Snepp's *Decent Interval* was released without PRB approval, the Carter administration's retaliation confirmed that the contract issue had mutated into more than the protection of classified information. Denied the opportunity to raise his misgivings internally, Snepp incorrectly assumed that his secrecy agreement was not binding, especially since his manuscript featured no classified material. After the book's release, the government filed a civil suit, again in the district court in Virginia, with a curious twist on the contract violation. The issue was not the revelation of classified information but profiteering. The court determined that publication "caused the United States irreparable harm and loss," with Snepp ordered to submit future work for review and surrender all monies earned from *Decent Interval*. The decision was upheld by the court of appeals, with Snepp's defense, based on First Amendment speech rights, roundly rejected. Unlike the Marchetti decision, the Supreme Court agreed to hear the case but quickly issued a judgment without receiving arguments that concurred with the lower courts. The *Snepp v. United States* ruling did resemble the Marchetti case in citing the DCI's mandate of "protecting intelligence sources and methods," thus tying the secrecy agreement even tighter to statute.[38]

The Snepp decision bore the hallmarks of an improvised official secrets act. Publishing any information related to national security, regardless of content, without permission was a criminal offense. Freedom-of-speech rights were suspended for any individual that had ever handled classified material. "The Court's treatment of the first amendment issues," commented a legal study, "represents a significant departure from prior case law."[39] If it did constitute an American official secrets act, it was a haphazard and inconsistent one. The PRB formally required all CIA employees to comply, but the rule was not systematically applied, with several instances of authors refusing or forgetting to engage with the process and the censors choosing to look away. Although the review process frustrated and afflicted Agency defenders as well as critics, anti-imperial whistleblowers bore the brunt of sanctions. Only Marchetti and Snepp were put on trial.[40]

Agee had evaded censorship earlier by publishing *Inside the Company* abroad, where he remained, posing a unique transnational challenge to the U.S. and European national security states. Moreover, he continued to champion the exposure of CIA officers around the world, disseminating the Marks methodology and collaborating with magazines like *Counter-Spy* and *Covert Action Information Bulletin* and with activists in Europe and Latin America. Governments on both sides of the Atlantic struck back through travel control and censorship. Several Western European countries deported him, and the Carter and Reagan administrations revoked his passport and brought an injunction in 1980 for his writing to be submitted to the PRB.[41] Yet the critical issue was to criminalize the "naming of names" tactic. "It is despicable that Philip Agee can publish the names of persons he claims are CIA officers," noted Senator John H. Chafee, "and yet the U.S. government has no legal mechanism to prosecute him for this act." Chafee was a leading congressional advocate for a new intelligence identities bill, which repeatedly cited the whistleblower and his collaborators in the context of the Welch murder. "At stake," noted a senior NSC figure, "is whether a small group of Americans who oppose all U.S. human intelligence capabilities can continue with impunity to ferret out and reveal the secret identities of American intelligence officers and agents."[42]

The 1982 Intelligence Identities Protection Act (IIPA) made it a federal crime to purposely unmask covert intelligence officers, whether through classified information or nonclassified sources. The act was another revision to the espionage statutes with the aim of prosecuting unauthorized disclosures. While sympathetic to the broader objective, opponents warned about the legislation's constitutional ramifications. Joseph Biden, one of a

FIGURE 5.2

The former CIA covert case officer Philip Agee talks at a press conference. Agee's whistleblowing and activism contributed to the passing of the 1982 Intelligence Identities Protection Act.

Source: Bettmann/Getty Images.

handful of dissenting senators, argued the bill "is so broadly drawn that it would subject to prosecution not only the malicious publicizing of agents' names but also the efforts of legitimate journalists to expose any corruption, malfeasance, or ineptitude occurring in American intelligence agencies." The press decried the impact on its First Amendment rights: the bill criminalized stories revealing information gleaned from public records, regardless of whether the author had served in government or handled classified documents.[43]

The state had developed mechanisms to preempt unauthorized disclosures that responded to the challenge of the 1970s generation. It established a process of censorship for individuals that had signed secrecy agreements and prosecution for those who failed to comply. New legislation also outlawed exposures to curb covert operations even when based on material in the public domain. This had not been a strategic government riposte but improvised maneuvers performed on the back of failed prosecution efforts via the Espionage Act. The legal rulings had a snowball effect, building on each case against whistleblowers and referencing one another. The judicial and legislative branches sided with the executive in restricting the First Amendment rights of national security officials. The measures had originated as a response to anti-imperial whistleblowing but soon saw applicability throughout the federal government. Meanwhile the state moved to coerce the language of whistleblowing itself.

COERCING THE WHISTLEBLOWING PHENOMENON

The legislative victories against the anti-imperial whistleblowers dovetailed with broader efforts to reassert executive power and strengthen the national security state. A hawkish turn in U.S. foreign relations from the late 1970s manifested in more aggressive policies abroad and a tougher stance on state security and information at home. The reputation of whistleblowers had been attacked to discredit them ever since Yardley, but accusations increasingly revolved on defection, theft, and profiteering. Focusing on character moved the debate from the substance of arguments to the notion of a crime being committed. The effort to delegitimize and neutralize individuals now blurred ideas of patriotism, morality, and criminality. It also served a broader goal of delineating unacceptable from acceptable forms of disclosure. While the 1970s generation was painted as radicals and reactionaries, figures like Fitzgerald were rehabilitated as model whistleblowers. The government attempted to frame whistleblowing as a legitimate drive to eliminate waste. Rather than abuse of power, the critical issue was improving the organization. Loyalty to the state was cloaked as efficiency.

By the end of the decade, both Democratic and Republican politicians praised Fitzgerald's exposure of waste and dishonesty, warning that his treatment should never be repeated. Notwithstanding the strong hint of anti-Nixon posturing, politicians were embracing a narrow version of whistleblowing that was politically acceptable and could generate popular support. Challenging wasteful spending by speaking to Congress was more palatable than criticizing the fundamental tenets of U.S. power. As new legislation to protect federal government whistleblowers was drafted, Carter cited Fitzgerald as someone who should have been rewarded rather than punished. The 1978 Civil Service Reform Act prohibited retaliation against employees who reported violations of laws, regulations, abuses of authority, and dangers to the public welfare, creating the Office of Special Counsel to manage complaints of unfair treatment against whistleblowers.[44] The legislation responded to the threat that Nader had outlined, but, crucially, there was no reference to whistleblowing involving classified information. Some officials expressed concern that the administration was not doing more to prosecute national security exposures. Carter, who had pledged greater government openness, instead issued an executive order that "balance[d] the public's interest in access to Government information with the need to protect certain national security information from disclosure."[45]

The exclusion of national security officials from state definitions of whistleblowing was criticized by federal employee interest groups and new legal advocacy organizations like the Government Accountability Project. As the cases of Marchetti, Snepp, and Agee demonstrated, the state made a sharp distinction between whistleblowing that protested as opposed to improved national security. Rejecting the notion that Snepp was a whistleblower at all, Carter reiterated he had "signed voluntarily a contract" that "the Attorney General has decided . . . ought to be honored." Snepp had deliberately evaded prepublication review that existed "to assure there were no revelations of secret material." The president tellingly remarked, "I don't believe that he has revealed anything that would lead to an improvement in our security apparatus or the protection of Americans' civil rights."[46]

The framing of a specific form of whistleblowing as honorable duty was starkly contrasted with "unauthorized disclosures." The issue was wrapped up in a broader drive to secure information, whether classified or simply given curiously opaque labels, and to prevent revelations throughout the U.S. government. As Reagan noted to all federal employees, "each of us has the right to leave our position of trust and criticize our government and its policies, if that is what our conscience dictates. What we do *not* have is the right to damage our country by giving away its secrets." Unauthorized disclosures were "improper, unethical, and plain wrong." In addition to passing the IIPA, the Reagan administration accelerated the clampdown through tighter control of national security information. A new executive order—examined by Matt Jones in these pages—reversed Carter's "balance test" and allowed for the reclassification of "information previously declassified and disclosed." Furthermore, National Security Decision Directive 84 required individuals to sign secrecy agreements as a precondition to accessing classified information, the violation of which would be "enforceable in a civil action." Officials would have to "submit to polygraph examinations" in the event of any investigation.[47]

An updated nondisclosure agreement reflected the changes as well as the growing scope of what constituted national security information. The CIA reworked its secrecy agreement with employees bound for life to submit to agency review, regardless of whether information was declassified, and widened the scope for prosecution under the violated-contract theory. It was potentially illegal for officials to discuss anything related to national security even as the epidemic of overclassification was producing ever-increasing amounts of information.[48]

* * *

By the early 1980s, the anti-imperial whistleblowing tradition had been caught in the crosshairs of renewed executive power. The state had clamped down on the challenge posed by the 1970s generation through a more imposing culture of secrecy. Prior restraint and censorship of national security officials were the means to control unauthorized disclosures. While freedom of speech as a whole was untouched, especially for the press, who continued to publish any information it obtained, the state had a tighter grip over national defense information. The U.S. government effectively suspended First Amendment rights for employees by enforcing the secrecy contract. All the legal risk lay with the individual who traversed the secrecy Rubicon.

The phenomenon of whistleblowing could not, however, be stifled or coerced. The PRB's ham-fisted censorship provided greater attention for authors and their works. Even in the face of state retaliation, whistleblowers provided insights that would not otherwise have circulated in the public realm. The 1970s generation was part of a political and cultural zeitgeist seeking transparency and emphasizing the public's right to know, which measures like the Freedom of Information Act addressed in an egalitarian manner.[49] The extent to which they encouraged an informed public that could bring about substantial reform nonetheless remained vague. There was certainly no emancipatory "truth shall set you free" moment. Yet judging impact through normative standards misses the crucial point of how the 1970s generation challenged the underlying structure of American power rather than tinker to enhance it.

The anti-imperial generation triggered profound political and legal anxieties. While the state backlash grappled with these concerns, the popular and cultural impact of whistleblowing informed public debates on secrecy, foreign relations, intelligence, and American power by injecting new perspectives into topics dominated by specialists and legalese. Moreover, the generation established a crucial precedent, which was revived in the early twenty-first century, of insiders feeling compelled to act out of conscience and blowing the whistle in full awareness of imminent government reprisal.

While commentators continue to map Ellsberg onto contemporary whistleblowers, the state has drawn a different historical analogy to the long 1970s. In his first public address as CIA director in 2017, Mike Pompeo outlined that the threat posed by Edward Snowden and Chelsea Manning originated not with the Pentagon Papers but with the likes of Agee. "Today, there are still plenty of Philip Agees in the world, and the harm they inflict on U.S. institutions and personnel is just as serious today as it was back then," Pompeo warned. "They don't all come from the Intelligence Community, share the same background, or use precisely the same tactics as

Agee, but they are certainly his soulmates." Indeed, national security whistle-blowers do not have a common background, nor do they copy one another exactly. Yet they are far from soulmates.[50] There are, nevertheless, important structural, thematic, and philosophical continuities around whistle-blowing. Hyperbolic executive rhetoric and prosecution still define the government approach as the state continues to wrestle with the anti-imperial tradition.

NOTES

1. Daniel Ellsberg, *Secrets: A Memoir of Vietnam and the Pentagon Papers* (New York: Viking, 2002), vii–x, 426; Nixon phone conversation, June 14, 1971, 7:13 pm, Conversation WHT 005-068, Nixon Tapes, http://nixontapeaudio.org/ellsberg/005-068.mp3.

2. Lloyd C. Gardner, *The War on Leakers: National Security and American Democracy, from Eugene V. Debs to Edward Snowden* (New York: New Press, 2016), 59–64.

3. Nicholas Thompson, "From Daniel Ellsberg to Edward Snowden," *New Yorker*, June 9, 2013; Malcolm Gladwell, "Daniel Ellsberg, Edward Snowden, and the Modern Whistle-Blower," *New Yorker*, December 19 & 26, 2016. Ellsberg has closely identified himself with Chelsea Manning and Edward Snowden: Ashley Fantz, "Pentagon Papers Leaker: 'I Was Bradley Manning,'" *CNN*, March 21, 2011; Ewen MacAskill, Daniel Ellsberg, and Edward Snowden, "Is Whistleblowing Worth Prison or a Life in Exile?" *Guardian*, January 16, 2018.

4. I draw here from Paul Kramer's concept of imperialism as a way of seeing and a historical category for analysis in "Power and Connection: Imperial Histories of the United States in the World," *American Historical Review* 116 (2011): 1348–91. See also Ian Tyrell and Jay Sexton, eds., *Empire's Twin: U.S. Anti-Imperialism from the Founding Fathers to the Age of Terrorism* (Ithaca, NY: Cornell University Press, 2015).

5. See Loch K. Johnson, *A Season of Inquiry: The Senate Intelligence Investigation* (Lexington: University Press of Kentucky, 1985); Kathryn S. Olmsted, *Challenging the Secret Government: The Post-Watergate Investigations of the CIA and FBI* (Chapel Hill: University of North Carolina Press, 1996).

6. Select whistleblowers have received brief attention in the narrow context of works on CIA retaliation: John Prados, *The Family Jewels: The CIA, Secrecy, and Presidential Power* (Austin: University of Texas Press, 2013), 236–56; Christopher Moran, *Company Confessions: Revealing CIA Secrets* (London: Biteback, 2015), 103–41, 179–214. Burgeoning bodies of scholarship on the 1970s do not discuss whistleblowing at all; for instance, see

Thomas Borstelmann, *The 1970s: A New Global History from Civil Rights to Economic Inequality* (Princeton, NJ: Princeton University Press, 2012); and Michael S. Foley, *Front Porch Politics: The Forgotten Heyday of American Activism in the 1970s and 1980s* (New York: Hill and Wang, 2013).

7. In addition to the first two chapters of this volume, see Kaeten Mistry, "Embarrassing Indiscretions: The Origins and Culture of U.S. National Security Whistleblowing" in *The Culture of Intelligence: Germany, Britain, France, and the USA*, ed. Andreas Gestrich et al. (Oxford: Oxford University Press, forthcoming); Ian MacDougall, "The Leak Prosecution That Lost the Space Race," *Atlantic*, August 15, 2016; Sam Lebovic, "The Forgotten 1957 Trial That Explains Our Country's Bizarre Whistleblower Laws," *Politico*, March 27, 2016.

8. Taylor Branch, "The Odd Couple: Ellsberg and Otepka," *Washington Monthly*, October 1971, 50–60; Eric Paul Roorda, "McCarthyite in Camelot: The 'Loss' of Cuba, Homophobia, and the Otto Otepka Scandal in the Kennedy State Department," *Diplomatic History* 31, no. 4 (September 2007), 747; Molly Moore, "A. Ernest Fitzgerald: Analyst Who Knows the Price of Exposing Cost Overruns," *Washington Post*, February 23, 1987.

9. Mistry, "Embarrassing Indiscretions"; Lebovic, chapter 2 in this volume.

10. "Otepka Dropped as Security Aide; Held Guilty of Passing Data—Congressmen Protest," *New York Times*, November 6, 1963, 1; Branch, "The Odd Couple"; "Tapes Show Nixon Role in Firing of Ernest Fitzgerald," *Washington Post*, March 7, 1979.

11. Ralph Nader, Peter Petkas, and Kate Blackwell, eds., *Whistle Blowing: The Report of the Conference on Professional Responsibility* (New York: Grossman, 1972), vii, 39–54; Charles Peters and Taylor Branch, *Blowing the Whistle: Dissent in the Public Interest* (New York: Praeger, 1972). See also chapter 1 in this volume.

12. Executive Orders 10290, September 24, 1951, and EO 10501, November 5, 1953, American Presidency Project, http://www.presidency.ucsb.edu/ws/?pid=78426, http://www.presidency.ucsb.edu/ws/index.php?pid=485.

13. On the cultural roots of the civic fraternity, see Robert Dean, *Imperial Brotherhood: Gender and the Making of Cold War Foreign Policy* (Amherst: University of Massachusetts Press, 2003). On state-press relations in the early Cold War: Gregg Herken, *The Georgetown Set: Friends and Rivals in Cold War Washington* (New York: Knopf, 2014); John Foran, "Discursive Subversions: *Time* Magazine, the CIA Overthrow of Musaddiq, and the Installation of the Shah," in *Cold War Constructions: The Political Culture of United States Imperialism, 1945–1966*, ed. Christopher Appy (Amherst: University of Massachusetts Press, 2000), 157–82; Hugh Wilford, *The Mighty Wurlitzer: How the CIA Played America* (Cambridge, MA: Harvard University Press, 2008), 225–28.

14. Nondisclosure agreements were standard in the CIA since 1947, although their use in other national security agencies varied enormously. In short, there was no uniform approach regarding NDAs in the national security state until the early 1980s.

15. Cutler, cited in Sam Lebovic, *Free Speech and Unfree News: The Paradox of Press Freedom in America* (Cambridge, MA: Harvard University Press, 2016), 174. On executive

privilege, see Mark J. Rozell, *Executive Privilege: Presidential Power, Secrecy, and Accountability*, 3rd ed. (Lawrence: University Press of Kansas, 2010).

16. Ellsberg, *Secrets*, 430; Daniel Ellsberg, "Secrecy and National Security Whistleblowing," *Social Research* 77 (2010): 773–804; author interview with Melvin Wulf (ACLU lawyer), New York, October 2011.

17. "U.S. Electronic Espionage: A Memoir," *Ramparts* 11 (August 1972): 35–50; John Marks and Victor Marchetti, *The CIA and the Cult of Intelligence* (New York: Knopf, 1974); Philip Agee, *Inside the Company: CIA Diary* (London: Penguin, 1975); Frank Snepp, *Decent Interval: The American Debacle in Vietnam and the Fall of Saigon* (New York: Random House, 1977); John Stockwell, *In Search of Enemies: A CIA Story* (New York: Norton, 1978); Ralph W. McGehee, *Deadly Deceits: My 25 Years in the CIA* (New York: Sheridan Square, 1983).

18. James Bamford, *The Puzzle Palace: A Report on America's Most Secret Agency* (Boston: Houghton Mifflin, 1982), 334–35; Peter Richardson, *A Bomb in Every Issue: How the Short, Unruly Life of Ramparts Magazine Changed America* (New York: New Press, 2009); Robert Baer, "Havana's Man in Havana," *Foreign Policy*, November 9, 2010; Scott Shane, "Philip Agee, 72, Is Dead; Exposed Other C.I.A. Officers," *New York Times*, January 10, 2008.

19. Snepp, *Decent Interval*, 485; Frank Snepp, *Irreparable Harm: A Firsthand Account of How One Agent Took On the CIA in an Epic Battle Over Secrecy and Free Speech* (New York: Random House, 1999), 87–88; Agee, *Inside the Company*, 589–614; Philip Agee, *On the Run* (Secaucus, NJ: Lyle Stuart, 1987), 92; David Shamus McCarthy, "The CIA & the Cult of Secrecy," Ph.D. diss., College of William & Mary, 2008, 16–22; Angus Mackenzie, *Secrets: The CIA's War at Home* (Berkeley: University of California Press, 1997), 58–60.

20. Snepp, *Decent Interval*, 13; David Wise and Thomas B. Ross, *The Invisible Government* (New York: Random House, 1964); Prados, *Family Jewels*, 203–5, 238.

21. "Public Meeting at Central Hall, Westminster, Speeches by Clark, Halperin, Wulf," February 4, 1977, Box 18, Philip Agee Papers, Tamiment Library & Robert F. Wagner Archives, New York University (henceforth PAP); Morton Halperin Oral History, Richard Nixon Library, Yorba Linda, CA (henceforth RNL); Morton Halperin, "CIA News Management," *Washington Post*, January 23, 1977; Howard Zinn, "Testifying at the Ellsberg Trial," in *The Zinn Reader: Writings on Disobedience and Democracy* (New York: Seven Stories, 1997), 420–26; Ellsberg, *Secrets*, 212–13, 230, 264; Kaeten Mistry, "A Transnational Protest Against the National Security State: Whistleblowing, Philip Agee, and Networks of Dissent," *Journal of American History* 106, no. 2 (September 2019): 370–78.

22. "U.S. Electronic Espionage: A Memoir"; Jim Mann, "CIA Says It Won't Prosecute Ex-Agent for Revealing Secrets," *Washington Post*, April 20, 1972.

23. Agee, *Inside the Company*, 616; Marks and Marchetti, *The CIA and the Cult of Intelligence*, 321–24; McGehee, *Deadly Deceits*, 194–95.

24. Stockwell, *In Search of Enemies*, 11; Gloria Emerson, "The Spy Who Rang My Doorbell," *New York Magazine*, January 23, 1978, 50.

25. John D. Marks, "How to Spot a Spook," *Washington Monthly*, November 1974, 5–11; Agee, *Inside the Company*, 617; Philip Agee, "Exposing the CIA," *Counter-Spy* 2 (Winter 1975): 19–20.

26. Stockwell, *In Search of Enemies*, 13; Snepp, *Decent Interval*, 9–10; Snepp, *Irreparable Harm*, 12, 26, 102–3, 300.

27. On the decade's transformative impact on foreign relations, see Daniel J. Sargent, *A Superpower Transformed: The Remaking of American Foreign Relations in the 1970s* (New York: Oxford University Press, 2015); Hal Brands, *Making the Unipolar Moment: U.S. Foreign Policy and the Rise of the Post–Cold War Order* (Ithaca, NY: Cornell University Press, 2016).

28. Jussi Hanhimaki, "Selling the 'Decent Interval': Kissinger, Triangular Diplomacy, and the End of the Vietnam War, 1971–73," *Diplomacy and Statecraft* 14 (2003): 159–94; Marks and Marchetti, *CIA and the Cult of Intelligence*, 319; Prados, *Family Jewels*, 239.

29. McGehee to Agee, August 25, 1987; Jonathan Markowitz (Citizens Opposed to Covert Action) to Agee, Stockwell, Retinger, and MacMichael, October 28, 1987; Oliver Stone to Agee, March 3, 1988; Bill Blum to Agee, December 14, 1988; Association of National Security Alumni Charter, January 13, 1989, Box 3, PAP; Pamphlet, "CIABASE: A Computer Database on the CIA" [n.d.], Box 14, PAP; Mistry, "Transnational Protest Against the National Security State," 362–63, 371–76, 385–88; *On Company Business*, dir. Allan Francovich (1980); *Snowden*, dir. Oliver Stone (2016).

30. Lebovic, *Free Speech and Unfree News*, esp. chaps. 7–8.

31. New York Times Co. v. United States, 403 U.S. 713 (1971), https://supreme.justia.com /cases/federal/us/403/713/case.html. For more, see James Goodale, *Fighting for the Press: The Inside Story of the Pentagon Papers and Other Battles* (New York: CUNY Journalism Press, 2013); David Rudenstine, *The Day the Presses Stopped: A History of the Pentagon Papers Case* (Berkeley: University of California Press, 1996).

32. David Young to John D. Ehrlichman, "Espionage Legislation," December 1, 1972, Box 2, David Young Papers, RNL.

33. Victor Marchetti, *Rope Dancer* (New York: Grosset & Dunlap, 1971); Mackenzie, *Secrets*, 43–48, 51–52; U.S. v. Victor L. Marchetti, Civil Action No. 179-72-A, May 19, 1972; U.S. Court of Appeals Fourth Circuit No. 72-1586, U.S. v. Marchetti, September 11, 1972, Box 34, Joseph Fred Buzhardt Papers, RNL.

34. David Rosenbaum, "Ex-Boss Says Writer on C.I.A. Has Not Revealed Any Secrets," *New York Times*, April 20, 1972; Alan Barth, "Muzzling Mr. Marchetti: Free Speech, Security, and the CIA," *Washington Post*, June 16, 1972; Mann, "CIA Says It Won't Prosecute Ex-Agent for Revealing Secrets."

35. Helms to Ehrlichman, May 23, 1972, Box 34, Buzhardt Papers, RNL; John S. Warner, "The Marchetti Case: New Case Law," *CIA FOIA Electronic Reading Room*, 2, 5, https:// www.cia.gov/library/readingroom/docs/CIA-RDP80S01268A000200020024-4.pdf.

36. Dean to Ehrlichman, "Secrecy Agreements for Government Employees Holding Security Clearances," January 15, 1973; Roy Ash to Ehrlichman, "Employment Contracts," January 29, 1973, Box 34, Buzhardt Papers, RNL; Warner, "The Marchetti Case," 5, 11.

37. McGehee, *Deadly Deceits*, 196–203.
38. Prados, *Family Jewels*, 253–54; Mackenzie, *Secrets*, 74–77; Snepp v. United States, 444 U.S. 507 (1980); Snepp provides a detailed account in *Irreparable Harm*, parts 3 and 4.
39. Diane F. Orentlicher, "Snepp v. United States: The CIA Secrecy Agreement and the First Amendment," *Columbia Law Review* 81, no. 3 (April 1981): 662.
40. In addition to Immerman's essay, see Prados, *Family Jewels*, 252–65; Moran, *Company Confessions*, 160, 202–11.
41. Mistry, "Transnational Protest Against the National Security State," 371–87.
42. Philip Bobbitt to Lloyd Cutler, "Identities," September 25, 1980, Box 210, Records of the White House Office of Counsel to the President, Jimmy Carter Library, Atlanta, GA (henceforth JCL); Kenneth DeGraffenreid, "Decision on Intelligence," October 1, 1981, RAC Box 14; Statement by John H. Chafee of Select Committee on Intelligence Before the 1980 Republican Platform Hearings, May 9, 1980, Box 11; John Chafee, "Need for an Intelligence Identities Bill," *Congressional Record*, Senate, 9703-4, July 24, 1980, Box 10, Kenneth DeGraffenreid Papers, Ronald Reagan Library, Simi Valley, CA (henceforth RRL).
43. Russell P. Napoli, *Intelligence Identities Protection Act and Its Interpretation* (New York: Nova Science, 2006); Jennifer K. Elsea, "Intelligence Identities Protection Act," April 10, 2013, Congressional Research Service; Joseph R. Biden Jr., "A Spy Law That Harms National Security," *Christian Science Monitor*, April 6, 1982; "President Signs Bill Making Disclosure of Agents a Crime," *Washington Post*, June 24, 1982.
44. Hannah Gurman, "National Security Whistleblowing: The Creation of a Legal Paradox," Navigating Law and Ethics at the Crossroads of Journalism and National Security, Center for Ethics and the Rule of Law, University of Pennsylvania, November 9, 2017; Jimmy Carter, August 3, 1978, *Public Papers of Presidents* (June 30–December 31, 1978), 1366–67.
45. Stansfield Turner to Zbigniew Brzezinski, "Leaks of Classified Information," November 13, 1978, Box 31, NSA 7, Office of the National Security Advisor, JCL; Carter Executive Order 12065, June 28, 1978, http://www.presidency.ucsb.edu/ws/index.php?pid =31009.
46. President's News Conference, March 2, 1978, https://www.presidency.ucsb.edu/docu ments/the-presidents-news-conference-1011.
47. Reagan Memo for Federal Employees, "Unauthorized Disclosure of Classified Information," August 30, 1983, Box 8, DeGraffenreid Papers, RRL; Executive Order 12356, April 2, 1982, http://www.presidency.ucsb.edu/ws/index.php?pid=42356; NSDD 84, "Safeguarding National Security Information," March 11, 1983, https://reaganlibrary .archives.gov/archives/reference/Scanned NSDDS/NSDD84.pdf.
48. Prados, *Family Jewels*, 255–56.
49. David E. Pozen, "Freedom of Information Beyond the Freedom of Information Act," *University of Pennsylvania Law Review* 165 (2017): 1097–1158.
50. Mike Pompeo Remarks, Center for Strategic and Intelligence Studies, April 13, 2017, https://www.cia.gov/news-information/speeches-testimony/2017-speeches-testimony

/pompeo-delivers-remarks-at-csis.html. On the similarities between the Snowden and Agee cases, see my "Whistleblowing Sans Frontières: Edward Snowden, Philip Agee, and the Transnational Challenge of National Security Dissent," *Process*, September 2019, http://www.processhistory.org/mistry-whistleblowing/.

6

WINTER SOLDIERS OF THE DARK SIDE

CIA Whistleblowers and National Security Dissent

JEREMY VARON

I N 1988, BROWN University was riven by the question: would CIA campus recruitment go off as planned or be thwarted by protests? Other universities from which the CIA drew its recruits were asking the same question.[1] The 1980s were the heyday of the CIA Off Campus movement.[2] Student activists zeroed in on CIA recruitment as a way to blast the Agency for violations of human rights and international law and denounce its often covert entanglements with the university itself. Pivotal in the dissent were special figures in American political life: ex-CIA officers turned critics—whistleblowers, by a familiar description.

In 1986, activists at University of Massachusetts–Amherst made headlines for their protest of CIA recruiters, resulting in nearly seventy arrests. Among arrestees were the 1960s rebel Abbie Hoffmann and Amy Carter, the daughter of President Jimmy Carter and a classmate of mine at Brown. At their trial the judge allowed the accused to argue that their acts were necessary to prevent future crimes. More remarkably, the jury acquitted them. The defense had laid out the recent history of CIA-sponsored assassinations, but perhaps most influential was testimony from Daniel Ellsberg, who famously exposed the Pentagon Papers, and ex-CIA covert operations officer Ralph McGehee.[3] With his 1983 memoir *Deadly Deceits: My 25 Years in the CIA*, McGehee had burst on the scene as an insider critic of the Agency.

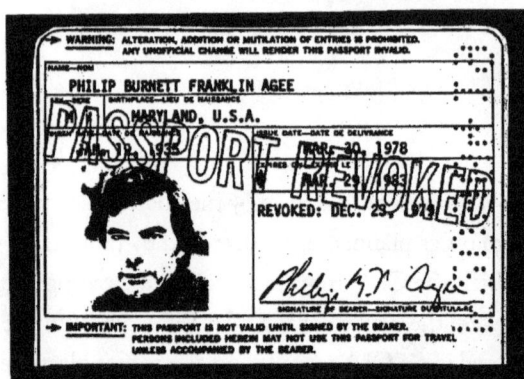

WHO EXPOSED CIA CRIMES AND BLEW
AGENTS' COVER IN 1974?

PHILIP AGEE

WHO HAD HIS PASSPORT REVOKED IN
1979 FOR CRITICIZING THE **CIA?**

PHILIP AGEE

PHILIP AGEE
TUESDAY, NOV. 29 8PM
SAYLES HALL
SPONSORED BY THE CENTRAL AMERICAN SOLIDARITY
ORGANIZATION

FIGURE 6.1

Flyer, prepared by the author and distributed by the student group People
Against the CIA, advertising a talk by Philip Agee at Brown University at
the height of Brown's CIA Off Campus efforts in the fall of 1988.

Source: Author.

Brown University had long been a valuable asset for the CIA. Its president from 1955 to 1966 had facilitated covert CIA research while in office. Brown alumni had risen high in the Agency's ranks.[4] But Brown also became a thorn in the CIA's side. In 1984, students performed a "citizen's arrest" of a CIA recruiter. Ending in only mild penalties, their disciplinary hearing featured the testimony of ex-CIA officer John Stockwell. His 1978 book *In Search of Enemies: A CIA Story* exposed the CIA's secret war in Angola and turned him into a renowned foe of the Agency.[5]

After a brief pause, open CIA recruitment at Brown made its return. Following months of protest in the fall of 1988, the coup de grâce in activist efforts to tilt campus opinion was a visit from Philip Agee, an ex-CIA officer whom I had invited to speak. Agee's 1975 book *Inside the Company: CIA Diary* had been an explosive bestseller. Published in the United Kingdom to escape U.S. censors, the book listed the true identities of more than 250 CIA personnel and paid agents in Latin America. Agee was branded a traitor by the intelligence community. CIA Director George H. W. Bush falsely accused him of contributing to the 1975 murder of the CIA's station chief in Greece, Richard Welch. Living at the time of our invitation in West Germany, Agee's passport had been revoked by the U.S. government.[6] Bringing him to Brown was itself an act of defiance.

I do not recall just what Agee said to a packed auditorium, but I remember the power of his address. A year before—in his first visit to the United States in nearly twenty years[7]—Agee had publicly confronted Arthur Hulnick, the CIA's campus liaison, at a nearby university:

> Mr. Hulnick, I ask you to describe how the CIA is working day and night with the security and intelligence services of El Salvador, the same services that either directly or through their death squads have murdered 70,000 people. . . . How do you justify CIA organization of, or support for, the overthrow of democratically elected civilian governments and their replacement with military dictatorships? . . . How dare you come to a university and try to entice the best of American youth into working for Murder, Incorporated.[8]

Activists at Brown did not prevent recruitment that year. But they did force a campus debate about the CIA. A few students were convinced to cancel their interviews; other meetings moved to secret locations. Agee's message briefly won the day.

My work as a CIA Off Campus activist instilled in me an enduring fascination with the ex-CIA patrons of the cause. In college I met Agee, Stockwell, and McGehee—three of the six most prominent CIA whistle-blowers of the era. Rounding out this tiny fraternity were Victor Marchetti, Sam Adams, and Frank Snepp, each of whom published damning revelations of government malfeasance. I grew to know McGehee best, performing research on the CIA at his Virginia home.

The attraction to the whistleblowers was at once personal and political. I grew up near the CIA in Northern Virginia. Its forest-ringed headquarters felt like an ominous Oz in the suburban midst, manipulating the world's destiny from just beyond the next highway exit.[9] But it was also a real place staffed by real people who might be one's neighbors. The whistleblowers, as I came to know them, testify to the vulnerability of institutions, no matter how powerful, when subject to the moral scrutiny of insider critics.

Above all, I grew to appreciate the whistleblowers' singular role in both educating and validating the public movement against the CIA. They could say with the authority of firsthand knowledge what advocates could only assert based on press accounts, government reports, and educated guesses, all of which could easily be disparaged as conspiracy theory. Although the whistleblowers' message was often attacked—and efforts were made by Agency loyalists to defame them personally—they could never be fully dismissed. They presented, moreover, a complicated kind of courage. To varying degrees, they declared themselves guilty of the very wrongs they disclosed. Revelation, for them, had the urgency of atonement, making it possible to admire, blame, fear, and pity them all at once.

This chapter explores the CIA whistleblowers' place in American society and history. Throughout, it toggles between the specific and the general: the particulars of their experiences and what we may learn from them about national security whistleblowing more broadly. The first point to stress is what can easily be occluded: the substance of their revelations and broader insights. That is, whistleblowers often become causes célèbres, especially as efforts to punish them intensify. Their cases can transform into a referendum on the ethics of disclosure and away from a reckoning with what they disclose. The CIA whistleblowers communicated what they saw as big and hard truths about the CIA and U.S. power. They were in fact careful not to reveal what they regarded as classified or legitimately secret information. Their greatest provocation arguably lay in their unique perspective on what they deemed the corruption of the American state.

The CIA whistleblowers, in addition, are fascinating as both character studies and individual instances of dissent. Their disclosures entailed deeply personal awakenings experienced at the elite echelons of the state apparatus, where such conversions are rare. They have, I argue, a rightful place in an American tradition of civil disobedience asserting the primacy of conscience in potential defiance of the law.

The chapter also considers the sociopolitical conditions that produce and support whistleblowing. If 1975 was the "Year of Intelligence," by virtue of congressional investigations of a seemingly rogue security apparatus, it was facilitated by a golden age of CIA dissidence. That age encompasses the whistleblowers' advocacy efforts beyond the publication of their books, pointing to a central contention of this essay: that the significance of whistleblowers is powerfully shaped by what their society does with the knowledge they share. I present the ex-CIA officers' engagement with civil society actors as integral to their whistleblower narratives. I track this legacy through the 1980s, when domestic grassroots resistance to the CIA reached historic heights. The eventual "fall" of the era's episodes of national security whistleblowing reflected state efforts to deter new whistleblowers but also a transformed political climate.[10]

To conclude, this chapter traces the return of CIA whistleblowers and other ex-government critics in the post-9/11 era. In their variety and resistance to precise labels, I suggest the value of seeing whistleblowing within a continuum of state dissent. Most importantly, their return underscores the amnesia of our time, defined by lessons unlearned and warnings ignored.

It raises with new urgency old questions posed by whistleblowers about the fundamental nature of American democracy and its place in the world.

* * *

The CIA whistleblowers are distinguished by the systemic and even radical nature of their critical perspectives. They communicated their views, most often, in book-length accounts of Agency operations in which they had a direct role. Retiring in 1969 from a senior position in the Office of the Director, Victor Marchetti was the first such whistleblower. He opened the gates for others with his 1974 *The CIA and the Cult of Intelligence*, coauthored with the State Department's John Marks. The book quickly grew notorious both for its content and the legal battles to get it published. In it, Marchetti and Marks assert: "There exists in our nation today a powerful and dangerous secret cult—the cult of intelligence. Its holy men are the clandestine professionals of the CIA. Its patrons and protectors are the highest officials of the federal government. . . . The purpose of this cult is to further the foreign policies of the U.S. government by covert and usually illegal means."[11] After detailing the CIA's modus operandi, they conclude: "The other countries of the world have a fundamental right not to have any outside power interfere in their internal affairs. . . . The United States is surely strong enough as a nation to climb out of the gutter and conduct its foreign policy in accordance with the ideals it was founded upon."[12]

Agee was next with his 1975 *Inside the Company*. Stationed in Latin America, he grew not only disdainful of the CIA but enthralled with the revolutionary socialism the CIA was fighting. Agee concluded, "Secret CIA operations constitute the usually unseen efforts to shore up unjust, unpopular, minority governments, always with the hope that overt military intervention . . . will not be necessary. . . . What counterinsurgency doctrine really comes down to is the protection of capitalists back in America."[13] In a prepublication press statement issued from the United Kingdom, Agee announced his goals: "First, to expose CIA officers and agents . . . to drive them out of the countries where they are operating; secondly to seek within the United States to have the CIA abolished."

Judging the CIA "the Gestapo and SS of our time," his rhetoric could be as inflammatory as his aims.[14]

Stockwell's master analysis in his 1978 *In Search of Enemies* was by parts jeremiad and lament:

> Cast as superpatriots, there were no rules, no controls, no laws, no moral restraints, and no Civil Rights for the CIA game-players. . . . Like any secret police, they became abusive of the people: they drugged American citizens; opened private mail; infiltrated the media with secret propaganda; lied to our elected representatives; and set themselves above the law. . . . The CIA presence in American foreign affairs will be judged by history as a surrender to the darker side of human nature. . . . Worst of all, by retaining the CIA we are accepting ourselves as a harsh and ruthless people.[15]

McGehee, a veteran of South Asian operations, concluded:

> The CIA is not now and has never been a central intelligence agency. It is the covert action arm of the President's foreign policy advisors [which] overthrows foreign governments. . . . [The CIA] labels the oppressed as lackeys of communism. . . . It is difficult to sell this story when the facts are otherwise, so the Agency plants weapons shipments, forges documents, broadcasts false propaganda, and transforms reality. Thus it creates a new reality it then believes.[16]

He later likened the intelligence apparatus to a "monster" that had to be stopped.[17]

Frank Snepp worked for the CIA at the U.S. embassy in Saigon until its fall in 1975. His main charge was that the U.S. government, including his CIA bosses, betrayed America's South Vietnamese allies, desperate to leave as the enemy advanced. He never issued a comprehensive broadside against the CIA or U.S. foreign policy as such. Snepp's cynicism, however, ran deep, increasing as Agency retribution intensified. He described his rearing in a Southern "culture that can blithely portray a war to preserve

WINTER SOLDIERS OF THE DARK SIDE

slavery as a crusade to protect states' rights" as "wonderful preparation for a career of endless charade."[18]

Veterans of different theaters and operations, the CIA whistleblowers never spoke with a fully unified voice. But they approached a shared analysis. Their foundational position is the rejection of the CIA's controlling myth—that the CIA is primarily an intelligence-gathering agency producing accurate information and dispassionate analysis so that elected leaders can form sensible policies. Instead, they insist, covert action lies at the heart of the CIA's mission, budget, and functioning. The goal of covert action is to manipulate foreign societies by political, economic, and military means. CIA "intelligence" is itself frequently manipulated to support preestablished policy imperatives.

In addition, the ex-officers maintained that the CIA was accountable neither to domestic and international law nor the constitutional system of checks and balances. Congress, in their view, had historically offered no meaningful oversight of the CIA. Even with the investigations of the mid-1970s, it lacked the will and means to enforce restraint. Essentially a privately held asset of the U.S. executive, the CIA ultimately did the bidding of U.S. economic interests and political and corporate elites. "American interests," as defined by those elites, are not in the interest of the majority of Americans, who benefit from a more egalitarian, peaceable world. The CIA is not therefore an aberrant institution that goes off book—a "rogue elephant," as famously described by the Church Committee investigations—but a central instrument of U.S. imperial power.

The ex-Agency critics stressed that the point of CIA deception was not to protect secrets vital to national security but instead to avoid oversight, embarrassment, and legal culpability. The American public is thus the primary object of CIA propaganda, with U.S. democracy its main victim.[19] Finally, the former Agency critics reject the moral logic that had underwritten the CIA's identity from the start. That logic, as stated in a secret portion of a 1954 report, held that "there are no rules in this game," that "hitherto acceptable norms of human conduct do not apply."[20] The CIA whistleblowers sharply broke with the conceit that a country can do no wrong if its cause is right.

The radical nature of their message even brings the adequacy of the term "whistleblower" into question. In common perception, whistleblowing entails either internally or externally exposing—and therefore seeking to stop or at least seriously question—some discrete, ongoing, dubious activity within an otherwise sound institution or objective. But the CIA veterans went beyond this. They declared the CIA immoral, argued that it should abandon covert action or be abolished, and condemned the imperial ends it served. And with the exception of Agee, who sought to disrupt current operations by naming names, the ex-officers addressed specific CIA misdeeds after the fact. Their primary means to affect present and future operations was to disclose patterns of CIA conduct. Potential victims would at least be alert to the threat. Given all this, we may even call them CIA dissenters, or even denouncers, or expand the definition of whistleblowing to accommodate their maximalist critique.

* * *

Whatever the best label for them, Marchetti, Agee, and the others were part of a historic surge of criticism of the CIA and the national security state, supported by a broader climate of dissent. That surge included state investigations of the intelligence community, the advent of magazines dedicated to combating the CIA, and vigorous social activism integrating anti-CIA themes. Several of the whistleblower memoirs were put out by America's leading publishing houses or magazines, who competed for the honor (and profits) of sponsoring critical exposés.[21]

The very existence of this golden age is remarkable. Between the formation of the CIA in 1947 and Marchetti's book in 1974 there had not been a single CIA whistleblower in the sense presented here. Several factors contributed to the absence of systemic, domestic criticism of the CIA before the 1970s. First among them was the strength of the anticommunist consensus during the early decades of the Cold War—the depth of belief among true believers, inoculating them against doubt about the morality of American power. In addition, there was a weak, nonskeptical domestic media. Closely aligned with the CIA, the press did little to disclose the controversial means, and often bitter effects, of American influence in the world. And McCarthyite repression reigned for years, discouraging expressions of criticism for fear that they might be regarded as acts of disloyalty. Finally, and notwithstanding the Bay of Pigs, there was no large-scale fiasco or publicly acknowledged instance of blowback during the first decades of the CIA's existence.

The climate for CIA dissidence changed dramatically with the Vietnam War, whose status as political and moral disaster became obvious to countless Americans. Equally important, there was fierce, overt, and visible opposition to the war. Much as for Ellsberg, who confessed that disclosing the Pentagon Papers was based in part on the inspiration of draft resisters, others in government might ask what their responsibility was to resist war and other state violence, whose direct burden was borne mostly by the young and the working class.

Resistance spread among active-duty and veteran soldiers, most famously Vietnam Veterans Against the War (VVAW). At its "Winter Soldier Investigation" in 1971, veterans provocatively testified to war crimes they witnessed or committed in Vietnam.[22] The counterculture seeped into military families and even those of CIA officers abroad.[23] Globally minded outfits like the Peace Corps were rife with antiwar sentiment. In the conflict's later stages, whole swaths of the federal workforce were antiwar, turning out for demonstrations and staging internal protests. Service to government, in short, ceased to be any guarantee of loyalty to its policies.[24]

Next came Watergate, exposing abuses of power many Americans had thought unimaginable. Watergate helped spawn the Church and Pike Committees' investigations of the intelligence community. The former became a telegenic freak show, with incredulous senators brandishing CIA poison-dart guns and other ghoulish paraphernalia while learning of CIA-backed coups and sinister drug experiments.[25] As never before in American history, government conduct was taken to account by government itself, and accountability enjoyed a new prestige.

In this climate, the ex-CIA officers found both general and specific motivation. Marchetti referenced Ellsberg in explaining his decision to publish a book. McGehee expressed the hope that his effort would help the millions of Americans whose idealism was similarly shattered by the Vietnam War.[26] He describes having desperately wanted, long before leaving the Agency, to join "the long-hair hippies" protesting the war in Washington, DC.[27] Agee made the chilling observation that when challenged the U.S. government would ultimately use the same repressive methods it encouraged or employed abroad against its own people, as the 1970 murders at Kent State University made plain to him.[28]

Stockwell confessed to being shocked by the revelations of the Church Committee. Through them he learned things about his employer he had not known; he also remained skeptical of Congress' ability to assert effective oversight. He justified breaking his secrecy oath by arguing it was "fraudulently obtained" because the CIA concealed from him that it drugged, terrorized, and murdered innocent people.[29] Snepp chose to write an exposé of the Vietnam War's end as it became clear to him that the CIA would not produce, and Congress would not demand, an honest account. Alleging in 1975 the willful suppression of knowledge of enemy troop strength in Vietnam, Sam Adams sought to disclose the disturbing story behind America's defeat as the country was still reeling from the war.[30] In short, the CIA whistleblowers seized on a moment of national reckoning and pushed it further.

To varying degrees, the whistleblowers found adoptive homes in the American and even global Left. Agee made common cause with international movements and foreign governments pushing back against U.S. hegemony.[31] Domestically, he allied with other government veterans and intrepid journalists in endeavors such as *CounterSpy*. Launched in 1973, the magazine was conceived that year at the fiftieth birthday party of Norman Mailer, famous for patronizing militant causes. It served as the "official bulletin" of the Committee for Action/Research on the Intelligence Community, which included former military intelligence officers.[32] Using public information, it too named clandestine CIA personnel. An early issue exposed the "F-6" counterinsurgency program in Vietnam—the successor to Operation Phoenix—replete with operational details.[33]

In 1978, after the demise of *CounterSpy*, Agee helped found *Covert Action Information Bulletin*. The magazine initially named names, exposed recruitment efforts, tracked CIA operations, and published broadsides against American power. Its second issue featured a lengthy address by its editor Louis Wolf at an international youth festival in Havana on how to research undercover CIA officers.[34] With Wolf, Agee edited a thick volume on CIA activity in Western Europe.[35] This was, in today's parlance, "weaponized" information disseminated by a coterie of CIA watchers intervening in a global political conflict bearing qualities of a war.

The bulk of other CIA whistleblowers emerged just a little later, by which point the revolutionary fervor of the 1960s had further waned; this later group did not share Agee's radicalism. "Anti-interventionism" largely replaced "anti-imperialism" as the governing construct for left-wing critics of U.S. foreign policy, and popular resistance was not nearly so militant. Their audience and allies spanned the nonsectarian Left: church groups, student organizations, NGOs, think tanks, and public-research endeavors. Even so, they were immersed as advocates and even activists in ongoing political struggles. CIA whistleblowing, in sum, is misunderstood as a solitary act, a cry in the bureaucratic wilderness. The CIA whistleblowers first emerged in a robust climate of protest, rife with truth-to-power politics and exemplary, self-sacrificing resistance. Their message further blossomed in the shifting sands of dissent.

In the 1980s, the CIA was on the defensive as never before, though not as the result of congressional investigations. Resistance, as evident in the CIA Off Campus movement, now came from the grassroots. After the fiasco in Vietnam, the United States was out of the business of bloody ground wars, relying instead on quick invasions and covert action to exert its influence. Activists viewed the CIA as the leading, often violent edge of the foreign policy outrages of the day. Anti-CIA campaigners thus had great overlap with the Central American solidarity and anti-Apartheid movements.

The ex-CIA officers Verne Lyon and David MacMichael emerged as vocal dissenters. MacMichael had resigned from the CIA in 1983 over pressure to falsify intelligence reports about the Contra war and in 1986 testified before the International Court of Justice in the case *Nicaragua v. the United States*.[36] They led the National Security Alumni Association, made up of retiree critics of U.S. policy. It lent gravitas to the arguments of activists and published its own bulletin, *Unclassified*.

In April 1987, students and others participated in large-scale civil disobedience at CIA headquarters. A staggering 550 people were arrested, including Daniel Ellsberg.[37] The only such protest in U.S. history, the action came a day after massive demonstrations at the Pentagon against U.S. interference in Central America.[38] Anti-CIA messaging was a fixture in campaigns geared to foreign affairs, where Stockwell, McGehee, and others were frequent lecturers. The CIA's Arthur Hulnick, who moved from CIA campus liaison to the Boston University faculty in 1992, all but confirmed the impact on public opinion. In a 2010 interview he revealed, "During the Reagan administration we gathered some polling data, and people said the CIA overthrows governments and kills people."[39] What impact such perceptions had on Agency conduct we can never know. But one may plausibly believe they constrained some CIA operations in some times and places.

The movement to stigmatize the CIA fell victim, over time, to larger political currents. Ironically, it was deflated by the conclusion of the Iran-Contra affair. Lieutenant Colonel Oliver North set up "the Enterprise" out of the National Security Council. It functioned as an "off-the-shelf" covert-operations cell that escaped legislative restrictions on U.S. involvement in Nicaragua and the standing policy of not cutting deals with hostage takers. The question burned as to whether the CIA had coordinated the Enterprise's activities, as some alleged.[40] If so, the CIA may well have set up a CIA outside itself precisely to avoid oversight and thus return to its "dirty tricks."

But North managed to quell the tempest. Before Congress and a national TV audience, he defended defying the law for the greater good of fighting communism. Taken in by his choir-boy patriotism and perverse charm, millions of Americans were persuaded. The alibi of the ends justifying the means was stepwise restored. The end of the Cold War, moreover, downsized covert action and blunted scrutiny of CIA excesses in the now-victorious struggle against communism. The swift U.S. triumph in the 1991 Persian Gulf War dramatically diminished post–Vietnam War skepticism about American military power. The American Left roared again to life only with the antiglobalization movement of the late 1990s. Addressing issues of rich and poor in a post–Cold War landscape, it targeted mostly institutions of American "soft power" like the International Monetary Fund. The CIA whistleblowers were largely forgotten as voices from a different world order.

By the early 1990s, the CIA had faded from either special public scrutiny or acclaim. It would be years before the blowback of CIA support for the Mujahideen in Afghanistan in the 1980s hit America in the face on 9/11; before the CIA regained its prestige, now as the nation's great protector from terrorism; and before the Agency again plunged into scandal with its global torture program, signaled by Vice President Dick Cheney as a necessary journey to "the dark side." And it would be nearly two decades before a new cohort of CIA officers emerged from that darkness to shed public light on CIA wrongs.

* * *

A broad sociopolitical climate of dissent encouraged the CIA whistleblowers to break ranks and speak out. But context alone cannot compel an individual to act, especially against an institution as powerful as the CIA. The CIA whistleblowers each went through profound transformations that were both political and deeply personal. Their narratives have the quality of conversion experiences, lending an air of religiosity to men steeped in the hyper-rational pursuit of the instrumental knowledge defining "intelligence." Such conversions are an essential foundation of their whistleblowing and a key to understanding whistleblowing more broadly.

Their cases bear some likeness to more familiar state dissenters, like soldiers turning against war and the war makers. Yet for this generation of CIA officers there was no precedent or easy account for protest in their professional ranks. These were not America's grunts, bitter at being sacrificed for the vanity, ambition, and obdurateness of the political class and the generals. Their shame was at being the shadowy middle-masters of U.S. policy, for which they bore managerial responsibility. They had special insight into not just the violent execution of American power but also its devious design.

Stockwell captioned his transformation as a journey from "belief, to doubt, to despair."[41] In truth, the process—shared by other CIA whistleblowers—was more complex. Crucially, a sense of it is derived largely from their *self-representation* in memoirs and interviews, pointing to the discursive nature of whistleblowing. "Discourse" is pertinent in two senses. First, the critical disclosure defining whistleblowing accretes all kinds of meanings, whether via the courts, official pronouncements, the press, public sentiment, or even popular culture. The conflict over the whistleblower's acts is fundamentally a war of interpretation. Voices in any of the forums just listed might deny that "whistleblowing" even took place. Critics, that is, may see only criminal activity, disloyalty, vanity, or personal grievance masquerading as conviction. The self-authored conversion story, by contrast, is a potent means for whistleblowers to positively define the meaning of their acts by establishing their credibility as initial loyalists forced by circumstance and conscience to share painful truths.

In a second sense of discourse, the whistleblower narratives are themselves retrospective reconstructions of their lives observing (consciously or not) literary and cultural tropes of guilt, sin, awakening, tragic-heroic truth telling, and even martyrdom. Their experience comes to life by means, in part, of a script. Its availability both enables their dissent and shapes or even constrains its articulation. In what follows, I offer a schematic of the CIA whistleblowers' conversion process. The stages, holding truer for some individuals than for others, are less a perfect sequence than overlapping dimensions of a trajectory toward public disclosure.

At its core, the whistleblower narrative entails the unmaking and remaking of the political and moral self. For this generation of CIA officers, that meant evolving past the patriotic archetypes they personified. Indeed, the CIA whistleblowers embodied powerful images of Cold War American manhood, each with a role in the protection of the American state and projection of its power.[42]

Stockwell had the no-nonsense demeanor of a Marine, which he had been before joining the CIA. He performed the rough work of running a secret war while navigating geopolitical machinations. McGehee was raised a Baptist in the Catholic Midwest. He had been a lineman at Notre Dame,

FIGURE 6.2

Flyer from student groups at the University of Massachusetts–Amherst advertising the invited lecture of ex-CIA officer John Stockwell during their campaign in the late 1980s to bar CIA recruiters from campus.

Source: In possession of author.

and in 1953, after being cut by the Green Bay Packers, was recruited by the CIA for its Directorate of Operations.[43] His memoir describes the near-religious fervor of his initiation into the CIA's anticommunist crusade. During the Vietnam War, he helped shape Thai hill tribes into fighting forces. When I met him in his retirement, he still wore a safari jacket and exuded a quiet intensity. It was easy to imagine him serving in a jungle redoubt as the hidden American hand behind an anticommunist militia.

Agee, by contrast, was dashing. Handsome, suave, and cosmopolitan, he had the aura of a master spy who used guile—backed by the American state—to move the levers of influence in foreign societies. Darkly handsome like Agee, Frank Snepp was raised in a Southern culture of patrician, martial fealty to country. While Columbia University was exploding in left-wing revolt in 1968, Snepp was graduating from its School of Foreign Service. Eschewing youth rebellion, he felt the pull of tradition and recruitment into the CIA, landing him in Saigon a year later.[44] Harvard-trained and with a WASP pedigree to match his name, Sam Adams was the epitome of the Kennedy-era technocrat. He joined the CIA in 1963, putting his facility with information in service to American prowess in the Congo and then Vietnam.[45]

Given these personae, CIA officers' transformation into whistleblowers was no small feat. Their narratives typically begin with their unquestioning loyalty as young men to a Cold War patriotic ideal. With recruitment, that loyalty is elevated into special service to the U.S. government and American people, with the CIA figured as their near-sacred guardian. McGehee describes himself as "gung ho" when joining the Agency.[46] Stockwell was attractive to the CIA by virtue of his unconventional boyhood in Africa. A supporter of the Republican presidential candidate Barry Goldwater in 1964, he confessed to being "naïve" but not quite "a moron," "swept along with the 'national security' and 'keep the world free' mentality" of so many of his generation.[47]

The next protracted stage is increasing misgivings instigated by uncomfortable episodes or insights within the performance of one's professional duties. Put otherwise, it is the disturbing perception that one is in the thrall of an agenda one cannot quite grasp, yielding to confirmation of one's suspicions. For McGehee and Adams, this sense first came from doing their jobs *too well*. Each was tasked with trying to understand the nature of South Asian enemies who, by prevailing calculations, should be losing. McGehee, charged with combating the Thai communist insurgency in 1965 through 1967, developed a technique for flushing out communist infiltrators at the village level. (The method entailed coercive interrogations and even the mock execution of detainees' loved ones—abuses he excused at the time.)[48] The good news, he initially thought, was that he had found a way to defeat the insurgency. The bad news, as he slowly surmised, was that by his estimation the Thai enemy was far larger than the CIA or Pentagon admitted or were prepared to defeat.[49] Instead of being rewarded for his potentially game-changing work, he was sidelined to paper pushing back at CIA headquarters in Virginia.

The analyst Sam Adams used credible intelligence to estimate the size of the Viet Cong enemy as vastly greater than what the top brass of the Pentagon was willing to concede or tell the U.S. president. Though CIA analysts agreed with him, the CIA leadership soon capitulated to Pentagon dictates. After early 1967 or so, when Adams communicated his findings to the relevant parties, the United States *knowingly* fought the Vietnam War without any true prospect of military success. Bureaucratic roadblocks and internal exile was Adams's fate, along with repeated suggestions that he resign should he press the matter.[50]

Agee's concern with the true intent of his mission intensified as he executed the CIA's operational goals in Latin America: to quietly subvert political parties and civil-society institutions—whether unions, student groups, the press, or the church—so as to toe the American line.

A next, fateful phase is apprehension of the pervasiveness of the deceit and the agendas behind it. Reassigned to Saigon in 1968, McGehee concluded that the CIA and the broader U.S. government were again deluded about the enemy they faced—one too big to defeat. Choked with garrisons, military traffic, and brothels, Saigon became for him a Goyaesque landscape of lethal cynicism. Adams came to believe that *hundreds* of people were involved in the falsification of enemy troop estimates. Even after the Tet Offensive, which validated his own estimates, the CIA and others refused to investigate the troop-strength issue, prompting him to take home and hide documents confirming the deception.[51]

Frank Snepp was part of the last CIA detail in Vietnam. His evolving observation was that the CIA station chief and Secretary of State Henry Kissinger had willfully deceived themselves into thinking that the United States could enjoy an honorable defeat that would leave its South Vietnamese allies mostly safe. The result was the absence of any official plan for Saigon's evacuation. Defying their superiors, Snepp and others managed a limited evacuation that left countless South Vietnamese in a perilous lurch. The great drama of his book is the tension between the self-serving optimism of his bosses contrasted with the encroaching danger on the ground. Stockwell, finally, grew suspicious of what he regarded as flimflam anticommunist wars in Africa, secretly directed by Kissinger and fought by the CIA through morally dubious proxies.

A related stage in conversion, experienced by some but not others, is the devastating awareness of complicity in wrongdoing, pressuring toward some life-changing choice. McGehee confessed great shame at participating in Operation Phoenix in Vietnam, a "country-wide assassination program" against alleged Viet Cong insurgents. (The program was akin to "shooting fish in a barrel" precisely because the insurgency was so popular.)[52] He broke down in a Vietnamese villa in 1968. With painful repetition, he writes: "I hated my part in this charade of murder and horror. My efforts were contributing to the deaths, to the burning alive of children. . . . The photographs of young Vietnamese children burned alive by napalm destroyed me. I wanted out of this massacre."[53] His fantasy was to throw himself off the roof of the CIA's Duc Hotel with sheets saying "THE CIA LIES" and "FUCK THE CIA" hanging from the building.

Agee had a bracing encounter with the suffering he helped direct. In Uruguay, he aided the arrest of a communist agitator, tarring him with false allegations of connections with the Soviets. The captive was tortured within earshot of Agee by the secret police, exuding a "horrible sound, I'll never forget it." "I began to question the work," he continued, "as the initial thrill of wielding secret power faded." At his next post in Mexico, the capstone to his transformation was hearing an activist, who later became his girlfriend, fulminate at the CIA-aided assassination in 1967 of Che Guevara, whom she considered humanity's greatest hope. "She was the personal factor which led me to say I'm quitting now."[54]

For Stockwell it was a lonely epiphany amid a futile, dirty war. After leaving a hapless African soldier from Joseph Savimbi's notorious, U.S.-backed UNITA army to die, Stockwell found himself "standing on the railroad tracks in the bare African veld [where] I felt an almost mystical objectivity about the CIA and the things I had done, the pointlessness of my operations in Lubumbashi, the brutality and betrayals of Vietnam, the empty cynicism of the case officer's role."[55]

The most dramatic revelation of a turning point came from Snepp. In *Decent Interval* he confesses great consternation at the CIA's betrayal of its South Vietnamese allies. It was only with his 1999 book *Irreparable Harm*, which chronicles the publication of his first book and the legal struggles that followed, that he disclosed his deepest motivations in writing *Decent Interval*. Snepp was father to a child by a Vietnamese woman. Both the mother—named My Lai by a seemingly cruel irony—and her child died, presumably at the mother's hand, following Saigon's fall.[56] The betrayal was Snepp's as well. Recounting the demise of My Lai and other South Vietnamese, he literally writes the words "Forgive me."[57]

The culminating stage is dedication to public criticism of the U.S. government as at once an account of the truth, a tribute to the victims, a bid to prevent future carnage, and a personal effort at a necessarily incomplete atonement. Adams quit the CIA so that he might tell his story, alleging in a 1975 *Harper's Magazine* article the deliberate suppression of reliable estimates of enemy troop strength. McGehee emerged from his despair with a new sense of purpose, whose seed was planted as he contemplated suicide in Vietnam. He dedicated his book to "those hurt by CIA operations."[58] Stockwell became a crusader against needless death, asserting Americans' "*unequivocal right* to know what their leaders are doing in America's name and with our tax dollars."[59] Agee framed his decision to go public with the passion of the civil disobedient answering the call of his own conscience and his responsibility to others: "Now, more than ever, indifference to injustice at home and abroad is impossible. . . . Each of us is forced to make a conscious choice whether to support the system of minority comfort . . . or to struggle for the . . . fair distribution of benefits for all society."[60]

Whistleblowing, in these cases at least, is more than just the act of disclosure. Instead, it is an act that also announces its own motivation through the telling of a narrative of transformation. That narrative typically presents cathartic moments of revelation and despair, pushing toward public revelation. The narrative helps render the act morally believable, if not politically justified. This happens in part through identification. At any point the reader or listener may ask: What would I have done in similar circumstances? The question may then follow: What can I do now, whatever my very different circumstances? Whistleblowing, by this sequence, ultimately resolves in an incitement to action for others. In this sense, whistleblowing can be a deeply intersubjective act, with the power to rally communities of resistance.

The decision to go public, however, may seem like the climax of the whistleblower saga, but it is not. In truth, the decision marked the beginning of a new ordeal: to have their revelations meet the public and to beat back state reprisals. Suppressive measures included the aggressive use of the courts to cloak their speech; the requirement of prepublication review of writing about the CIA to the CIA itself; the extremely broad determination of what constitutes protected information to include even nonclassified material; public defamation; and, for those publishing without prior review, the enjoining of the author's profits. But the suppression efforts had a second, ironic effect: it both propelled and intensified their criticisms, coloring their entire identity as whistleblowers. The legal struggles in particular protracted their battles with the CIA, crippling them financially. This meant the whistleblowers needed to earn income through public speaking, which enhanced media interest in them and made them all the more determined to share their insights. Repressive applications of the law helped *produce* their dissent.

★ ★ ★

CIA-sponsored assassinations and coups, macabre mind-control research, the training of foreign governments in torture, support for dictators and unscrupulous guerrillas, and the spinning of lies to justify U.S. intervention—all this may seem the ignominy of a bygone era, justified in its day by the imperative of slaying communism. Yet many Americans, including in the national security apparatus, never accepted such behavior as necessary for either security or freedom.

Some of the moral rot of the Cold War returned with the U.S. response to the September 11, 2001, attacks. Among the most notorious measures was the Bush administration's torture program, authored by the CIA. With it has also come the return of CIA whistleblowers, for example, John Kiriakou, among a much larger cohort of national security dissenters. Their diverse profiles conform to and deviate from the patterns I have outlined here, revealing both historical continuities and shifts in legacies of state dissent.

Since 9/11, national security professionals have both drawn from and contributed to a climate of protest against aspects of the "War on Terror." In the main, they are not engaging in "unauthorized disclosure" but are government personnel drawing on insider information and perspectives to condemn—most often after amicable retirements—state conduct. Notable figures include Richard A. Clarke, the counterterrorism official who exposed Bush administration duplicity justifying the Iraq War; Lt. Col. Lawrence Wilkerson, the former chief of staff of Secretary of State Colin Powell, who became a fierce critic of the war and the torture program; Navy General Counsel Alberto Mora, who battled torture proponents within the Bush administration; Col. Morris Davis, who resigned as the chief prosecutor of the Military Commissions in Guantanamo in protest of their feeble due process; Sergeant Joseph Hickman, a guard at Guantanamo who alleged that in 2006 three detained men were tortured to death in a secret facility at the prison camp;[61] and Mark Fallon, the former lead criminal investigator of al-Qaeda suspects, who authored an exposé on how diverse government branches "conspired to torture."[62]

These dissenters provided stunning rebukes to the policies they were supposed to endorse and the leaders they were meant to follow. Their voices have been valuable in public activism that—if never on par with Vietnam War–era protests—has arguably helped constrain the "War on Terror." Now professors, lecturers, authors, and pundits, they have reinvented themselves as professional advocates for human rights and the public's right to know. Lesser-known figures have banded together as Veteran Intelligence Professionals for Sanity (VIPS), addressing everything from state surveillance to drone strikes to current U.S. military engagements. And some ex-government personnel—like Col. Ann Wright, who resigned from the State Department over the Iraq War, and the CIA analyst Ray McGovern, who cofounded VIPS—have fully crossed over to the grassroots protest culture, including its civil disobedience.[63] All these figures occupied a space for professional dissent that opened decades ago.

It is difficult to draw any definitive conclusions about the relative impact of public criticisms by state officials versus the revelation of state secrets. Indeed, the very accusation of unauthorized disclosures can dramatically amplify the notoriety of the putative whistleblower. This was the case with Agee, who named names, and Edward Snowden, who disclosed massive amounts of data to journalists. But insider critics operating fully within the law can also create huge firestorms depending on the content and timing of their message. Clarke became a national sensation for charging in early 2004 that claims of Iraqi WMD were a mendacious pretext for war. His revelations before Congress and a worried public came as the U.S. occupation failed to turn up WMD and met growing, violent resistance. By the same token, assuming legal risks to expose state conduct is no guarantee of widespread public attention. The prison guard, Hickman, went to great lengths both to document and publicize allegations of murder at Guantanamo, which he insisted were being covered up. His efforts entailed extensive sleuthing with attorneys and FOIA requests, all amid fears of state reprisal. Yet his revelations, first surfacing in 2010, were only a minor story, as public interest in Guantanamo had greatly faded.

These cases help illuminate the place of whistleblowing within a spectrum of national security dissent and the dependence of notoriety on a wealth of variables. Whatever their exact position among post-9/11 national security dissenters, whistleblowers exist in a special class: they are prosecuted or otherwise strongly attacked by the state for their disclosures and heralded by their defenders. Snowden and Thomas Drake top the list for NSA whistleblowers, while Chelsea Manning does for the U.S. military. For the CIA the key figure is Kiriakou.

I first met Kiriakou in January 2017 as a copanelist at a press event pleading for the preservation of the full Senate Torture Report just before Donald Trump was sworn in as president. Republican lawmakers had threatened to destroy all copies of the document, most of which remains classified. I was representing a group dedicated to closing the prison at Guantanamo. Kiriakou was present as one of only two CIA whistleblowers to denounce torture. He had served two years on a plea deal in federal prison for alleged secrecy violations—payback, he insists, for his "revelation" in 2007 of a torture program already known by the world to exist. He remains the only CIA employee to go to prison for torture, though his "crime" was to criticize it. I later invited him to give a lecture at the New School, where I am a professor.

Much had changed since I brought Agee to campus as a student decades ago. There is today no large-scale public outcry against the CIA. The United States faces real terrorist threats. Dismantling or even disarming the elite U.S. intelligence agency is unthinkable to nearly all Americans. Kiriakou, moreover, is vastly more accessible than Agee and his cohort ever were. Before the internet, it was difficult to access their writings, which might be found only in specialized magazines and used bookstores. Yet with a few keystrokes one can call up half a dozen interviews with Kiriakou and download his three books. Even so, it was a thrill to present for my students the officer who first took down Abu Zubaydah and then took on the CIA. Now woven into the history of CIA whistleblowing, Kiriakou's very public narrative is worth recounting.

Like his forebears, Kiriakou grew up a true believer in the American project. But his was a fresh-faced patriotism distant from the baggage of the Cold War. From a line of Greek-American Democrats, he joined the CIA in 1990 as a defender of liberal democracy just as the Soviet empire was crumbling.[64] There was, Kiriakou reports, little institutional memory in the CIA of past struggles over its lawfulness and integrity. He was only vaguely aware of Marchetti and Snepp, whom he saw as "disgruntled former employees who had nonetheless done an important public service by challenging the Agency." Stockwell had lingering respect among some of his colleagues. "You can be a good and honorable guy," a superior told him of Stockwell, "and go a separate way." With Agee things were different. In the 1990s, Kiriakou landed an assignment in Greece to capture the members of the November 17 guerrilla group who killed Richard Welch. When handed the autopsy photos, he was bluntly told "Agee did this." Agee was seen as a "traitor and murderer."[65]

When 9/11 hit, Kiriakou pleaded to join the front lines. He soon led the capture in Pakistan of Abu Zubaydah, then thought to be al-Qaeda's third in command.[66] Kiriakou's emergence as a whistleblower was all but accidental. In 2004, he left the CIA in good standing. In September 2007 there was an uptick in denials by the Bush administration that torture had occurred, with the caveat that rogue agents may have done unauthorized things. Kiriakou learned that the White House was falsely suggesting that he had tortured Zubaydah.

To set the record straight, he did a TV interview. In it, he asserted that he knew that Zubaydah had been waterboarded, though only once; that his treatment—clearly torture—was authorized at the highest levels of government; that the torture had extracted vital intelligence; and that he thought it was wrong. "At the time I felt that waterboarding was something we needed to do [but] I think I changed my mind," he told his ABC interviewer. "We are Americans and we're better than that."[67] More media appearances followed, given Kiriakou's newfound status as the first former CIA operative to confirm the findings of journalists and human rights groups that torture had taken place. He would not be excused for his modest revelation.

The FBI, he later learned, immediately put him under investigation. It concluded that he had neither violated his secrecy oath nor disclosed classified information. Nonetheless, he was subject to years of surveillance, schemes to entrap him, and absurd efforts by the CIA to censor his proposed memoir. The manuscript was cleared only with the switch to the Obama administration, though with the most critical parts excised. *The Reluctant Spy: My Secret Life in the CIA's War on Terror* (2010) mostly reads like a standard professional yarn, with opinions about his bosses and tributes to the good people who overwhelmingly populate the CIA. The discussions of torture are highly equivocal. He reiterates that it was wrong and notes, as the CIA inspector general's 2004 report revealed when made public in 2008–2009, that Zubaydah was waterboarded eighty-three times, yielding information of questionable valuable.[68] But Kiriakou praises the Obama administration for declining to prosecute CIA personnel.[69] The book is a far cry from the earlier, sharply critical memoirs.

The Kiriakou tale did not end there. Tensions had been raised in 2009 when he reached out to the CIA in conjunction with investigations he was conducting as a staff member of the Senate Foreign Relations Committee. It concerned possible CIA involvement in the 2002 killing of two thousand captives by a notorious U.S. Afghan ally. "I'm not sure if I was doing [the investigations] subconsciously" to strike at the CIA for its torture program, he later allowed.[70] Far from an epiphany, his moral misgivings came only gradually.

It would be several years until the boom was fully lowered on him. In January 2012, Kiriakou was arrested on multiple breaches of the Espionage Act and other serious allegations. One year later, he pleaded guilty to a single violation of the Intelligence Identities Protection Act of 1982—itself a direct product of Agee's disclosures—and sentenced to federal prison. He was released in 2015.

For all its distinctiveness, Kiriakou's story has a stinging familiarity within the history of CIA whistleblowing. Most readily, there is the tenacity of his CIA and Justice Department pursuers. The attempt to prosecute him under the Espionage Act was more aggressive even than the measures brought against a prior, far more hostile generation of CIA dissenters. Like them, he concludes that the purpose of such actions was "to make an example of me, to deter anyone else."[71] Kiriakou's case also speaks to the irony of suppression efforts. Without the crackdown, his public comments on torture would have ended there. Instead, he has become an outspoken critic of torture, interviewed by the world's leading media and invited to lecture before countless student, church, and advocacy groups. He states outright that "the CIA made me a human rights activist."[72] Directly connecting with the whistleblowing legacy, in 2016 he received the Sam

Adams Award, given by the Sam Adams Associates for Integrity in Intelligence to government personnel distinguished by their ethical conduct.[73]

The deeper continuity is the behavior Kiriakou addressed: systemic torture by the CIA, uniting the Cold War and the "War on Terror." A wealth of research has demonstrated the origins of post-9/11 torture in Cold War–era CIA research on torture and the training of foreign security services in torture methods.[74] Whatever the whistleblowing and public condemnations of the past, some of the worst of the CIA's behavior remains.

Kiriakou's whistleblowing is significant, finally, for the lessons and challenges he articulates. In these, he is joined by his ex-colleague in the CIA Glenn L. Carle. Carle was also tasked to hunt down al-Qaeda suspects. Unlike Kiriakou, he participated to an unspecified extent in "enhanced interrogations." He too wrote a memoir, *The Interrogator: An Education* (2011), subject to extensive redactions. For months the CIA brutalized a detainee who, Carle came to suspect, was in fact a nobody. In a scene reminiscent of Stockwell's epiphany in the African veld, Carle realized while gazing at "the bleak landscape" in a Middle Eastern desert that

> we were becoming—in secret and out of sight except to the few of us involved in the "dark side," if you will, of the Global War on Terror—no longer the government of checks, balances, the law I had proudly sworn to "preserve and protect." . . . We denounce these procedures as totalitarian in other countries. I feared that I had become part of what constituted elements of a de facto American junta.[75]

He concludes that "coercive interrogation policies have corrupted our government's institutions, eroded our society's most deeply cherished values, undermined our laws, and do not work."[76]

One of Kiriakou's most striking judgments about torture was among the simplest. To an interviewer in 2015 he noted that one day the United States lectures a foreign government about its human rights abuses and the next day asks that it rough up a prisoner during interrogation and share the transcript. Reflecting on the hypocrisy, he asked: "As a country we are going to have to make a decision . . . whether we are going to be this beacon of human rights that we'd like to think we are . . . or are we going to be the biggest, toughest bully on the block? Because we can't be both at the same time."[77]

The early returns are not encouraging with respect to Kiriakou's query. There has been no national reckoning with torture, let alone prosecution of CIA personnel for likely crimes. CIA torture has been immunized, culminating in the promotion in 2018 of Gina Haspel to CIA director. Haspel had supervised the first CIA torture site in Thailand in 2003 and later helped destroy video evidence of torture. Before her confirmation hearing, Kiriakou warned in an op-ed, "the message [her nomination] sends to the CIA workforce is simple: Engage in war crimes, in crimes against humanity, and you'll get promoted. Don't worry about the law. . . . Go ahead and do it anyway. We'll cover for you."[78] The seventy-eight-year-old former CIA analyst Ray McGovern was brutally removed for disrupting the hearing, where Haspel refused to call the post-9/11 interrogation methods immoral.[79]

Circumstances may be more dire than Kiriakou's question suggests. Openly backing torture, Trump and some of his supporters appear unapologetically to relish being the bully and dropping a commitment to human rights as a guiding principle in America's foreign and even domestic affairs. Trump's notorious embrace of authoritarianism has led to the surreal spectacle of the former CIA directors Michael Hayden and John Brennan and the former director of national intelligence James Clapper frequently blasting Trump as a great enemy of American democracy and the rule of law. The kinds of officials against whom national security dissidents have railed are now ubiquitous defenders of democracy, slandered by their conservative detractors, including the president.[80] Brennan was implicated in the CIA torture program, thwarting his first bid to become CIA director in 2009.[81] In March 2013 Clapper denied before the Senate what Snowden's disclosure later revealed: that the NSA was collecting data on millions of Americans.[82] All three men supported Haspel's nomination.

At issue in the very real and consequential conflict between the former agency heads and Trump is whether U.S. power will rest on liberal or illiberal foundations. Cast in cynical terms, at stake is the degree and brazenness with which America may continue to violate its own laws and historic ideals. The whistleblowers pushed for a much deeper alignment of American conduct and values while questioning whose interests the national security apparatus ultimately served. Until such a reconciliation occurs, there will be more grave violations of law and morality and more whistleblowers like Stockwell and McGehee, Kiriakou and Carle. If the United States ever resolves to fulfill its better nature it may have in part the CIA whistleblowers—the winter soldiers of the dark side—to thank.

NOTES

1. The classic work on the origins of the Office for Strategic Services and then the CIA in Ivy League universities is Robin W. Winks, *Cloak and Gown: Scholars in the Secret War, 1939–1961* (London: Harvill, 1987). On the evolving nature of CIA campus recruiting in the 1980s, see David Wise, "Campus Recruiting and the C.I.A.," *New York Times*, June 8, 1986, http://www.nytimes.com/1986/06/08/magazine/campus-recruiting-and-the-cia .html.

2. The sole book on 1980s-era anti-CIA campus protests is Amy Chen Mills, *CIA Off Campus: Building the Movement Against Agency Recruitment and Research* (Boston: South End, 1991).

3. On the UMASS protests and resulting trial, see http://scua.library.umass.edu/ead /muph012; https://blogs.umass.edu/radicalumass/histories-of-radical-actions-at-umass /the-cia-on-trial/.

4. The Brown president was Barnaby Conrad Keeney; his involvement with the CIA is reported in Doug Cumming, "Brown's Ties Date Back to 1950s," *Providence Journal*, December 6, 1987; *CounterSpy*, Spring 1980, 45; and Ernest Volkman, "Spies on Campus," *Penthouse*, October 1979, http://www.namebase.net/campus/volkman.html. In 1962, Keeney helped establish funding for the notorious MK-ULTRA mind-control experimentation program and then served as chairman of the Human Ecology Fund, a front for the research and other projects. Brown alumni who then worked for the CIA, also profiled in the *Providence Journal*, include Duane "Dewey" Clarridge ('53), instrumental in the mining of Nicaraguan harbors in 1984 and support for the Contra armies, and E. Howard Hunt and Charles Colson of Watergate fame.

5. On the 1984 Brown protests, see "Students Punished for Protest," *New York Times*, December 9, 1984, http://www.nytimes.com/1984/12/09/us/students-punished-for-protest .html; "Sanctions Upheld Against Brown CIA Protesters," *UPI*, December 22, 1984, https://www.upi.com/Archives/1984/12/22/Sanctions-upheld-against-Brown-CIA -protesters/2126472539600/; Cory Dean, "Student Activism Alive at Brown U.," *New York Times*, February 15, 1985, http://www.nytimes.com/1985/02/14/us/student-activism-alive

-at-brown-u.html. Three years prior, in 1981, students disrupted a lecture of CIA head William Casey by reciting Lewis Carroll's nonsense poem *Jabberwocky*. "Six Students at Brown Charged for Disrupting Casey Speech," *New York Times*, October 26, 1981, http://www.nytimes.com/1981/10/26/us/6-students-at-brown-charged-for-disrupting-casey-speech.html. I have written a detailed brief on the CIA and Brown, which narrates the protests based on news accounts, interviews, and my own participation, titled "The Company We Keep: Brown University and the CIA" (unpublished manuscript).

6. Agee's passport was revoked in 1979 by Secretary of State Cyrus Vance. The government claimed national security damage from his cross-country haranguing of the CIA. Agee challenged the measure, eventually resulting in the case Haig v. Agee, settled by the Supreme Court in the government's favor in 1981. See Kaeten Mistry, "A Transnational Protest Against the National Security State: Whistleblowing, Philip Agee, and Networks of Dissent," *Journal of American History* 106, no. 2 (September 2019): 362–89.

7. Ex-CIA chief George Bush described Agee's return to the United States as "disgraceful" and "despicable." Daniel Brandt, "Little Magazines May Come and Go," *National Reporter* 11, no. 2 (Fall 1988): 5.

8. Mills, *CIA Off Campus*, xiv.

9. See, for example, Bonnie Jacob, "Spies Among Us: Old Spooks Never Die . . . They Just Retire to Northern Virginia—and Keep Right on Working," *New Dominion*, July/August 1988, 22–27. On the political geography of Northern Virginia, see Andrew Friedman, *Covert Capital: Landscapes of Denial and the Making of U.S. Empire in the Suburbs of Northern Virginia* (Berkeley: University of California Press, 2013).

10. See Kaeten Mistry in this volume and his "A Transnational Protest Against the National Security State."

11. Victor Marchetti and John D. Marks, *The CIA and the Cult of Intelligence* (New York: Knopf, 1974), 1.

12. Marchetti and Marks, *The CIA and the Cult of Intelligence*, 324.

13. Philip Agee, *Inside the Company: CIA Diary* (London: Stonehill, 1975), 484.

14. Agee, quoted in Judith Schenck Koffler and Bennett L. Gershman, "Symposium: National Security and Civil Liberties: The New Seditious Libel," *Cornell Law Review* 69 (April 1984): 16.

15. John Stockwell, *In Search of Enemies: A CIA Story* (New York: Norton, 1974), 251–53.

16. Ralph McGehee, *Deadly Deceits: My 25 Years in the CIA* (New York: Sheridan Square, 1983), 192–94.

17. McGehee, *Deadly Deceits*, 194; and James Otis, *Secrets of the CIA*, documentary film (1998), https://www.youtube.com/watch?v=ut3UF9TlJ_E.

18. Frank Snepp, *Irreparable Harm: A Firsthand Account of How One Agent Took on the CIA in an Epic Battle Over Secrecy and Free Speech* (New York: Random House, 1999), xiv.

19. Agee is the exception here. He turned strongly internationalist, framing his dissent as solidarity with the world's poor and not fidelity to American principles.

20. James Doolittle et al., "Report on the Covert Activities of the Central Intelligence Agency," in *The Central Intelligence Agency: History and Documents, ed.* William M. Leary (Tuscaloosa: University of Alabama Press, 1984), 143.

21. Alfred A. Knopf published Marchetti and Marks's *The CIA and the Cult of Intelligence,* Random House published Snepp's *Decent Interval,* and *Harper's* published Adams's initial exposé.

22. The history of the term "winter soldier" is discussed in Veterans for Peace, "Who Are the Real Winter Soldiers?" April 4, 2014, https://www.veteransforpeace.org/pressroom/news/2014/04/04/who-are-real-winter-soldiers.

23. McGehee discusses the drug use and other rebellion of the children of U.S. personnel in Thailand in *Deadly Deceits,* 163–65.

24. Opposition to the Vietnam War in the military and civil service is a through line in the epic account of the antiwar movement. See Tom Wells, *The War Within: America's Battle Over Vietnam* (Berkeley: University of California Press, 1994).

25. Nicholas M. Horrock, "Colby Describes C.I.A. Poison Dart Gun," *New York Times,* September 17, 1975, https://www.nytimes.com/1975/09/17/archives/colby-describes-cia-poison-work-he-tells-senate-panel-of-secret.html.

26. McGehee, *Deadly Deceits,* xii.

27. McGehee, *Deadly Deceits,* 161–62.

28. Agee, *Inside the Company,* 486.

29. Stockwell, *In Search of Enemies,* 9.

30. Adams made the initial public allegation in Sam Adams, "Vietnam Cover-Up: Playing with the Numbers," *Harper's,* May 1975.

31. Mistry, "A Transnational Protest Against the National Security State."

32. The history of *CounterSpy* is briefly retold in a successor publication. Brandt, "Little Magazines May Come and Go."

33. *CounterSpy* 1, no. 2 (May 1973). The issue, sold for 75 cents, has as its cover a menacing picture of a Vietnamese phoenix, symbolizing the state terror program.

34. "Who We Are," *Covert Action Information Bulletin,* July 1978, 3; "Researching Undercover CIA Officers," *Covert Action Information Bulletin* 2 (October 1978): 11–14.

35. Philip Agee, Louis Wolf, Karl van Meter, and Louis Wolf, eds., *Dirty Work: The CIA in Western Europe* (New York: Dorset, 1978). A companion volume was soon published by others affiliated with *Covert Action*: Ellen Ray and William Schapp, eds., *Dirty Work 2: The CIA in Africa* (London: Zed, 1980).

36. For a brief biography of MacMichael, see "Interview with David MacMichael, Former CIA Analyst, US Marine and Historian," RThieme, 2006, http://www.thiemeworks.com/interview-with-david-macmichael-former-cia-analyst-us-marine-and-historian/.

37. "550 Protestors Arrested Outside CIA Headquarters," *Los Angeles Times,* April 27, 1987, http://articles.latimes.com/1987-04-27/news/mn-978_1_cia-headquarters.

38. Information of the protest action is contained in an organizer's manual, "NONVIOLENT CIVIL DISOBEDIENCE AT CIA HEADQUARTERS, Langley, Virginia"

(author's possession). The manual's background section on the CIA includes a brief interview with Stockwell.

39. Susan Seligson, "CIA Veteran Hulnick Slams Agency's Critics," *BU Today*, January 22, 2010, https://www.bu.edu/today/2010/cia-veteran-hulnick-slams-agency's-critics/.

40. On the question of Casey's alleged confession, see Richard Zoglin, "Did a Dead Man Tell No Tales?" *Time*, October 12, 1987.

41. John Stockwell, "A C.I.A. Trip—from Belief, to Doubt, to Despair," *Center Magazine: Center for the Study of Democratic Government* 7, no. 5 (September/October 1979): 18–19.

42. On the masculine personae and gendered sensibility of U.S. state officials, see Robert Dean, *Imperial Brotherhood: Gender and the Making of Cold War Foreign Policy* (Amherst: University of Massachusetts Press, 2002).

43. Otis, *Secrets of the CIA*.

44. Snepp, *Irreparable Harm*, xii–xv.

45. Adams's background and career are detailed in Michael Hiam, *Who the Hell Are We Fighting: The Story of Sam Adams and U.S. Intelligence Wars* (Hanover, NH: Steerforth, 2006).

46. McGehee, *Deadly Deceits*, 1.

47. Stockwell, "A C.I.A. Trip," 18–19.

48. McGehee, *Deadly Deceits*, 105–6.

49. McGehee records the disappointing response of his higher ups, including Far East Division Chief William Colby, in *Deadly Deceits*, 109–14.

50. Sam Adams, *War of Numbers: An Intelligence Memoir* (1996; repr. Hanover, NH: Steerforth, 2012), preface.

51. Adams, *War of Numbers*, preface.

52. Otis, *Secrets of the CIA*.

53. McGehee, *Deadly Deceits*, ix–x.

54. Otis, *Secrets of the CIA*.

55. Stockwell, *In Search of Enemies*, 150.

56. Snepp, *Irreparable Harm*, 1–9.

57. Snepp, *Irreparable Harm*, 10.

58. McGehee, *Deadly Deceits*, dedication.

59. Stockwell, *In Search of Enemies*, 15.

60. Agee, *Inside the Company*, 516.

61. Hickman's allegations were first recorded in Scott Horton, "The Guantanamo 'Suicides': A Camp Delta Sergeant Blows the Whistle," *Harper's*, June 18, 2010. Hickman expanded on the allegations and narrated his dangerous sleuthing in Joseph Hickman, *Murder at Camp Delta: A Staff Sergeant's Pursuit of the Truth About Guantanamo Bay* (New York: Simon and Schuster, 2014). The riskiness of Hickman's exposé and the struggles to publish his allegations place him closer to a classic whistleblower revealing state secrets.

62. Mark Fallon, *Unjustifiable Means: The Inside Story of How the CIA, Pentagon, and U.S. Government Conspired to Torture* (New York: Reagan Arts, 2017).

63. Ann Wright coauthored a book on criticism of the Iraq War by government and former government officials. Ann Wright and Susan Dixon, *Dissent—Voices of Conscience:*

Government Insiders Speak Out Against the War in Iraq (Kihei, HI: Koa, 2008). In 2006, McGovern famously confronted Secretary of Defense Donald Rumsfeld about his false claims of Iraqi WMD. It is captured at https://www.youtube.com/watch ?v=v1FTmuhynaw. McGovern has a website with a bio and various of his writings: http://raymcgovern.com/.

64. The following sketch, except when noted, is drawn from two main sources: his own memoir, John Kiriakou, *The Reluctant Spy: My Secret Life in the CIA's War on Terror* (New York: Bantam, 2009); and the multipart interview with Paul Jay for "Reality Asserts Itself" (*The Real News Network*) in 2015, https://www.youtube.com/watch?v=E82OrQF 9nkY&index=15&list=RDyL8rVbWniW4%20 (see side-links for the URL of other installments of the interview). Hereafter RAI interview.

65. Material about his regard for prior dissidence is from a phone interview I conducted with Kiriakou on January 8, 2018.

66. Joseph Hickman and John Kiriakou, *The Convenient Terrorist: Two Whistleblowers' Stories of Torture, Terror, Secret Wars, and CIA Lies* (New York: Skyhorse, 2017).

67. The original ABC footage is shown in the RAI interview.

68. Authored in 2004, large portions of the CIA inspector general's report were made public by the Bush administration in 2008. In August 2009, the Obama administration released additional portions of the report that, among other things, cast doubt on the value of the intelligence gained from CIA interrogations. On the differences between the two versions of the report, see the National Security Archive blog from August 25, 2009, https://nsarchive2.gwu.edu/torture_archive/index_ig.htm.

69. John Kiriakou, *The Reluctant* Spy, 190–92.

70. RAI interview.

71. Author interview with John Kiriakou.

72. Author interview with John Kiriakou.

73. The purpose, history, and recipients of the award are recorded at http://samadamsaward .ch/. Other notable awardees include Lawrence Wilkerson (2009), WikiLeaks founder Julian Assange (2010), National Security Agency whistleblowers Thomas Drake (2011) and William Binney (2015), Edward Snowden (2013), Chelsea Manning (2014), and the legendary investigative journalist Seymour Hersh (2017), who has reported heavily on the CIA since the 1960s.

74. Key texts are Alfred W. McCoy, *A Question of Torture: CIA Interrogation, from the Cold War to the War on Terror* (New York: Metropolitan, 2006); Jane Mayer, *The Dark Side: The Inside Story of How the War on Terror Turned Into a War on American Ideals* (New York: Anchor, 2008); and the U.S. government's own "Report of the Senate Select Committee on Intelligence—Committee Study of the Central Intelligence Agency's Detention and Interrogation Program," 2014, https://www.intelligence.senate.gov/sites /default/files/publications/CRPT-113srpt288.pdf.

75. Glenn L. Carle, *The Interrogator: An Education* (New York: Nation, 2011), 300–1.

76. Carle, *The Interrogator*, 299.

77. RAI interview.

78. John Kiriakou, "I Went to Prison for Disclosing Torture. Gina Haspel Helped Cover It Up," *Washington Post*, March 16, 2018, https://www.washingtonpost.com/outlook/i-went-to-prison-for-disclosing-the-cias-torture-gina-haspel-helped-cover-it-up/2018/03/15/9507884e-27f8-11e8-874b-d517e912f125_story.html.

79. Among dozens of articles on Haspel's record, see Annabelle Timsit, "What Happened at the Thailand 'Black Site' Run by Trump's CIA Pick," *Atlantic*, March 14, 2018, https://www.theatlantic.com/international/archive/2018/03/gina-haspel-black-site-torture-cia/555539/; and Patrice Toddonio, "CIA Director Nominee Supported Destruction of Torture Tapes," *PBS Frontline*, May 9, 2018, https://www.pbs.org/wgbh/frontline/article/cia-director-nominee-supported-destruction-of-torture-tapes/. On Haspel's confirmation hearing, see Jeremy Varon, "'Bloody Gina,' the CIA, and Torture," *Public Seminar*, May 15, 2018, http://www.publicseminar.org/2018/05/bloody-gina-the-cia-and-the-senate/. A video of McGovern's treatment is at: https://www.youtube.com/watch?v=CE1hTokoseg.

80. See John Brennan, "I Will Speak Out Until Integrity Returns to the White House," *Washington Post*, June 1, 2018, https://www.washingtonpost.com/opinions/john-brennan-i-will-speak-out-until-integrity-returns-to-the-white-house/2018/05/31/afbccafa-64e8-11e8-a69c-b944de66d9e7_story.html; and "Former DNI Clapper Questions Trump's 'Fitness' to Be President," *Daily Beast*, https://www.thedailybeast.com/former-dni-chief-clapper-i-question-trumps-fitness-to-be-potus. In April 2018, President Trump revoked Brennan's security clearance as retaliation against his public criticisms.

81. Michel Crowly, "John Brennan's Zig-Zag on Torture," *Politico*, December 9, 2014, https://www.politico.com/story/2014/12/john-brennan-cia-torture-113456.

82. See "James Clapper Says He Misspoke, Didn't Lie About NSA Surveillance," *CBS News*, September 18, 2014, https://www.cbsnews.com/news/james-clapper-says-he-misspoke-didnt-lie-about-nsa-surveillance/.

7

FROM THE MUNDANE TO THE ABSURD

The Advent and Evolution of Prepublication Review

RICHARD H. IMMERMAN

VERY AMERICAN WHO participates in the formulation or implementation of U.S. national security policy, and as a consequence can potentially access classified information, must sign a nondisclosure, or as more commonly known, a secrecy, agreement (NDA). This requirement, which covers current and former employees as well as contractors, applies most transparently to members of the U.S. intelligence community. But State Department, military, National Security Council, congressional staff and personnel, and thousands of others in and out of Washington are likewise subject to it. Beginning in 1976, the requirement also covered executive-branch employees with "access to information containing sources and methods of intelligence."[1] The wording of the NDA may vary slightly depending on the year, the government branch or agency, and the classification level. The intent and parameters are nevertheless consistent. The agreement's introduction at a minimum reads along the lines of, "Intending to be legally bound, I hereby accept the obligations contained in this Agreement in consideration of my being granted access to classified information. . . . I understand and accept that by being granted access to classified information, special confidence and trust shall be placed in me by the United States Government."

The template then continues with the more operative words:

> I have been advised that the unauthorized disclosure, unauthorized reten-
> tion, or negligent handling of classified information by me could cause
> damage or irreparable injury to the United States or could be used to
> advantage by a foreign nation. I hereby agree that I will never divulge clas-
> sified information to anyone unless: (a) I have officially verified that the
> recipient has been properly authorized by the United States Government
> to receive it; or (b) I have been given prior written notice of authorization
> from the United States Government Department or Agency (hereinafter
> Department or Agency) responsible for the classification of information or
> last granting me a security clearance that such disclosure is permitted.

The agreement makes explicit near the end that it will remain in effect not
only during the time when the individual official has authorized access to
classified information but also "at all times afterward." In other words, an
NDA is a lifetime contract that threatens the signatory with prosecution
should she or he ever violate its terms.[2]

Who, when, and why someone originally conceived of an NDA remains
a mystery. As one authority writes, "There is no origin story for the nondisclosure agreement, no Edison or Franklin who lays claim to the form."[3]
What we can claim with confidence is that NDAs began to appear more
frequently in the 1940s in connection with maritime law. The requirement
that an employee sign one became widespread throughout the government
during the early years of the Cold War and acquired increased notoriety in
the wake of Watergate and the Year of Intelligence (1975). It was at that
time that revelations about Central Intelligence Agency (CIA) abuses precipitated eye-opening congressional hearings that rivaled those on the
Nixon administration's abuses.

Yet what drew state attention to NDAs preceded those dueling sets
of hearings and was a catalyst for both: Daniel Ellsberg's disclosure in 1971
of what came to be called the Pentagon Papers, the Department of
Defense's top-secret study of U.S. policy and strategy in Vietnam from
1945 to 1967, and the legal battles that ensued. Even then, the issue for

most of the public, and for that matter for Ellsberg, was not that he was violating his NDA. Rather, the issue was that he was revealing secrets. The NDA received consideration only in so far as it represented a potential instrument for prosecuting and punishing him.[4] Only after the government's case against Ellsberg collapsed did it seek to exploit that potential.

Other essays in this volume explore that defining moment in the "long 1970s" in more depth. It is sufficient for my purposes to point out the obvious: the Pentagon Papers that Ellsberg and his former RAND colleague Anthony Russo photocopied were composed of classified information to which Ellsberg had privileged access. That Ellsberg, as both a RAND analyst who worked on nuclear strategy and former official in Robert McNamara's Pentagon, had signed an NDA was to the government of less significance than the harm to U.S. national security it claimed he caused and the precedent he might establish. Further, many in the legal community held that NDAs were unenforceable, especially if the plaintiff is not willing to disclose additional classified material through discovery.[5]

Consequently, the government initially sought to prosecute Ellsberg for violating the 1917 Espionage Act in addition to stealing government records and engaging in a conspiracy. The Nixon administration's illegal efforts to gather evidence against him led to the dismissal of all charges against him. Nevertheless, the government's campaign, which of course included its unsuccessful attempt to prevent the publication of the documents, laid down a marker for the future. NDAs could prove a more effective means than the Espionage Act to censor authors because they did not leave it to the courts to determine the legality of the government's conduct, the extent to which the disclosure of information damaged national security, or whether arriving at a verdict required the disclosure of additional—including classified—information.

While perhaps the most notorious, the legal jeopardy precipitated by Ellsberg's disclosures was among that era's multiple episodes that garnered headlines by pitting national security "whistleblowers" against the government they had served. Victor Marchetti, Philip Agee, Frank Snepp, and John Stockwell all gained far more notoriety than they would have otherwise had the publication of their books about their CIA careers—books critical of the CIA, it must be noted—not collided with the terms of the NDAs they had signed as a requirement of employment. In contrast to Ellsberg and the Pentagon Papers, one can make a strong case that the government's efforts to prevent publication of these books was not so much driven by a concern with protecting national security as to muzzle whistleblowers: to censor their criticism or undermine their capability to shine a light on behavior that for various reasons the government sought to keep secret. Ironically, to at least some degree that case rests on the government's decision to rely on the provisions of NDAs as opposed to the Espionage Act to suppress publication. Equally if not more ironically, the increased reliance on NDAs proved ineffective in silencing whistleblowers but caused the greatest hardship to those who most conscientiously sought to honor the spirit as well as the letter of the NDA.[6]

THE ADVENT OF PREPUBLICATION REVIEW

Because of the government's success in the 1970s in weaponizing secrecy agreements to promote secrecy, by the 1980s the requirement to sign an NDA had become standard for national security officials throughout the federal government. Yet as the Vietnam War and then the Cold War receded from the American consciousness, and perhaps because the hardships experienced by those who wrote in the 1970s deterred subsequent writers from following suit, fewer controversies surfaced in the news or were graphically illustrated by blacked-out (redacted) passages in publications.[7] But the clash between security and privacy that followed the 9/11 tragedy and U.S. declaration of a "Global War on Terror" dramatically increased the tension between secrecy and transparency. The whistleblowers John Kiriakou and Chelsea Manning were sent to jail for revealing classified information; Edward Snowden, to exile. And although the charges against him were dropped, Thomas Drake had his security clearance suspended; was indicted for obstructing justice, giving false statements, and mishandling (not disclosing) classified information; and spent a year clearing his name.[8]

What these cases all had in common is that the protagonist self-identified as a whistleblower who directly challenged, or in extreme cases willingly violated, the NDA in order to serve what she or he considered the greater public good by exposing behavior that would otherwise remain secret. Important as these cases are, they fail to capture the broader impact of the national security establishment's efforts to censor the public writings of current and former employees. Shortly after the CIA's ad hoc intervention to prevent the publication and control the contents of Marchetti and Marks's *The Cult of Intelligence* and Agee's *Inside the Company*, the environment changed. Many members of America's national security community, who not only never intended to violate their NDAs but also judged that they had conscientiously adhered to the terms, found themselves victims of the federal government's expanding and intensifying culture of secrecy. Seemingly treated more as suspected outlaws than faithful civil servants or other government employees, they were compelled to choose between the same kind of legal jeopardy that Ellsberg and his successors confronted or the sanctity of their integrity.

The reason for this development was not complicated. In the wake of the judicial proceedings that enveloped *The Cult of Intelligence* and an extraordinary increase of the number of aspiring authors who were agency employees or former employees, the CIA determined that the structure of the existing mechanism for ensuring against the disclosure of classified information, the Office of Security, was insufficiently rigorous to enforce NDAs. Hence on June 10, 1976, it created a unit, the Publication Review Board (PRB), composed of senior officers representing each of the CIA's four directorates—labeled at the time Administration, Intelligence, Operations, and Science and Technology—plus officers responsible for cover and for personnel security and a legal counsel. CIA Headquarters Notice 178, the directive that established the PRB, mandated that all present and past, and by some interpretations future, Agency personnel, regardless of the position held, submit to it for inspection any book, article, interview, lecture, screenplay, press release, résumé or curriculum vitae, or other text intended for public dissemination. Failure to fulfill this obligation was not only cause for denying publication in full but also for legal prosecution.[9]

Vested in the PRB was the authority to detect—and quarantine—any and all unauthorized disclosure of information that it judged to be classified. Over the subsequent years the CIA's PRB expanded its full-time personnel, centralized its work, and assumed responsibility for reviewing texts written by current as well as former employees. Until the burden became too great because of the spike in the number of manuscripts written by working CIA personnel following 9/11, their reviews had been entrusted to their managers. Since the Reagan administration, virtually every pillar that composes America's national security architecture has adopted some form of PRB, each with its own standards.[10]

Many in the public are vaguely aware of this process, although very few possess more than the barest understanding of how it operates. Further, fewer still are aware of its burdens, its imperfections, and its costs. The CIA's PRB and comparable offices throughout the national security state evolved in an era of unprecedented abuse of government power, when publicly exposing these abuses seemed to many witnesses the most effective remedy. These witnesses, who often proudly claimed the title of whistleblower, assessed NDAs as invalid contracts because the government had forfeited a legitimate claim to have entered into them in good faith. The purpose of the prepublication review boards was to enforce these contracts in what the government defined as a hostile environment. The way to remedy lawlessness, government officials claimed, was to reinforce those laws. Hence disclosing classified information of any nature could not be tolerated regardless of the circumstances.

In the subsequent decades, however, the volume of government-produced information exploded, the classification guidelines became ever more ambiguous, and as a result overclassification grew rampant. The federal government's prepublication review boards were powerless against whistleblowing. Most government employees or former employees who intend to express themselves in the public sphere do not hesitate to submit their writings, speeches, or even talking points to an appropriate PRB. If the PRB requests that they omit material because it remains classified (or highly sensitive—for example, "Formerly Restricted Data" or "Controlled Unclassified Information"), they may appeal, but in the end they oblige. Their priority is avoiding a long-drawn-out process, let alone a penalty. Neither whistleblowers nor their opposites, government-sanctioned "leakers," however, think for a second about submitting for review the information that they intend to disclose publicly. Although they, too, want to avoid a penalty, particularly but not exclusively jail time, they all but dare the government to take them to court and accept the risks of that choice.

What comes before the review boards are the writings, speeches, diaries, and similar texts of memoirists, scholars, and current and former national security officials who for a variety of motives seek to publish their stories, interpretations, and analyses. The consequences of their getting ensnared in a process that is ill-designed for its most common usage can be Kafkaesque. A recent case is that of Sarah Carlson, a retired analyst with the CIA's Counterterrorism Center who submitted a book manuscript about a single incident about which she had firsthand knowledge. The incident remains classified. That's because more than two years after she submitted her manuscript to the PRB, and after receiving its approval twice, she dutifully submitted it one final time after adding one additional page of text. This time the PRB vetoed the publication of the entire manuscript.[11]

The grief encountered by Carlson and others,[12] however, none of whom fit even the most elastic definition of whistleblower, occurs too frequently. In the interest of full disclosure, I am one of five plaintiffs in a lawsuit filed by the Knight First Amendment Institute at Columbia University and the American Civil Liberties Union against the director of national intelligence, director of the CIA, director of the NSA, and acting secretary of defense. The lawsuit challenges the constitutionality of the prepublication review system because of the restraints it imposes on free speech and due-process rights. The complaint includes testimony from each of the plaintiffs about the hardships each encountered when seeking permission from their respective prepublication review authorities.[13]

Nevertheless, the trials and tribulations of Carlson, the lawsuit's plaintiffs, and others are more the exception than the rule. In the course of any given year, the CIA's PRB and parallel offices and divisions across the government and military review hundreds if not thousands of texts. According to one authority, in the 1990s the CIA's PRB alone reviewed 18,000 pages of text annually; by 2004, that number had risen to 30,000.[14] The vast majority of these pages cover anodyne topics unlikely to attract attention or controversy, in part because the writers consciously seek to avoid triggering PRB redlining. First-time authors are especially conservative, and more experienced ones acquire the skill necessary to mask sensitive material; they omit words, provide cover names and otherwise conceal identities, that sort of thing. Therefore, most of these reviews are perfunctory and completed in a reasonable amount of time.

To get a better sense of the actual workings of the system, I interviewed, corresponded with, and/or distributed a questionnaire on their interactions with the PRB or its equivalent to some two dozen individuals who are or were employed by the CIA, the Defense Intelligence Agency, the National Intelligence Council, the National Security Agency, the National Reconnaissance Office, the Department of State, and the Department of Defense. While this sample is far too small to meet the criteria of statistical significance, and indeed in most cases I chose my subjects because I knew them and their publication histories, I am confident that, with the exception of covert operatives, my "set" is fairly representative of a cross-section of those who submit texts for a PRB review. Most of the respondents reported that while on occasion they ran into a problem, those problems did not rise to the level of serious. As a consequence, they judged their prepublication review experiences as satisfactory. But nearly each person with whom I spoke or corresponded did report at least one snafu. Individually, these are manageable. But collectively they can produce a nightmare. That's what happened to Sarah Carlson and others who have written about their ordeals. It's also what happened to me and explains my participation in the lawsuit.[15]

In this chapter, I draw on my experience and that of others, along with published government and nongovernmental sources, to walk the reader through the prepublication review process. My aim is twofold. First, I shine a light on a process that is obscure, opaque, and all but absent from the scholarly literature. Second, and relatedly, I aggregate accounts of prepublication reviews in order to bring to the public's attention the pitfalls that inhere in the process. In conjunction with their complaint challenging the constitutionality of the prepublication review process, the Knight First Amendment Institute and American Civil Liberties Union filed Freedom of Information Act requests to obtain documentation about different intelligence agencies' review practices for the purpose of promoting their reform.[16] My goal is parallel to theirs. My premise is that by explaining prepublication review policies and procedures, this essay will raise public consciousness and thereby prompt the multiple agencies to reexamine those policies and procedures. Put another way, I seek to blow the whistle on the prepublication review process in the hope of improving it. An artifact of the exaggerated perceptions of internal as well as external threats spawned by the era of Vietnam, Watergate, and the Year of Intelligence, PRBs exacerbate the culture of secrecy that I argue erodes America's image and democratic institutions and consequently is detrimental to its national security interests. Improving the process will accordingly serve the national interest by promoting transparency.

THE PREPUBLICATION REVIEW PROCESS

The first step in the process is for the national security employee to learn what is required of him or her should he or she seek to publish a book, book chapter, article, opinion piece, or any other text with public visibility, receive a request to comment publicly on anything related to his position or agency, accept an invitation to speak or lecture, or undertake an equivalent activity. When and how the employees receive this indoctrination varies. When they first start work, personnel hired by the Executive Office of the President, most departments, the intelligence community, and elsewhere in the federal government where access to classified material is either expected or likely receive a security briefing. At that time, they sign the NDA (in most instances even if they have already signed an NDA for a previous position) and learn the dos and don'ts of working in a classified environment.

This briefing normally, but not always, includes an introduction to the mandates of prepublication review. The same holds true for consultants and contractors once they have received their clearances. Two of the former federal employees whom I interviewed, however, learned about the prepublication process after they left their government positions, not when they began them.[17] In some instances, moreover, the employee, often a consultant or contractor, only learns about prepublication review when she or he has completed a manuscript or informed his or her supervisor that one is in preparation. This less systematic introduction can also apply to military personnel and, until relatively recently, many in the State Department.[18]

In almost all cases the introduction to prepublication review is just that—an introduction. The briefer, who may or may not be intimately familiar with the process, explains in general terms what material must be submitted for prepublication review. Because the criteria are by definition ambiguous, that translates into virtually everything—whether fiction or nonfiction and regardless of the author's personal involvement with the subject matter and access to classified material that may be relevant. The briefer also provides the employee with a point of contact for the board or other mechanism responsible for conducting the reviews and the URL for the particular agency's or department's prepublication review policy guidelines.[19]

Because the policies are complicated, differ among agencies, and are open to interpretation, how they become operational only becomes apparent after the employee, or former employee, submits a text for review. While this first step may seem straightforward, it is not. The author and the reviewer can easily disagree as to whether the text falls within the category that requires a review. To quote one authority, the decision is "entirely a judgment call." What is more, certain requirements are written in such fine print that even the most conscientious individual is likely to be unaware of it. For example, if a federal employee is listed as a coauthor of a text with someone with no government connections, even if his or her contribution was extremely minor or divorced from his or her access to classified material, the manuscript must still undergo prepublication review. Hence the prudent course of action is to submit it—and to do so before sending it to colleagues, a press agent, or of course a publisher. This sequencing is easy to forget.[20]

But where and how to submit may not be any clearer. Some agencies, such as the CIA and the ODNI, stipulate that all present and past employees submit their texts to the same review authority.[21] The State Department, however, not only distinguishes among current and former personnel but also among titles and locations. State's Bureau of Public Affairs (PA), for example, reviews material for employees, including but not limited to both the foreign and civil service, who work within the United States, whereas the Chief of Mission's office conducts the final review for personnel posted overseas. The Chief of Mission is also responsible for reviewing the work of USAID employees living abroad, but the prepublication review authority for domestic employees is USAID's Bureau of Legislative and Public Affairs (LPA). Former State Department personnel must have their manuscripts cleared by the Office of Information Programs and Services, Global Information Services, Bureau of Administration (A/GIS/IPS). So, too, must former employees currently working for the department on a temporary or part-time basis (formerly WAEs, "When Actually Employed"; the designation was recently renamed to "Reemployed Annuitants" to promote clarity) with the exception of those who must submit their texts to PA. No document explains this bifurcation. Especially because changes in assignments are so common in the State Department, the potential author or speaker must conduct the required research.[22]

Because of its size and decentralization, determining the locus for review is even more complicated in the Department of Defense and its components. DoD Directive (DoDD) 5230.09, "Clearance of DoD Information for Public Release," August 22, 2008, and DoD Instruction (DoDI) 5230.29, "Security and Policy Review of DoD Information for Public Release," August 13, 2014, govern the department's prepublication review process. It vests the authority for reviewing material from current, former, and retired employees in the Defense Office of Prepublication and Security Review (DOPSR). DoD's intelligence components, however, such as the DIA and NSA, have their own prepublication review authorities. The DIA's is classified. The review authority for the NSA and its subagency, the Central Security Service, is the Office of Policy and Records. But often NSA/CSS required multiple reviews before providing permission to publish. Other components of the Department of Defense, such as the U.S. Army and the different Combatant Commands, each have their own review policies and authorities. According to a 2016 report by the DoD's inspector general, these policies do not comply with DoD policies as codified in DoDD 5230.09 and DoDI 5230.29. The U.S. Army War College regulations differ from that of the U.S. Army. They are compliant.[23]

This cacophony of authorities and guidelines does not make it easy for the employee to identify where to submit his or her text. The question of how to submit can likewise produce uncertainty. Most guidance directives provide an email or postal address. Classified material, however, should be hand delivered. But, of course, the purpose of the prepublication reviews is to determine whether the text includes any classified information. Most employees, confident that their manuscripts contain exclusively material that's available to the public, do submit by email or a postal service. Delivering the manuscript personally is more appropriate, nevertheless. For this reason one of those whom I contacted about this project arranged, as if following espionage tradecraft, to hand off a manuscript outside a museum.[24]

While virtually all the reviewing authorities promptly acknowledge receipt of a submitted text (although one of those whom I contacted reported that on one occasion it took months to receive an acknowledgment), the following weeks and even months can be exasperating. The guidelines normatively stipulate that the review will be completed in thirty days. The NSA/CSS is the outlier: it sets the deadline at twenty-five days. But whether the suspense is twenty-five days or thirty days makes no difference in practice. There is a significant divergence among agencies. For example, the ODNI is as a rule more efficient than the CIA or DoD. Still, patterns do emerge. For short pieces, such as an op-ed essay or press release, especially those that are time sensitive, the turnaround time can be a matter of a day or two. Based on those I interviewed, moreover, the review time for an article or book chapter normatively falls in line with the twenty-five-to-thirty-day requirement, although on relatively rare occasions the wait can extend to several months.[25]

But books are another matter, and in these instances the policy guidelines are almost always ignored without apology. It is not that the reviewers don't act in good faith. None of the sources that provide the foundation for this chapter claim that the aim is anything other than to complete their reviews as rapidly as possible and approve the dissemination of all permissible information. Rather, the responsible boards or offices lack resources adequate to shoulder the workload generated by the explosion of information and individuals or organizations intent on disseminating it—and the overclassification of that information. Moreover, because of the ambiguity—and many would argue the irrationality and impracticality—of the classification guidelines, the reviews can prove to be complicated. For this reason, the decisions arrived at during those reviews can be highly subjective and dependent on the individual reviewer's, or reviewers', interpretations of the guidelines, own experiences and priorities, and time constraints.

Thus depending on the book's length, its coverage (covert actions or counterintelligence, for example, or past and especially current foreign policy flashpoints require much closer attention than such subjects as analytic tradecraft or intelligence community management), the diversity of agencies with "equities" (meaning those agencies that are integral to or have a vested interest in the story), and the frequent need to appeal mandated redactions, a book can often take six months or more to review. My own experience with papers, quotes, articles, and books is in line with this standard. Further, some authors have provided accounts of nightmarish scenarios. It took a full year for one State Department foreign service officer to receive clearance to publish his book. It took more than a year for the CIA's PRB to approve the publication of a book manuscript written by a former CIA analyst. And as mentioned earlier, more than two years passed after another CIA analyst submitted her manuscript; finally she received authorization to publish, and it became available in June 2019. And a clandestine operative from the Agency who has submitted for prepublication review her memoir has hired a lawyer. Her book is scheduled for imminent publication, and she has made the changes in the manuscript required by the reviewers. But the CIA has yet to give her the green light to publish.[26]

Some of the reasons for these delays are understandable and acceptable. Some are neither. And the latter can evoke such frustration, irritation, and anxiety that it deters authors from writing in the first place.[27] I suspect that this deterrence function may be among the purposes of the prepublication requirements, at least in so far as they deter someone from whistleblowing. After all, the CIA established the PRB within two years of the publication of *The Cult of Intelligence* and *Inside the Company*. But a more pervasive and powerful motive is that of preempting a publication that would make public an operation, relationship, undercover agent or foreign "asset," or, most likely, information that would reveal intelligence sources or methods. Whistleblowers, it goes without saying, seek to disclose precisely this kind of information because of the purpose they are committed to serving. They therefore cannot be expected to submit manuscripts or anything else for prepublication review. For this reason, the U.S. government recognized the futility of trying to halt or even restrict publication of Edward Snowden's memoir, *Permanent Record*. Instead, drawing on the precedent established when Frank Snepp violated his NDA with the publication of *Decent Interval*, the Justice Department is suing to recover all of Snowden's potential earnings from the book.[28] Most of those who submit material for prepublication review, however, are as convinced of the need to keep these secrets secret as the reviewers.

Therein lies the problem. The texts' authors have with very few exceptions bent over backward to avoid including anything that would not only violate the NDA they signed but also serve as a red flag to the reviewer. Heading their list of prohibited information is any reference, even an indirect one, to classified information or the citation of a classified document. Perhaps because they'd gone through a review previously, spoken to someone who has, or read an account, many go even further. They obscure the identities of individuals or organizations by using cover names or another strategy. They omit material that may alert the reader to a source or method even if it's not part of the narrative. And they assiduously locate a book, memoir, article in the press, or other open source that supports their account, claim, or argument. The author will "wear" these "fig leaves," to quote a former head of the CIA's PRB, "as a way of indicating to readers that the information is in the public domain and does not necessarily come from unique, inside knowledge." For this purpose, some authors do not consider themselves sufficiently protected unless they cite at least two fig leaves, one of which, in the best of all possible worlds, is a senior government official.[29]

The presumption of the reviewers, at least as perceived by many who have submitted texts for reviews, is nevertheless that authors are presumed "guilty" of including *verboten* material unless they, the reviewer, can prove them innocent. Some critics of the process allege that within this category falls anything that might embarrass the agency or department.[30] Should this criticism be valid, such a deletion would not only constitute an abuse of the reviewer's authority but also be unconstitutional. While I won't rule out the possibility that such an abuse has occurred, I have no evidence that it has. I do have evidence that the fig leaf proposed by the CIA's former PRB chief is often a chimera. That's in part because of the government's, above all the intelligence community's, adherence to the "mosaic theory," which states that by piecing together a sufficient volume of unclassified material an adversary can acquire classified information.[31]

A reviewer devoted to the mosaic theory, consequently, can take an inordinate amount of time going through a manuscript with a fine-tooth comb, imagining what material can be strung together to disclose something that should not be. But no less time consuming, and a more conventional reason for both delays and frustration, is the government's definition of classified information—and that definition's challenge to common sense. For example, FRD (Formerly Restricted Data) is primarily information that the Department of Defense or Department of Energy no longer considers should be classified but also is not prepared to release to the public. Hence currently it might as well remain classified. In an effort to standardize practices across the more than one hundred agencies that classify documents, the federal government established the classification "Controlled Unclassified Information." CUI applies to information that does not meet the threshold of classification for reasons of national security but according to the relevant agency requires some protection. It literally defies a common definition. Imagine the problem this poses for reviewers. For the sake of simplicity, I will draw primarily from my own experience to explain and illustrate. Both published and unpublished sources, however, attest that what I confronted was anything but exceptional.

THE HIDDEN HAND OF THE PRB

Before and after my service as an assistant deputy director of national intelligence (ADDNI), I was employed as a tenured faculty member at a university. As such, I was expected to produce and disseminate scholarship that reflected my training as a historian. Central to that training was the identification of reliable sources that I could cite to support accounts and my interpretations of these histories. My training included locating the sources, distinguishing among them, and assessing their respective reliability. Having signed a contract to write a history of the CIA virtually simultaneous to my appointment as an ADDNI, I knew I must be careful lest I violate my NDA. But I also knew, because of my training as a historian, that *all* of the information on events and developments that occurred during my tenure in government would remain classified. The United States only declassifies documents twenty-five years after their date of issue unless released after a Mandatory Declassification Review or Freedom of Information Act request. And because my tenure coincided with the Global War on Terror, I knew better than to waste anyone's time by filing such requests.

So I didn't. Even for my coverage of the decades before 2001, I relied exclusively on secondary sources, the press, and government publications, particularly publication by the CIA's Center for the Study of Intelligence or comparable authority. If anything, I was more systematic than I otherwise might have been in citing my evidence in order to make transparent its origin. Before turning in my book on the CIA's history for review (which I did through email—it never occurred to me that I might be risking a hacker gaining access to classified information, and no one ever cautioned me against doing so or alerted me that my behavior was reckless if not illegal), I had submitted (likewise by email) multiple papers I prepared for delivery, articles, and an earlier book on U.S. expansion from colonial times to the present. (At the instruction of the CIA's PRB, which conducted prepublication review for the ODNI, I even submitted the chapters on the eighteenth and nineteenth centuries.) In each instance, I received approval to publish within a few days or weeks (three weeks for the book manuscript).

The only requested revisions were very minor—adding "former" to the title of a senior officer for a talk I was giving on the intelligence community, for example, or correcting an acronym, that sort of thing. On occasion I was asked to delete a reference to a location, which I found puzzling. Still, I readily obliged. Because of my precautions I expected the same response after submitted my CIA book.[32]

Three days after submitting that manuscript I received an acknowledgment that read, "Received your manuscript. DNI Pre Pub will review it as quickly as possible." Two months passed without my hearing another word. With my patience reaching its limit, I contacted "DNI Pre Pub." I learned that the individual who had acknowledged receipt of my manuscript was on medical leave, and "we have no record of your submission." Although disappointed and surprised over this development, my only response was to resubmit that same day. A week later I was informed that the first two chapters had been approved, with one small revision required for each. The email I received the week after that read, "We should have the final four chapters reviewed by COB [close of business] Friday [this e-mail was sent on Monday]. We did send Chapter 3 to CIA as it had some of its equities—and we cannot control how long it will take for its review. But, since we highlighted these sections in Chapter 3, ideally, they will be able to quickly review those sections." I was confident in the outcome; I should not have been.[33]

Because the book was a history of the CIA, I still do not understand why its "equities" only surfaced in chapter 3. I assume that someone at the ODNI who had not been involved with the review previously now was. And that's critical, because my experience and that of others suggests the results are very much dependent on individuals. The individual who wrote me to expect the review of my manuscript within a week had no control over the individual or individuals to whom he or she sent it.

I cannot determine whether my manuscript became the victim of CIA culture or the individual(s) assigned to review it for its PRB. I suspect it was a combination of both. What I do know is that several weeks later I learned that the CIA's PRB was now reviewing the entire manuscript, that "It is not the Agency's practice to communicate a date when the review will be complete," and that "our preliminary review has found classified CIA information that will require deletion prior to your being able to publish." The level of my anxiety escalated exponentially. After several futile attempts to reach the CIA's PRB by phone in order to gain insight into the problems, I finally received permission to speak with someone on the board. She told me that she could not explain the issues because doing so would require referring to classified information over an insecure line. Shortly thereafter I received an email reinforcing that point: "too much detail would make the explanation itself classified." Several weeks later I received word from the CIA's PRB that it had completed the review and would communicate its judgments to the DNI.[34]

About a week after that I received an e-mail from the DNI with the outcome. It read in part, "DNI Pre Pub, in coordination with all equity holding Agencies [i.e., the CIA], has completed the review of your manuscript and has found material that is not suitable for public release. . . . Once these offending articles are removed from your manuscript, DNI Pre Pub approves for release. If you would like to re-word any of the offending sections, you are required to re-submit those updates for final review." Attached was a file with scores and scores of blacked-out "offending articles." Although the ODNI's guidance that was in effect at that time required that I receive *in writing* the reasons for why the articles "were not suitable for release," I received not a word of explanation.[35]

Reviewing the files literally made me sick to my stomach. Page after page was bathed in black. Because the offending sections were blacked out, I could receive the text via email without risk of revealing classified information. But because they were blacked out, I had to painstakingly compare those pages with my originals in order to identify the redacted words. What I discovered sickened me further. In many cases the problem was my fig leaves. For my sources I had cited countless articles that appeared in major press outlets—the *New York Times, Washington Post,* and so on. Most of this information was common knowledge; some of it had appeared in headlines. I had no idea how the journalists acquired it; the bulk of journalism covered events that took place before I entered government service or after I had left. I knew no more than any other newspaper reader.

But the government's position is that any information that reaches the public through an unauthorized channel, no matter how widespread its circulation, remains classified. If a historian or political scientist cites Mark Mazzetti's article in the *New York Times* about a subject that the government has not officially declassified, for example, or, for that matter, cites the National Security Archive's website, she or he is commended as a scholar. If a government employee who has signed an NDA does the same, even a temporary employee, she or he can be charged with a criminal offense. Not only is she or he disclosing classified information, but according to the government, she or he also is "giv[ing] the information more weight." My position as a senior government official reinforced that premise. Shortly before I published my book Mazzetti published his. He included information identical to what I could not.[36]

At least there was a logic to these redactions of information that I had culled from journalists who had evidently received it through an unauthorized channel (of course, I had no way of knowing that). Other redactions had no logic whatsoever. To illustrate, I mentioned a well-known CIA site. It had been written about widely and featured prominently in major Hollywood films. I was allowed to refer to it by its formal name or nickname but not both. I also had to delete the source I cited about it, an article from a local newspaper. And then there were the many "offensive sections" that included information previously published—by government agencies themselves, including the CIA. Reviewers don't have access to a database of government publications on previously classified information, and they lack both the expertise and time to check carefully. With me they made many mistakes, and I am not alone. What is more, reviewers themselves are not always on the same page. One of my subjects reported an incident when an individual from one branch of an agency identified material as being in the public domain but another from a different branch of the same agency insisted that nevertheless it could not be acknowledged. In the end the author had to excise that material.[37]

I never considered accepting the deletions or abandoning my plans to publish *The Hidden Hand*. I did consider filing a legal action, but the prospect terrified me. I imagined months if not years of further delay. So after seeking advice from both current and former government officials and other scholars, I decided the best response was "simply" to appeal to the ODNI's Information Management Office (IMO) and its Office of General Counsel (OGC). I place "simply" in quotes because the process was arduous. I challenged every required redaction, provided support for every one of my challenges, and pointed out the multiple violations of the prepublication review requirements. Fortunately for me, a change of leadership had occurred at the ODNI's IMO, and I now received more attention—and consideration. The office's new head managed to elicit some explanation from the CIA's PRB, some modification of its demands, and, most important, arrange a face-to-face meeting with the CIA reviewer of my manuscript and one more senior member of its PRB in a "secure" environment (my hotel room). That resulted in more explanations and more modifications. In the end the PRB determined that by recrafting a few sentences, I could restore about 80 percent of the "offending articles." I am confident that with the commitment of more time and effort I could have restored more. But I decided that, albeit still dissatisfied, I could live with what I had "won." Already close to a year had passed since I had submitted the manuscript. About six months later the book finally came out—with conspicuous redactions.

THE WAY AHEAD

That my appeal led to the restoration of so much of the deletions, and did so with remarkable efficiency in light of the time required for the review, underscores how flawed the prepublication review process was. Indeed, that my ordeal lasted months longer than it should have because one individual at the ODNI's IMO required a medical leave of absence and one individual at the CIA's PRB was overworked and insufficiently informed testifies to the vulnerability of the process to a single point of failure. It can and should be improved. The House Permanent Select Committee on Intelligence (HPSCI) acknowledged this need in 2016. Recognizing "the perception that the pre-publication review process can be unfair, untimely, and unduly onerous" and that "the review process must yield timely, reasoned, and impartial decisions that are subject to appeal, HPSCI recommended that "the pre-publication review process should be improved to better incentivize compliance and to deter personnel from violating their commitments." As 2018 drew to a close, the Office of the Director of National Intelligence announced that in response a new policy would be forthcoming. When remains in question, as does what revisions the policy will include. As of this writing, President Trump has yet to nominate a DNI to succeed Dan Coats; whoever that is (should she or he get confirmed) could reverse Coats's decision.[38]

They should be extensive and applicable beyond the intelligence community. Staffing must increase, personnel conducting the reviews should be better informed and have access to the resources they need, and the uncontrolled overclassification of information in the United States must be reformed. This last point is acknowledged by most experts. In the aftermath of the Cold War, Congress established the Public Interest Declassification Board expressly for this purpose, and the PIDB has proposed multiple recommendations to reform the classification process. Both the legislative and executive branches of the federal government must finally summon the political will to implement them.[39] Further, the NDAs should not be lifelong contracts. Someone who has been out of government and therefore without access to classified information for twenty years, to set an arbitrary number, should be exempted from the prepublication review requirement. These are just some of the many suggestions I received from my respondents.

But the fundamental reform must be based on trust. The managers of America's national security must trust that those who have pledged to protect the national security intend to honor that pledge. One can debate whether that holds true for whistleblowers. But the fact of the matter is that there are few whistleblowers. Most government personnel are committed to keeping whatever secrets are entrusted to them. And if they make a mistake, it will be minor and benign. Rather than place obstacle after obstacle in their path to publication, the government should encourage those who serve to write and speak. They will add to the historical record and public understanding, both cornerstones of good citizenship. In the United States, transparency is the ally, not the enemy, of national security. The recognition of that relationship, in and out of Washington, won't eliminate the need for NDAs as a safeguard against the inadvertent disclosure of information that should remain secret. But it will lessen the burden—and discomfort—associated with enforcing them. The United States should not be in the business of controlling information, and it is a testament to its ideals and values that it is not good at it.

NOTES

1. Rebecca H., "The 'Right to Write' in the Information Age: A Look at Prepublication Review Boards," *Studies in Intelligence* 60 (September 2016): 16, https:/www.cia.gov /library/center-for-the-study-of-intelligence/csi-publications/csi-studies/studies/vol -60-no-4/the-right-to-write.html.
2. Classified Information Nondisclosure Agreement (SF-312) (Rev 1-00) [July 2013], https:// fas.org/sgp/isoo/new_sf312.pdf.
3. Michelle Dean, "Contracts of Silence: How the Non-Disclosure Agreement Became a Tool for Powerful People to Stymie Journalists from Informing the Public," *Columbia Journalism Review*, Winter 2018, https://www.cjr.org/special_report/nda-agreement .php/.
4. Although Ellsberg barely gave the NDA he signed in the 1960s a second thought when he provided the *New York Times* journalist Neil Sheehan with the Pentagon Papers he copied in the 1970s, he subsequently likened the "psycho-social" meaning of his secrecy agreement to the "Mafia code of *omertà*." Daniel Ellsberg, "Secrecy and National Security Whistleblowing," *Social Research* 77 (Fall 2010): 780.
5. Dean, "Contracts of Silence."
6. John D. Marks and Victor Marchetti, *The CIA and the Cult of Intelligence* (New York: Knopf, 1974); Philip Agee, *Inside the Company: CIA Diary* (New York: Farrar, Straus & Giroux, 1975); Frank Snepp, *Decent Interval: The American Debacle in Vietnam and the Fall of Saigon* (New York: Random House, 1977); John Stockwell, *In Search of Enemies: A CIA Story* (New York: Norton, 1978). For valuable insight into the legal and constitutional issues inherent in the Snepp case and pertinent to the others as well, see Diane F. Orentlicher, "Snepp v. United States: The CIA Secrecy Agreement and the First Amendment," *Columbia Law Review* 81 (April 1981): 662–706.
7. A notable exception is Ralph McGehee, who in 1983 published *Deadly Deceits: My 25 Years in the CIA* (New York: Sheridan Square, 1983).

8. Reality Winner is the most recent government employee to be prosecuted successfully under the Espionage Act for disclosing classified information. Although some label her as a whistleblower, she has not self-identified as such, and her motives remain obscure.

9. At my security briefing upon entering on duty at the Office of the Director of National Intelligence (ODNI), I asked whether I should submit a manuscript of a forthcoming article that I had written months before for review. At that time the CIA's PRB was responsible for reviewing ODNI manuscripts. The response was yes, which, it turns out fortunately, I did. The article, which received attention in the press and generated controversy in the intelligence community, was cleared without a single comment. The fallout, at least for me personally, would almost certainly have been more severe had the article not been cleared. Author's email correspondence with the ODNI's Information Management Office (IMO), September 5 and September 10, 2007.

10. John Hollister Hedley, "Secrets, Free Speech, and Fig Leaves: Reviewing the Work of CIA Authors," *Studies in Intelligence*, Spring 1998, https://www.cia.gov/library/center-for -the-study-of-intelligence/csi-publications/csi-studies/studies/spring98/Secret.html; John Prados, *The Family Jewels: The CIA, Secrecy, and Presidential Power* (Austin: University of Texas Press, 2013), 256–58; CIA News and Information, "Helping Safeguard our Nation's Secrets—The Publication Review Board [Interview with the PRB chair]," 2014, https://www.cia.gov/news-information/featured-story-archive/2014-featured-story -archive/helping-safeguard-our-nations-secrets-the-publication-review-board.html; Rebecca H., "The 'Right to Write' in the Information Age," 17; and Jack Goldsmith and Oona Hathaway, "The Government's Prepublication Review Process Is Broken," *Washington Post*, December 25, 2015.

11. Spencer Ackerman, "The CIA Cleared Her Book Twice. Then It Took It Back. Why? It's a Secret," *Daily Beast*, May 1, 2018, https://www.thedailybeast.com/the-cia-cleared -her-book-twice-then-it-took-it-back-why-its-a-secret.

12. Nada Bakos and John Nixon, "The CIA Is Delaying Our Books' Publication, and That Hurts Our Democracy," *Washington Post*, December 22, 2016.

13. Charlie Savage, "Ex-National Security Officials Sue to Limit Censorship of Their Books," *New York Times*, April 2, 2019, https://www.nytimes.com/2019/04/02/us/politics /prepublication-censorship-system.html; Deanne Paul, "These Former Officers Say the CIA and NSA Are Censoring Them. Now They're Suing," *Washington Post*, April 2, 1019, https://www.washingtonpost.com/nation/2019/04/02/these-former-agents-say-cia -nsa-are-censoring-them-now-theyre-suing/. The text of the complaint is available at https://int.nyt.com/data/documenthelper/727-edgar-v-coats-d-md-no-19-cv-98 /ba6f2a420dae17154f55/optimized/full.pdf.

14. Prados, *Family Jewels*, 262–63.

15. Because some of my sources are current government employees and most if not all are likely to submit future manuscripts and other texts to their appropriate agencies for prepublication review, they will remain anonymous, identified only by a letter (for example, "Subject A"). If the subject communicated with me in writing or completed a questionnaire, I retain copies. As a former assistant deputy director of national security

and current chair of a State Department advisory committee, I have signed two nondisclosure agreements and submitted multiple manuscripts for prepublication review. The most serious difficulty I encountered concerned my book, *The Hidden Hand: A Brief History of the CIA* (Boston: Wiley-Blackwell, 2014).

16. Jack Goldsmith, "A Request for Intelligence Community Employees with Bad Prepublication Review Experiences," *Lawfare*, September 5, 2018, https://www.lawfareblog.com /request-intelligence-community-employees-bad-prepublication-review-experiences.

17. Subjects D, L, and R.

18. Subjects B, C, F, and V. I interviewed several State Department employees collectively. All stressed how informal was their initial exposure to prepublication review and agreed that over the past several years the process from beginning to end has become more rigorous.

19. I base this paragraph on my two briefings I received on prepublication review, but it is consistent with the reports of those who shared their experiences with me and published accounts.

20. Yaniv Barzilai, "Publishing in the Foreign Service," *Foreign Service Journal*, June 2014, http://www.afsa.org/publishing-foreign-service; Subjects I and T.

21. Rebecca H., "The 'Right to Write' in the Information Age"; Office of the Director of National Intelligence Instruction 80.04, "ODNI Pre-Publication of Review of Information to Be Publicly Released, April 8, 2014, https://fas.org/irp/dni/prepub.pdf.

22. U.S. Department of State Bureau of Public Affairs, 3 FAM 4170, "Review of Public Speaking, Teaching, Writing, and Media Engagement," March 27, 2017, https://fam.state .gov/fam/03fam/03fam4170.html; Office of Information Programs and Services, Global Information Services, Bureau of Public Affairs, "Manuscript Clearance Procedures for Retirees," October 11, https://www.afsa.org/sites/default/files/Portals/0/man_clear _proc_ret.pdf. I have in my possession a copy of the January 2018 slight revision of this guidance, which is not available online.

23. U.S. Department of Defense, Defense Office of Prepublication and Security Review Brochure, https://www.esd.whs.mil/Portals/54/Documents/DOPSR/Docs/DOPSR%20 BROCHURE.PDF?ver=2017-07-05-142406-460; U.S. Department of Defense, Executive Services Directorate, Defense Office of Prepublication and Security Review, http:// www.esd.whs.mil/DOPSR/; Defense Intelligence Agency, DIAI 5400.300, "Prepublication of Review of Information to Be Publicly Released," August 18, 2006, http://www .dia.mil/FOIA/FOIA-Electronic-Reading-Room/FileId/39658/; National Security Agency/National Security Service NSA/CSS Policy 1-30, January 9, 2012, https://fas.org /irp/nsa/prepub-2012.pdf; Thomas Reed Willemain, "A Personal Tale of Prepublication Review," *Lawfare*, January 10, 2017, https://www.lawfareblog.com/personal-tale -prepublication-review; U.S. Department of Defense Inspector General, Report No. DODIG-2016-101, "Review of the Policies for Prepublication Review of DoD Classified or Sensitive Information to Ensure No DoD Sensitive or Classified Information Is Released to the Media," June 17, 2016, https://media.defense.gov/2016/Jun/17/2001714248

/-1/-1/1/DODIG-2016-101.pdf; and US Army War College, CBks Regulation No. 360.1, "Public Release of Information and Engagement," April 26, 2017 (author's possession).

24. Subject M.

25. Subjects B, D, J, L, R, and N. I submitted my chapter for this volume to PPR on a Friday. It was acknowledged the following Monday and cleared for publication a week later.

26. Subjects J and M; Willemain, "A Personal Tale of Prepublication Review"; Barzilai, "Publishing in the Foreign Service"; Bakos and Nixon, "The CIA Is Delaying Our Books' Publication"; Ackerman, "The CIA Cleared Her Book Twice." Bakos wrote in 2016 that the PRB had delayed publication of her book for fourteen months. It was finally published in June 2019. Nada Bakos, *The Targeter: My Life in the CIA, on the Hunt for the Godfather of ISIS* (New York: Little Brown, 2019). On the ordeal Amaryliss Fox is undergoing in effort to publish her *Life Undercover: Coming of Age in the CIA*, see Mary Louise Kelly, "A Look Inside the CIA That the Agency Isn't Ready for You to See," *Washington Post*, September 11, 2019.

27. Subject O; Rebecca H., "The Right to Write."

28. U.S. Department of Justice press release, "United States Files Civil Lawsuit Against Edward Snowden for Publishing a Book in Violation of CIA and NSA Non-Disclosure Agreements," September 17, 2019.

29. Hedley, "Secrets, Free Speech, and Fig Leaves"; Subject R.

30. Subject D; Jack Goldsmith and Oona Hathaway, "More Problems with Prepublication Review," *Lawfare*, December 28, 2015, https://www.lawfareblog.com/more-problems-prepublication-review.

31. David E. Pozen, "The Mosaic Theory, National Security, and the Freedom of Information Act," *Yale Law Journal*, December 2005, https://www.yalelawjournal.org/note/the-mosaic-theory-national-security-and-the-freedom-of-information-act; About CIA, "Keeping Secrets Safe: The Publications Review Board," February 2, 2017, https://www.cia.gov/about-cia/publications-review-board.

32. Author's e-mail correspondence with the ODNI's IMO, September 10, 2007; February 5, 2009; February 9, 2009; February 12, 2009; July 13, 2009; January 25, 2013.

33. Author's e-mail correspondence with the ODNI's IMO, January 28, 2013; April 16, 2013; April 22, 2013; April 29, 2013.

34. Author's e-mail correspondence with the ODNI's IMO and the CIA's PRB, May 7, 2013; May 14, 2013, June 14, 2013, July 3, 2013.

35. Author's e-mail correspondence with the ODNI's IMO and the CIA's PRB, July 12, 2013; Office of the Director of National Intelligence Instruction No. 2007-6, "ODNI Prepublication of Review of Information to Be Publicly Released," April 8, 2014, July 25, 2007, https://fas.org/irp/dni/prepub-2007.pdf.

36. Hedley, "Secrets, Free Speech, and Fig Leaves"; Mark Mazzetti, *The Way of the Knife: The CIA, a Secret Army, and a War at the Ends of the Earth* (New York: Penguin, 2013). When I ultimately met with PRB personnel to plead my case, I learned explicitly that my position as an ADDNI had affected decisions about what to exclude from my manuscript.

37. Willemain, "A Personal Tale of Prepublication Review"; Rebecca H., "The 'Right to Write' in the Information Age"; Subject D. About a quarter of my respondents reported that review boards had insisted on deleting material that has been made public in government publications.

38. Steven Aftergood, "New Pre-Publication Review Policy Is Coming," Federation of American Scientists' *Secrecy News*, December 12, 2018, https://fas.org/blogs/secrecy/2018/12/ic-pre-pub-review/.

39. See, for example, "Transforming the Security Classification System, Report to the President by the Public Interest Declassification Board," November 2012, https://www.archives.gov/declassification/pidb/recommendations/transforming-classification.html.

8

THE PUBLIC SPHERE HERO

Representations of Whistleblowing in U.S. Culture

TIMOTHY MELLEY

W HEN DID IT become *heroic* to publish secrets? When, more exactly, did popular narrative begin to celebrate the subversive disclosure and dissemination of institutional secrets?

In the United States, the answer seems to be in the mid-1970s, when modern whistleblowing emerged as a potent countermeasure to the deceptions of the national security state and corporate public relations practices. In the wake of shocking revelations over CIA programs, official lies about the Vietnam War, and the Watergate affair, popular narrative began to represent the leaking of official secrets as selfless national service rather than treason. It also increasingly featured the publication of secrets as a dramatic denouement that rescues an ailing democracy. Since then, heroic disclosure has become increasingly central to popular narrative, both fictional and nonfictional. Many protagonists of the post-Nixon cultural imaginary are investigative journalists and virtuous insiders—spies, politicians, detectives, soldiers, and bureaucrats—who risk career and personal safety to shine light into the swamp of corporate and state corruption.

The roots of this trend lie in Nixon-era exposé journalism and whistleblowing by figures like the RAND analyst Daniel Ellsberg, FBI Deputy Director Mark ("Deep Throat") Felt, and former CIA operatives Victor Marchetti and Philip Agee. Entering public discourse through reporting and memoir, many of these cases were later dramatized in a surprisingly consistent form that I call the "public sphere hero narrative." This narrative suggests, first, that the public sphere has become a deceptive and comforting spectacle masking the brutal exercise of sovereign power and, second, that the fate of democracy hinges on the dramatic revelation of hermetic *arcana imperii*. The public sphere hero narrative usually pairs an institutional "insider" with a journalist, lawyer, politician, or publisher able to authenticate and disseminate organizational secrets. Its more specific tropes, which I will explain in detail later, run through a large body of memoir, journalism, and fiction, but they are probably best recognized in popular films such as *Serpico* (1973), *Three Days of the Condor* (1975), *All the President's Men* (1976), *The China Syndrome* (1979), *The Prince of the City* (1981), *Hopscotch* (1980), *Absence of Malice* (1982), *Silkwood* (1983), *The Package* (1989), *The Firm* (1993), *A Few Good Men* (1993), *The Pelican Brief* (1993), *The Insider* (1999), *Erin Brockovich* (2000), *Syriana* (2005), *North Country* (2005), *Good Night and Good Luck* (2005), *The Constant Gardner* (2005), *Michael Clayton* (2007), *Frost/Nixon* (2008), *State of Play* (2009), *The Informant!* (2009), *Fair Game* (2010), *The Green Zone* (2010), *The Whistleblower* (2011), *The Newsroom* (2012–2014), *We Sell Secrets* (2013), *Safe House* (2012), *Citizenfour* (2014), *Concussion* (2015), *Spotlight* (2015), *Miss Sloane* (2016), *Snowden* (2016), *Mark W. Felt: The Man Who Brought Down the White House* (2017), and *The Post* (2017), among many others.

In the pages that follow, I trace the growth of this narrative from prominent cases of whistleblowing in the 1970s into an increasingly salient aspect of U.S. political culture. Public sphere heroism, I argue, is now essential to the idea of American citizenship in an age of anxiety and confusion about the relations of secrecy and transparency to contemporary democracy. In advancing this claim, I want to emphasize that I am concerned with a *cultural* narrative, a set of tropes and conventions circulating through many texts, genres, and productions, often in different configurations and with implications that exceed the politics of individual texts. My aim is not a comprehensive history of this form but an account of its influence on democracy and political agency. These effects are complex. On the one hand, the public sphere hero narrative has fostered a growing admiration

THE PUBLIC SPHERE HERO

for whistleblowing. By renarrativizing it as heroic public service rather than treason, it has not simply made acts of resistance more attractive but has also provided a social script for others who wish to come forward. More than simply the "reflection" of real acts, in other words, it has been an essential force in the growth of whistleblowing as a social phenomenon. As I will suggest at the conclusion of this essay, for instance, Edward Snowden seems to have been influenced by the fictions of public sphere heroism.

On the other hand, the public sphere hero narrative has encouraged the political fantasy that sovereign power can be halted by the simple "hand-off" of hermetic secrets to the public. In the melodramatic precincts of this narrative, secrets rule the world, and they speak for themselves. The dysfunction in democracy is caused not by ideology—the collective disavowal of undemocratic practices—but by public unknowing. If we only *knew*, the public sphere hero narrative suggests, then all would be well. The problem with this proposition, of course, is that the post-Watergate public *does* know about clandestine agencies, covert action, corporate public relations strategies, and political influence schemes—if not the operational details, then the general logic of institutional secrecy and plausible deniability. These things are not secret; they are *public secrets*, the objects of intense public fascination, discussion, and fantasy. They have entered public discourse not only through whistleblowing, leaks, and investigations but through incessant representation in television serials, novels, comics, electronic games, and films.[1] The narrative of public sphere heroism is essential to this system of representation. Endlessly depicting shocking institutional malfeasance, it nonetheless suggests that what democracy needs most is not collective action or structural reform but just one more dramatic disclosure.

THE GENEALOGY OF REVELATION

The association of *heroism* with disclosure is a notable departure from tradition. To be sure, heroes have always doggedly pursued truth and fought corruption, and there is certainly nothing new about heroic sacrifice for the public good.[2] But heroism is a masculinist construct that has tended to idealize reserve rather than disclosure. The traditional heroes of Western culture suffer the slings and arrows of outrageous fortune with a minimum of whining and yakking. They zip it not only because modesty is a masculine virtue but because heroic honor rests on a moral code in which "one's word is one's bond" and "actions speak louder than words." (Hamlet is not much of a hero until he puts a sock in the suicidal dithering and starts killing people.) Within this paradigm, actions, not words, are what change the world, and heroes are both "people of action" and "people of few words" (among them, often, "I'm no hero"). The conventional opposition between words and action is what distinguishes the "strong and silent" hero from more voluble figures like the poet and the politician. Telling the hero's story is the worry of the poet (or, nowadays, the journalist). Protagonists who tell their own tales or seek to manipulate public opinion are traditionally seen as politicians, a more calculating type who is traditionally less a hero than a traitor, a dissembler, a villain.[3]

The "public sphere heroism" of the past half-century is thus a significant social development. It is the symptom of a society worried about institutional secrecy. It is no accident that the public sphere hero narrative emerged in the 1970s and resurged again during the U.S. "Global War on Terror," periods of intense public concern about state secrecy. Cracks in the system of plausible deniability had appeared earlier in the Cold War—most notably in Eisenhower's public lie about U-2 flights over the USSR, Kennedy's Bay of Pigs fiasco, and the assassinations of the 1960s—but the period between the publication of the Pentagon Papers in 1971 and the Church Committee hearings in 1975 was a high-water mark in more than a decade of rising skepticism about the activities of a massive U.S. national security state. As the public began to grasp the scale and power of the new "invisible government," the cultural understanding of "informing" shifted, recognizing the possibility of an ethically motivated disclosure distinct from espionage and treason. Inside information—leaked by former Cold Warriors like Ellsberg, Felt, Marchetti, and Agee and framed in the aggressive reporting of John Marks, Seymour Hersh, Christopher Pyle, Neil Sheehan, Bob Woodward and Carl Bernstein, and others—helped bring down a president, reveal what *Time* magazine in 1971 called "the secret war" in Southeast Asia, and expose CIA programs of assassination, regime change, and domestic political interference.[4]

Of course, the McCarthy era had also been a period of extraordinary concern over institutional secrecy, and it too had a script for ideological conversion and public confession. In his 1952 memoir *Witness*, the preeminent American Cold War informer Whittaker Chambers fashioned himself not only as a converted ex-communist but also as a "confessor" of sorts to the many former colleagues who had divulged their communist sins in his office. But unlike the whistleblowing of the Vietnam era, such public testimony supported, rather than undermined, state power. McCarthy-era informing was in fact state sponsored, encouraged by high-profile "atom spy" trials, official allegations of communist conspiracy, and an elaborate congressional apparatus for the extraction of public confessions. Likewise, the major McCarthy-era dramas of informing—*On the Waterfront* (1954) and *The Harder They Fall* (1956), themselves products of the infamous Hollywood informant Budd Schulberg—were about working stiffs ratting out illegal union and sports-betting schemes.[5] These "insiders" renounced underworld codes of silence to become *agents of the state*.

Nixon-era whistleblowing was, by contrast, subversive and illegal. It attacked the Cold War state. In so doing it not only revealed scandalous institutional secrets but also the massive new system of state secrecy and the lengths to which the state would go to shield undemocratic activity from public view. As Kaeten Mistry and Sam Lebovic suggest in this volume, whistleblowing only became a recognizable form of activism in the context of this byzantine system of laws, Cold War–era "classification" protocols, and regulatory bureaucracies. Unlike many Western nations, which have mechanisms for censoring the public press, the United States approached the problem of state secrecy by sanctioning individuals under the 1917 Espionage Act, the classification apparatus, and the increasing use of nondisclosure agreements (NDAs). This emphasis on the punishment of individuals, rather than institutions, helped whistleblowing become culturally legible as a *privileged* form of leaking—politically charged and controversial but widely understood to be motivated by an ethical commitment to the public good rather than a desire for wealth, fame, revenge, or something darker.

The structure of U.S. law gave a biographical character to public debates over secrecy. It conferred a rare celebrity on midlevel bureaucrats, allowing them to tell the public why they felt compelled to break secrecy laws under threat of severe government sanction and at such significant personal cost. As their stories moved through cycles of reporting, memoir, and popular dramatic entertainment, they were increasingly grafted onto long-standing American models of heroic individual agency as an antidote to social influence, and their stories were often melodramatized through familiar heroic types—the martyr, the renegade, the penitent, the good soldier. Over the past fifty years, major Hollywood motion pictures have celebrated the leaks of former intelligence officials (Ellsberg, W. Mark Felt, Edward Snowden, Chelsea Manning), corporate watchdogs (Karen Silkwood, Jeffrey Wigand, Erin Brockovich, Mark Whitacre), and a wide array of other insiders (Frank Serpico, Robert Leuci, Valerie Plame, Robert Baer, Kathryn Bolkovac).[6]

Blockbuster biopics about these figures are the bread and butter of the public sphere hero narrative, but they are hardly its only source or exemplars. The tropes of public sphere heroism also developed from memoirs and novels of espionage, and they fed a burgeoning postwar culture of conspiracy in which celebrated American writers embraced "creative paranoia" as a reasonable form of suspicion about state and corporate power.[7] As Richard Hofstadter observed in 1964, the "paranoid style in American politics" involves a fascination with the figure of the renegade, "the man or woman who has been in the secret world of the enemy, and brings forth with him or her the final verification of suspicions which might otherwise have been doubted by a skeptical world."[8] There is, in other words, an internal connection between the whistleblower and the "conspiracy theorist"—the self-appointed (and potentially paranoid) hero eager to warn the public of secret plots. The desire to expose corruption to a sleepy public is now a central theme in a cultural imaginary organized around the erotics of revelation. It would be one thing if this obsession were confined to Hollywood melodrama or tabloid news, but even the mainstream news teems with reports of corporate scandal, covert operations, disinformation campaigns, and hacked documents. Media outlets vie to deploy the Pulitzer-scented rhetoric of exposé to the next "Travelgate," "Nannygate," "Pizzagate," or "Gamergate." From the drama of public hearings (Iran-Contra, Clarence Thomas, the Clinton-Lewinsky affair, Big Tobacco, Benghazi, Enron, AIG, NSA warrantless surveillance) to the daily drumbeat of moral turpitude by priests, politicians, and corporate chieftains, American public life is mired in what Mark Danner calls "frozen scandal."[9] In this regime, politics is organized around the hermeneutics of suspicion, and the fate of democracy seems to hang on the revelation of secret malfeasance by self-appointed guardians of the public sphere: amateur historians, bloggers, and social media warriors. Even the president of the United States now participates in this national fantasy-work, regularly alleging nefarious plots—election tampering, fabricated news, and rogue "deep state" conspiracy—that, not coincidentally, are important features of the major political dramas of the day: *Scandal*, *Mr. Robot*, *House of Cards*, and others.

THE MAKING OF HEROES

What are the conventions of the public sphere hero narrative?

First and foremost, it is a story of conversion. It dramatizes the transformation of a committed organizational insider into a reluctant rebel and public advocate. The organization has many antagonists on the outside—journalists, politicians, watchdogs, even spies—but the *insider* is a good soldier wholly committed to its mission. Only later is she or he scandalized and transformed from naïveté, or jaded apathy, into heroic resistance. This conversion is crucial in establishing the authenticity of the insider's evidence or testimony. While outsiders can be dismissed as partisan and uninformed, the insider knows the organization and often believes deeply in its mission. The heroic insider is not a grandstander but a conflicted servant struggling to do the right thing. In his famous letter exposing the My Lai massacre, for example, Ron Ridenhour agonizes over the problem of publicity: "I have considered sending this to newspapers, magazines and broadcasting companies, but I somehow feel that investigation and action by the Congress of the United States is the appropriate procedure, and as a conscientious citizen I have no desire to further besmirch the image of the American serviceman in the eyes of the world."[10]

But of course, whistleblowers do ultimately need newspapers, magazines, and broadcasting companies, and this is why, second, the public sphere hero narrative is a tale of *publication*. It almost always pairs the insider with a journalist, lawyer, or publisher. Like the concept of whistleblowing, the public sphere hero narrative conflates the activities of leaking and publishing, informing and reporting, disclosing and disseminating. In some cases, such as *All the President's Men*, *The Insider*, and *The Post*, the narrative virtually erases the whistleblower, concentrating instead on the heroic aspects of exposé journalism. Even in such cases, however, it tends to minimize the work of writing—of sorting, framing, explaining, and contextualizing raw evidence or data. In the public sphere hero narrative, *revelation itself* is transformative. The most important convention of the form is the dramatic handoff or data dump, followed by a triumphant explosion of breaking news. In this soaring and decisive moment, the machinery of publicity takes center stage, and the public is visibly jolted by shocking revelations. Newspapers shoot through giant platens in uncut streams; they rifle through massive sorters and rise in spectacular columns. Delivery trucks trundle from the bowels of printing facilities like columns of tanks into the predawn dark. Stacks of papers thud to the pavement at newsstands. Delivery boys hurl them onto the stoops of middle-class houses. High-profile meetings halt as the cell phones of important people ring in unison. On televisions, computers, and jumbotrons around the world, a flood of alerts interrupts regular programming to signal a dramatic transformation of public consciousness.

Third, the narrative prepares its audience for this transformation by explicitly invoking public sphere theory. One or more characters diagnose the dysfunction of democracy as a lack of transparency and assert the value of a critical press. This statement is often delivered as a didactic speech at the dramatic crux of the narrative and highlighted with the filmmaker's full arsenal of visual and sonic weapons. The defense of transparency is often given in public testimony (*Ms. Sloane*, *The Whistleblower*, *The Insider*), and

FIGURE 8.1

In Steven Spielberg's *The Post* (2017), the thud of newspapers outside
U.S. government buildings visualizes the exposure of the Pentagon
Papers as the triumphant restoration of democracy.

it is often juxtaposed with footage of official lying or misdirection. Both
Snowden and *Citizenfour*, for instance, show General James Clapper,
director of national intelligence, testifying falsely to Senator Ron Wyden
on March 12, 2013, that the NSA does not ("willingly") collect metadata on
American citizens. *The Whistleblower* shows a UN official denying the
human sex trafficking in Bosnia. *The Informant* reprises C-Span video of
lying tobacco officials.

Finally, the public sphere hero narrative is, paradoxically, both melodramatic and veridical. The moral struggle of the whistleblower and the individual struggle of the journalist/advocate merge in a high-stakes battle to
bring critical information into public view. Time is short, the organization's
misdeeds are dramatic in size and scale, and the consequences of their exposure are extraordinary. At stake is an entire industry (*The Insider, State of
Play, Northland*), an institution (*Spotlight, The Firm*), or the complete archive
of state secrets (*Hopscotch, Snowden, Mission Impossible!, Atomic Blonde, Safe*

House). In the hero's possession these secrets have the power to reorganize society. This is a melodramatic formula best suited to the conspiracy thriller, but the public sphere hero narrative also appeals aggressively to its own veridicality. It is often marketed as a "true story," and it often contains news footage, testimony, archival material, or fictional footage featuring real news anchors. The narrative positions itself as a powerful political statement capable of revealing real secrets and making a real political intervention. It is part of a melodramatic mode in American politics.

The whirlwind hagiography of Edward Snowden illustrates how public sphere hero narratives emerge and circulate. The initial public reaction to Snowden's leak of NSA documents to the filmmaker Laura Poitras and *Guardian* journalists Glenn Greenwald and Ewen MacAskill was mixed. Greenwald's initial June 2013 *Guardian* articles elicited waves of both condemnation and praise for Snowden from experts and the public.[11] Although the *Guardian* called Snowden a whistleblower, *Time*'s June 24, 2013, issue featured him, Bradley Manning, and Aaron Swartz as "The Informers," a "New Generation of Hacktivists . . . Driven to Spill the Government's Secrets." This portrait differed notably from *Time*'s December 30, 2002, "Persons of the Year" cover, which featured Cynthia Cooper of Worldcom, Coleen Rowley of the FBI, and Sherron Watkins of Enron as "The Whistleblowers." Lighted from above, wearing smart business attire, and standing back to back with arms crossed, "the whistleblowers" are presented as nononsense, self-sacrificing civil servants. "The Informers," by contrast, are a trio of bad boys whose disembodied heads float atop redacted lines of computer code, all in grayscale. This far more ambivalent presentation suggests both a mysterious allure and a vague threat. The term "informers" has a disquieting Cold War residue that captures public uncertainty about the nature of electronic surveillance after a decade of "War on Terror."

Laura Poitras's brilliant 2014 documentary *Citizenfour* intervened dramatically in the formation of Snowden as a public sphere hero. The film squarely places Snowden in the tradition of national security whistleblowing, framing his act as a brave and exceedingly thoughtful personal sacrifice to protect modern democracy. *Citizenfour* is not a full-blown public sphere hero narrative, as I have sketched it. (The melodrama of Snowden's conversion would be supplied in 2016 by Oliver Stone.) Yet it is notable how many conventions of the public sphere hero narrative inform *Citizenfour.* Poitras creates a chilling urgency about her plan to meet the mysterious "citizenfour." Over images of a gargantuan NSA data-collection site under construction in Bluffdale, Utah, Poitras reads Snowden's offer to provide proof of a vast program of NSA surveillance authorized by the secret "Presidential Policy Directive 20." Already fluent in the language of self-sacrifice, Snowden adds, "I already know how this will end for me. . . . I ask only that you ensure this information makes it home to the American public." Using archival courtroom and congressional footage, Poitras then painstakingly lays out the history of legal and legislative inquiries into NSA surveillance activity after 9/11. She also incorporates interviews and footage of public activism by privacy advocates, including the "legendary NSA crypto-mathematician" and whistleblower William Binney, who joined other high-ranking colleagues—Thomas Drake, J. Kirk Wiebe, and Edward Loomis—to raise questions about NSA data mining.[12]

With this framework in place, *Citizenfour* moves to the Mira Hotel in Hong Kong, where Greenwald and Poitras meet Snowden for a series of interviews. Poitras punctuates Snowden's calm, technically brilliant, and philosophically astute commentary with the central convention of the public sphere hero narrative: the drama of publicity itself. As soon as the first interview is over, the screen goes dark, and a deep voice intones, "This is *CNN Breaking News.*" Wolf Blitzer appears, gravely announcing "an explosive new report." This story gives way to others from CNN, ABC, and BBC, the primary content of which is the discussion of public sphere theory. We see footage from the *Guardian* newsroom, a montage of newspaper headlines, and charged hearings from the German and European parliaments. Eventually, Poitras captures the essence of public sphere heroism in a single striking juxtaposition. Snowden sits on his hotel bed, calmly watching television pundits debate his action; meanwhile, literally outside the room where he is hiding, a giant projection of Snowden's face towers surreally over pedestrians on the HK Jumbotron.

If Poitras allowed the public to understand Snowden's act as a technically and philosophically sophisticated act of courage, then Oliver Stone's

FIGURE 8.2

Borrowing heavily from Laura Poitras's *Citizenfour* (2014), Oliver Stone's *Snowden* (2016) compiles archival footage of "breaking news" to signal the global effect of Snowden's stunning revelations.

Snowden (2016) offered a thoroughly melodramatized version of the public sphere hero narrative. Stone borrows substantially from *Citizenfour*, overlaying a fictionalized version of Poitras's film with a second narrative strand about Snowden's ideological conversion from committed patriot to radical activist. Stone's Snowden is a wide-eyed conservative who enlists in the Marines and the CIA after 9/11. A brilliant mathematician and programmer, he rises swiftly but is increasingly disturbed by clandestine recruitment methods, drone strikes, and surveillance technologies. A turning point comes when he discovers that his invention, a data "backup system," is being used to intensify drone strikes. What ultimately drives him to action, however, is NSA Director Clapper's bald-faced lies about this program in congressional testimony. Stone stages this moment in a dimly lit NSA operations room, where Snowden and his comrades watch a television monitor, aghast as Clapper denies the existence of the surveillance systems at work all around them.

The second strand of *Snowden* repurposes Poitras's Mira Hotel scenes. Like the courtroom portion of Stone's *JFK*, this part of *Snowden* is an embedded "essay" of sorts in which Snowden explains the theory of democracy and the threat posed by warrantless surveillance. Like Poitras, Stone makes whistleblowing a central theme, hammering home the notion that even questioning state methods will result in severe punishment. In *Snowden*, NSA employees express alarm about the conviction of John Kiriakou, the career CIA officer sentenced to prison for exposing CIA torture after 9/11. Stone also includes a character named Hank Forrester (Nicholas Cage), a sort of fictional stand-in for the NSA whistleblower William Binney, who is so crucial to Poitras's film. Forrester is a technical genius who once voiced constitutional concerns to the NSA leadership and was swiftly demoted to curator of the agency's basement museum of spy gadgets.[13] Stone's script has Forrester mentoring Snowden in order to highlight the stakes of Snowden's sacrifice and set the stage for the final montage of breaking news that will signal the effect of that sacrifice.

SECRET SHARERS

At first glance, the representation of whistleblowing, especially in fiction, would seem secondary to the matter of whistleblowing itself. If narratives of whistleblowing merit serious attention, this is because real whistleblowers have had a lasting influence on the popular imagination. But this view is mistaken. Representation is integral, not secondary, to whistleblowing. Whistleblowing can only have political effects through representation, and this representation includes both the description of leaked material and the biographies of whistleblowers.[14] After all, leaks are a dime a dozen. Some are motivated by revenge, narcissism, or greed; others are strategic in nature: acts of espionage or disinformation by hostile institutions or even ploys of the "exposed" institution itself. Hence, the truth value and political efficacy of a leak rests significantly on the ethos of the leaker, and this ethos rests in turn on the way the leaker's actions are described and narrativized. Leaks that can be authenticated as acts of rebellion by once-committed insiders stand out sharply from the ever-mounting slush pile of rumors and conspiracy theories.

The conflation of leaks with their representation in narrative and image in fact haunts the very concept of whistleblowing. Consider, for instance, the timeline of U.S. whistleblowing curated by the Government Accountability Project (GAP), a nonprofit whistleblowers-advocacy organization. In addition to now-famous cases of military and corporate rebellion from John Paul Vann through John Kiriakou, GAP's timeline includes the muckraking journalism of Julius Chambers and Nellie Bly (who had themselves admitted to New York insane asylums in 1872 and 1887, respectively, and whose articles and books about their experiences led to the release of prisoners and reform of the lunacy laws), the fiction of Upton Sinclair (whose 1906 novel *The Jungle* exposed conditions in Chicago slaughterhouses), and Rachel Carson's *Silent Spring* (1962), a work of long-form journalism on the effects of DDT on animals and humans.[15] None of these cases are whistleblowing in the strict sense—the disclosure of protected information by insiders, for the public good, under threat of significant individual sanction. Carson, Chambers, and Sinclair were all outsiders, not insiders, and none of them disclosed "secrets" in the sense of compartmentalized knowledge secured by force of law. Their main contributions lay in the construction of narrative. Carson collated and explicated disparate and overlooked technical information. *The Jungle* revealed to the reading classes the horrifying daily experience of tens of thousands of meatpackers. This experience was hardly a secret, but it may have seemed like one to those who had never experienced, or read about, factory conditions. What the public perceives as "secret" is thus often ideologically, rather than juridically, repressed. It is "hidden," in other words, less by deliberate censorship or concealment than by collective repression. This repression is a function of the *narratives* that circulate (or do not circulate) in public discourse, and hence the tendency for large classes of human experience to be substantially unrepresented or underrepresented has often been conceptualized as a problem of historical "amnesia," "invisibility," and public secrecy.[16]

This is why exposé narrative is so often conflated with whistleblowing. Both attempt to reveal socially repressed knowledge in order to jog a tranquilized public into action. The public sphere hero narrative reflects this entwinement by emphasizing the role of writers, publishers, lawyers, and other public advocates. Indeed, it often subordinates the contribution of the whistleblower proper to that of the journalist, publisher, or filmmaker. Moreover, the public sphere hero narrative *imitates* whistleblowing in its desire to expose corporate and state corruption to an unaware reading or viewing public. Among the most sophisticated examples of this tendency is Michael Mann's 1999 film *The Insider.* The film is the story of Jeffrey Wigand (Russell Crowe) and his relationship to a gritty *60 Minutes* producer, Lowell Bergman (Al Pacino). As Bergman tells his colleagues at CBS, Wigand is "the ultimate insider . . . the top scientist at the third-largest tobacco company in America." In 1995, after being fired from Brown and Williamson, Wigand takes a consulting job for *60 Minutes.* Alarmed, the corporation begins surveilling him and demands that he sign a more restrictive nondisclosure agreement or lose his severance. Under Bergman's careful guidance, Wigand decides to testify in court that the company had manufactured cigarettes to be more addictive. Later, he sits for a *60 Minutes* interview, accusing Brown and Williamson's CEO, Thomas Sandefur, of perjury and explaining the process of chemical "impact boosting" that make cigarettes a "nicotine delivery device."

Wigand's testimony could be the end of the story, but it is not. After the interview is filmed, Brown and Williamson sue CBS News for "tortious interference." If the court finds in their favor, a CBS lawyer explains, then the truth of Wigand's testimony will not mitigate the damages: "they own the information he's disclosing. The truer it is, the greater the damage." Because the company is being sold, CBS executives kill Wigand's explosive interview. This the film's pivot point: it places Bergman in precisely the position he earlier ascribed to Wigand: "in possession of vital insider stuff that the American people for their welfare really *do* need to know" and told by every member of his organization to suppress it.

Caught in this secondary crisis of public deception, Bergman is remarkably decisive and heroic. He goes to war against CBS, doggedly pursuing the story and refusing to quit when asked. He meets with a *Wall Street Journal* reporter to kill a hatchet piece about Wigand. He calls in favors with FBI agents, cops, and judges, ensuring that bogus judgments against Wigand are reversed. When Mike Wallace bends to the corporate pressure, Bergmann himself becomes a whistleblower, leaking the entire scandal to the *New York Times*, which publishes an op-ed arguing that *60 Minutes* has "disgraced the legacy of Edward R. Murrow." This stinging rebuke brings a repentant Wallace back to his senses, and soon CBS is airing the Wigand interview along with a confession about CBS corporate cowardice.

The Insider is thus a double public sphere hero narrative. Its *real* insider is not Wigand but Bergman. Mann works hard to distinguish Bergman from both Mike Wallace, the morally callow journalist, and Jeffrey Wigand, the vengeful whistleblower.[17] This is why the film opens with Bergman riding blindfolded among Hezbollah gunmen to arrange an interview with a sheik for Mike Wallace and why it ends with Bergman figuring out the location of the Unabomber so he can pressure FBI leaders into letting CBS scoop the story. A supremely competent "fixer" with deep inside knowledge across multiple areas of expertise, Bergman is also the film's public sphere theorist. At one point he tells Wigand, "You go public and thirty million people hear what you got to say? Nothing, I mean nothing, will ever be the same again. That's the power you have." Wigand is unmoved by this fantasy. He shrugs and replies, "You believe that because you get information to people, something happens?"[18] For Bergman—the true public sphere hero—this is not even a question. Bergman is so committed that in the moment of his greatest triumph, lauded by CBS brass and surrounded by monitors displaying breaking news of the Unabomber's arrest, he resigns his job for a position in what Mike Wallace earlier scorned as "the wilderness of NPR."

A key implication of *The Insider* is that representation itself is heroic. Just as the GAP sees Rachel Carson and Upton Sinclair as "whistleblowers," Mann suggests that the exposé journalist can outdo even the whistleblower in changing society. This argument implies the same thing about the heroic public sphere biopic: if the journalistic representation of secrets is heroic public service, then so perhaps is the filmic. Making a film like *The Insider* itself appeals to the fantasy of public sphere heroism. Perhaps this is why journalists and publishers have been so central to public sphere hero biopics from *All the President's Men* to *The Post*. Indeed, the desire to do something *like* whistleblowing in one's film *about* whistleblowing is reflected not only in biography but also in fiction. Consider, for instance, Tony Gilroy's 2007 thriller *Michael Clayton*. The film is about the murder of a corporate whistleblower, Arthur Edens (Tom Wilkinson), a corporate attorney for the Monsanto-like corporation United Northfield. In the course of defending "U-North" against a class-action lawsuit, Edens discovers a secret "internal research memorandum" warning corporate leadership that its farm product, Culcitate, poisons well water, causing "significant human tissue damage." No longer willing to defend the company, Edens threatens to publish the report if the company does not settle the lawsuit. In the film's most arresting scene, he leaves a brilliant and threatening speech on the voicemail of U-North's chief counsel, Karen Crowder (Tilda Swinton). He first makes an audiotape of U-North's slick public relations advertisement, in which lush images of farmland, dewy plants, and playing children are the backdrop over which a soothing baritone intones, "we find the seed, we shape the soil, we speed the harvest, we feed the planet." With this message looping in the background, Edens shouts into the phone: "Let's have a big, paranoid, malignant round of applause for United North Culcitate Internal Research Memorandum #229. . . . Not only is this a great product, it is a superb cancer delivery system." The memo, he adds, mandates that this horrifying knowledge *"must* be kept within the protective confines of United Northfield's trade secret language."

After hearing the message, a shaken Crowder has Edens murdered, and the cause of public advocacy falls to an even more unlikely public sphere hero, Michael Clayton (George Clooney). The firm's legendary "fixer," Clayton has built his entire career on moral compromise. He spends his days ushering rich clients around legal hurdles and helping corporations twist out of legal binds. Crippled by gambling debts and family problems, he desperately needs the patronage of the firm's corrupt managing partners, but he cannot accept Edens's apparent suicide, and when U-North's team blows up his car he is converted into a zealous enemy of the corporation. Presumed dead, he confronts a terrified Crowder with a copy of the memo and a list of her crimes. Secretly wearing a wire for the New York City Police Department, he extracts a five-million-dollar bribe for his silence, then slaps the memo into her hand and says, "You're so fucked."

One of the unstated goals of productions like *Michael Clayton* is to do something much like whistleblowing—that is, to bring to public consciousness corporate misbehavior that is widely presumed but often unproven. The film may be fictional, but it echoes cases in which Monsanto, Dupont, and other multinational conglomerates have concealed the dangers of consumer products. The use of fiction not only allows for a more melodramatic story; it also sidesteps the problem of libel, a legal consideration that has been crucial to national security representations, to which I now turn.

UNQUIET AMERICANS

I have been tracing the development of public sphere heroism from reports of whistleblowing into dramas that aim to shock the public with florid accounts of institutional corruption. I now want to examine a second strand of public sphere heroism as it emerged from espionage memoirs in the 1970s and fed a mushrooming national security imaginary.

Espionage has a paradoxical relation to heroism. It is the epitome of modern heroic agency, especially as fantasied in spy fiction, yet as a real practice it *cannot* be the basis of public heroism, for spies can never reveal their work. This, at least, was the general practice in the United States until 1974, when Victor Marchetti and John Marks published their explosive exposé *The CIA and the Cult of Intelligence*. They were soon joined by other disaffected CIA insiders, most notably Philip Agee, John Stockwell, and Ralph McGehee, whose exposé memoirs excoriated the agency for extortion, disinformation, assassination, and regime change. So radical were these indictments of the CIA's core mission that, as Jeremy Varon notes, the term "whistleblowing" may be inadequate to describe them, because it presumes a basic desire to reform an institution.[19] Marchetti called the CIA a "dangerous secret cult." Stockwell described it as "an experiment in amorality, a real-life fantasy island" with "no rules, no controls, no moral restraints." Agee, believing that he had permanently sabotaged Latin American democracy, attempted to do penance by publishing the names of 250 active CIA agents.[20]

The CIA was damaged not only by the revelations of these accounts but by the public battles that unfolded around them. Marchetti's *CIA and the Cult of Intelligence* was the subject of a brutal censorship fight in which the CIA asserted its right to redact a full quarter of the text. Knopf successfully challenged these cuts in federal court, and the agency was forced to restore the majority of the excised material. Eventually, Knopf published the text with 168 blank spaces, but it also bolded 141 passages that had been stricken by the CIA but later restored by the court. Readers could thus see that most were redacted only to avoid agency embarrassment.[21] In response to this history, the CIA created its Publication Review Board (PRB) in 1976. The creation of the PRB routinized the state's oversight of talkative spies, erecting significant new roadblocks to intelligence memoirs. In 1982 Congress helped, by outlawing the naming of clandestine U.S. officers. Yet these changes hardly suppressed the publication of espionage memoirs. On the contrary, there has been an extraordinary boom in the genre.

How can we explain this paradox? One possibility is that public sphere heroism has made the disclosure of espionage work more intelligible, attractive, and exciting. Consider, for instance, Robert Baer's *See No Evil* (2002), "the true story that suggested [*sic*] the major motion picture *Syriana*" (2005), according to the paperback version's cover. *See No Evil* is both a record of PRB scrutiny and an assertion of public sphere heroism. The text is full of redactions—many absurd in their suppression of widely known information. Baer captures this absurdity, along with his own heroism, in a single bitter anecdote: several years after his retirement, he learned that the CIA had *secretly* awarded him a Career Service Medal for valorous service. He only learned of the award because ex-colleagues leaked the information to him. While Baer bristles at the absurdity of a career recognition kept secret from its very recipient, he is no Edward Snowden, and his book is far less critical of the U.S. security state than Stephen Gaghan's bleak and conspiratorial film *Syriana*. Indeed, Baer writes admiringly of the CIA and explains the value of PRB review. He justifies his memoir as an attempt to enhance post-9/11 CIA effectiveness, motivated by a "growing rage" at leaders who only care to "keep the bad news from the newspapers" (266). His publisher frames the project as whistleblowing; an approving foreword by Seymour Hersh, the dean of American exposé journalism, praises Baer's story as "the stuff of Clancy thrillers" though "the dangers were real" (xiv). Baer, too, casts himself as a modern-day James Bond, promising tales of "places most Americans will never travel to" (xvii), a "cast of characters no novelist could create" (267), and revelations "almost none of which has appeared outside government files" (xvii). In short, like many contemporary espionage memoirs, Baer's "exposé" is strangely conflicted: marketed as nonfiction with all the pleasures of *fiction* and, despite some criticisms of the agency, exceedingly deferential to its mission.

In this regard, *See No Evil* demarcates the challenges of publishing, and marketing, the exposé of intelligence. It also helps explain why, for all the growth in spy memoirs, fiction has ultimately become a more important medium for public sphere hero narratives. For one thing, classification enforcement itself revolves around a simplistic distinction between fiction and nonfiction. As a senior PRB member explains in the CIA's in-house academic journal, the PRB uses "what is colloquially termed 'the James Bond literary genre test.' In short, if the manuscript is deemed to fit in the category of current spy novels, the board applies a more lenient standard to publication approval."[22] This standard has made fiction an increasingly attractive medium for former intelligence officials eager to avoid the difficulty (and embarrassment) of PBR review.[23] Fiction is also often a more coherent form of critique. Lloyd Gardner notes:

> The best historical commentaries on our age are being offered as fictional accounts. I am talking about novelists who have served in the intelligence community at one post or another. I have in mind Edward Wilson, Barry Eisler, Valerie Plame, Bob Graham, and, yes, even Casper Weinberger, Secretary of Defense in the Reagan Administration.[24]

In fact, fiction has from the beginning been essential to the public sphere heroism of espionage agents. Victor Marchetti's indictment of the CIA, for instance, began not with *The CIA and the Cult of Intelligence* but with *The Rope Dancer* (1971), a novel about a "National Intelligence Agency" whose corrupt leaders closely resemble their counterparts in the CIA and whose hero, Paul Franklin, sells secrets to the Soviets. The novel enraged CIA Director Richard Helms, who launched a surveillance operation against Marchetti. A year later, the agency learned that Marchetti had also pitched a nonfiction exposé to New York editors, and the agency obtained court orders quashing publication of the book before any of it had been written.[25]

It was amid this battle and the subsequent public tumult of Watergate and the Church Commission hearings that espionage fiction began to develop the conventions of public sphere heroism. Whereas early Cold War spy fiction tended to end on the smug silence of James Bond or an exhausted acceptance of espionage's dizzying "wilderness of mirrors," espionage films after Watergate began to end in disclosure. The first notable title in this tradition is Sidney Pollack's *Three Days of the Condor* (1975). A loose adaption of James Grady's novel *Six Days of the Condor* (1974), the film introduced what would become the classic denouement: its hero, the CIA analyst Ronald Malcolm (Robert Redford), exposes a CIA conspiracy by delivering a packet of evidence to the front door of the *New York Times*. Crucially, Malcolm only stumbles upon the conspiracy because of his unusual assignment: he analyzes *fiction* for the CIA. It is his discovery that novels are being used to communicate secret information that leads to the assassination of his entire unit. This is precisely the sort of self-aggrandizing premise one might expect of a novelist, but on a figurative level it is true: fiction *can* reveal the logic of state secrecy if one knows how to read it—that is, as a site of public secrets. Indeed, while Grady claims to have invented his novel's premise out of whole cloth (based in part on his reading of Marchetti), the film version alarmed Soviet agents. As Pete Earley reports, the USSR so feared the potential of a U.S. cultural-analysis branch that it built a new two-thousand-person unit to do the sort of cultural analysis described in *Three Days*.[26] Not only had a fiction inspired a real KGB operation, but that operation itself suggested that fiction was a legitimate concern for state intelligence services.

As the case of *The Rope Dancer* suggests, the CIA also takes fiction seriously. While the PRB is permissive of espionage melodrama, other elements of the agency are keenly interested in representations of agency activity.[27] In 2013, CIA leaders invited the cast and producers of the CIA drama

Homeland to a day-long meeting in its secure Langley headquarters. The CIA and Department of Defense gave considerable clandestine support to the makers of the film *Zero Dark Thirty*, which celebrated the risky operation to kill Osama bin Laden. It is no accident that so many notable representations of the national security state are fictionalizations of intelligence reports, memoirs, and journalism. In addition to *Argo* and *Zero Dark Thirty*, the most sophisticated and appreciated films of covert action in recent years—*Syriana*, *The Green Zone*, and *Fair Game*—have loudly proclaimed their nonfiction origins in long-form journalism and CIA memoir.[28] They have also adapted the conventions of public sphere heroism—mourning the lack of transparency that requires a reliance on fiction while at the same time lionizing whistleblowing and journalistic exposure. In *The Green Zone*, for example, Paul Greengrass examines how bad journalism and falsified intelligence leaks helped justify the U.S. invasion of Iraq in 2003.[29] The film purports to be based on Rajiv Chandrasekaran's savage account of U.S. hubris in Iraq, *Imperial Life in the Emerald City*, but it is more about the hoodwinking of the Pulitzer Prize–winning *New York Times* reporter Judith Miller by Ahmad Chalabi, the Iraqi politician who provided U.S. neocons with falsified reports of Iraqi WMD programs.[30] *The Green Zone* adapts this case of disinformation into a story of public sphere heroism. Its protagonist, chief warrant officer Roy Miller (Matt Damon), heads a U.S. Army unit searching for weapons of mass destruction around Baghdad shortly after the U.S. invasion in 2003. After harrowing firefights, Miller's team finds suspected WMD sites empty and long unused. He begins to fear that the intelligence provided to U.S. forces is false. His suspicions are shared by a thirty-year CIA veteran, Martin Brown (Brendan Gleeson), who is viewed as an obstructionist "dinosaur" by the brash young Pentagon Special Intelligence Unit coordinator Clark Poundstone (Greg Kinnear).

Poundstone in some ways resembles L. Paul Bremer, the U.S. head of the Coalition Provisional Authority in Iraq, but he also turns out to be the source of strategic leaks about WMDs in the run-up to the war. He has slipped the *Wall Street Journal* reporter Lawrie Dayne (Amy Ryan) details said to come from a high-level Baathist codenamed "Magellan." But

Poundstone has been lying, and Dayne—a thinly disguised Judith Miller—has published erroneous articles as a result. It is of course Roy Miller who roots out this journalistic failure. "Jesus Christ," he shouts at Dayne, "this is the reason we went to war! How could somebody like you write something that's not true?" Miller has already deduced that "Magellan" is General al-Rawi, the Jack of Clubs in the infamous U.S. deck of "high-value targets," and he correctly suspects that al-Rawi told U.S. authorities that there were no WMDs in Iraq. To prove it, however, he must *literally* battle his own organization, the U.S. Army. Miller launches a rogue nighttime mission to bring in al-Rawi from a safehouse far outside the Green Zone. This plot harnesses the conventions of the thriller to public sphere heroism: what is at stake in this dangerous and traitorous mission is not the capture of a dangerous enemy but rather the production of *evidence* that U.S. officials deceived the American public. When al-Rawi is shot dead at the end of the mission, this goal seems to slip away. But in the public sphere hero narrative, disclosure is only a keyboard away. The film ends with Miller typing a report entitled "Falsification of WMD Intel: The Truth About 'Magellan.'" He sends it to reporters at the *New York Times, Washington Post, Wall Street Journal, Newsweek, Time,* NBC News, Fox News, *60 Minutes,* and others. To the sound of thundering drums and triumphant music, he presses the send button.

Greengrass explains that he imagined *The Green Zone* as an extension of his blockbuster Jason Bourne films. He wanted viewers of *The Green Zone* to "consider whether the mistrust and paranoia that characterized Bourne's world was so far-fetched after all."[31] In other words, the goal of this quasi-historical project was to legitimate spy fiction—to suggest that the paranoid espionage thriller is an appropriate way of conceptualizing contemporary politics. Or to put it somewhat differently, the project was to legitimate what is often called "conspiracy theory" by assimilating it to whistleblowing. If this seems a rather bizarre inversion of the more obvious project—using historicist narrative to represent real events—it nonetheless seems to reflect a world in which real politics seems already infused with the "far-fetched" elements of the conspiracy thriller.

Such fantasies of transformative disclosure are now stock elements of the conspiracy imaginary. The 2012 CIA thriller *Safe House*, for instance, does not seem at first glance to be a film about the public sphere. It is a dark, action-packed espionage tale about a rookie operative charged with guarding "one of the most notorious traitors we've got," a dangerous and brilliant veteran who is trying to sell state secrets to a foreign agent. Both men end up in a CIA safehouse that is attacked by other agents, and for the next twenty-four hours the veteran, Tobin Frost (Denzel Washington), attempts to elude and manipulate the rookie, Matt Westin (Ryan Reynolds). But for all the action, the film is in fact a whistleblowing narrative. After Westin saves Frost from a group of CIA-funded assassins, Frost reveals that, many years earlier, he had participated in the assassination of a CIA whistleblower. His team was told their target was a Bermudan drug dealer but later learned "the whole thing was about stopping him from testifying about wetworks [assassinations] to a congressional hearing."[32]

Frost's decision to sell secrets is a sort of revenge against the agency, but he is too jaded and selfish to be heroic. Like Forrester in *Snowden*, he represents the future Westin must avoid, and the confrontation with him transforms Westin from a naïve and ambitious patriot to a cagy public advocate. At the end of the film, after a brutal gun battle has killed Frost and almost every other agent in the field, Westin finds himself facing Deputy Director Harlan Whitford (Sam Shepherd), who suggests altering his report and destroying any files Tobin may have given him. This is all Westin needs to blow the whistle. Standing in the very lobby of CIA headquarters, he sends Frost's files to news outlets around the world. The film ends in the familiar symphony of breaking news on CNN ("Intelligence Agencies Exposed: Documents Shed Light on International Corruption"), BBC ("Parliament Incriminates MI6 Officials"), and others.

This is what spy fiction looks like when there is not even a vestigial trace of a foreign enemy: the work of the CIA is to reveal the work of the CIA. Dramatic conflict becomes organized around a battle with the repressive apparatus of the security state, and three days of the condor are no longer needed to convert the good agent into whistleblower: three hours will do. In this version of the public sphere hero narrative, deep secrecy, not ideology, is still the primary ill of democracy, and disclosure is still the antidote. We need only await the next transformative revelation—even if we already know its sordid contents.

Such fantasies may seem trivial. After all, public sphere heroism is only the stuff of popular melodrama. What possible effect could it have on the real workings of democracy?

Consider, as a final example, the few personal objects that Edward Snowden brought with him to the Mira Hotel in Hong Kong: a Rubik's cube, a multifunction knife, and a young-adult novel. The novel, which Poitras captures amid Snowden's computer peripherals, is Cory Doctorow's *Homeland* (2013).[33] It is the sequel to Doctorow's popular hacktivist thriller *Little Brother* (2008), in which a seventeen-year-old Marcus Yallow singlehandedly exposes the unconstitutional excesses of a runaway Homeland Security Department. *Homeland* finds Marcus in a similar pickle. His onetime rival, Masha, has given him a million secret documents revealing corporate and state corruption. The material is a safeguard; if she goes missing, he is to release it to the press—and shortly after the book opens, Masha is kidnapped. But Marcus is also working for a reformist candidate for the California Senate, a man who can make serious changes for the better. If Marcus releases the scandalous material, he will torpedo his boss's campaign by associating it with illegal hacking.

"*Homeland*," its dust jacket declares, is a "fast-paced, passionate . . . paean to activism, to courage, to the drive to make the world a better place." This advertisement captures the essence of public sphere heroism, the cultural fantasy that a daring individual act of exposure will heal a democracy corrupted by state surveillance. In retrospect, it seems a strangely prophetic description of Edward Snowden's daring act of revelation. If there is a lesson here, however, it is not only that political fictions can inspire political action. They can also condition a collective inaction in which the public passively admires a real hero's "courage to make the world a better place"— and then wonders why so little has changed.

NOTES

1. On "public secrecy," see Michael Taussig, *Defacement: Public Secrecy and the Labor of the Negative* (Stanford, CA: Stanford University Press, 1999). For a discussion of this idea in the context of national security leaks, see Timothy Melley, *The Covert Sphere: Secrecy, Fiction, and the National Security State* (Ithaca, NY: Cornell University Press, 2012).

2. There is also nothing new about the public's fascination with *arcana imperii*. As Martin Heidegger explained, the very notion of truth is connected to disclosure, unconcealment, revelation, and that which is evident through the Greek notion of *alethia* (ἀλήθε ι): "The Origin of the Work of Art," in *Poetry-Language-Thought*, trans. Albert Hofstadter (1971; New York: Perennial, 2013), 15–86.

3. These sweeping generalizations about heroism have obvious counterexamples. Roland, for instance, is a voluble braggart. Odysseus and many other heroes are skilled wordsmiths. Yet, as Lida Maxwell notes in her essay in this volume, celebrity often has a paradoxical relation to heroism. Ellsberg needed to embrace celebrity in order to protect his heroic status from smears, yet celebrity threatened that status by replacing the ethos of quiet sacrifice with an obsession with public image. Attempting to manage one's public is traditionally unmasculine and unheroic. A corollary of the masculinized construction of heroism is that leaking is often feminized and associated with excessive volubility, emotional lability, and insufficient emotional reserve. Such associations are a well-documented thread in Cold War stereotypes of the homosexual spy and the femme fatale, for example.

4. David Wise and Thomas B. Ross, *The Invisible Government* (New York: Random House, 1964). By emphasizing the 1970s and early 2000s, I don't mean to suggest that the decades between these lacked notable cases of whistleblowing. As Hannah Gurman demonstrates in her essay in this volume, the thematics of whistleblowing were crucial to the 1980s and the Iran-Contra era.

5. C. P. Trussell, "Schulberg Tells of Red Dictation: Move to Control His Writing Cause Him to Leave Party," *New York Times*, May 24, 1951. On this era, see Ellen Schrecker, *Many Are the Crimes: McCarthyism in America* (Boston: Little, Brown, 1998); and Stephen Whitfield, *The Culture of the Cold War* (Baltimore, MD: Johns Hopkins University Press, 1991).

6. Films about these figures, respectively, are *The Post* (Steven Spielberg, dir; 20th Century Fox, 2017), *All the President's Men* (Alan J. Pakula, dir.; Warner Bros., 1976), *W. Mark Felt: The Man Who Brought Down the White House* (Peter Landesman, dir.; Sony, 2017), *Citizenfour* (Laura Poitras, dir.; HBO/Participant/Praxis, 2014), *Snowden* (Oliver Stone, dir.; Endgame/Krautpack/Vendian, 2016); *The Fifth Estate* (Bill Condon, dir.; Disney, 2013); *Silkwood* (Mike Nichols, dir.; 20th Century Fox, 1983); *The Insider* (Michael Mann, dir.; Touchstone/Spyglass/Forward Pass, 1999); *Erin Brockovich* (Steven Soderbergh, dir.; Universal/Columbia, 2000); *The Informant!* (Steven Soderbergh, dir.; Warner Bros,

2009); *Serpico* (Sidney Lumet, dir.; Paramount, 1973); *The Prince of the City* (Sidney Lumet, dir.; Orion/Warner, 1981); *Fair Game* (Doug Liman, dir.; Riverroad, 2010); *Syriana* (Steven Gaghan, dir.; Warner Bros., 2005); and *The Whistleblower* (Larysa Kondracki, dir.; Goldwyn, 2010).

7. Thomas Pynchon, *Gravity's Rainbow* (New York: Viking, 1973), 638. See Timothy Melley, *Empire of Conspiracy: The Culture of Paranoia in Postwar America* (Ithaca, NY: Cornell University Press, 2000); Mark Fenster, *Conspiracy Theories: Secrecy and Power in American Culture* (Minneapolis: University of Minnesota Press, 1999); and Peter Knight, *Conspiracy Culture: From Kennedy to the X-Files* (London: Routledge, 2000).

8. Richard Hofstadter, "The Paranoid Style in American Politics," in *The Paranoid Style in American Politics and Other Essays* (New York: Knopf, 1965), 35. "The renegade," Hofstadter adds, "is living proof that all the conversions are not made by the wrong side. He brings with him the promise of redemption and victory" (35).

9. Mark Danner, "Frozen Scandal," *New York Review of Books*, December 4, 2008, https://www.nybooks.com/articles/2008/12/04/frozen-scandal/.

10. Ron Ridenhour, "Letter," March 29, 1969, http://www.digitalhistory.uh.edu/active_learning/explorations/vietnam/ridenhour_letter.cfm.

11. Mirren Gidda, "Edward Snowden and the NSA Files—Timeline," *Guardian*, August 21, 2013, https://www.theguardian.com/world/2013/jun/23/edward-snowden-nsa-files-timeline. The *Guardian* called Snowden a "whistleblower" in the first week of its coverage. Greenwald, Glenn, Ewen MacAskill, and Laura Poitras, "Edward Snowden: The Whistleblower Behind the NSA Surveillance Revelations," *Guardian*, June 11, 2013, https://www.theguardian.com/world/2013/jun/09/edward-snowden-nsa-whistleblower-surveillance.

12. Peter Eisler and Susan Page, "3 NSA Veterans Speak Out on Whistleblower: We Told You So," *USA Today*, June 16, 2013, https://www.usatoday.com/story/news/politics/2013/06/16/snowden-whistleblower-nsa-officials-roundtable/2428809/.

13. Binney left the NSA in October 2001, before Snowden joined the agency. Forrester seems to be intended to suggest his general type. The CIA officer John Kiriakou was sentenced to prison for exposing CIA torture after 9/11.

14. Consider, for instance, how the public might have responded to the 2.5 *million* words of the Pentagon Papers without the brilliant and focused explication of Neil Sheehan and others in the press. Neil Sheehan, "Vietnam Archive: Pentagon Study Traces 3 Decades of Growing U.S. Involvement," *New York Times*, June 13, 1971, https://archive.nytimes.com/www.nytimes.com/books/97/04/13/reviews/papers-overview.html.

15. GAP's timeline also includes the somewhat anomalous case in which Ben Franklin is said to have given Thomas Cushing, speaker of the Massachusetts Assembly, letters in which the governor of Massachusetts, Thomas Hutchinson, suggested "an abridgement of . . . English liberties" in the colonies and increased military resources to control the fractious colonists. Cushing then passed the letters to Samuel Adams, who not only published them but highlighted the inflammatory phrases so effectively that Hutchinson was burned in effigy. If Franklin was the source of the letters, a point of some

historiographic contention, his disclosure looks like textbook diplomacy—a quiet, strategic leak made for political advantage. (Bernard Bailyn speculates that it was former colonial governor Thomas Pownall who gave Cushing the letters. See his *The Ordeal of Thomas Hutchinson* [Cambridge, MA: Belknap, 1974], 231–35.) What made the material incendiary was Adams's framing of it as evidence of a British plot "to overthrow the Constitution of Government." See http://www.historynet.com/stolen-letters-benjamin-franklin-and-the-hutchinson-affair.htm. Franklin asserted that his goal was not revelation or political gamesmanship but "Reconciliation, which for the common Good I earnestly wished." *Tract Relative to the Affair of the Hutchinson Letters*, 1774, in *The Papers of Benjamin Franklin*, 21:414; "Benjamin Franklin to Thomas Cushing," London [December 2, 1772], in *The Papers of Benjamin Franklin*, 19:399; http://www.yale.edu/franklinpapers; http://franklinpapers.org/franklin/framedVolumes.jsp.

16. Notable explorations of these metaphors for public unknowing are Ralph Ellison, *Invisible Man* (New York: Viking, 1951); and Russel Jacoby, *Social Amnesia: A Critique of Social Psychology from Adler to Laing* (Boston: Beacon, 1975). For further discussion, see Melley, *Covert Sphere*, esp. 6–7.

17. The film is based on Marie Brenner, "Jeffrey Wigand: The Man Who Knew Too Much," *Vanity Fair*, April 1, 2004, https://www.vanityfair.com/magazine/1996/05/wigand199605. The script distinguishes the more self-interested Wigand from a deeply ethical Bergman by suggesting that Bergman is almost "too" willing to lose his story in order to allow Bergman to make his own decision about testifying. Eric Roth and Michael Man, *The Insider*, November 5, 1999, http://www.dailyscript.com/scripts/the-insider_shooting.html.

18. Even at the end of his interview, when Mike Wallace asks if he "wishes he hadn't blown the whistle," an exhausted Wigand—his marriage gone, family in tatters, career destroyed—is ambivalent. "Yeah, there are times I wish I hadn't done it. There are times I feel compelled to do it," he says. Hesitating, he concludes, "I think it's worth it."

19. Varon's point is that whistleblowers, as commonly understood, are reformers intent on fixing their organization rather than obliterating it.

20. Victor Marchetti and John Marks, *The CIA and the Cult of Intelligence* (New York: Knopf, 1974), 4, 251; Philip Agee, *Inside the Company: CIA Diary* (London: Stonehill, 1975); John Stockwell, *In Search of Enemies: A CIA Story* (New York: Norton, 1984); Ralph McGehee, *Deadly Deceits: My 25 Years in the CIA* (New York: Sheridan Square, 1983).

21. Christopher Moran, *Company Confessions: Secrets, Memoirs, and the CIA* (New York: Thomas Dunne, 2015), 114–22. A more detailed account of CIA whistleblowing in this period is provided in the essays by Varon and Mistry in this volume, while Immerman explains the PRB in detail.

22. [Redacted], CIA, "Prepublication Review in the Information Age," *Studies in Intelligence* 55, no. 3 (September 2011). Confidential. *Studies in Intelligence* is the CIA's in-house academic journal. The NSArchive describes the author as "first senior representative of the Directorate of Intelligence on the CIA Publication Review Board (PRB)." See https://nsarchive2.gwu.edu/NSAEBB/NSAEBB493/.

23. J. Patrick McGarvey, *The CIA: The Myth and the Madness* (New York: Penguin, 1972). Ted Gup, "Down on 'the Farm': Learning How to Spy for the CIA," *Washington Post*, February 19, 1980, https://www.washingtonpost.com/archive/local/1980/02/19/down-on-the-farm-learning-how-to-spy-for-the-cia/fbe2f23c-ab8d-4fba-aab2-1c1da55f1c53/.

24. Lloyd C. Gardner, *Roundtable Review* 18, no. 14 (2017), http://www.tiny.cc/Roundtable-XVIII-14. This assertion is a major argument of Melley, *The Covert Sphere*.

25. Moran, *Company Confessions*, 114–22.

26. In an essay on the creation of the novel, Grady cites his influences as Ross and Wise, *The Invisible Government*; Marchetti, *The Rope Dancer*; Richard Condon, *The Manchurian Candidate*; Charles McCarry and Noel Behn, *Kremlin Letter*; and Alan Pakula, *Scorpio*, *The Parallax View*, and *Killer Elite*. See James Grady, "Confession," in *Six Days of the Condor*, rev. ed. (New York: Open Road, 2011); Pete Earley, *Comrade J: The Untold Secrets of Russia's Master Spy in America After the End of the Cold War* (New York: Berkeley, 2008).

27. This claim is explained at length in Melley, *Covert Sphere*, esp. intro. and chap. 6.

28. *Body of Lies* is based on a novel of the same name by the *Washington Post* correspondent David Ignatius. *Fair Game* is based on the memoirs of the former CIA officer Valerie Plame Wilson and her husband, Ambassador Joseph Wilson (*Fair Game* and *The Politics of Truth*, respectively). *Argo* is based on a 1999–2000 article in the CIA's internal journal, *Studies in Intelligence*, by the CIA officer Antonio Mendez. Department of Defense and CIA officials held several long meetings with the filmmakers of *Zero Dark Thirty*. CIA, "Documents Related to 'Judicial Watch, Inc. v. DOD, et al.,' Case No. 1:12-cv-00049-rc (ddc)," 113 pg., Judicial Watch Press Room (2013), http://www.scribd.com/doc/94447731/Judicial-Watch-Bin-Laden-Movie-CIA; Department of Defense, "Documents Related to 'Judicial Watch, Inc. v. DOD, et al.,' Case No. 1:12-cv-00049-rc (ddc)," 153 pg., Judicial Watch Press Room (2013), http://www.scribd.com/doc/94447718/Judicial-Watch-Bin-Laden-Movie-DoD.

29. *The Green Zone* (Paul Greengrass, dir.; Universal, 2010).

30. Franklin Foer, "The Source of the Trouble," *New York Magazine*, June 7, 2004, http://nymag.com/nymetro/news/media/features/9226/: "During the winter of 2001 and throughout 2002, Miller produced a series of stunning stories about Saddam Hussein's ambition and capacity to produce weapons of mass destruction, based largely on information provided by Chalabi and his allies—almost all of which have turned out to be stunningly inaccurate." Lloyd Gardner discusses this case in his essay for this volume.

31. Paul Greengrass, "Foreword," in Rajiv Chandrasekaran, *Imperial Life in the Emerald City: Iraq's Green Zone* (2006; New York: Vintage, 2010), xiii.

32. *Safe House* (Daniel Espinosa, dir.; Universal, 2012).

33. Cory Doctorow, *Homeland* (New York: Tor Teen, 2013); Cory Doctorow, *Little Brother* (New York: Tor Teen, 2008).

9

CREATING UNCERTAINTY, CASTING DOUBT

U.S. Intelligence Leaks from Reform to Spyware for Sale

MATTHEW L. JONES

1981

LESS THAN A month and half into the new Ronald Reagan administration, the *Washington Post* regaled readers with leaked information about a new executive order to unshackle the U.S. intelligence services and, specifically, expand the Central Intelligence Agency's (CIA) domestic authorities. "The suggested new rules," sources said, "would allow infiltration of domestic groups when that is deemed 'necessary' instead of ruling out such infiltration unless it is 'essential.'"[1] Just a few weeks later, on March 17, 1981, Counselor to the President Edwin Meese defensively declared in the *New York Times*, the "White House is absolutely opposed to the C.I.A. getting into domestic spying." Admiral Bobby Ray Inman, the new deputy director of the CIA and former National Security Agency (NSA) director, told the paper "he was doing his utmost to prevent 'a series of repugnant changes.'"[2] These leaks helped key career intelligence officials and, in all likelihood, congressional staff members who opposed such measures to outplay newly arrived political appointees in the National Security Council (NSC)—in the media, in internal turf wars, and in the circulation of draft orders within the executive and legislative branches over the course of 1981.[3]

These disclosures and others in 1981—as copious internal documentation obtained through the Freedom of Information Act (FOIA) reveals— prevented the CIA from being given a broad array of new domestic authorities. The leaks made it challenging for the new administration to remove numerous restrictions on U.S. intelligence agencies in the executive order (EO 12333) that Reagan ultimately signed. Yet even as the general contours of restrictions remained, the intelligence community (IC) saw many other more subtle reworkings of its authorities. These changes are at the heart of current controversies around surveillance precipitated by the unauthorized disclosures of Edward Snowden.

Like most reporting based on leaks from trusted but unnamed sources, the *Washington Post* articles did not question the truthfulness of the material. But others challenged their motivations. In his discussion with the paper the day after the story's publication, Inman provided a folk-sociological account to explain the disclosures. Civil liberties were but a pretense. "A cottage industry has grown up in this town in various agencies and locales," consisting, he explained, of "people whose full-time jobs depend on the time they spend searching for infractions of existing regulations, providing interpretations of policy . . . [and] shaping and forming other ones." With the intelligence restrictions of the mid-1970s came new bureaucracies. "As best I can trace those alarms," Inman continued, "they are being fed by people who are worried about the impact on their current status or jobs."[4] The leakers were defending bureaucratic turf, not protecting civil liberties.

Inman impugned the motives of the leaker(s) but did not deny the authenticity and utility of their disclosures in the internecine turf war among Langley (CIA), Fort Meade (NSA), and Pennsylvania Avenue (the White House). The *Post*, he argued, had been played by a bureaucratic faction within the U.S. government. For his part, Inman too was playing the media—outflanking Reagan political nominees in the NSC who were set on rolling back a swath of restrictions on the CIA and intelligence-oversight mechanisms created in the mid-to-late 1970s. For their part, the NSC appointees, earnest torchbearers of the Reagan revolution, were livid about Inman's comments to the press. He had undermined their efforts to control the interagency battle to revise the executive order. Nothing suggests

Inman was the source of the leaks. But he knew how to use the press to push the process in a way that reduced restrictions on the CIA, gave the Agency cover for future morally and legally ambiguous situations, and would not needlessly inflame civil-libertarian critics or intelligence hawks.

2017

On November 8, 2017, Wikileaks released a cache of CIA malware code, including software allowing the agency to hack into computers to collect information and code that could possibly allow one to impersonate the Russian antivirus firm Kaspersky.[5]

The microblogging website Twitter—a foremost place for discussion in the information-security (infosec) community—was afire with questions around this disclosure. Two years earlier, many in the infosec community, a curious mélange of nonstate and former spook hackers, might have been less suspicious, even gleeful about the disclosures of this information. No longer, however, was Wikileaks primarily understood as a potent forum for illuminating the nefarious practices of the United States, its military allies, and their private contractors. After 2016, growing suspicions about Wikileaks, and especially its leader Julian Assange, cast the authenticity and integrity of the leak into considerable doubt. @conspiratoro noted, "I'm assuming discrediting the accusations involving Kaspersky is why Julian/ Wikileaks released it in the first place. #StuckInAnEmbassy."[6] According to this view, widely repeated within the infosec community, Assange published information about the CIA's ability to impersonate a Russian firm in order to cast doubt on the IC's conclusion that Kaspersky had been working on behalf of the Russian intelligence services, wittingly or unwittingly, to exfiltrate NSA documents via their antivirus product. By the middle of 2017, a growing consensus emerged, even among many erstwhile Assange supporters, that he and his organization had always been or had become a Russian agent, whether unintentionally or deliberately. Everything that had smelled a bit fishy about Assange a few years before now stank.

More than just Assange's sources, motives, and potential place in a Russian cyberwar operation were questioned. The respected cyberpolicy analyst Mara Tam noted in a thread of tweets:

No matter how cool you think the [most recent Wikileaks release of CIA hacking software] are, we KNOW Julian pumps altered docs through Wikileaks.[7]

If you have faith in the integrity of source or documentation released [by Wikileaks in this disclosure], you are failing at evidence-based reasoning.[8]

In tweet after tweet, respected voices from across the civil and quasi-governmental twittertariat impugned the authenticity, integrity, motives, and sources behind the latest Wikileaks files.

MAKING UP UNCERTAINTY

Separated by some thirty-five years, these two examples came in the wake of the two golden moments of disclosures about the U.S. national security state: the early-to-mid 1970s and the mid-2010s. Both periods saw a dramatic uptick in public awareness and scrutiny of intelligence activities, their legal foundations, and demands for reform. They dramatically illustrated the cultural impact and political ramifications of the disclosure of secrets. And they both illustrated the need to move beyond the stories of individuals to reconstruct how the media, in their respective moments, received or ignored, promoted or undermined the disclosures and the sources behind them.

These two episodes underscore the endemic uncertainty around the disclosure of government secrets. Someone making a disclosure, which I will generally call a "leak" for short, could be a government plant, a whistle-blower as narrowly defined in law, an operator working for a foreign power, or a public-interest hacker based anywhere in the world. Scholars such as

David Pozen and Stephen Hess have put domestic leaks into a typology based on the motivations of leakers:

> the *ego leak*, meant to satisfy the leaker's "sense of self-importance"; the *goodwill leak*, meant to curry favor with a reporter; the *policy leak*, meant to help, hurt, or alter a plan or policy; the *animus* leak, meant to settle grudges or embarrass others; the *trial balloon* leak, meant to test the response of key constituencies, members of Congress, or the general public; and the *whistleblower* leak, meant to reveal a perceived abuse and, unique among the list, usually employed by career personnel.[9]

To this list can be added leaks by or on behalf of a foreign power, the deliberate exposure of something gained through espionage, as well as what Gabriella Coleman calls the "public interest hack," some of which may very well be foreign influence operations.[10]

Leakers may know where they fit within this typology, but everyone else argues about it. This uncertainty about motivation is a crucial nescience surrounding any disclosure and is therefore essential to its historical effects. Other forms of uncertainty abound around leaks: the authenticity and integrity of the information, the identity of the insider source, the potential that the leaker and the news or advocacy organizations are unwittingly working toward nefarious purposes, the classification of the exposed material, and the relevance of statutory and case law pertaining to its disclosure. Often these uncertainties remain latent and are foregrounded only when a disclosure is particularly sensitive or contested, or used, as Inman did, as a potent political tool. Such uncertainty is often productive: government officials use it as a veil to protect themselves and advance their agendas but also to deny the existence of leaks; law enforcement, as Lloyd Gardner and others have documented in detail, uses the opacity and capriciousness around prosecutions of unauthorized disclosures as a bludgeon against low- and midlevel sources while typically leaving higher-placed officials largely alone.

Legitimate whistleblower? Egomaniacal leaker? Russian or Chinese agent preying on fears of the national security state? Edward Snowden continues to be celebrated and vilified as each of these. Debates about Snowden's significance nearly always involve a narrativization of what sort of leaker, virtuous or vicious, he was. For example, soon after the first wave of disclosures, a top lawyer for the intelligence community, Bob Litt, argued, "Some people claim that these disclosures were a form of 'whistleblowing.' But let's be clear. These programs are not illegal."[11] On Litt's account, a whole domain of secret law vindicated the government, and thus Snowden did not fit into the narrowly drawn state category of a legal whistleblower. While the initial Snowden revelations focused primarily on the expansion of national security intelligence into domestic communications, many of the subsequent disclosures revealed novel aspects of the NSA's foreign intelligence, especially hacking into the computer systems of foreign states. As reporting based on Snowden documents increasingly detailed such missions, intelligence insiders and their public supporters pushed even harder against the notion that Snowden was a whistleblower, increasingly portraying him as working in tandem with—if not on behalf of—foreign intelligence services.

As other chapters in this volume illustrate, the example of Snowden followed a familiar script, in which demonization of a whistleblower overtakes "public consideration of the contents of the revelation."[12] This chapter similarly concerns the process of retelling the stories about unauthorized disclosures, as seen in the two opening examples; the conflict of stories told *about* those exposing information are as important to the cultural and political ramifications of leaks as the content of the disclosures and the underlying motivations behind them. The case studies illustrate two key forms of recasting the narrative around disclosures—or offering alternative stories about them—that blunt their effects by impugning the revelations and the motives behind them. On the domestic plane, the narrative recasts leaks about government waste or abuse as an expression of bureaucratic politics or the self-interest of the leaker. On the foreign axis, the story takes a set of disclosures that claim to be whistleblowing, such as the Snowden revelations, and reframes them as foreign influence operations.

The first half of this chapter focuses on debates around the motivations of leaks on the *domestic* plane in debates about IC reform in 1981; the second half turns to more recent arguments around the potential *foreign* motivations of contemporary leakers. The chapter examines the intense conflict and revelations surrounding the drafting of EO 12333, the Reagan administration's effort to strengthen the powers and responsibilities of intelligence agencies. Drawing on a mass of archival documents from the Reagan library and CIA Records Search Tool (CREST) archive, it reconstructs a crucial episode of policy making in a world of regular domestic "pleaking"— planted leaks intended to influence policy making.[13] The chapter then explores disclosures of U.S. government malware in the two years after Snowden's revelations, highlighting how the authorization for more recent IC activities was rooted in EO 12333, especially reworking interpretations over signals intelligence to justify worldwide state-sanctioned hacking.

THE FOG OF DISCLOSURE AND THE WORK OF CLOSURE

The case of Snowden underscores that the lack of clarity around the status of disclosures is not incidental or something to wait around to be resolved but fundamental to the phenomenon and its effects, both in the moment and often for some time after. The *lack* of clarity is thus historically important, whatever the facts about the leaker are. This is true even if one is certain about the motivations and moral quality of the individual making disclosures. Daniel Ellsberg or Chelsea Manning may have been perfectly certain of their motivations, and we might have extremely robust evidence about their reasons, yet "Ellsberg" and "Manning" as social phenomena exist in a haze of uncertainties, amplified by divergent groups with different political and ethical aims. Opponents of a leaker or her political or institutional position work to intensify this uncertainty, either as a substitute for legal action or in tandem with it, as seen with Inman and Mara Tam. The amplification of uncertainty around leaks and whistleblowing often involves further disclosure and authorized leaking. Richard Nixon took such a tack in ordering the break-in to the office of Ellsberg's psychologist to gain discriminating evidence and thus "convict the son of a bitch in the press."[14]

Whatever one's opinion of Manning or Snowden—leaking traitors or ethical whistleblowers—the *absence* of certainty around their motivations is crucial to their historical and political significance. To understand the importance of the lack of clarity around leaks, we have to track how closure around the status of leakers emerges not simply on the basis of facts but through the historical process of forging consensus. We need not identify false positives or false negatives—leakers that aren't or are really something other than they claim—but also adjudicate the status of an unauthorized disclosure over time in various communities: foreign-policy wonks, the general newspaper-reading public, civil libertarians, information-security practitioners. This approach enables us to escape what Mistry calls "a crude patriot-traitor dichotomy."[15] To understand the work of leaks and other forms of disclosure, we must go beyond investigating the true motives of leakers to acknowledging the perplexing state of indecision when leaks inform policy making and broader political questions.[16]

SOCIOLOGY OF LEAKS AND INTELLIGENCE REFORM IN THE EARLY 1980s

As the Reagan administration prepared to enter office, key members of the transition team claimed that unauthorized disclosures and subsequent public scrutiny throughout the 1970s had profoundly weakened and demoralized the intelligence agencies. The presidential transition team explained that the IC "has been buffeted for years by investigations, accusations, probes and a relentless campaign of adverse publicity."[17] In a 1981 Heritage Foundation volume sketching policies for a conservative presidency, staff member Samuel Francis, later famous as a white-supremacist paleoconservative, outlined the many challenges facing the IC in the 1980s. Calling for domestic authorities for the CIA, more robust counterintelligence, and the return of Internal Security committees, Francis explained the revelations about the CIA and FBI abuses were inspired not just by civil libertarians but the bureaucracy:

> It would be comforting—but wrong—to believe that the only problems of American Intelligence derive from the mid-1970s enterprising journalists, irresponsible congressional investigations, bad publicity, a few defectors, the Hughes-Ryan Amendment, and the Freedom of Information Act.... Surely these things contributed to the downfall. But the decline was under way earlier. Its causes are deeper. The information which both the press and congressional committees used against American intelligence was provided to them by factions within the intelligence community intent on laying low their bureaucratic adversaries. They succeeded.[18]

Francis claimed to be summarizing the views of many in the IC: civil-libertarian claims were but a facade for bureaucratic gamesmanship. The incoming Reagan administration echoed this account of the decline of intelligence and the sociology of leaks that had contributed to it. Whistle-blowing and leaks were in bad faith and harmed national security. The advocates for loosening IC constraints framed much of their work as undoing the damage that a generation of leakers, along with allies inside and outside government, had wrought.

Transition planning documents noted that the "new national security team" was to "scrutinize existing excessive restraints on intelligence activities, particularly the imposition of courtroom standards on intelligence-gathering and counterintelligence activities." These restraints had been introduced following congressional inquiries in the mid-1970s, most famously the Church Committee, into intelligence misdeeds.[19] The new team took to the task with gusto, albeit without political and bureaucratic savvy.[20] The NSC staffer for intelligence programs, Kenneth deGraffenreid, excoriated Executive Order 12036, the Carter administration's edict restricting the intelligence agencies. "Drafted in the emotional wake of the Church Committee's attack on the intelligence agencies by an unholy alliance of smug, comfortable bureaucrats and those on the political left committed to radically curtailing our capabilities," he noted, EO 12036 "is a deeply flawed document. It is punitive, demeaning and in some ways silly."[21] Threats from the Soviet Union and terrorists, at home and abroad, meant that pious civil-liberty concerns around domestic surveillance would have to go. Embodying these convictions proved far more challenging than deGraffenreid and NSC staffers imagined.

While no identifiable leakers directly shaped the writing of the Reagan executive order, anonymous leaks punctuated the entire process. The mainstream press drew on the leaks to challenge the national security state, in what seemed like a reprise of the 1970s. The new NSC political appointees quickly found they had to reform the IC legal structure, since draft policies were quickly leaked by actors aiming to shape the internal process. Leaking wasn't an accidental feature but, to their dismay, constitutive of how policy was made among the White House, executive agencies, and Congress. The conservative appointees' anticipation that it would be easy to reassert executive power faded quickly in the face of opposition from Congress, the press, and CIA bureaucrats. National Security Advisor Richard Allen was explicit: "The press is sure to receive copies" of the draft executive order. "Comments will not be made during the course of interagency deliberations."[22]

The media uproar in March 1981 about the leaked EO draft led to a dramatic shift within the IC toward a lighter revision of the Carter executive order. Three NSC political appointees thought the administration had dramatically overreacted to the leaks and undermined its hawkish approach to intelligence gathering and covert action. In memo after vitriolic memo, the appointees sought to reframe the leaks and cast doubt on their significance:

First, reports of the first firestorm have been greatly exaggerated. What pyrotechnics there were resulted from a masterfully orchestrated leak (e.g. simultaneous editorials, op-ed pieces by former Administration people, etc., *one day* after the draft was distributed.) What noise occurred was notable only for its predictability: the ACLU [American Civil Liberties Union], Mort Halperin; Joe Biden. The operative question in that regard is: so what?

This reading suggested that the reaction to the leaks lacked any grounding with voters. Rather, the leaks and discussion of them emerged from special-interest organizations and groups that did not represent a substantial number of voters. "Second, the outcry which did occur was based on the wildly exaggerated and grossly distorted interpretation of the revision prepared in advance by the ACLU and the anti-intelligence lobby. We made no effort to set the record straight and indeed Administration witnesses on the Hill *added* to the damage by certain nearly-hysterical comments about 'repugnant changes.'"[23]

According to NSC officials, the press was viewing these documents through the distorting hermeneutic of 1970s skepticism toward intelligence. Inman and others had only made things worse by using the leaks for their own purposes to take out "repugnant changes" while inserting issues central to CIA's turf battles with the Department of Justice. The real political danger, they insisted, came from the right wing and centrist constituency that had just elected Reagan. "The thunder on this issue will be on the right, not the left." The administration will take "heat," and "the anti-intelligence lobby *will* make noise, if only for the sake of their own constituencies, while secretly grinning from within. . . . The enemy is clever."[24]

CIA memos and working documents revealed an agency insisting upon an extremely cautious position from the start. In a February 1981 letter, Director of Central Intelligence William Casey praised modesty in making changes to the existing executive order precisely because leaking had to be assumed: "The approach . . . was to retain as much of the substance of EO 12036 as possible. . . . A more radical revision of the Executive Order could be characterized, however inaccurately, as a wholesale scrapping of legal control on intelligence activities, raising unnecessary public fears and opposition."[25]

A few months later, the CIA general counsel explained that the "elimination of public guidelines may engender strong criticism and lead to renewed calls for comprehensive legislative charters for the Intelligence Community."[26] CIA staff had come to celebrate that when things went wrong the buck stopped at the White House, not at Langley, and embraced detailed outlines of specific authorities rather than the vast authority that conservative NSC activists sought. Casey and his deputy Inman consistently maintained this line, whose prudence was confirmed when initial proposals leaked in early March 1981. Inman, as we saw earlier, leveraged them to focus the process along the CIA's preferred, gradualist path.

Internal NSC correspondence revealed ever greater paranoia about Inman's machinations. Rumors about what Inman might do seemed as potent as anything he in fact did. Soon NSC staffers were passing unverified intelligence to superiors. In a memo labeled "Eyes Only" and "Outside the System," Michael A. Berta, Donald Gregg, and deGraffenreid reported rumors from a U.S. Senate Select Committee on Intelligence (SSCI) source: the committee was under the "impression that Admiral Inman was suggesting that the White House would not be forthcoming with any further drafts" of the executive order. The source added, "he felt that Admiral Inman would resign as a result of this exercise" and that "there would very soon be press on this issue" to the effect that the "White House was pushing an Executive Order which would include no protections for civil liberties."[27] Concerns about past and potential leaks were crucial to the deliberations within the White House and the CIA.

As predicted, subsequent drafts of the EO repeatedly leaked over the course of 1981. As the process neared a conclusion in October, with the semblance of agreement among the NSC, CIA, and congressional committees, a new series of leaks and denunciatory op-eds appeared. NSC staffers collected and annotated the full range of clips. An editorial in the *Washington Post* argued that the very haplessness of the White House in the face of the leaks fueled suspicion:

> At each critical leak the administration complains that its position is being unfairly presented and maligned. Yet it declines to explain or defend its drafts in public, even when the leaked language raises as many questions as it answers, and such official explanations as people without security clearances are permitted to hear tend to be murmured and cursory. We would not argue that the administration ought to do all its drafting and consulting with Congress in the noonday sun. The visible result of midnight toil, however, is the cloud of suspicion now gathering over the Reagan order.[28]

By the end of October, the SSCI, led by Barry Goldwater and Daniel P. Moynihan, issued a bipartisan report recommending changes to the order, while respecting the executive's prerogative to issue it. "The committee recommends that the Administration rethink its position on this section and consider whether the benefits derived from the apparent expansion of CIA authority is off-set by the possible controversy this section may generate."[29] Like the executive, the members of the congressional committee framed their discussion in terms of public reaction and the media's response.

What was the long game for the CIA and Inman? While the disparate parts of the IC had divergent goals in rolling back restrictions in 1981, they agreed on one thing. All wanted to fundamentally weaken the Carter-era enhancements to the Freedom of Information Act. When the IC was asked to put together requests for changes to the executive order regulating intelligence, the CIA General Counsel noted the "unanimous view" that section 3-303 of Carter EO 12065 should be revoked:

> The section in question establishes the so-called "balancing test" under which it was intended, in relatively rare cases, that classifying officials, with respect to materials that concededly meet the criteria for classification, nonetheless balance whether the public interest in disclosure outweighs the damage to the national security that might reasonably be expected from disclosure. . . . A concerted campaign is being made by groups hostile to the Intelligence Community to introduce the "balancing test" as part of the courts' scrutiny of agency classification decisions used as the basis for withholding documents under the FOIA.[30]

The Reagan administration subsequently undermined the "balancing test" inscribed in EO 12065. Reforming FOIA was so important that Inman was "willing to live with demeaning provisions if this will bring greater Congressional support for FOIA and agent identities legislation."[31] Restrictions on intelligence work were sufferable, for the moment, as part of a long game, so long as transparency was eluded. This meant exposing some details about the legal regime around intelligence while defanging the means through which citizens might systematically gain access to knowledge about their government. The public learning a little about the agencies now was a price worth paying for the public being systematically unable to learn more in the future.

Ultimately EO 12333 did not prevent numerous intelligence malfeasances in the 1980s, most notably the Iran-Contra affair. There was a tremendous expansion of activities based on secret interpretations of carefully inserted clauses, most of which remain classified. The CIA and national security lawyers knew how to write authorities in such a way to allow them to proceed even if leaked. For instance, the IC inserted a seemingly innocuous clause about "incidental collection" that is now at the heart of debates about spying on U.S. citizens. In ways still little known, the "War on Drugs," once declared a national security issue, led to secret interpretations of EO 12333 in the mid-1980s. This allowed greater "transnational" intelligence gathering involving U.S. persons; these likely provided key precedents for mass metadata collection two decades later.

LEAKS AND THE CONSTITUTION OF POLICY

The legal scholar David Pozen argues that the incessant leaks pervading the U.S. government—both within senior policy-making circles and the bureaucracy—plays a de facto role in ensuring citizens accept the vast secret state.[32] The democratic process continuously extends outside government through a nonsystematic but sustained process of leaking, a bizarre but essential form of publicness and ersatz transparency. The series of leaks prompting intelligence reforms in the 1970s and the 2010s suggests that the secrecy state maintains legitimacy precisely because the "pressure valve" of leaking is *integral, not ancillary*, to the process of governance.

Yet this presupposes that the media is willing to push back when the government claims the need to preserve national security. Stressing "the fragility of whistleblower-press relations," Hannah Gurman underscores "how quickly they can break down under changing historical and political circumstances."[33] The press reacts to leaks and whistleblowers in highly situated ways, with dramatic changes from the 1970s to the mid-1980s leading to less press skepticism of the state's invocation of national security. In 1981, NSC staffers recognized that press distrust of secret government activity was rooted in events of the 1970s. Yet by the mid-1980s, the Reagan administration had nurtured a decidedly less hostile press.[34]

The de facto legitimacy of the secret administrative state thereby may rest in its unclear, irregular, but real porousness and propensity to leak over time, particularly about major abuses or illegal activities and with a press culture willing to challenge it on national security issues. The creation of EO 12333 exemplifies this: the restructuring document of the IC went through a complex interagency process marked by leaking and a skeptical press. Whatever officials publicly say, leaking is a feature, not a bug, of the system. The more extreme proposals for unshackling the IC were knocked down by leaks, often imprecise leaks, over the course of 1981. NSC staffers were outraged and decidedly outplayed. And the very threat of leaks was used by more experienced CIA hands to retain most of the form and much of the content of Carter EO 12036, while inserting their own revisions. Neither CIA nor NSC staffers could get all they wanted, of course. Leaking and the potential for leaking enabled the imperfect interaction among agencies and with Congress.

If leaks are ordinary operative procedure, so are attacks on unauthorized disclosure. Regular denunciations, prohibitions, and initiatives against leaking are as integral to our leaky constitutional order as efforts to foreclose unauthorized disclosures. And the uncertainty around the proper bounds of leaking likely serves both to encourage and discourage leaking. The amplified government war on leaking in recent years might, in this analysis, best be understood as a constitutional power grab to return to a less porous if more literally de jure state of affairs.

Creating uncertainty around leaks is part of the normal give-and-take of the extrainstitutional decision-making process within many democratic polities. To make the sources of unauthorized disclosures foreign—or to seem potentially foreign—is to cast them as outside the domestic plane of contestation and bureaucratic infighting, to make them into foreign influence operations. With that, we now turn to the very recent past, where the ramifications of EO 12333 have been felt in the world of "cyber" warfare and espionage.

A FOREIGN AXIS? MUDDYING THE WATERS
AROUND UNAUTHORIZED DISCLOSURES

Stoking doubt about the character and allegiance of the NSA leaker Reality Winner, a U.S. prosecutor described her with a farrago of innuendo about activities deemed "not criminal, but . . . of interest." For instance, how to change a phone SIM card; owning "four phones, two laptops, and one tablet"; traveling by herself in Belize. "Nothing criminal about that," the prosecutor stated in court, "but it seems odd."[35]

Although the prosecutor proved nothing, he sought to create a cloud of uncertainty around Winner's leak of NSA evidence about Russian influence operations in the 2016 U.S. presidential election. To be "criminal" is to occupy a clear location; to seem "odd" is to be in a dispersed haze of potential positions. Without explicitly saying so, the prosecutor located Winner as a potential foreign agent, one that made odd trips, has an odd amount of computer gear, and knows the very basic procedure of changing SIM chips, practiced by criminal masterminds and regular travelers alike, but here given the patina of potential action to injure the United States. As revealing as it is transparent, the prosecutorial legerdemain sought to move the classification of Winner in a new dimension: not simply as someone who broke the law but as a potential foreign agent who did so in the course of espionage on behalf of a foreign power. She is thus lifted, with vague suspicions, from the plane of domestic leaks and whistleblowing into an axis of foreignness.

In the wake of a major leak exposing potential malfeasance, different parties fight over the appropriate classification of the individual disclosing information and of the material itself. The figures and organizations who engage in contests over exposures often work proactively to redefine a leaker and his or her disclosures. One typical move is to argue that a disclosure, while formally illegal, constitutes whistleblowing in the *spirit* if not letter of the very narrowly cast law. In the domestic plane, a leaker might be classified as a virtuous whistleblower, a bureaucratic backstabber, or someone seeking self-aggrandizement. In the national security realm, there are often attempts to cast an apparently virtuous whistleblower as a foreign spy in all but name. Contestation around the classification of leakers tends to be unresolved in the short term, even if it reaches closure in time.

Much of the discussion of leakers occurs in a largely domestic plane, with the axis of media and the axis of government. The cases of Winner and Snowden, among others, require another z-axis, the axis of foreignness, of potential espionage and suspect foreign motives. Creating doubts around the foreign connections and motivations of leakers is an old strategy of the Justice Department, parts of the news media, and indeed other leakers.

Coming back to the classification of different forms of leaking, let us consider the contrast between national security whistleblowing and espionage. Gurman and Mistry note the former involves "an insider" who discloses "privileged information . . . in the name of the public interest, breaking the rules of a system to dissent from the status quo."[36] Whistleblowers are defined by their allegiance to some more fundamental principles underlying a polity, and thus they are domestic actors, by their reporting of violations of the law (or perhaps the true spirit of the constitutional order) and the purpose in violating confidentiality or classification. (The far narrower formal legal category of an official whistleblower works through institutional means of oversight.) To claim publicly that a leaker of unauthorized information is a whistleblower is to locate that person within the constitutional order, quite precisely a person *of* the state, not an enemy of it, at worst a violator of *domestic* laws, not someone challenging the integrity of the security of the state. In Pickering v. Board of Education, the Supreme Court insisted on a balancing test weighing "the interests of the [individual], as a citizen, in commenting upon matters of public concern" against "the interest of the State, as an employer, in promoting the efficiency of the public services it performs through its employees."[37] To be a whistleblower who breaks the law is to operate within a utilitarian logic of the greater good of the domestic polity, in a classic form of civil disobedience, as discussed by Gurman and Mistry and Pozen in these pages.

Meanwhile, a key facet of the U.S. Espionage Act is that it casts the accused outside the domestic political order even as it works within domestic courts, including military ones.[38] It infamously excludes any utilitarian logic of the domestic good by including no balancing test between the interest of the public and the need for secrecy. The *domestic* logic of the U.S. constitutional order precludes an Official Secrets Act; although statutory, the Espionage Act works outside the constitutional order as an emanation of the sovereign authority of the president, as reflected in Article II. The inchoate quality of the legislation, long demonstrated in learned law reviews and examined by Sam Lebovic, is not just an accidental quality of poor drafting but the result of shoving it into the U.S. legal system.[39] Thus to charge someone under the act—Ellsberg, Manning, Snowden—is essentially to push them outside of the domestic plane. Civil disobedience is out of the question, since the leaker has challenged the sovereignty and imperiled the security of the state, not just broken its domestic laws.

Associating leakers with espionage, the state denies them any sort of whistleblower status and casts them as threats to national security. Yet the U.S. government has experienced repeated difficulties successfully prosecuting through the Espionage Act, as Lebovic and Mistry explore, in no small part because of the limits of the statutes, the risks of revealing further secrets, and violations of the First Amendment.[40] In the case of the NSA whistleblower Thomas Drake, the government was forced to shift registers and abandon prosecution under the Espionage Act, but only after entirely destroying his career and life. Even Michael Hayden, the former NSA and CIA director, remarked, "He should have been fired for unauthorized meetings with the press. Prosecutorial overreach was so great it collapsed under its own weight."[41]

Adding a foreign dimension highlights how important *uncertainty* about leakers' motivations and sources is in the wake of a leak. Uncertainty fundamentally characterized leaks in the early Cold War, the 1970s, and the twenty-first century with the material released by Snowden and via

Wikipedia. The international axis is thus a dichotomy. A friend-foe, domestic-foreign dichotomy is the end product of an effort to impose certainty where often none exists, to achieve closure about the status of someone making unauthorized disclosures. It's not so clear with everyday leaks who is a friend or foe. To claim clarity is to make a move around the leak, to defend a classification and justify the actions that accompany it.[42]

THE PUBLIC-INTEREST HACK AND THE QUICKLY CHANGING FORTUNES OF WIKILEAKS

Wikileaks exemplifies the expansion of the pool of leakers to include hackers capable of extracting documents from governmental and corporate systems and releasing them en masse. Unlike classic government leakers and whistleblowers, the individuals and groups releasing this information were never authorized for any access. Nevertheless, they play an increasingly important role in the contemporary politics of disclosure. In the past fifteen years, third parties have regularly released privileged government information, with both short-term and long-term effects. Much of our knowledge of the markets for electronic surveillance tools, for example, rests on a series of hacks into contractors to governments, democratic and despotic alike, that were published on Wikileaks and other websites. Coleman introduced the category of the "public interest hack" to capture the nature of such leaks. Such a hack "entails a computer infiltration for the purpose of leaking documents that will have political consequence."[43] Like leaks, they are forms of information operations.

In 2017, the latest big Wikileaks revelation, providing details about CIA hacking tools, got a muted reception. They showed that the CIA and MI5, Britain's domestic security service, had developed capacities to exploit Smart TVs and other "internet of things" (IoT) devices (refrigerators, coffeemakers, thermostats, etc.). Supporters of the national security establishment responded predictably, noting that espionage is what the CIA is supposed to do, that the tools are simply the natural evolution of espionage in the

Internet Age, and that details ought not to be revealed to the world. The reaction among many of Assange's earlier avid readers in the civil-libertarian and hacker communities was also muted. The exposed CIA tools exploited fairly well-known vulnerabilities, often using variants of available software. In the wake of Snowden, there was little doubt that the United States has exploited computer vulnerabilities on a vast scale. In 2016, the danger posed by insecure computers embedded into everyday appliances had increasingly become a preoccupation of the infosec community, whose predictions were affirmed with the success of the Mirai botnet, which used thousands of IoT devices to orchestrate denial-of-service attacks.

As the case of Wikileaks suggests, state actors are now exploiting the public-interest hack to unsettle the current information environment. Little is certain in the gray area between large-scale state-sponsored hacks and disclosures and public-interest hacks. Uncertainty around who hacked Sony in 2014 presaged questions around the far more significant hack of the Democratic National Committee during the 2016 presidential campaign. Coleman argues that whether a "government masterminded the hack or only later piggybacked on its coattails may prove unimportant; this hack offered another public statement that conveyed in effect that a government or other entity *could* use this method for a motley array of purposes, such as retribution, a raw display of aggression and power, or other geopolitical machinations."[44] The uncertainty around attribution amplified the potential power of the hack, particularly as a politically significant act.

The main communities that have valorized Wikileaks' 2016 revelations are clustered around the defense of Donald Trump against allegations of Russian active measures in support of his election, in particular, online communities associated with the "alt-right" (the libertarian, "redpilled" white-supremacist right), such as the Reddit subreddit r/the_donald, the infamous message board 4chan.org/pol, and alternative news media such as Infowars. Here leaks are understood to reveal the capacities that allowed U.S. intelligence services to undertake massive false-flag operations, especially to create the appearance of Russian interference in the 2016 election and to secure mainstream political support for the IC. In other words, these communities argued that the leaked tools demonstrated that the putative Russian meddling was in fact a domestic operation by the "deep state."

My interest here is not to achieve closure about Assange and Wikileaks but to illustrate the historical and political significance of the growing uncertainty around his operation and the renewed effort to end debate about him. The polarization around Assange has now gathered a group of zealous alt-right followers but also made him considerably less valuable as an intelligence asset to the Russians or anyone else wanting to use Wikileaks for information operations. Despite the increased uncertainty around Assange, there is growing closure across many communities that he is acting or being used to act on behalf of the Russians. This certainly now extends beyond the national security centrists and hardliners who always distrusted him to encompass erstwhile electronic civil rights and libertarian allies. Anything Assange now makes available is suspect, even among long-standing progressive critics of the U.S. government, and far more than when Wikileaks published the Manning material.

SHADOWBROKERS AND BLURRING THE DOMESTIC-FOREIGN DISTINCTION

An even more significant leak of U.S. government malware became public around the same time as the CIA warez that disappointed the information-security community. In August 2016, a group calling itself the "Shadowbrokers" announced they had hacked the NSA, stolen its "cyber weapons," released some files, and put the rest up for auction. The Shadowbrokers frequently communicated in a highly stylized and exaggerated bad English—in the style of Sasha Baron Cohen's Kazakh naïf Borat—denouncing various elites and castigating the world for not buying the pilfered goods.[45] The goods, a devastating release of the NSA's prized hacking software, were certainly real. Snowden's revelations had described some of the tools, to the horror of the spooks; now the code was available, and precious U.S. exploits were soon built into worldwide ransomware. The consensus was that the Russians had done it, albeit at great cost to their access to these tools.[46] Uncertainty around attribution, however, proved useful.

In one over-the-top blog post, "Boceffus Cleetus" attempted to muddy the waters around the Shadowbrokers by arguing that the leak sprung from an entirely domestic internecine rivalry and was no Russian operation. By focusing on domestic rivalry, Cleetus recast the leaks in the opposite direction of those painting Winner or Snowden as foreign spies. "What if the Russian's ain't hacking nothin? [*sic passim*] What if the shadow brokers ain't Russian? Whatcha got as the next best theory? What if its a deep state civil war tween CIA and ole NSA?" In moving the leaks to the domestic plane, Cleetus invoked the sociology of the two agencies, this time focused on their radically different demographics: "NSA is Department of Defense, military. The majority of the military are high school grads, coming from rural 'Red States', conservatives," whereas "CIA is college grads only and has the traditions of the urban yankee northeastern and east coast ivy leaguers, 'Blue State', liberals." Here was a more plausible, entirely domestic narrative for the DNC hack and the Shadowbrokers. "What if the NSA leaked the emails to Wikileaks to help Trump? What if the CIA discovered NSA was leakin emails? What would they go and do about it?" CIA has no legal recourse here: "Enter the shadow brokers. I rekon the shadow brokers is CIA. What if the shadow brokers incident is CIA tit-for-tat retribution against NSA email leaks? Hack or steal NSA tools? Embarrass them? Get them broken up, fired? Sounds far fetched?"[47]

Not content to expose code, the Shadowbrokers began exposing former NSA employees now working in the hacking community. In so doing, they set forth their own alternative explanation of government malware leaks: they were not CIA but classic anarchist cyberlibertarians content to trash all the pieties of defenders of the American intelligence agencies within the Westphalian state order. In a profanity-laced message, the Shadowbrokers mocked the well-known infosec researcher Jake Williams, who had been "doxxed" (outed) as a former NSA hacker.[48] "Poor Jake is being naive if thinking there is good guys and bad guys. Jake is being naive if thinking his hacking for US IC not result in collateral damage against innocent peoples somewheres at sometimes [*sic passim*]."[49]

Following the ideological posture of most of their writings, the Shadowbrokers cast themselves as cyberlibertarians or anarchists critical of the state system and the increasing use of hacking worldwide: "TheShadowBrokers is evil monster bad guys because realizing there is being no good or bad and no rules, only controllers and controlled. Some peoples is being angry with theshadowbrokers because [TheShadowBrokers] rejects this system the peoples let control them." They painted the former NSA hacker Williams as deluded by the putative claims of lawful hacking for a sovereign state: "But is being ok Jake you are being like small child sleeping well at night, you are good guys because you hacking for Merica and following rules, right? Presidential Executive Orders. What's is value of Presidential Executive Order these days?" The messaged riffed on—we might say exploited—civil-libertarian claims about the illegality of U.S. intelligence, particularly claims of those likely to see EO 12333 as simply a legal veneer for the sorts of activity every other state engages in.

The Shadowbrokers remain elusive. During the writing of this chapter, a new voice emerged, claiming, in a now deleted tweet, "TheShadowBrokers is not a foreign operation." The writer(s) blamed the confusion on the esteem and lucre that commentators might accrue from casting tall tales. "Stupid amerikanski talking heads too concerned about getting famous from #shadowbrokers leaks making up all kinds of crazy theories."[50] Indeed, they explained, "You don't know our names, we dont work for another country, and we weren't in it for profit. If [sic] course you shitbird charlatans had all your stupid fucking theories that sound like a script from some shitty spy movie."[51] Commentators beguiled by their own narrative forms had made accounts fit standard forms of espionage tales.

In the wake of Snowden and other disclosures, EO 12333 served as the touchstone in the defense that the United States has, since the 1970s, sharply differentiated foreign intelligence from domestic intelligence and that, unlike most other nation-states, publicly declared limits on collecting intelligence on its own citizens. Yet EO 12333 provides extraordinarily broad authorizations for foreign intelligence, allowing U.S. agencies to act like every other geopolitical power. Over the course of the 1990s, American government hacking into foreign computers became doctrinally understood as authorized espionage and portrayed as a "natural extension" of the collection authorities enshrined in the Reagan-era edict.[52] The Shadowbrokers drew on the distrust in many media subcultures of such legal pretexts, to pollute the information environment and undermine their most informed opponents in the public sphere.

FORENSICS, UNCERTAINTY, AND HISTORY

When Inman spoke to the *Washington Post* in 1981, he asked its staff to be more critical of sources, to act more like an intelligence service with greater suspicion not only about the information but about the motives for its dissemination. Claims of influence and deception operations around the 2016 U.S. election and British referendum on EU membership placed everyday citizens in the epistemic place of professional intelligence analysis. Increasingly, we need the full range of forensic capacities to cut through the uncertainty created when documents are leaked.

In November 2017, the infosec practitioner and analyst "the grugq" noted, "If I were assembling a counter cyberwar team, rhetoric, lit crit and discourse analysis would be skills I'd want pretty high up there."[53] The hacking community focused far too much on technical computer skills, which the spooks—whether Russian, British, or American—would not do. In a brilliant forensic analysis combining deep technical and cultural knowledge, the grugq translated and unpacked the wordplay, associations, and limitations of the Shadowbrokers to attribute the hack to the Russian security services, denying the claim of a CIA operation on the NSA. Following a hermeneutic practice going back to Quintilian, the grugq identified the key audiences (alt-right, deep-red infowars fans, and infosec geeks) and showed the "Matryoshka Doll Messaging" involved.[54]

To focus on the historic importance of uncertainty is not to insist on an inescapable historical relativism. The protocols of academic historical practice emerged in response to crippling uncertainty about the validity of legal documents, indeed of all documents, at the end of the seventeenth century.[55] Yet many of the actors in this history sought systematically to make documentation *unavailable* to posterity and, it would seem, to any serious scholarly attention. For this reason, there is something especially delicious, indeed, in reading through the efforts of national security officials so dedicated to stymieing the release of documents and the settling of historical accounts.

NOTES

My thanks to the editors, for the detailed comments on this chapter, and to Anders Stephanson, for his insightful commentary.

1. "Task Force on Intelligence Proposes to Ease Restrictions on Domestic Spying," *Washington Post*, March 10, 1981.

2. Hedrick Smith, "President Opposes Domestic C.I.A. Role," *New York Times*, March 18, 1981, http://www.nytimes.com/1981/03/18/us/president-opposes-domestic-cia-role.html.

3. For a delightful survey of the Reagan administration's struggles with leaking, see Stephen Hess, *The Government/Press Connection: Press Officers and Their Offices* (Washington, DC: Brookings Institution, 1984), chap. 7.

4. "Reagan to Ease Curb on Domestic Spying, CIA Official Confirms; CIA: Reagan to Ease Curb on Spying in U.S.," *Washington Post*, March 11, 1981.

5. Wikileaks, "Vault 8," November 9, 2017, https:/wikileaks.org/vault8/. Ironically, it now appears that Kaspersky helped the U.S. government identify a thief of massive amounts of classified data. Kim Zetter, "How a Russian Firm Helped Catch an Alleged NSA Data Thief," *Politico*, January 9, 2019, https://politi.co/2FfagBv.

6. Conspirador Norteño (@conspiratoro), November 9, 2017, https://twitter.com/conspiratoro/status/928680845950574594.

7. мара-яга (@marasawr), November 9, 2017, https://twitter.com/marasawr/status/928675263617097728.

8. мара-яга (@marasawr), November 9, 2017, https://twitter.com/marasawr/status/928676328517357568

9. David E. Pozen, "The Leaky Leviathan: Why the Government Condemns and Condones Unlawful Disclosures of Information," *Harvard Law Review* 127 (2013): 532; Hess, *The Government/Press Connection*, 77–78. Following Pozen and Hess, I depart from the sharp dichotomy of leakers and whistleblowers used in the editors' introduction and in chapter 1.

10. Gabriella Coleman, "The Public Interest Hack," *Limn* (blog), May 9, 2017, https://limn.it/the-public-interest-hack/.

11. Robert Litt, "Privacy, Technology, and National Security: An Overview of Intelligence Collection," July 13, 2013, https://www.dni.gov/index.php/newsroom/speeches-interviews /speeches-interviews-2013/item/896-privacy-technology-and-national-security-an -overview-of-intelligence-collection-by-robert-s-litt-odni-general-counsel.

12. See the editors' introduction.

13. Given the hostility of Reagan administration officials to FOIA, it's ironic that a FOIA request led to the release of a remarkably complete set, at least by FOIA standards, of records around the drafting of EO 12333. The final version of Executive Order 12333, "United States Intelligence Activities," December 4, 1981, is available at https:/www .archives.gov/federal-register/codification/executive-order/12333.html.

14. Lloyd C. Gardner, *The War on Leakers: National Security and American Democracy, from Eugene V. Debs to Edward Snowden* (New York: New Press, 2016), 59–60.

15. Kaeten Mistry, "A Transnational Protest Against the National Security State: Whistle-blowing, Philip Agee, and Networks of Dissent," *Journal of American History* 106, no. 2 (September 2019): 362–89.

16. Analyzing the phenomenon of closure allows us to bracket questions of moral and legal culpability. This can be admittedly unsettling, for it often pushes up against our moral and legal convictions, whatever they may be, say, about the need to protect civil liberties against the expanding security state or the need to defend the security state in order to protect liberty. Such a move can be even more unsettling when returning to a case that already has substantial closure (such as Ellsberg) than still actively debated examples such as Snowden or Manning.

17. "Issues of Intelligence," box 300, folder 6, William J. Casey Papers, Hoover Institution, Stanford, CA.

18. Samuel Francis, "The Intelligence Community," in *Mandate for Leadership: Policy Management in a Conservative Administration*, ed. Charles L. Heatherly and Heritage Foundation (Washington, DC: Heritage Foundation, 1981), 907.

19. "Strategic Overview," December 25, 1980, box 300, folder 6, Casey Papers.

20. Reagan's National Security Council, especially in the early years, was denuded of clout and power. To the dismay of staffers, it played a far less fundamental role in policy formation than they had hoped. Christopher C. Shoemaker, *The NSC Staff: Counseling the Council* (Boulder, CO: Westview, 1991), 60–63.

21. deGraffenreid to Richard V. Allen, "Son of E.O. 12036," EO12036 Revisions April–May 1981 (2), RAC box 4, Kenneth deGraffenreid Papers, Ronald Reagan Library, Simi Valley, CA. DeGraffenreid was NSC Staff on Intelligence from 1981 to 1983 and senior advisor to the president and senior director for intelligence from 1983 to 1987.

22. Richard. V. Allen to Edwin Meese, "Proposed Revision of Executive Order 12036," c. May 1981, EO12036 Revisions April–May 1981 (5), RAC box 4, deGraffenreid Papers.

23. Michael A. Berta, Kenneth deGraffenreid, and Robert Kimmitt to Richard V. Allen, "E.O. 13026 Revision, 13.5.1981," EO12036 Revisions April–May 1981 (7), RAC box 4, deGraffenreid Papers.

24. Berta, deGraffenreid, and Kimmitt to Richard V. Allen.

25. Casey to Richard V. Allen, February 13, 1981, CIA-RDP84B00890R000400070079-3. pdf, CIA Records Search Tool (CREST), https://www.cia.gov/library/readingroom /collection/crest-25-year-program-archive.

26. Sporken (CIA) to DCI, "Analysis of National Security Council Draft Executive Order on United States Intelligence Activities," May 28, 1981, EO 12036 Revisions (4 of 12), RAC box 4, deGraffenreid Papers.

27. Donald Gregg, Michael A. Berta, and Kenneth deGraffenreid to Richard V. Allen and James W. Nance, "Latest Developments on Admiral Inman and Executive Order 12036," May 20, 1981, EO12036 Revisions April–May 1981 (10), RAC box 4, deGraffenreid Papers.

28. "The Reagan Intelligence Order," *Washington Post*, October 21, 1981.

29. "Report of the Select Committee on Intelligence," October 30, 1981, 9, EO12036 Revisions October 1981 (10), RAC box 4, deGraffenreid Papers.

30. Sporlick to Richard V. Allen, February 18, 1981, EO12036 Revisions April–May 1981 (5), RAC box 4, deGraffenreid Papers.

31. Donald Gregg to Richard V. Allen, "Executive Order 13026 Restrictions," March 27, 1981, EO12036 Revisions April–May 1981 (1), RAC box 4, deGraffenreid Papers.

32. Pozen, "The Leaky Leviathan," 559.

33. See chapter 10 in this volume.

34. David Shaumus McCarthy, *Selling the CIA: Public Relations and the Culture of Secrecy* (Lawrence: University Press of Kansas, 2018).

35. Quoted in Kerry Howley, "The Story of Reality Winner, America's Most Unlikely Leaker," *Daily Intelligencer*, December 22, 2017, http://nymag.com/daily/intelligencer/2017 /12/who-is-reality-winner.html.

36. See chapter 1 in this volume.

37. 391 U.S. 563, 568 (1968), quoted in "Brief of Amicus Curiae American Civil Liberties Union in Support of Appellant, US vs. PFC Chelsea Manning," May 18, 2016, 22.

38. For the improvisatorial quality of the understanding and use of the Espionage Act, see chapter 2 in this volume.

39. The locus classicus here is Harold Edgar and Benno C. Schmidt Jr., "The Espionage Statutes and Publication of Defense Information," *Columbia Law Review* 73, no. 5 (May 1973): 929–1087. My argument suggests a greater awareness on the part of Congress of the peculiarities of the legislation.

40. In addition to chapters 2 and 5 in this volume, see Mistry, "Transnational Protest Against the National Security State."

41. Quoted in Gardner, *The War on Leakers*, 135.

42. Including the foreign axis allows us to put U.S. active measures or perception management of various sorts in the same analytical space with non-U.S. operations designed to influence and transform U.S. policy, policy makers, morale, and voters.

43. Coleman, "The Public Interest Hack." This issue of *Limn* features several sharp accounts of the transformations around leaking and journalism associated with the development of Wikileaks and other online platforms.

44. Coleman, "The Public Interest Hack."

45. Shadowbrokers, "REPOST: TheShadowBrokers Message#1—August 2016," Steemit, August 2016, https://steemit.com/shadowbrokers/@theshadowbrokers/repost-theshadow brokers-message-1-august-2016.

46. the grugq, "The Great Cyber Game: Commentary," *The Grugq* (blog), December 16, 2016, https://medium.com/@thegrugq/the-great-cyber-game-commentary-3f821f0db749.

47. Shadowbrokers, "REPOST: TheShadowBrokers Message#1—August 2016."

48. Scott Shane, Nicole Perlroth, and David E. Sanger, "Security Breach and Spilled Secrets Have Shaken the N.S.A. to Its Core," *New York Times*, November 12, 2017, https://www.nytimes.com/2017/11/12/us/nsa-shadow-brokers.html.

49. Shadowbrokers, "Response to Response to DOXing," Steemit, June 30, 2017, https://steemit.com/shadowbrokers/@theshadowbrokers/response-to-response-to-doxing.

50. LexingtonAluminum (@LexingtonAl), February 17, 2019, https://twitter.com/lexingtonal/status/1097121717204471810?s=11 (since deleted).

51. LexingtonAluminum, (@LexingtonAl), February 16, 2019, https://twitter.com/Lexington Al/status/1096906785582137344.

52. For the making of hacking into a form of internationally licit espionage, see Matthew L. Jones, "The Spy Who Pwned Me," *Limn*, June 22, 2017, http://limn.it/the-spy-who-pwned-me/.

53. the grugq (@thegrugq), November 21, 2017, https://twitter.com/thegrugq/status/933108673110450176.

54. the grugq, "The Great Cyber Game: Commentary (2)," *The Grugq* (blog), December 16, 2016, https://medium.com/@thegrugq/the-great-cyber-game-commentary-2-33c9b79ca8ac.

55. Anthony Grafton, *Forgers and Critics: Creativity and Duplicity in Western Scholarship* (Princeton, NJ: Princeton University Press, 1990).

10

UNFIT TO PRINT

The Press and the Contragate Whistleblowers

HANNAH GURMAN

Flacko knows too much and it would do no one any good if he went to the press.

He has got to be finessed out.

—ROBERT OWEN TO OLIVER NORTH, JULY 31, 1985

OWEN'S SUSPICIONS WERE prescient. In the fall of 1985, Flacko began to tell the press what he knew. He had decided to become, in his own words, "a high-profile whistleblower."[1] On June 15, 1986, he appeared on the CBS television show *West 57th*. He revealed that despite a congressional ban, White House officials were secretly funneling money, arms, and mercenaries to the Contras—a coalition of right-wing militias seeking to overthrow the socialist Sandinista government in Nicaragua. "We've got a cancer here. It's like Watergate. It's not going away."[2] The man behind these revelations was the head field commander of a U.S. mercenary group that organized illegal military raids in Nicaragua. Flacko was his nickname. His actual name was Jack Terrell.

This was one of the public's first glimpses into the "Enterprise," the elaborate international network run by Oliver North from within the National Security Council (NSC). North worked as an aide in the NSC; Owen served as his liaison to the Contras. The emerging scandal, dubbed "Contragate," brought to light the network's involvement in drug trafficking, gun running, and money laundering, belying the Reagan administration's public rhetoric of a righteous struggle against the evils of communism.[3] Terrell was one of several rank-and-file insiders who helped reveal the Contra war from the inside. As the scandal broadened, he and other mercenaries continued to share their stories with the press and with federal and congressional investigators. The following decade, an employee of the Drug Enforcement Administration (DEA) came forward with similar stories about the Enterprise.

The individuals who exposed Contragate from the inside expected the press would give voice and legitimacy to their claims. Instead, coverage of the story fostered an attitude of incredulity and suspicion. In newspaper and magazine articles as well as radio programs, journalists raised doubts about the credibility of the aspiring whistleblowers. A story on NPR characterized Terrell as a low-class criminal: "Everything Jack Terrell told us was a lie. He himself said he served time in prison and that was about the only truth he told us."[4] A piece in the *Los Angeles Times* portrayed the mercenaries as "lost Rambos" and quoted a source who characterized one individual as "the dregs of humanity."[5] These depictions contributed to the general rejection of Terrell's and others' claims to whistleblower status. Reviewing Terrell's 1992 memoir, *Publishers Weekly* concluded that the author's attempt to portray himself as a whistleblower "ultimately fails to convince."[6] Subsequent histories of whistleblowing excluded the individuals who exposed Contragate and glossed over the 1980s and 1990s more generally.[7]

This chapter suggests that the overlooked tale of Contragate should be used to rethink major questions about the relationship between whistleblowers and the press. Are national security whistleblowers and the press natural allies? How do relations between the press and the state in matters of national security affect responses to aspiring whistleblowers? What role does social status—particularly in terms of class and race—play in the assessments of credibility the press makes? Do professional standards alleviate social prejudices?

The case of the Contragate whistleblowers upends several presumptive answers to these questions. Challenging the assumption of a natural alliance between the press and whistleblowers, it highlights the historical and political contingencies of this relationship. Pushing up against mythologies of the free press, it reflects the close bonds that historically tie the journalists who cover national security issues and officials inside the national security state. Complicating the idea of the press as a neutral arbiter of credibility, it underscores the role of social prejudices in journalists' assessments of aspiring whistleblowers. And upending the presumption that professional journalistic standards alleviate social biases, it foregrounds the ways in which these standards can also exacerbate underlying prejudices.

In the following pages, I examine a labyrinthine information war waged against the individuals who revealed Contragate from the inside. This war originated in the White House as a deliberate campaign to smear individuals who threatened to disclose the Contra operation to the public. It was continued by congressmen and journalists who, in the course of investigating Contragate, refused to acknowledge Terrell and others as whistleblowers. And it was expanded a full decade later by major national newspapers that employed racist and classist ideology to discredit a new generation of Contragate whistleblowers and journalists as conspiracy theorists. This antagonism was shaped by professional as well as partisan politics. Powerful figures within the journalistic establishment pitted the paranoid conspiracy theories of Contragate against the rational conclusions of the press.

Delving into the details of this often ruthless and sometimes macabre credibility battle forces us to move beyond clichéd conceptions of the relationship between whistleblowers, the state, and the press. Only in so doing can we approach a true understanding of both the possibilities and limits of national security whistleblowing.

STATE-PRESS RELATIONS AND OLIVER NORTH'S WAR AGAINST WHISTLEBLOWERS

Terrell and the other mercenaries who blew the whistle on Contragate had all joined the covert war through Civilian Military Assistance (CMA), a private military training organization headquartered in Decatur, Alabama. CMA recruited down-and-out veterans and adventurers seeking to prove their mettle and find their purpose. Foot soldiers in the Reagan revolution, many of them were lost souls in a post-Vietnam American purgatory who wanted their country to regain confidence in its global mission and military power. Born and raised in Alabama, Terrell was a lifelong conservative. When he joined CMA in 1984, he was working as a manager of a condominium in the town of Gulf Shores. "I was 43 and going nowhere. I was alone and bitter about my life."[8] A precocious but troubled youth, at age fifteen, he had been sentenced to eighteen years in prison for stealing a car. Following a series of business ventures, marriages, and divorces, becoming a soldier offered the promise of a fresh start and a newfound meaning in life.

CMA's fantasy of war quickly dissolved in the face of the reality on the ground. In the training camp in Honduras, Terrell observed sick, hungry, and ill-equipped campesinos struggling to stay alive while the Contra leadership embezzled funds to support their luxurious lifestyles. He became frustrated by the willingness of U.S. officials to overlook or even participate in this corruption for political and personal gain. Most of all, though, he grew disillusioned when he realized that the press was collaborating in the state's official lies to the public about these realities.

Within days of his arrival in Honduras, Terrell met Fred Francis, an NBC reporter who produced pro-Contra pieces after participating in a staged visit to the Contra military bases in Honduras. "I didn't know much about journalism," Terrell later wrote in his memoir, "but I thought this was tampering with the truth."[9] In contrast to CMA's self-image as a "cadre of freedom fighters," he concluded that the mercenary outfit was just a "propaganda organ for interests within the government."[10] While Terrell never lost faith in the cause of the war, he stopped believing in the image of the war being marketed to the American people. The journalists Terrell met in Honduras were part of a broader public relations campaign organized by the Reagan administration. Created in 1983 and overseen by North, who collaborated with propaganda experts in the Central Intelligence Agency (CIA), the Office of Public Diplomacy for Latin America and the Caribbean produced and disseminated pro-Contra news stories to garner support for the Contras in the media, Congress, and the public. Insiders referred to the campaign as "perception management."[11]

Although Reagan's Hollywood background imbued him with a particularly keen sense of how to use the media to advance his agenda,[12] the collaboration between the U.S. national security state and the press during the Contra War was shaped by a much longer history. The modern national security state and mass media developed in tandem during the early decades of the twentieth century. During World War I, senior policy makers asserted significant control over the frames in which the media operated. Despite the failure of proposed legislation to censor the press, informal agreements, social networks, and shared ideologies between the national security establishment and the media blurred the line between state propaganda and the free press in the interwar period. Published in 1922, Walter Lippmann's *Public Opinion* argued that the press serves to "manufacture consent" for the agenda of political and economic elites.[13]

In the aftermath of World War II, a small group of senior policy makers and elite journalists who went to the same private schools, moved in the same social circles, and even lived in the same neighborhood collaborated with one another to forge public support for the emerging Cold War. Members of this group, who dubbed themselves the "Georgetown set," would frequently gather for dinner parties at the home of the journalist Joseph Alsop, a nephew of Theodore Roosevelt whose "Matter of Fact" column appeared in more than a hundred newspapers around the United States.[14] Phil Graham, the publisher of the *Washington Post* and one of the Georgetown set, described these parties as a "form of government by invitation," concluding that "more political decisions get made at Georgetown suppers than anywhere else in the nation's capital, including the Oval Office."[15]

Using leaks and personal ties to policy makers, Joe and his brother Stewart emblematized the practice of "access journalism." From the late 1940s to the late 1960s, they helped garner public support for more aggressive political and military intervention in Southern Europe, Eastern Europe, China, Korea, Latin America, and the Middle East. To his subsequent regret, Joe Alsop, who popularized a culture of paranoia over the 1949 "loss" of China, also inadvertently helped stoke the rise of McCarthyism and anti-communist hysteria in the United States.[16]

In this period, mutual bonds were also forged between elite foreign policy journalists and the newly formed CIA. Alsop was a close friend of Frank Wisner, who headed the agency's covert-operations unit from 1948 for well over a decade. On many occasions, he wittingly served as a vehicle for CIA information and disinformation campaigns. Wisner also worked closely with Cy Sulzberger, the *New York Times'* foreign affairs columnist and nephew of the paper's publisher, and Frank Murphy, a journalist for *Fortune* magazine. Wisner "spelled out in more detail what he wanted me to do, and I agreed to help him," wrote Murphy in his private diary. Although the press relied heavily on the CIA as a source, it did not disclose this collaboration to the public.[17]

In addition to rewarding friendly journalists, the CIA also punished those who dared to be more critical. At the behest of Wisner and CIA Director Allen Dulles, Sydney Gruson of the *New York Times* was moved off the Guatemala desk after publishing a story that characterized Jacobo Arbenz, the president ousted by a CIA-backed coup, as a patriot and nationalist rather than as a Marxist. During the Kennedy administration, Alsop, a strong supporter of the president, agreed to sit on a story about the upcoming Bay of Pigs invasion, and Graham unwittingly published misleading information leaked to him from the White House about negotiations with Khrushchev to resolve the Cuban Missile Crisis. Continuing the carrot-and-stick approach, Jack and Robert Kennedy also directed the CIA to spy on journalists who used leaked information to challenge the administration's foreign policy line.[18]

By the end of the 1960s, the Cold War consensus that the Georgetown set had helped forge was being challenged by a younger generation of journalists who were more critical of the escalating war in Vietnam. This generation, which included David Halberstam, Neil Sheehan, and Frankie Fitzgerald, distrusted senior foreign policy makers and the journalists who parroted their views, identifying the state-press connection as a major factor in the war's escalation. By 1968, as the failures of the war mounted, the press became less willing to corroborate the claims of senior policy makers. Katharine Graham, who took over the *Washington Post* after her husband's death, privately began to question her staunch support of the war.[19]

In 1971, the *New York Times* and the *Washington Post* began publishing articles from a top-secret historical study of U.S. intervention in Vietnam that undermined the official progress narrative. The study, which became known as the Pentagon Papers, had been given to Sheehan by Daniel Ellsberg, an analyst at RAND. More than any other, the Pentagon Papers has shaped the idea that journalists can be counted on to throw their lot in with whistleblowers in a mutual effort to expose the truth.[20] While the story is inspiring and firmly lodged in the popular imagination, it is also limiting. In focusing so heavily on this event, memoirists, filmmakers, and historians have neglected the deeper ties between the state and the press and their effect on whistleblower-press relations.

Press criticism of the Vietnam War turned out to be more the exception than the rule. By the end of the 1970s, as hostilities between the United States and the Soviet Union resumed and the broader political winds shifted to the right, the press muted its critique of the Cold War, covert operations, and the national security state. If the failures of the Vietnam War inspired journalists to adopt a more critical attitude toward U.S. military intervention and presidential power, the Reagan era motivated the press to get over the "Vietnam Syndrome" and the distrust of executive power induced by Watergate.[21] Witnessing these developments first hand, the journalist Robert Parry concluded that the Reagan era marked the decline of the "skeptical journalist" and the rise of the "patriotic journalist."[22] North's perception-management operation thus restored the bonds between the press and the state that had been temporarily severed during the crisis in Vietnam.

While this put strains on the relationship between whistleblowers and the press in general, the low social status of Contragate whistleblowers made them particularly vulnerable. Unlike Daniel Ellsberg, a Harvard graduate and member of the national security elite, who had the ear of Robert McNamara and other senior policy makers, the Contragate whistleblowers were low-class drifters who operated in the dark interstitial spaces of the U.S.

imperial apparatus. Their disreputable backgrounds exacerbated the underlying tensions between whistleblowers and the national security press.

Nonetheless, Jack Terrell decided to challenge the Reagan administration with a perception-management campaign of his own. When the Contra leadership rebuffed Terrell's efforts to support the Miskitia Indian tribe, which was intent on waging its own war against the Sandinistas, he went to the press. In March 1985, Terrell contacted Brian Barger, an ABC TV-correspondent, who traveled to Nicaragua to document corruption in the Contra operation. By the summer of 1985, Terrell had left Honduras for good and was regularly feeding information to the press that hinted at ongoing White House collaboration with the Contras.[23]

Meanwhile, in Costa Rica, two other disillusioned CMA soldiers were also reaching out to the press. They were an unlikely duo. Steven Carr, a twenty-six-year-old alcoholic and cocaine addict, joined CMA after being kicked out of the U.S. Army and Navy and doing a stint in prison. Peter Glibbery, a twenty-five-year old British veteran, was a more sober, studious type; he'd studied engineering in college. Carr and Glibbery both went to Costa Rica to help open a southern front of the war. Six weeks after their arrival, they were arrested by the Costa Rican police after a botched raid and charged with illegal possession of weapons and explosives. Resentful at being left to languish in prison, they gave a press conference in which they claimed that John Hull, a wealthy American rancher in Costa Rica, was using his farm as a Contra supply hub in coordination with the NSC.[24]

Between the fall of 1985 and the summer of 1986, Terrell, Carr, and Glibbery were named as sources in a series of stories that narrowed in on North's Contra network.[25] On December 20, 1985, Barger and Parry, both of whom were now working for the Associated Press (AP), exposed the Contras' involvement in cocaine trafficking.[26] On April 10, 1986, they cited Terrell and Carr as sources in a story about a federal inquiry into the Contras' smuggling operations.[27] The whistleblowers also began to collaborate with lawsuits involving the Contras. In early 1986, Terrell, Carr, and Glibbery agreed to cooperate with U.S. attorneys in Miami who were investigating the matter. This brought them into closer contact with journalists and with the staff of John Kerry, the junior senator from Massachusetts and

Congress' most vocal opponent of the Contras. In March 1986, an assistant federal public defender in Miami, a staffer from Kerry's office, and a journalist from the *Boston Globe* went to Costa Rica to interview Carr and Glibbery. The whistleblowers also agreed to testify in a civil suit against John Hull launched by the Christic Institute—a liberal legal group that opposed the Contras.[28] On June 13, 1986, NBC's Tom Brokaw ran a story on Contra gun running in which Carr and Glibbery named Hull as a CIA asset and identified North as the main coordinator of Contra aid after the congressional ban.[29]

Owen and North had been unable to prevent the whistleblowers from going to the press. However, in the spring of 1986, as the news coverage homed in on their operation, they launched an aggressive information campaign to silence and discredit the whistleblowers. One aspect of this campaign consisted of internal surveillance and the spreading of disinformation about Terrell within the executive branch. In May 1986, under the auspices of the Terrorist Incident Working Group, North directed the FBI to investigate Terrell, engaging a dozen agents in a full-time surveillance operation.[30] Following Terrell's appearance on *West 57th*, North also recruited Glenn Robinette, a former CIA agent, who posed as a Hollywood producer interested in making a movie about Terrell's life as a mercenary.[31] On July 28, North escalated his campaign against Terrell, sending a memo to National Security Advisor John Poindexter in which he accused Terrell of attempting to assassinate the president and identified him as a "terrorist threat." The memo was initialed by Reagan.[32]

In addition to spreading disinformation inside the White House, North attempted to discredit Terrell in the press. The *Washington Times*, a right-wing news outlet and staunch ally of the administration, played a particularly important role in this effort. On June 3, 1986, under the headline "Anti-Contra Witness Said to Fabricate Story," the paper characterized Terrell as an unreliable source and challenged the veracity of his account.[33] Tom Posey, the head of the CMA whom North had recruited to spy on Terrell, also played a key role in this campaign. Posey was the source who attempted to discredit Terrell on NPR. John Hull launched a parallel campaign against the whistleblowers who exposed him. Carr had fled

Costa Rica without explanation one day before his scheduled testimony against Hull. He later claimed that Hull had threatened to send him back to jail if he testified. Hull also went to the press. He was the source who characterized Carr as the "dregs of humanity."

Operating in the dark and informal spaces of the vast U.S. military empire, the rough-and-tumble whistleblowers were the easiest targets in a broader war of credibility aimed at anyone who exposed the U.S.-Contra network. This included the journalists and investigators with whom Terrell, Carr, and Glibbery collaborated. At North's request, the FBI conducted surveillance of Barger and Parry. Elliott Abrams, the assistant secretary of state for inter-American affairs, directed his press secretary to lead a parallel smear campaign in the press. Right-wing news outlets reported that Parry was undermining the Contra struggle and even suggested that the reporters had poisoned North's dog. Congress soon began to cast doubt on Parry's and Barger's reports, precipitating an internal investigation within the Associated Press. Unable to withstand a temporary demotion during the investigation, Barger resigned from the AP.[34]

The information campaign also targeted Senator Kerry after he launched a subcommittee in April 1986 to investigate the Contras' involvement in drug trafficking. Conceding that he initially found their story to "strain credibility,"[35] Kerry highlighted the value of insiders as participant witnesses: "When you're trying the devil, you don't go to Heaven for your witnesses. . . . You're going to find the participants."[36] In 1986, the U.S. Justice Department, which had secretly halted the federal investigation of the Contra network, nonetheless concluded that Kerry's sources lacked credibility. The *Washington Times* called Kerry's investigation a "witch hunt."[37]

These attacks put an added strain on the emerging but volatile relationship between Terrell and the press, in which journalists intermingled classist and ideological judgments in their assessment of the aspiring whistleblower's credibility. Several left-wing journalists did not trust Terrell, who hailed from the white working class that comprised Reagan's base. Leslie Cockburn, who coproduced *West 57th*, suspected he might be part of the administration's propaganda network. "She thought I could be a disinformation agent posing as a friend to the liberal cause," Terrell later recalled. Cockburn and Terrell eventually became good friends. However, the journalist Scott Armstrong, who moved in elite liberal circles in Washington and worked closely with Kerry's staff, continued to harbor suspicions. According to Terrell, Armstrong "began a campaign in Washington to discredit everything I said" and advised other journalists not to collaborate with Terrell. "To the righties I was a traitor who had gone over to the other side and become a left-wing mercenary nut. To the lefties I was a right-wing mercenary nut who would kill anybody who looked at me the wrong way."[38] Casting doubt on Terrell's credibility, the propaganda outlets of the Reagan administration knowingly supported North's information war, and the mainstream press unwittingly reinforced it.

THE RISE OF OLIVER NORTH AND THE FALL OF THE CONTRAGATE WHISTLEBLOWERS

In the fall of 1986, the scope of Contragate expanded significantly. On October 7, a Contra supply plane was shot down over Nicaraguan air space. The sole survivor, an American pilot named Eugene Hasenfus, appeared at a Nicaraguan press conference and told the world he had been working for the CIA.[39] On November 3, the Lebanese newspaper *Ash-Shiraa* revealed that the Reagan administration had illegally exchanged arms for hostages with Iran. Three weeks later, Attorney General Edward Meese gave a press conference in which he acknowledged that the proceeds of this transaction had been funneled to the Contras.[40]

Rather than strengthening the credibility of the whistleblowers, the media's coverage of the Iran-Contra scandal paradoxically eroded it further. When North emerged as an unexpected populist hero, journalists continued to distance themselves both from the whistleblowers and from the macabre premises of their stories, ignoring an opportunity to challenge North from within his own base of support. As details of the Iran-Contra scandal unfolded, journalists continued to use the whistleblowers as sources while simultaneously holding them at bay. The *Miami Herald*, for instance, relied heavily on Terrell's information but rarely used his name. In his memoir, Terrell claims that he alerted journalists to the diversion of funds weeks before the administration's public acknowledgment. For a brief time afterward, "I became an oracle," he remembers. To the public, however, he remained largely unknown.[41]

In December 1986, two weeks after Reagan fired North in an attempt to limit the damage of the scandal, Steven Carr was found dead in his apartment in Van Nuys, California. Upon his return to the United States, Carr had served a six-month prison sentence for a former violation of parole. In a prison interview with Michael Fessier, a reporter for the *Los Angeles Times*, Carr reiterated his portrait of Contra corruption: "The public is being lied to about what is going on down there. The money that is supposed to be going for the contras is actually going into the pockets of certain politicians." He also portrayed himself as a political martyr who would pay the ultimate price for his revelations. "I'm not too popular with a lot of people because I tell the truth. One of these days they're going to find my body. They'll call it a cocaine overdose." Convulsing in his driveway before his death, Carr confessed, "I paranoided out."[42] Fessier was one of the few journalists to highlight Carr's paranoia as a reflection of a self-reinforcing truth about the Contra war. The war's "slightly fictional aura" allowed for plausible deniability, which only exacerbated the paranoia of those who tried to expose the conspiracy, making it easier to discredit them.

The media's tendency to hold the whistleblowers at arm's length continued after Congress organized a bicameral committee to investigate the Iran-Contra affair. Preoccupied with national stability and their own political fortunes, the co-chairs of the congressional investigation promised, "This will not be another Watergate."[43] In addition to political forces, the medium of television played a central role in shaping the investigation. Both the White House and Congress hoped to focus the blame on North. Instead, the televised hearings turned North into a hero. As the press sought in vain to undermine North's narrative of militaristic masculine patriotism, few journalists called attention to his own campaign to silence and discredit the foot soldiers of the Contra War.

Over the summer of 1987, the testimonies of White House officials displaced daytime soap operas and preoccupied the nation. The drama came to a climax in July, when North testified. Hollywood film director Steven Spielberg would later observe that the staging of the hearing room considerably favored the witness. On television North appeared "at the hero's angle, looking up as though from a pit at the committees, who resembled two rows of judges at the Spanish Inquisition."[44] North was more than ready to play the part of a rank-and-file patriot willing to break the law for his country. Wearing a perfectly pressed military uniform that highlighted his chiseled aquiline features, he stared firmly at the committee as he delivered his opening statement. Stressing that fealty to his superiors constituted a higher duty, North simultaneously defended himself and pointed an accusatory finger at Congress.[45] On the second day of his testimony, North admitted that he lied to Congress about ongoing White House support of the Contras but defended his actions in the name of national security.[46] The hearings dramatically shifted public opinion in North's favor.[47]

Although North had working-class roots and was ideologically aligned with the mercenaries who exposed Contragate, he had become a member of the military and political elite. As details of North's war against the lowly members of his entourage emerged, the press largely ignored them. In August, both Glenn Robinette and Richard Secord, a retired Air Force commander and key member of the Contra network, disclosed North's attempt to sic the security apparatus on the internal critics who threatened to expose his operation. These testimonies revealed that North had personally requested FBI surveillance of Terrell. They also made public the memo in which North had accused Terrell of attempting to assassinate Reagan. Overly conciliatory and lacking in teeth, the committee's final report nonetheless concluded that North's investigation of Terrell constituted a ruthless effort to discredit and silence internal critics who challenged North on his own terms.[48]

Journalists were even more cautious than the congressional committee. Christopher Drew of the *Chicago Tribune* was one of the few to comment on the revelations about Terrell. Drew observed that efforts to suppress dissidents within the operation were much more extensive than previously known. "It raises echoes of the Watergate scandal," he concluded.[49] As the independent prosecution of the Iran-Contra scandal hobbled along, Terrell found himself facing criminal charges of his own. On July 13, 1988, he and seven other members of the Contra operation were indicted for violations of the U.S. Neutrality Act, facing up to thirty-three years in jail and $33,000 in fines. The application of the Neutrality Act, which forbids individuals to engage in acts of war with countries that are not officially at war with the United States, itself reflected the distinction between professional whistleblowers—civil servants and contractors such as Ellsberg, who were prosecuted for disclosing classified documents—and itinerant grunts like Terrell, who carried out the dirty work but lacked access to the official documentation of their operations.

Terrell regarded the charges as a transparent act of retaliation. "When you blow the whistle, when you talk against the policy and start exposing corruption. . . . Then they go after you with everything they got," he said in an interview shortly after his indictment.[50] Although the press was largely hesitant to support Terrell, one whistleblower-turned-journalist was not. The former CIA agent Frank Snepp had helped expose the intelligence agency's dirty secrets to the public in the 1970s. In the wake of his best-selling memoir *Decent Interval* (1977), Snepp was sued by the federal government. Ruling on the government's behalf, the Supreme Court forced Snepp to return the proceeds of his book. Facing financial ruin, he turned to journalism partly out of necessity. In a *New York Times* op-ed he penned on Terrell's behalf, Snepp observed that the central players in the Iran-Contra scandal remained unaccountable and asked, "Where is the justice in this tangled and mysterious affair?"[51]

The press also gave a cool reception to Senator Kerry's report, which concluded that federal officials involved in the clandestine war knew about the Contras' involvement in drug trafficking.[52] In addition to being distracted by North's trial, journalists took the lead from congressional Republicans who refused to attend Kerry's press conference. The *Washington Post* buried its coverage of the report on page 20; the *New York Times* didn't cover it at all.[53] Two months after North was convicted of interfering with a congressional investigation, destroying government documents, and accepting illegal gratuities, the judge in the Neutrality Act case dismissed all charges against Terrell, chastising the Justice Department for prosecuting soldiers who served in and then blew the whistle on the nation's secret wars.[54]

The moment came too late for the first generation of Contragate whistleblowers. Carr did not live to see it. After his indictment, the remainder of Terrell's liberal support network dried up. Alienated and unable to find work, he moved to the Philippines, where he dabbled in business ventures and once again enlisted in mercenary work.[55] Glibbery vanished from the scene without a trace. The majority of the press never acknowledged these individuals as whistleblowers, and, within a short time, the media largely forgot about them.

CONTRAGATE REDUX: THE LIBERAL PRESS DISCREDITS CASTILLO AND WEBB

In 1994, three years after an appeals court dismissed all charges against North, who emerged as an aspiring politician, another whistleblower and journalist attempted to revive Contragate. A new and particularly virulent credibility battle ensued in the press. This time it was not the fringe right-wing press but the journalistic establishment that moved most aggressively. In addition to class biases, racial prejudices informed judgments about credibility. Ironically, the press framed its attack as an exercise in the professional principles and ethics of journalism. In addition to rejecting yet another Contragate whistleblower, this campaign also precipitated the death of an accomplished journalist.

In 1994, capitalizing on his popularity among military and evangelical conservatives, North secured the Republican candidacy for the 1994 U.S. Senate race in Virginia. Celerino Castillo privately fumed as he watched television coverage of North's campaign. More than ever, he was determined to speak out. In contrast to the earlier Contragate whistleblowers,

Castillo had the benefit of institutional affiliation and personal integrity. In addition to being a respected employee of a federal law-enforcement agency, he was also a decorated Vietnam veteran. But he was not a member of the national security elite.[56]

A former DEA agent who had been stationed in Central America in the 1980s, Castillo had spent several years investigating a drug-smuggling operation that the Contras had been running out of a CIA-controlled air base in El Salvador. Between the fall of 1986 and the winter of 1989, he detailed his findings in a series of internal reports that traced the planes being used for drug shipments directly to North's Enterprise. Castillo's superiors had repeatedly warned him not to speak up. When he tried to share his information with George H. W. Bush at a cocktail party at the U.S. embassy in El Salvador, the vice president smiled politely before shaking Castillo's hand and walking away. When Kerry's committee investigated, the DEA ordered

FIGURE 10.1

Celerino Castillo with Vice President George H. W. Bush
at a cocktail party at the home of the U.S. ambassador
in Guatemala, January 14, 1986.

Source: Courtesy of Mosaic Press.

Castillo to keep his files open, so that the agency could deny Freedom of Information Act requests from the senator's staff. Castillo was eventually transferred to San Francisco, after the DEA discovered that a Guatemalan military officer with ties to the CIA had targeted him for assassination. Castillo retired from the DEA in 1992 and was about to publish his memoir when North won the Senate nomination.[57]

By this time, scholars and journalists had already exposed a long history of entanglement between the U.S. foreign policy apparatus and global drug trafficking, dating back to the Vietnam War. Al McCoy's *The Politics of Heroin in Southeast Asia* (1972) meticulously documented the U.S. fields used by heroin traffickers, the corruption of the U.S. allies who directly profited from the trade, and the U.S. officials who turned a blind eye to these operations.[58] Jonathan Marshall's *Drug Wars* (1991) updated this story, examining how, in its war on communism in the Third World, the U.S. frequently aligned with drug traffickers and tacitly supported the expansion of global drug smuggling.[59] North's knowledge of Contra drug trafficking had also been well documented by Kerry's committee, whose report quoted fifteen instances in which North referred to these activities.[60] In a recent interview on *60 Minutes*, even the former head of the DEA admitted CIA complicity in the drug trade.[61]

Castillo's claims further confirmed these findings and fleshed out additional details drawn from his personal experience. Nonetheless, in responding to Castillo, the media ignored the established evidence and cast doubt on his allegations. The *Washington Post* was the first to challenge Castillo's credibility. The editorial board argued there wasn't enough evidence to conclude that North knew about the drug operation. In a separate piece, Howard Kurtz, the *Post*'s media analyst, echoed these doubts and cast suspicion on Castillo's motives.[62] After North lost the election, his image once again faded from the national spotlight, and the attacks on Castillo ebbed.

Castillo's story was largely forgotten until a little-known journalist from Sacramento cracked the biggest story on the Contras and drug trafficking to date. In a series published by the *San Jose Mercury News* in August 1996, Gary Webb traced the links between the Contras and the crack-cocaine epidemic in Los Angeles. Telling the story of an LA-based cocaine smuggler with ties to the Contras who was protected from prosecution by federal agents, Webb mapped a matrix of connections between the U.S.-backed Contras and cocaine traffickers in America's cities.[63] Posted on the *Mercury*'s website, his story quickly went viral, gaining national attention and heralding a new age in which small media outlets could compete with major national newspapers. Webb's exposé struck a special chord in the black community, which was disproportionately affected by crack and the regime of mass incarceration that rose along with it. The story galvanized a group of black politicians, journalists, and activists to demand the government address Webb's claims.

Castillo's visibility grew dramatically in the context of the black community's reactions to Webb's story. Joe Madison, a syndicated radio host and columnist, repeatedly cited Castillo as a key source whose own investigative work within the DEA corroborated Webb's claims. In September 1996, Castillo appeared as a featured speaker at press conferences and demonstrations with Madison and the activist Dick Gregory. Madison went on a hunger strike, demanding that the CIA and DEA release Castillo's files and all of its information concerning ties to the Contras' drug-trafficking operations. High-profile black politicians, including Jesse Jackson and Maxine Waters, a congresswoman from California, spoke out in support of the campaign.[64]

Caught off guard by this alternative-media blitz, the major national newspapers styled themselves as the calm and professional voice of reason struggling against the crazed agents of conspiracy theory. Although Webb's analysis focused on the larger structure of connections between the federal government and drug traffickers and abstained from making claims about what the CIA did or didn't know, journalists erected Webb as a straw man of "deep state" conspiracy theory. Participating in a long tradition in which elites pathologize conspiracy theories and associate them with poor whites and racial minorities, such claims carefully avoided any acknowledgment of the fact that Contragate had been an actual government conspiracy.[65]

Howard Kurtz again took the lead, arguing that Webb's story was not credible because the CIA had not corroborated it.[66] Simplifying Webb's argument, they dissected its logical leaps in copious detail, schooling readers in the relationship between claims and evidence.[67] Responding to the outcry among black politicians and media outlets, journalists condescend-ingly analyzed the pathology of conspiracy in the black community. "The biggest shock wasn't the story," wrote Robert Suro and Walter Pincus in the *New York Times*, "but the credibility the story seems to have generated."[68] The principles of responsible journalism were invoked to advance what Alexander Cockburn called a "manic literalism"[69] that shifted the investi-gative gaze away from Contragate and toward the Mexican-American whis-tleblower and small-town journalist who attempted to expose it. This par-alleled the response of journalists to the whistleblowers. Out of a desire to avoid dealing with the content of the revelation, the focus was placed on the individual making it.

The media's characterization of Webb and Castillo as agents of over-blown conspiracy theory once again gave plausible deniability to senior officials implicated in the scandal. In June 1997, Duane "Dewey" Clarridge, the chief of the CIA's Latin America division from 1981 to 1987, appeared on *Dateline-NBC* and growled at the claim that the CIA had been involved in the drug trade. "Don't give me the conspiracy bullshit. Come on. You're a more intelligent man than that. There has never been a conspiracy in this country."[70] Following a barrage of criticism, NBC canceled its scheduled follow-up on this story. Reporting on subsequent government investigations of the charges, the major national newspapers treated the conclusions of the agencies as definitive truths. In December 1997, upon the release of the CIA inspector general's report, the *Los Angeles Times*, *Washington Post*, and *New York Times* simply relayed the agency's conclusion that an internal investigation had found no proof of a connection between the CIA and the Contras' drug-trafficking operations.[71] Six weeks later, in yet another expo-sure of the open secret, the inspector general testified to Congress that the CIA knowingly did business with drug traffickers.[72]

Increasingly ostracized by the journalistic establishment and no longer supported by his editor, who retracted the story under pressure from the national newspapers, Webb was forced to resign from the *Mercury News*. Alienated and despondent, he disappeared from the public eye. On December 10, 2004, he was found dead in his home with two self-inflicted bullet holes in his head. Webb's death prompted several journalists to reflect critically on the culture of professional journalism that shaped the press's refusal to examine the connections between the Cold War in the Third World and the explosion of the global drug trade. In 2006, Nicholas Shou published *Kill the Messenger*, a book about Webb that shined a light on the bullying culture of the establishment media. The book was adapted into a film in 2014, once again reviving the credibility wars of Contragate. The *Washington Post* published a scathing review of the film under the headline "Gary Webb Was No Journalism Hero."[73] Ten years after Webb's death, the establishment media still made a point of discrediting Webb's story in the name of responsible journalism.

As the mainstream press continued to distance itself from Contragate, the radical fringes of the right-wing press increasingly embraced figures like Webb and Castillo, using their experiences to advance their own war against the "deep state" establishment. After 9/11, the radio firebrand and rabid conspiracy theorist Alex Jones became Castillo's most vocal and influential supporter, periodically interviewing him on segments about the CIA's involvement in drug trafficking. In 2008, when Castillo was arrested at a gun show for selling firearms without a license and sentenced to thirty-seven months in prison, several libertarian websites published articles in his defense, explaining that the government had exacted revenge on a truth-telling whistleblower.[74]

The story didn't gain much traction elsewhere. *Fox News*, which had become the central organ of right-wing power, was busy turning North into a media personality in his own right. In addition to making regular appearances on Fox's *Sean Hannity Show*, North hosted the long-running series *War Stories with Oliver North*, which brought the mission of ending the Vietnam Syndrome into the post-9/11 era. The mainstream press largely ignored the story. Having dismissed Castillo's claims as conspiracy theory, the *Washington Post* and *New York Times* overlooked that the government might actually be retaliating against a whistleblower. To entertain this possibility, the press would have to question two decades of its own judgments about the credibility of the Contragate whistleblowers.

* * *

At the height of the U.S. wars in Iraq and Afghanistan, the journalist Mark Danner used the term "frozen scandal" to draw a contrast between the Watergate period and the post-9/11 era. In the "Global War on Terror," he lamented, political scandals "begin in revelation and white-hot controversy and end with our learning to live with our secret wrongdoing that is in fact no secret at all. This is our new normal." Danner argued that the press deserved some of the blame for the fact that the George W. Bush administration was never held accountable for its deceitful invasion of Iraq, support of torture, and countless other war crimes.[75]

Contragate draws our attention to the longer history of frozen scandal and the role that whistleblowing has played in this history. The 1960s and 1970s marked the heyday of whistleblower-press relations. But that dynamic did not last. When the Reagan administration restored press-state relations to their pre-Vietnam status, it challenged the tentative alliance that had developed between whistleblowers and journalists in this period. Historians and journalists have largely overlooked this important legacy of the Reagan era.

Contragate reveals the fragility of whistleblower-press relations and how quickly they can break down under changing political circumstances. It also shows that the principles of professional journalism and the imperative to vet the credibility of sources can serve to suppress legitimate whistleblowers and produce a distorted politics of credibility. Focusing so myopically on the whistleblowers' disreputable pasts and attraction to conspiracy theory, mainstream journalists advanced class and racial prejudices, paradoxically neglecting the deep corruption of power and the actual conspiracy of North's Enterprise. In discrediting the whistleblowers, the press played a key role in making Contragate a frozen scandal.

More broadly, Contragate highlights how the press's response to whistleblowers helps perpetuate the power of the national security establishment. Following 9/11, the elevation of false whistleblowers and the rejection of real ones worked to advance the agenda of the George W. Bush administration. In the lead-up to the Iraq War, the *New York Times* reporter Judith Miller legitimated the Iraqi exile Ahmed Chalebi as a whistleblower, although his claims that Saddam Hussein harbored weapons of mass destruction proved to be false. In 2010, when WikiLeaks published footage of an Apache helicopter casually gunning down a dozen civilians in a Baghdad suburb, the press relied heavily on gender and class prejudices in its assessment of the whistleblower. The press pathologized Chelsea Manning's sexuality, while defenders of professional journalism raised concerns about the legitimacy of WikiLeaks and the stability of its founder, Julian Assange, a nomadic outsider who openly attacked the establishment press.[76]

Since the election of Donald Trump, the mainstream press has been energized to reclaim its role as agents of truth in the face of White House lies. As establishment journalists dug deeper into the ties between the Trump campaign and Russian interference in the 2016 presidential election, allusions to Watergate once again proliferated.[77] High hopes were raised that whistleblowers inside the White House and national security agencies would help the press expose a scandal that could bring down the administration. In an ironic twist, however, the dynamics of the Contragate credibility wars were inverted. Despite publishing numerous accounts of corruption and criminal behavior in the Trump administration, many of which were supplied by insiders, the press could no longer take its own credibility for granted. Pro-Trump news outlets accused the press of inventing the scandal it claimed to be exposing. The administration's routine accusations of "fake news" pose grave dangers to press freedom. They also serve as reminders of how easily the idea of credibility can be manipulated and distorted by those in power.

At a conference on whistleblowing in 2019, the former *Guardian* journalist Ewen MacAskill said, "The journalists are secondary here. It's the whistleblowers who have the courage to take that step."[78] It is thus fitting that in the Trump era, whistleblowers are stepping up to defend press freedom. Edward Snowden, who disclosed the NSA's surveillance program to MacAskill in 2013, is currently president of the Freedom of the Press Foundation, a position he uses to call global attention to Trump's attack on journalists and the current "dark moment for press freedom."[79] As journalists increasingly face dangers that have historically faced whistleblowers, their mutual trust and collaboration is becoming more important than ever.

NOTES

1. Jack Terrell, *Disposable Patriot: Revelations of a Soldier in America's Secret Wars* (Bethesda, MD: National Press Books, 1992), 326.

2. *West 57th*, CBS, June 25, 1986.

3. For comprehensive histories of Contragate and the Iran-Contra Affair, see Malcolm Byrne, *Iran-Contra: Reagan's Scandal and the Unchecked Abuse of Presidential Power* (Lawrence: University Press of Kansas, 2014); Theodore Draper, *A Very Thin Line: The Iran-Contra Affairs* (New York: Hill & Wang, 1991); Lawrence E. Walsh, *Firewall: The Iran-Contra Conspiracy and Cover-Up* (New York: Norton, 1997).

4. *All Things Considered*, NPR, May 15, 1986. For a transcript, see U.S. Congress, Senate, Committee on Foreign Relations, Subcommittee on Terrorism, Narcotics, and International Operations, 100th Cong., 2d sess., S-Prt 100-65, 1988 (hereafter cited as Kerry Report), 436–41.

5. Terrell, *Disposable Patriot*, 343; Michael Fessier, "An American Contra: The Confused Life and Mysterious Death of Steven Carr," *Los Angeles Times*, May 31, 1987.

6. *Publishers Weekly*, October 12, 1991, 62.

7. See, for example, Lloyd Gardner, *The War on Leakers: National Security and Democracy from Eugene V. Debs to Edward Snowden* (New York: New Press, 2016); Malcolm Gladwell, "Daniel Ellsberg, Edward Snowden, and the Modern Whistleblower," *New Yorker*, December 19 and 26, 2016.

8. Terrell, *Disposable Patriot*, 22.

9. Terrell, *Disposable Patriot*, 98.

10. Terrell, *Disposable Patriot*, 128.

11. Byrne, *Iran-Contra*, 22; Robert Parry, *Lost History: Contras, Cocaine, the Press, and Project Truth* (Arlington, VA: Medium Consortium, 1999), 56–78.

12. Mark Hertsgaard, *On Bended Knee: The Press and the Reagan Presidency* (New York: Schocken, 1998); Parry, *Lost History*, 11–13.

13. Walter Lippmann, *Public Opinion* (New York: Free Press, 1997), 158.

14. Gregg Herken, *The Georgetown Set: Friends and Rivals in Cold War Washington* (New York: Knopf, 2014), 89.

15. Herken, *The Georgetown Set*, 62.

16. Herken, *The Georgetown Set*, 86–126.

17. Herken, *The Georgetown Set*, 177–80.

18. Herken, *The Georgetown Set*, 218, 219, 264–83; Hugh Wilford, *The Mighty Wurlitzer: How the CIA Played America* (Cambridge, MA: Harvard University Press, 2008), 29–51.

19. Herken, *The Georgetown Set*, 285–87, 324–27.

20. *The Most Dangerous Man in America: Daniel Ellsberg and the Pentagon Papers* (dir. Judith Ehrlich and Rick Goldsmith, First Run Features, 2009); *The Post* (dir. Steven Spielberg, Twentieth Century Fox, 2018); James Goodale, *Fighting for the Press: The Inside Story of the Pentagon Papers and Other Battles* (New York: CUNY Journalism Press, 2013).

21. Susan Carruthers, *The Media at War*, 2nd ed. (New York: Palgrave, 2011), 96–141.
22. Robert Parry, "Rise of the Patriotic Journalist," *ConsortiumNews*, October 20, 2005, https://www.consortiumnews.com/2005/101905.html.
23. Terrell, *Disposable Patriot*, 311.
24. Fessier, "An American Contra"; Colin Smith, "Soldiers' Story Blows Costa Rican Façade," *Observer*, July 7, 1985.
25. Joel Brinkley, "Nicaragua Rebels Getting Advice from White House on Operations," *New York Times*, August 1985. For a full list of news reports, see Kerry Report, 820.
26. Robert Parry and Brian Barger, "Contras Funded by Cocaine Trafficking," *Associated Press*, December 20, 1985.
27. Brian Barger and Robert Parry, "Cocaine, Gun Charges Probed: Contras and U.S. Backers Subjects of FBI Inquiry," *Washington Post*, April 11, 1986.
28. Terrell, *Disposable Patriot*, 400, 343.
29. *NBC Evening News*, "Central American/Noriega/Nicaragua and Contra Aid," 550456, NBC, June 13, 1986.
30. Kerry Report, 159, 163.
31. David Hoffman and Joe Pichirallo, "Critic of Contras Was 'Terrorist Threat,'" *Washington Post*, September 22, 1987; Christopher Drew, "How North Waged War on His Critics," *Chicago Tribune*, August 30, 1987.
32. John Poindexter to the President Re: Terrorist Threat: Terrell, July 28, 1986, box CFOA 1129, Arthur B. Culvahouse Files, Ronald Reagan Library, Simi Valley, CA.
33. James Morrison, "Anti-Contra Witness Said to Fabricate Story," *Washington Times*, June 3, 1986.
34. Alexander Cockburn and Jeffrey St. Clair, *Whiteout: The CIA, Drugs, and the Press* (New York: Verso, 1997), 299–301; Parry, *Lost History*, 114–15.
35. Kerry Report, 762–63.
36. U.S. Congress, Senate, Committee on Foreign Relations, Subcommittee on Terrorism, Narcotics, and International Operations, Hearings, 100th Cong., 2d sess., February 10, 199, S Hrg 100-773, Pt. 2, 156.
37. Kerry Report, 161–62; Terrell, *Disposable Patriot*, 405.
38. Terrell, *Disposable Patriot*, 336–41.
39. James LeMoyne, "Nicaragua Shows Reporters Man It Says Is Flier," *New York Times*, October 8, 1986.
40. Byrne, *Iran-Contra*, 1–3.
41. Terrell, *Disposable Patriot*, 377, 383.
42. Fessier, "An American Contra."
43. Byrne, *Iran-Contra*, 281.
44. Byrne, *Iran-Contra*, 290.
45. *Washington Journal*, "Iran-Contra Investigation Day 25," CSPAN, July 9, 1987, https://www.c-span.org/video/?9534-1/irancontra-investigation-day-25.
46. *Washington Journal*, "Iran Contra Investigation Day 24," CSPAN, https://www.c-span.org/video/?9533-1/irancontra-investigation-day-24&start=20511.

47. Richard J. Meislin, "Iran Contra Hearings: A Majority in New Poll Still Find Reagan Lied on Iran-Contra Issue," *New York Times,* July 18, 1987; Byrne, *Iran-Contra,* 298.

48. Report of the Congressional Committees Investigating the Iran-Contra Affair, 100th Cong., 1st sess., H Rpt 100-43, 1987, 107–16, 569.

49. Drew, "How North Waged War on His Critics"; Christopher Drew, "North Put FBI Heat on Critic," *Chicago Tribune,* September 17, 1987.

50. "Indicted in Plot to Recruit for Contras," *Los Angeles Times,* July 13, 1988.

51. Frank Snepp and Jonathan King, "Iran-Contra Folly," *New York Times,* July 31, 1988.

52. Kerry Report, 36.

53. Peter Kornbluh, "The Storm Over Dark Alliance," *Columbia Journalism Review* 35 (1997): 33–39; Cockburn and St. Clair, *Whiteout,* 307–8.

54. "6 Cleared of Illegal Aid to Contras," *Associated Press,* July 14, 1989; Terrell, *Disposable Patriot,* 421.

55. Terrell, *Disposable Patriot,* 423–43; Bob Drogin, "Manila Official Denies Plot of Murder Rebel Leaders," *Los Angeles Times,* October 18, 1991.

56. Celerino Castillo, *Powderburns: Cocaine, Contras, and the Drug War* (Oakville: Mosaic, 1994), 24–43.

57. Castillo, *Powderburns,* 126–234.

58. Al McCoy, *The Politics of Heroin: CIA Complicity in the Global Drug Trade* (New York: Harper & Row, 1977).

59. Jonathan Marshall, *Drug Wars: Corruption, Counterinsurgency, and Covert Operations in the Third World* (Forestville, CA: Cohan and Cohen, 1991).

60. Kerry Report, 145–46.

61. "The CIA's Cocaine," *60 Minutes,* CBS, November 21, 1993.

62. Howard Kurtz, "North Coverage Heading South," *Washington Post,* June 24, 1994.

63. Gary Webb, "Crack Plague's Roots Are in Nicaragua War," *Mercury News,* August 18, 1996.

64. Washington Linn Jr., "Black Press Aiding in Hault of CIA Crime," *Philadelphia Tribune,* October 22, 1996; Joe Madison, "We Are Not Going to Back Off CIA Drug Dealing Issue," *New Pittsburgh Courier,* November 23, 1996.

65. Richard Hofstadter's 1964 essay remains the defining and most influential example of this tradition. Richard Hofstadter, "The Paranoid Style in American Politics," *Harpers,* December 12, 2017, https:/harpers.org/archive/1964/11/the-paranoid-style-in-american-politics/. For a study of this tradition, incorporating the history of actual government conspiracies, see Kathryn Olmsted, *Real Enemies: Conspiracy Theories and American Democracy, WWI to 9/11* (New York: Oxford University Press, 2009). Iran-Contra also raised the concept of conspiracy as a legal issue. The independent prosecutor initially charged White House officials with "conspiracy to defraud the government." However, he was forced to drop this charge after the Reagan Justice Department argued that Congress had no constitutional ground to investigate the executive branch. Byrne, *Iran-Contra,* 309–25.

66. Howard Kurtz, "Running with the CIA Story," *Washington Post,* October 2, 1996.

67. Tim Golden, "Though Evidence Is Thin, Tale of CIA and Drugs Has a Life of Its Own," *New York Times*, October 21, 1996.

68. Robert Suro and Walter Pincus, "The CIA and Crack: Evidence Is Lacking of an Alleged Plot," *Washington Post*, October 4, 1996.

69. Cockburn and St. Clair, *Whiteout*, 35.

70. *Dateline NBC*, "A Crack in the Story," June 13, 1997.

71. Tim Weiner, "CIA Report Concludes Agency Knew Nothing of Drug Dealers' Ties to Rebels," *New York Times*, January 30, 1998; Cockburn and St. Clair, *Whiteout*, 54–55.

72. Cockburn and St. Clair, *Whiteout*, 391.

73. Jeff Leen, "Gary Webb Was No Journalism Hero," *Washington Post*, October 17, 2014.

74. Bill Conroy, "U.S. Government Finally Exacts Revenge on Iran/Contra Whistleblower Cele Castillo," *Narcosphere*, http://narcosphere.narconews.com/notebook/bill-conroy /2008/11/us-government-finally-exacts-revenge-irancontra-whistleblower-cele-cast.

75. Mark Danner, "Frozen Scandal," *New York Review of Books*, December 4, 2008.

76. See, for example, the *New York Times* e-book *Open Secrets: WikiLeaks, War, and American Diplomacy* (2011).

77. Peter Baker, "In Trump's Firing of Comey, Echoes of Watergate," *New York Times*, May 9, 2017; Jonathan Chait, "Comey's Memo Is the Smoking Gun of Trump's Watergate," *New York Magazine*, May 16, 2017.

78. "Exposing Secrets: The Past, Present, and Future of Whistleblowing and Government Secrecy," London, January 17, 2019, https://wp.nyu.edu/whistleblowing/conference/.

79. "Assange Arrest a 'Dark Moment' for Press Freedom: Snowden," *Reuters*, March 15, 2019, https://www.reuters.com/article/us-ecuador-assange-snowden-idUSKCN1RN1D4.

11

THE CHALLENGE OF JOURNALISM
AND THE TRUTH IN OUR *TIMES*

James Risen, Judith Miller, and National

Security Reporting

LLOYD C. GARDNER

S EPTEMBER 11, 2001, WAS not the beginning, of course, of the argument over reporters' obligations to the public as against government claims of priority for secrets essential to protecting national security. The point man in this debate on the government side during the George W. Bush administration, General Michael V. Hayden, director of the National Security Agency (NSA), liked to put it this way: "The Public's Right to Know . . . and Be Safe."[1]

Despite his role as chief guardian of government secrets, Hayden was not an absolutist. "This legitimate free press–legitimate government secrets thing is a condition we will have to manage," he wrote, "not a problem we will solve."[2] In the post–World War II years, government had the upper hand in the argument, until Vietnam and Watergate. After revelations that the 1964 Gulf of Tonkin Resolution had been obtained from a largely uninformed Congress that did not inquire too deeply into whether the supposed North Vietnamese attack on U.S. Navy ships that launched the war and sent half a million troops to Southeast Asia had actually taken place, the balance began to shift—dramatically so with the uproar over the 1971 release of the Pentagon Papers by a former government official, Daniel Ellsberg. He took upon himself the responsibility for revealing how policy makers at each step of the way had documented a different and pessimistic view of America's role while misleading the public. The breakdown of trust then reached a crisis level over the Watergate tapes, which President Richard Nixon did not wish to reveal. He was forced to resign, ushering in a period when congressional investigations multiplied and expanded into all the clandestine and covert activities of the Central Intelligence Agency and other intelligence agencies back to the early postwar era.[3]

Yet even as such criticism prompted congressional inquiries and public debate, the technical capabilities available for collecting information on more and more individuals were increasing exponentially, and the numbers of people empowered to stamp SECRET or CONFIDENTIAL on a document was growing into a vast army of classifiers. In some ways, the 1966 Freedom of Information Act had marked a turning point in the debate, resulting from growing doubts about government veracity as the Vietnam "credibility gap" undermined President Lyndon Johnson's public statements about the war's progress. This new law put the burden on the government to prove that the documents it generated really were privileged as vital national secrets and not classified to protect politicians and agencies from subsequent embarrassment. It provided added stimulus to reporters not only to request documents but to go beyond FOIA (Freedom of Information Act) requests and seek out individuals willing to talk about what went into the documents.[4] FOIA was not the endgame for reporters, however, for there had been a long tradition of "whistleblowing" and "leaking" by government officials who believed they were acting in the public's interest (or, it should be said, for other reasons). But things done either in the public interest or for private satisfaction are an inevitable aspect of democratic government. Moreover, high government officials have always enjoyed the largely risk-free ability to leak information by "trial balloons," or with sotto voce whispers to discredit some rival in another office, or through one-on-one interviews with favored journalists to advance a policy under the anonymous imprimatur of off-the-record opinions, without being called out as leakers.

The *New York Times* reporter James Risen began reporting on the CIA after the end of the Cold War and the fall of the Soviet Union. In those two decades before 9/11, access to "intel" sources proved relatively easy. "I was the first reporter many of them met." What paid off for finding newsworthy stories was his willingness just to sit and listen. A whole generation was leaving the agency, and many wanted to talk about Cold War days gone by. "They had fascinating stories to tell."[5] Then came the terrorist attacks on a crystal-clear morning at the end of the summer of 2001. An American Airlines Boeing 767 captured by al-Qaeda terrorists smashed into the North Tower of the World Trade Center. Eighteen minutes later, terrorists flew United Airlines Flight 175 into the South Tower. An hour after the first attack, a third plane targeted the Pentagon, diving into the nerve center of American military planning. In a fourth plane seized by hijackers, passengers wielding a fire extinguisher broke into the flight deck. We will never know for sure what its objective had been, but with no one in control the plane flipped upside down, plummeting into a rural Pennsylvania field at five hundred miles an hour.[6]

This was the most serious attack by an enemy on American soil since Pearl Harbor, December 7, 1941. More died on 9/11 than at Pearl Harbor. The Japanese navy and air force carried out the attack on Pearl Harbor, yet it took fewer than twenty terrorists using only box cutters and knives smuggled on board to carry out the 9/11 raids that shocked the nation to its core. Even worse in terms of intelligence failures, several of the men had received flight training in the United States sufficient to enable them to steer the large planes into their targets. How could this have happened? The repercussions of that intelligence failure would shape the debate over what was safe for the public to find out and what government officials argued was only safe for the government to know.

Congress passed legislation in late 2002 creating a commission to find out why the plot and those who carried it out had not been detected. The White House was not eager for such a body poking around in intelligence matters, fearful both of a distraction from its determination to confront Iraq's leader Saddam Hussein and of the political ramifications of a blame game in the run-up to the 2004 election. Much of the commission's time was spent trying to figure out whether the entire structure of American intelligence needed top-to-bottom revamping or whether appointing a national director could remedy the situation so that in the future there would be better information sharing among individuals and agencies in need-to-know positions. But the commission was secretly riven by disagreements about what the Bush administration should have known in advance of 9/11 and about threats of new attacks even as it finished its deliberations in an election year.[7]

Under this pressure, the Bush administration reacted by devising new means for the NSA to track down terrorists through various sorts of wiretapping procedures, that, as Hayden's aptly titled memoir *Playing to the Edge* acknowledged, raised serious constitutional questions. Several government officials had grave doubts. Fourth Amendment protections against warrantless searches were one issue, but Justice Department officials also began to contend there was no First Amendment privilege for reporters, reaching toward a means of prosecuting reporters for receiving classified information from sources through unauthorized disclosures.

A book on the 9/11 Commission by the *New York Times* reporter Philip Shenon illustrated what Hayden meant about the blood, sweat, and tears of managing the gap between the right to know and the right to be safe and government's proper role in both. Shenon revealed secrets about apparent government failures to follow up on information before 9/11 and about threats of new attacks. He used anonymous sources, although he did not like doing so, he said, and the *Times* did not even allow the phrase to be used in its reporting. "But in any sort of reporting on the inner workings of the government, especially when it involves intelligence agencies and classified information, there is almost always a need to depend on sources who cannot be identified by name."[8]

Shenon would not pay any price for these revelations. However, reporters that he relied upon for some of his material, Risen and Judith Miller, found themselves in the middle of a series of controversies. Their stories would illustrate how the "Global War on Terror" has become the greatest challenge to journalists writing about national security affairs today.

* * *

"In the intel community, when someone runs a story that threatens to win a Pulitzer Prize . . . everyone holds their breath to see if the political leadership that told you to do this in the first place is going to man up and back you."[9] Once again, Hayden offered the best summary of the issues. Left out in Shenon's description of his sources were the confusing distinctions (or labels) government officials sometimes use for identifying and separating whistleblowers and leakers. According to government standards—albeit unwritten—a whistleblower is a legitimate public servant who detects and reports on malfeasance in his or her department, while a leaker is someone who acts out of pique or self-interested motives for revenge or money. By this definition, leakers are disloyal betrayers of the national interest and, therefore, subject to harsh laws dating back to the 1917 Espionage Act. Conversely, from this perspective, the reporters who receive information from leakers are either naïve or Pulitzer hunters without a conscience, and they have no business deciding on their own whether the information they hold will harm the nation if it is revealed. But the government more often than not fudges over these supposed distinctions to label anyone it pleases a leaker. Thus, Hayden's comment about secrecy and being backed up applies to both categories, not just leakers, as well as to sources and reporters alike. And there's the rub.[10]

At the time of the 9/11 attacks, Judith Miller had been with the *New York Times* since the 1970s; James Risen was a relative newcomer, having come from the *Los Angeles Times*. Miller said she had been hired because the *New York Times* had a woman problem—not enough of them, especially working on national security issues. A leftist rebel in college, Miller now did much of her reporting through contacts with men placed well within the inner circles of power. Colleagues had given her the title "Miss Run Amok." She took it as a compliment because, she said, that really meant no one dared to get in her way on the hunt for a front-page story. In contrast, Risen worked outside that perimeter, patiently cultivating sources, sometimes over months at a time, who had indicated they had a story to tell but had to be certain of their listener. He liked to fit in, not stand out. The two had worked together on stories about intelligence failures before 9/11 that earned the *New York Times* Pulitzers in 2002.[11]

Although Risen and Miller would part ways on questions arising out of Gulf War II, they continued to respect each other. She would not have thought about writing an article on weapons of mass destruction (WMD) and the CIA, she noted, without consulting "Jim." "A beat reporter had contacts and context that roving investigators like me lacked. Their input made our stories richer and usually more accurate." Still, she liked to think of herself always as the glass-ceiling breaker, earning solo bylines for nearly all her work and replacing the male monopoly wherever she trod.[12]

Miller established herself as a book author as well. Her 1990 bio *Saddam Hussein and the Crisis in the Gulf*, written with Laurie Mylroie, gave a rapid-fire account of the man the authors contended ruled like a mafia don, and then the 2002 exposé *Germs, Biological Weapons, and America's Secret War*, coauthored with the *Times* reporters William Broad and Stephen Engelberg, carried the story forward and helped make the case for military action against the Iraqi leader. In short, Miller had considerable standing with her bosses at the newspaper when she started writing stories after 9/11 that suggested Hussein had never given up his desire for nuclear weapons after Gulf War I.[13]

By now she was the confidant of White House aides at the highest level. In her memoir *The Story*, she writes that by midsummer 2002 it was clear the hardliners in the Bush administration had won the debate over whether to go to war to remove Hussein. As a reporter she was simply recording the chain of evidence that led to this conclusion, not making news herself. The consensus spread across to Democrats, including the defeated presidential candidate Al Gore, a point she wished to emphasize because by the time her memoir was published she had been accused of being an unwitting salesperson for the calamitous aftermath of the invasion.[14]

The Miller controversy centered on stories that developed out of a Bush campaign to convince the public of Hussein's nuclear intentions, as encapsulated in a slogan by the speechwriter Michael Gerson. The United States could not wait to see the full proof, Gerson warned, because "the first sign of a 'smoking gun' might be a mushroom cloud."[15] Picked up and repeated endlessly by policy makers in the months before Gulf War II, most dramatically by National Security Adviser Condoleezza Rice, that chilling warning first appeared in a *New York Times* article by Miller and Michael Gordon on September 8, 2002. Even amid all the speeches by members of Bush administration, it was this sound bite that stood out.

The title of their article was "Threat and Responses: The Iraqis; U.S. Says Hussein Intensifies Quest for A-Bomb Parts." "Mushroom cloud" was the most quoted phrase from the article, which led off with the assertion that Hussein had indeed embarked on a "worldwide hunt for materials to make an atomic bomb" and had sought to buy thousands of specially designated aluminum tubes for use in centrifuges to process uranium up to weapons-grade material. Several efforts had been made to block the shipment of those tubes, whose specifications "had persuaded American intelligence experts that they were meant for Iraq's nuclear program."[16]

The source(s) for this and other assertions were, as had become usual, anonymous "intelligence experts." After this introduction, the article reminded readers about the failed intelligence before Gulf War I that underestimated how far along Hussein's nuclear and other WMD programs had been at that time. Quoting the anonymous officials, the article then posed the issue not as "why now?" but as "why is waiting better if it made Hussein harder to deal with?" The article did include comments by administration critics that the threat was being exaggerated, but these were more than diminished by the editors' title and the repetition of the "mushroom cloud" warning.

The final fillip for the article was Vice President Dick Cheney's appearance on *Meet the Press* the following Sunday:

> What we've seen recently that has raised our level of concern to the current state of unrest, if you will, if I can put it in those terms . . . is that he now is trying, through his illicit procurement network, to acquire the equipment he needs to be able to enrich uranium to make the bombs.
>
> Aluminum tubes? [moderator, Tim Russert]
>
> Specifically, aluminum tubes. . . . There's a story in the *New York Times* this morning . . . and I want to attribute the *Times*. I don't want to talk about, obviously, specific intelligence sources, but it's now public that, in fact, he has been seeking to acquire, and we have been able to intercept and prevent him from acquiring through this particular channel, the kinds of tubes that are necessary to build a centrifuge. And the centrifuge is required to take low-grade uranium and enhance it into highly enriched uranium, which is what you have to have in order to build a bomb.[17]

It was all marvelously worded by Cheney: pretending the information in the article had been something of a security leak. But this was a "secret" the administration badly wanted to leak. And the reporters accomplished this for White House hardliners, adding a whiff of mystery. Gordon had been responsible for the sections dealing with the aluminum tubes; Miller discussed chemical and biological weapons. But the writers said that their sources told them an A-bomb was Hussein's "ace in the hole" to make all his other weapons threats credible.

The aluminum-tubes rationale for invasion was subsequently debunked. The *New York Times* repudiated it in a 2004 article:

> Senior administration officials repeatedly failed to fully disclose the contrary views of America's leading nuclear scientists, an examination by *The New York Times* has found. They sometimes overstated even the most dire intelligence assessments of the tubes, yet minimized or rejected the strong doubts of nuclear experts. They worried privately that the nuclear case was weak, but expressed sober certitude in public.[18]

Another story, also later proved false, concerned alleged Iraqi purchases of "yellowcake" uranium from Niger. This story would have grave ramifications for Miller down the line in connection with the perjury trial of I. Lewis "Scooter" Libby, a key aide to Cheney. In the meantime, Miller's articles kept up a steady flow of alarmist headlines to the newspaper, most often based on supposedly crucial secret information supplied by the exile leader Ahmad Chalabi, who introduced her to other exile figures, including those who had supposedly worked on WMD and knew where Hussein was hiding them from the world. Ironically, Miller's long-standing irritation at being ignored by male reporters and editors would lead her into ambiguous relationships with power brokers in the Bush war cabinet.[19]

★ ★ ★

But if Miller was "played" by those desiring war or other means of removing Hussein, she was hardly alone, albeit her access and position gave her special importance. The *New York Times* and *Washington Post* published article after article and editorial after editorial advocating a showdown with the Iraqi dictator. It was in some ways a startling moment for the American public: the newspapers that had published the Pentagon Papers, against heavy pressure from the Nixon administration, and had pursued the Watergate story from the start until Nixon's resignation were now falling in line behind the Bush administration's claims. There were few dissenting reporters and no front-page stories challenging the accuracy of the White House's assertions. A reasonable explanation, of course, is the trauma of 9/11 and how it changed American feelings about vulnerability to future attacks by determined terrorists aided by a supposedly unfriendly government possessing weapons of mass destruction. A simple desire for revenge for the attacks added to the fever unsettling the nation and spreading through the newspaper headlines. If doubts were raised, they were in a few places and buried in the back pages.

James Risen got this treatment when he began to write stories based on information that intelligence experts had doubts about the administration's claims of contacts between Iraq and al-Qaeda. He managed to sneak one onto the front page of the Sunday edition, he said, when senior editors often were not around. Another story sat in the *New York Times* computer system for days, and then weeks, untouched by editors. It finally ran but was badly cut and buried deep inside the paper. "I wrote another one, and the same thing happened. I tried to write more, but I started to get the message."[20]

In the aftermath of 9/11, the press seemed to retreat to the early Cold War years, when stories covering up the CIA's role in overthrowing an elected government in Guatemala or lies about the Bay of Pigs invaders as an autonomous force went down with a spoonful of sugar. And for a few moments longer the spell lasted, until reality soured promises of "Mission Accomplished." The bombing and invasion of Iraq started in March 2003 with great fanfare. In May, President Bush alighted on an aircraft carrier to proclaim victory. Once "Mission Accomplished" became "What Happened to Those WMD?" however, the reversal in the tone of the war's press coverage was dramatic.

For Risen the war had become secondary. He had started working on his biggest story: how the administration had begun wiretapping American citizens. In the wake of revelations about Cold War misbehavior by intelligence agencies, the 1978 Foreign Intelligence Surveillance Act had established a secret FISA court specifically to rule on applications for such warrants. Risen was told by a source that the wiretapping program he later learned was code-named Stellar Wind was warrantless. "The Bush administration's program was probably illegal and unconstitutional," and "only a handful of carefully selected people in the government knew about it," he later wrote. "I left that meeting shocked, but as a reporter, I was also elated. I knew that this was the story of a lifetime."[21]

This opened another front in the contemporary struggle between journalists and the government. NSA wiretapping was part of the Bush administration's self-declared "Global War on Terror." Clearly, a fear of another 9/11 attack was the driving force. On the one hand, internal critics of the program in the Justice Department, especially Thomas Tamm, Risen's principal source, would insist that the government had gone much too far in violating the privacy rights of American citizens, which were guaranteed under Article IV of the Constitution. And, they argued, such a program looked too much like ones the communist regimes of Eastern Europe had imposed during the Cold War. On the other hand, defenders of NSA's Stellar Wind and other programs in the White House offered various arguments: that these were not messages intercepted *between* American citizens, since one end of the communication link had to be outside the United States; that journalists who planned to write about the programs were arrogating to themselves the right to determine when national security secrets could be made public; and that publication would provide suspected terrorists with a tipoff that their communications were being monitored.

Risen and his coauthor Eric Lichtblau drew on these debates in preparing their blockbuster story in the fall of 2004. A long struggle over publication thus began when Risen placed a call to NSA headquarters to speak to Director Hayden on an urgent matter. When Risen read him the first paragraphs of the story, Hayden let out an audible gasp, stammered a bit, and then said that whatever the NSA was doing was legal and "operationally effective." Then he hung up. Delighted that Hayden had actually confirmed their story, the *New York Times* reporters went to their Washington editor, Philip Taubman, who would act as a go-between with Hayden in the drawn-out discussions that followed. But Hayden had already called Taubman to ask that the paper not print the story. Taubman had more sympathy for the NSA's argument that publishing "might" undermine efforts to prevent another 9/11. Hayden claimed he told Risen that, as head of the NSA, he was duty bound to be as aggressive as possible in protecting American lives. Hayden said that during their phone call Risen had asked for a private meeting to discuss the whole question "off the record," adding that he had been following intelligence questions for a long time and that it behooved the director to sit down and talk with him. Hayden bristled; that sounded like a threat.[22]

A meeting was arranged, but with CIA officials, who took a different tack than Hayden, confirming nothing while putting the whole question in the hypothetical: "if there were such a program, etc., etc." Those on the administration side noted, according to Hayden's memoirs, that Taubman thus understood by their manner how serious the issues were, while "Risen doesn't give a shit, frankly." In any event, the *New York Times* agreed not to publish the article—at least not immediately. Risen had already made many enemies in the administration besides Michael Hayden. With the aid of another whistleblower, Jeffrey Sterling, formerly of the CIA, he had previously unearthed a botched scheme to sabotage the Iranian nuclear program that depended on a planted formula that would derail the Iranian scientists' calculations. In both cases, Risen believed that the government was not protecting American security but instead hiding its mistakes and malfeasance from public awareness.[23]

The Sterling story later led to the biggest confrontation on press freedoms and obligations in the Bush administration, triggering a showdown over journalists and whistleblowers, with continuing repercussions from Bush to Obama and beyond. It was the NSA story that began the hunt for leakers. Sterling was not involved in that wrestling match, and his role in the Iranian kerfuffle was complicated by questions of racial prejudice and revenge motives. But there were several additional reasons why the *New York Times* did not publish the wiretapping story in the fall of 2004, besides the proximity to 9/11, including concern that the paper would have intervened with a sensational story in the weeks before a presidential election. Risen did not help his case for publication, finally, by hinting that the *Washington Post* would scoop the *New York Times* as it had with the Pentagon Papers. As it turned out later, Edward Snowden would not offer the *New York Times* his revelations about the NSA's programs because it had held up publication of the Risen/Lichtblau story for over a year. Because of that earlier decision, Snowden did not trust the paper to print the story and the documents.[24]

Meanwhile, in all this haze of conflicting motives, Risen and Lichtblau kept working on the story as directed by their editor, doing research and adding new details, and the *New York Times* kept finding reasons not to publish. A year later, Risen forced the issue by announcing to the editors in Washington and New York that he planned to publish a book that would include both stories: Stellar Wind and the Iranian mishap. The *Times* editors gave the administration notice that they were planning to run the story, and yet another meeting was called—this time with Bush presiding. The *Times* upped its team as well, to include Arthur O. Sulzberger Jr., its chief executive and namesake son of the legendary publisher who had resisted government pressure not to publish the Pentagon Papers. Sulzberger made an effort to break the ice by joking that they were both now in their fathers' offices. No ice broke. When Sulzberger then began to explain why the *Times* planned to publish the story, the president cut him short, saying they were there to hear why going ahead with the story was wrong. Bush then noted if another attack was successful he expected the newspaper's "leadership to be up on the Hill right hands in the air along with the leadership of the intelligence community, explaining to Congress how they permitted it to happen."[25]

The rest of the meeting proved anticlimactic. The president signaled Hayden to present an example of how Stellar Wind had prevented a disaster. "It could have gone better," Hayden mused afterward. Someone else at the meeting recalled that Hayden had cited the instance of a would-be terrorist's plan to knock down the Brooklyn Bridge with a tool similar to a blowtorch. Everyone at the meeting in addition to Hayden realized that was a weak case. "*How long would it take to knock down the Brooklyn Bridge with a blowtorch? Hours? Days? And no one would notice?* Sulzberger glanced at Bush and thought he seemed to be snickering at the notion too." The *New York Times* contingent left the Oval Office feeling that the administration had made no real case for the program's secrecy. It was hard to imagine that al-Qaeda militants were not assuming their calls were tapped, warrants or no, "so the most compelling issues were the legal questions. Had Bush and Cheney exceeded their powers? Where were the lines to be drawn in a democracy during wartime?"[26]

What finally convinced the *New York Times* editors was a story that the White House was planning an injunction akin to the Nixon administration in 1971 to prevent publication of the Pentagon Papers. That settled it. The article, "Bush Lets U.S. Spy on Callers Without Courts," appeared on the newspaper's website on December 15, 2005, to prevent prior restraint from being an option: "Under a presidential order signed in 2002, the intelligence agency [NSA] has monitored the international telephone calls and international e-mail messages of hundreds, perhaps thousands, of people inside the United States without warrants over the past three years in an effort to track possible 'dirty numbers' linked to Al-Qaeda, the officials said."

The article reported somewhat ambiguously that warrants were still required to monitor entirely domestic communications but did not say what the government was required to show to obtain such warrants. "This is really a sea change," it quoted one former official who specialized in national security law. "It's almost a mainstay of this country that the N.S.A. only does foreign searches." Clearly—and much to the anger of the Bush administration—the article focused on that aspect of Stellar Wind, not the foreign aspects. It even reported White House pleas not to publish the article on grounds it would "jeopardize continuing investigations and alert would-be terrorists that they might be under scrutiny." But after one year's delay, the decision had been made to go ahead with the story. By foregrounding the issue of publication, the *New York Times* thus put itself in the position of overruling the administration and the president on a matter of national security.

Moreover, the reporters cited "nearly a dozen current and former officials, who were granted anonymity" to talk about the program "because of their concerns about the operation's legality and oversight." Thus the contention was that the government was split over the long-term implications of Stellar Wind, another thing sure to stir the administration's ire. Bush responded with a speech from the White House defending the program and calling it a vital tool in safeguarding the nation from terrorist attacks. Subsequently, as Risen wrote, "Teams of FBI agents were soon trying to hunt down our sources."[27]

The search did not produce the principal source for the story, Thomas Tamm. Two NSA employees, however, Thomas Drake and William Binney, who had offered a less intrusive alternative to Hayden's Stellar Wind, got caught up in the furor by FBI agents, who raided their homes in search of evidence that they had been the leakers. In the case of Drake, they effectively ruined his government career. Drake had made every effort to contest Stellar Wind inside the government and had gotten nowhere. Finally, he went the route of talking to a correspondent for the *Baltimore Sun*. After the government pursued a conviction under the Espionage Act for Drake—an effort that failed—he was then convicted of the nearly meaningless crime of bringing home and storing classified materials on his computer. Nevertheless, his career in government was over. Drake and Binney became crusaders challenging what they saw as the NSA's overreach into Fourth Amendment rights against improper searches. By the time of the Snowden revelations, they were prominent figures in the effort to expose the ongoing government surveillance of American citizens. At a Berlin Conference in the wake of Snowden's dramatic actions in 2013, which had given evidence that Stellar Wind was only one of the government's ongoing and enlarged listening-post programs, Binney compared NSA surveillance to that of dictatorships. "They really want to have information about everything. This is really a totalitarian approach. The goal is control of the people." Drake asserted that the NSA's "monitoring regime has grown into a system that is strangling the world."[28]

Did anything change because of the publication of the NSA article? Risen and Lichtblau won another Pulitzer Prize, a sure sign that the national mood was shifting against the Iraq War or was at least uneasy about the ultimate aims of national security policy. Congressional investigations were launched, and, along with subsequent newspaper articles in other papers by other reporters, it may have had some effect on the Democratic victory in the 2006 congressional elections. But that is speculative. What was certain was the administration's absolute determination to continue its pursuit of nearly a dozen "current and former officials" who had supplied the authors with the information they needed to write their exposé.

The final government effort to retaliate for the Stellar Wind leak, Risen always believed, was the later threats of imprisonment for his refusal to testify against the whistleblower Jeffrey Sterling, whom the government wished to convict under the Espionage Act for being the source of Risen's chapter on Iran in his 2006 book *State of War: The Secret History of the CIA and the Bush Administration*. The interconnection of the NSA story and the Iranian exposé was at the heart of Risen's journalistic campaign—just as it was for the government. Along with the Iran story, *State of War* contained the version of the NSA story that Risen had threatened to publish if the *New York Times* had not relented as well as the story he and Lichtblau had fought over with editors for more than a year. Risen always believed that the two cases were linked by the government's original determination to seek out and punish the Stellar Wind whistleblowers and its growing determination to protect itself against embarrassment no matter the costs and risks to democracy.

* * *

Judith Miller, Risen's colleague and former coauthor, actually did go to jail for twelve weeks to protect another source, "Scooter" Libby. That story unfolded alongside Risen's long quest. In these debates, journalists' claims to a First Amendment right to protect confidential sources became a central issue with unusual twists. A White House vow that all leakers would be punished—even those who worked in the vice president's office—proved how something could boomerang after the former diplomat Joseph Wilson wrote an op-ed piece in the *New York Times* on July 6, 2003, entitled "What I Didn't Find in Africa." In the article Wilson identified himself as the unnamed envoy mentioned in various news stories about a mission to verify that Iraq had sought large quantities of yellowcake uranium—in some accounts upward of five hundred pounds.[29]

Inquiries about the transaction from Vice President Cheney's office had prompted Wilson's trip to Niger in February 2002. He returned from the country convinced it was "highly doubtful" such transactions ever took place. The American ambassador, Barbro Owens-Kirkpatrick, had debunked allegations of uranium sales even before Wilson reported his findings to CIA debriefers; he thought the matter was settled. Then came President Bush's dramatic assertion in his State of the Union message to Congress in January 2003: "The British government has learned that Saddam Hussein recently sought significant quantities of uranium from Africa."

Surprised by the president's statement, Wilson was told that perhaps the president was not referring to Niger but other African countries in these notorious sixteen words. Not so. Upset about the White House's insistence, Wilson's op-ed asked, "Did the Bush administration manipulate intelligence about Saddam Hussein's weapons programs to justify an invasion of Iraq?" He answered in the next sentence, "I have little choice but to conclude that some of the intelligence related to Iraq's nuclear weapons program was twisted to exaggerate the Iraqi theat." The article appeared at a time, moreover, when the administration was beginning to have a hard time explaining where Hussein's supposed WMD had gone, if they ever existed.

Wilson's revelations were dramatic and as consequential as those about Stellar Wind or efforts to stymie Iran's nuclear program. Cheney wanted his revenge against Wilson even more as embarrassments piled up. The article set off a flurry of activity. CIA Director George Tenet confessed in public on July 11 that "These 16 words should never have been included in the text written for the President. . . . This did not rise to the level of certainty which should be required for Presidential speeches, and CIA should have ensured that it was removed."[30]

"The Wilson matter was now Topic A inside the Beltway," wrote Michael Isikoff and David Corn in *Hubris*. Soon a full-on campaign to discredit Wilson was underway, with Cheney's office again looking to manipulate Miller, as they had with the story of Hussein's aluminum tubes. Cheney gave his annotated copy of Wilson's article to Libby, with the suggestive comment, "Do we ordinarily send people out pro bono to work for us? Or did his wife send him on a junket?"[31] Cheney's pointed query set in motion a series of events that ultimately led to Miller's twelve-week imprisonment for refusing to testify about what Libby had told her and the latter's conviction for lying to the FBI. It unfolded when Robert Novak, a conservative reporter, published his column "Mission to Niger" in the *Washington Post* on July 14, 2003, in which he mentioned that Wilson's wife, Valerie Plame, was a CIA operative working on WMD. "Two senior administration officials told me Wilson's wife suggested sending him to Niger." The column did not identify her as a covert agent, but it did give her maiden and cover name. This potentially violated the 1982 Intelligence Identities Protection Act.

But the administration's Wilson "bashing" was in full gear, so much so it even alarmed White House aides. "Scooter and Karl [Rove] are out of control," Adam Levine, a press aide, complained to another official. "You've got to rein these guys in." Here was an irony to top all ironies in the efforts to shut down whistleblowers and leakers. Cheney and others had employed leaks they had planted with Judith Miller to launch a war; they were now seeking to use leaks to destroy critics of that war.[32]

After his conversations with Wilson, with the Novak column having stirred up other stories about Valerie Plame, David Corn published a question on his *Nation* blog: "Did senior Bush officials blow the cover of a US intelligence officer working covertly in a field of vital importance to national security—and break the law—in order to strike at a Bush administration critic and intimidate others?"[33]

Among those with whom Libby had been planting the information about Wilson's wife working at the CIA was Miller. She never wrote a story about it, but she did tell an editor, Jill Abramson, that it was worth finding out if

Libby's revelations really meant there was a Wilson/Plame plot, so to speak, to undermine Bush or whether the Libby information was merely a White House attempt to discredit a truth teller. What Libby had plainly done was to commit a serious federal offense by revealing the identity of a covert operative.[34]

The CIA sent a formal complaint to the FBI about what had happened, and the Justice Department opened an investigation. Ironically, given events in later years, the deputy attorney general who appointed a special counsel in the Plame investigation was James Comey. Attorney General John Ashcroft had recused himself because some of the possible targets of the investigation posed a potential conflict of interest. Patrick Fitzgerald had a strong reputation for independence and was far enough away, in the Chicago federal attorney's office, not to be seen as part of the Bush executive leadership.

The CIA complaint put the Justice Department in a tight spot: how to assure the public that the investigation of a high-level White House figure would be fair. When he appointed Fitzgerald, Comey assured him it was a piece of cake and would take no more than a few months, half a year at most. It took four years, and Fitzgerald would be attacked both by Libby supporters and newspapers defending Miller's decision to go to jail rather than reveal Libby as a leaker of Plame's name.[35]

Libby's defense was that he had gotten Plame's name from reporters, specifically, Tim Russert. But Russert told the FBI that was not the case; Libby had instead given it to him. Russert died before he could testify at Libby's trial for perjury. Therefore, Miller's testimony about her conversations with Cheney's confidant became all the more important as confirmation about one side of the story or the other. Further complicating matters, Libby's case became intertwined with the debate over whether it had been right to go to war against Iraq. Miller's reputation was beginning to be an issue, moreover, and some hoped to strike a blow against the war by attacking Libby's activities—any and all of them—and were eager to see the Cheney aide convicted. If that meant abandoning Miller, so be it. Besides, she had led the war cry, hadn't she?

Risen thought it was a terrible mistake to refight the Iraq War question by proxy over Miller's prewar stories.[36] When Miller refused to testify about what Libby had told her about Plame, the presiding judge gave her an opportunity to make a statement about the need for a free press. She quoted Jefferson, who had said if forced to choose between having a government and a free press, he would choose the latter. She went on to discuss her years of reporting in and about the Middle East as further confirmation of Jefferson's essential creed. Without confidential sources, she said, a truly free and independent press was impossible. Hence democracy could not survive.[37]

Miller never really admitted that she had been manipulated. She contended that her stories included criticism about the drive to war, even as a consensus supported the campaign to take down Hussein. Regardless, Risen backed her up, despite their differing views on the war, and would certainly subscribe to her invocation of Jefferson at her trial. The intertwined careers of these two reporters well illustrated the complications of the free press in the context of national security.

Judge Thomas F. Hogan heard her out and sent the reporter off to jail, shackled like a convicted felon. There she stayed for eighty-five days. Fitzgerald had no intention of letting her out until she relented and offered up what he wanted. "This is a proud but awful moment for *The New York Times* and its employees," began the paper's editorial on Miller's jailing. She had taken a lonely and painful path, it continued. "We wish she did not have to choose it, but we are certain she did the right thing." Like Miller's statement to the court, it connected her with the great traditions of civil disobedience "that began with this nation's founding." Then the editorial turned to the Novak article, suggesting it was indeed possible that someone had "told Mr. Novak" to undermine Wilson's credibility by revealing his wife's name, in order to "send a chilling signal to other officials." It then declared, "if Ms. Miller testifies, it may be immeasurably harder in the future to persuade a frightened government employee to talk about malfeasance in high places, or a worried worker to reveal corporate crimes."[38]

Then came a somewhat curious half-nod in the direction of those who believed that Miller had been trapped in her own coziness with Bush officials. Had Libby sought her out as a sympathetic listener? It was highly possible, as she was a desirable outlet with *New York Times* credentials to provide greater credibility with its audience than Novak. "To be frank," it read, "this is far from an ideal case." "We would not have wanted our reporter to give up her liberty over a situation whose details are so complicated and muddy."

Nonetheless, it proved impossible for the paper to provide a sympathetic home for Miller after she was released, having obtained a personal waiver from Libby that freed her from her self-imposed confinement by not testifying. Others already had, and the case, as the *New York Times* editorial said, was among the murkiest of episodes surrounding the whole sequence of events, including others in the administration, especially Vice President Dick Cheney, who were just as deeply involved in the "outing" of Valerie Plame as Libby and Novak.[39]

At the conclusion of the Libby trial, Special Prosecutor Patrick Fitzgerald made it clear that the vice president was the real target of the investigation: he was the promoter of a series of leaks to out Valerie Plame. Fitzgerald had imperfect evidence that Libby had been the leak to Robert Novak, but it was Libby's perjury that prevented him from getting the full story of how Cheney manipulated the news as he had in planting stories about Iraq's nuclear capabilities before the second Gulf War. There was a cloud over the vice president, Fitzgerald said at the conclusion of the Libby trial. "We didn't put that cloud there. That cloud remains because the defendant obstructed justice and lied about what happened," Fitzgerald added.[40]

Libby was convicted but would not go to jail: Bush commuted his thirty-month sentence, citing his many years of public service. It was not a pardon, however, and the order that Libby pay a $250,000 fine remained in place. Bush went out of his way, moreover, to say that the punishment was still harsh because his reputation had been forever damaged. In 2018, President Donald Trump pardoned Libby, satisfying a long-desired outcome for a segment of his base supporters. But that only raised new questions about Trump's hope of setting a precedent to pardon those who had lied to the FBI in connection with the Russia investigation about collusion in the 2016 election.[41]

* * *

Miller left the *New York Times* and eventually moved to *Fox News* as a commentator. Risen also left the *Times* and began writing for the *Intercept* an online news outlet. These two places could not be further apart politically. Risen's last big battle came over a subpoena to testify in the trial of Sterling for exposing the story of the CIA's embarrassing effort to sabotage the Iranian nuclear weapons program, which he covered in *State of War*. Risen always believed that the subpoenas he fought had to do with the Stellar Wind story more than the Iran affair. His fight against government actions had stretched from the Bush administration to the Justice Department during the Obama years. Like Miller, Risen also believed the issue was not "which side were you on" over the Iraq War but the integrity of reporters who gave their word that a source would remain confidential. The government's use of the minatory Espionage Act to imprison leakers and intimidate reporters formed a two-front attack on an independent press, the foundation of the American democratic state. The threat of the penalties under that 1917 act had been invoked several times in the twentieth century, as discussed in other chapters of this volume. Obama's Justice Department invoked it more often than all previous administrations. Despite failures to convict, it brought results in the form of career-ending punishments on lesser charges.[42]

Risen would not go to jail, as a last-minute compromise was reached that did not require him to divulge his source. Asked on CBS News if he would ever give up a source, Risen replied: "Never, no. Basically, the choice the government's given me is: give up everything I believe or go to jail. So, I'm not going to talk."[43] Attorney General Eric Holder stopped the pursuit by declaring that no reporter would go to jail for doing his or her job. How definitive that was as a reporter's protection was open to question, especially when that job involved reporting on information about secret national security matters.

These were magnified by the government prosecutor's closing argument in the Sterling trial: "Jeffrey Sterling was the hero of Risen's story. Don't let him be the hero of this one." Whatever the jury thought about the ambiguously worded threat to Risen and other reporters who would follow in his tracks, Sterling was convicted and sentenced to forty-two months in prison. When Bush declared a "Global War on Terror," he said that the enemy hated the American way of life and was determined to destroy it. "Al-Qaeda is to terror what the Mafia is to crime," he said on September 20, 2001, "But its goal is not making money, its goal is remaking the world and imposing its radical beliefs on people everywhere."[44] It was a justification for what Cheney said had to be done on the "dark side" to defeat this menace. The Mafia mention was interesting, as a reference to a threat to the nation's integrity from within in years past. It was now for debate whether democracy could survive attacks on an independent press, the challenge to Truth in our Times.

The travails of Judith Miller and James Risen are an unfinished story that transcends the presidencies when the events recounted here took place. The challenge has shifted shape, but the stakes are the same. Miller's reliance on inside sources to produce sensational stories was not unique and continues today as reporters rely on leaks deliberately planted by government officials; Risen's fight against precisely such efforts is also a timeless obligation of journalism in a democracy.[45]

* * *

A few weeks after Donald Trump's surprising victory in November 2016, Risen wrote an op-ed piece for the *New York Times*. He was about to leave the newspaper to join the *Intercept* as senior national security correspondent; he was also to become director of First Look Media's Press Freedom Defense Fund. Entitled "If Donald Trump Targets Journalists, Thank Obama," Risen wrote that if the presidential campaign was a good indicator, the new president was likely to "embrace the aggressive crackdown on journalists and whistle-blowers that is an important yet little understood component of Mr. Obama's presidential legacy." Risen offered as proof the nine cases his administration had prosecuted, invoking the "Espionage Act, a relic of World War I–era red-baiting, not to prosecute spies but to go after government officials who talked to journalists." His own experience and struggle in the Jeffrey Sterling case provided the backdrop for the op-ed piece, but he supported this claim (one that seemed overly harsh to Obama supporters) with a 2013 report from the Committee to Protect Journalists, authored by Leonard Downie, a former executive editor of the *Washington Post*. Downie wrote that the Obama war on leaks and other efforts to control information was "the most aggressive I've seen since the Nixon administration, when I was one of the editors involved in the *Washington Post*'s investigation of Watergate." Trevor Timm, executive director of the Freedom of the Press Foundation, added, "Obama has laid all the groundwork Trump needs for an unprecedented crackdown on the press."[46]

When Trump then went after WikiLeaks's Julian Assange, Risen was not surprised. Assange had all the qualifications government censors—of either party—love for a test case. He was not widely loved, to put it mildly. His role as head of WikiLeaks during the 2016 presidential campaign when he dumped Democratic Party e-mails onto his website brought cries of outrage even from those who had earlier defended his role in distributing secret documents given to him during the Iraq War by Chelsea Manning. But there was a bizarre twist to the hacking of the Democratic Party computers that entangled the already fraught story of Hillary Clinton's separate "missing" e-mails from her private computer when she was secretary of state. The Clinton e-mails had become a controversy all on their own when, at a crucial point in the election campaign, FBI Director James Comey stigmatized her behavior as careless in a press conference.

Donald Trump then called on WikiLeaks to publish those e-mails. "Russia, if you're listening," he said at a press conference on July 27, 2016, "I hope you're able to find the 30,000 e-mails that are missing." He added, "I think you will probably be rewarded mightily by our press." That comment has been widely interpreted then and now to mean he welcomed Assange's forays into classified secret documents and his willingness to publish them. The interpretation gained weight when postelection investigations demonstrated that within hours of Trump's call—whether meant that way or as a sarcastic jibe at the press—the Russians did send pilfered Clinton messages to WikiLeaks. But in his comments Trump had gone on to say no one really knew if the Russians had been the culprits in the leak of Democratic Party documents. "It could be somebody sitting in his bed. *But it shows how weak we are, it shows how disrespected we are . . . the leaders throughout the world have no respect for our country anymore and they certainly have no respect for our leader.*" Then, to add yet another layer to this muddled piece of campaign rhetoric, Trump closed with, "Why should I tell Putin what to do?"[47]

The call on Russia to publish the e-mails provided headlines for months, and now years, before and after the Mueller Report on interference in the 2016 election. But there was also the implication that as soon as he became president he would do something about America's standing in the world so that foreign dictators would not be able to traffic in state secrets. However that may be, the Trump administration decided to make the unpopular Assange a test case. The WikiLeaks founder had been inside Ecuador's embassy in London as an asylum seeker since 2012, after Swedish prosecutors had attempted to extradite him to face a rape charge. There were rumors that the Swedish indictment was trumped up in order to get him out of the United Kingdom and make it easier to extradite him to the United States to face charges under the Espionage Act for publishing the secret documents Manning had provided WikiLeaks.

Ecuador revoked Assange's asylum after a series of murky events, including confrontations inside the embassy and government changes in Quito. Chased from the embassy, he was immediately arrested and then convicted of violating his bail and sentenced to fifty weeks in prison. Three *New York Times* reporters considered rumors about what President Barack Obama intended but concluded, "The Obama administration had explored whether to bring charges against Mr. Assange but decided not, in part because of fears of creating a precedent that could chill traditional journalism."[48]

When the Trump administration then issued a warrant for Assange's arrest to begin extradition proceedings, it at first attempted to skirt the press issue. The Justice Department did not charge him under the Espionage Act, as Obama had done in at least nine other cases, but with conspiring to commit "unlawful computer intrusion" through an agreement with Manning to break an encoded password so that she could log onto a classified military network. It was a head-scratching indictment in convoluted lawyerese. Assange's lawyers sounded a warning to all journalists about "these unprecedented criminal charges." The administration apparently agreed and moved quickly to simplify matters—with a new indictment charging Assange with seventeen different counts under the Espionage Act. As for endangering press freedom, the Justice Department was having none of it. A spokesman for the department declared, "Julian Assange is no journalist." No mainstream reporter would put human lives "at a grave and imminent risk" of harm.[49] Asked by a reporter if anyone had been killed because of what WikiLeaks had published, a senior official "speaking on the condition of anonymity" replied that the government's burden was only to establish the "potential" for harm.[50]

Risen responded to this event with a stinging call for action. "A TRUE DEMOCRACY does not allow its government to decide who is a journalist. A nation in which a leader gets to make that decision is on the road to dictatorship." Reviewing the actual material Manning had supplied WikiLeaks and then what had been published by the *New York Times* and the *Guardian*, Risen reminded everyone of some of the things that had been revealed about "long-hidden truths" in the wars in Iraq and Afghanistan. What had occurred was "almost a textbook definition of the job of a reporter covering national security at a major news organization." It was interesting, moreover, that the charges against Assange had nothing to do with his role in laundering documents from Russian spies to help Trump win. "It is exceedingly unlikely that this Justice Department would choose to go down that road."[51]

Mike Pompeo, Trump's CIA director before he became secretary of state, had called WikiLeaks a "nonstate hostile intelligence service." The conservative columnist Marc Thiessen picked up on that charge after Assange's indictment under the Espionage Act, claiming the damage he had done in releasing more than a quarter of a million classified State Department cables was "unfathomable." "Assange is not a journalist. He is a spy."[52]

The debate over press freedom and responsibility is an old one. But Risen's warning about who gets to decide who is a journalist has never seemed more pertinent to the fate of democracy. With presidential tweets constantly calling the press "fake news" purveyors and the "enemy of the people," we are living in dangerous times, and there is no sure conclusion that the outcome will be in democracy's favor.

NOTES

1. This is the title of chapter 7 of Hayden's memoir, *Playing to the Edge: American Intelligence in the Age of Terror* (New York: Penguin, 2016), 113.
2. Hayden, *Playing to the Edge*, 126.
3. For more on this point, see John Prados, *The Ghosts of Langley: Into the CIA's Heart of Darkness* (New York: New Press, 2017), beginning with chap. 5, "The Consiglieri," 195, and later chapters.
4. An overview is in Lloyd C. Gardner, *The War on Leakers: National Security and American Democracy from Eugene V. Debs to Edward Snowden* (New York: New Press, 2016).
5. James Risen, "My Life as a *New York Times* Reporter in the Shadow of the War on Terror," *Intercept*, January 3, 2018, https://theintercept.com/2018/01/03my-life-as-a-new-york-times-reporter-in-the-shadow-of-the-war-on-terror/.
6. History.com, "9/11 Attacks—Facts & Summary," https://www.history.com/topics/21st-century/9--11-attacks.
7. Philip Shenon, *The Commission: The Uncensored History of the 9/11 Investigation* (New York: Twelve, 2008), 372–76.
8. Shenon, *The Commission*, 424.
9. Hayden, *Playing to the Edge*, 103–4.
10. For an excellent summary of the issue, see Michael Walzer, "Just and Unjust Leaks," *Foreign Affairs* 97, no. 2 (March/April 2018): 48–59; see also responses to Walzer by Peter Feaver and Allison Stanger, "The Secret Sharers: Leaking and Whistle-Blowing in the Trump Era," *Foreign Affairs* 97, no. 6 (November/December 2018): 199–206.
11. See, for example, James Risen and Judith Miller, "The Spies: Pakistani Intelligence Had Links to Al Qaeda, U.S. Officials Say," *New York Times*, October 29, 2001. In this article, the two authors cited anonymous "American officials" who contended the Pakistani intelligence service (ISI) had turned "a blind eye for years to the growing ties between Osama bin Laden and the Taliban."
12. Judith Miller, *The Story: A Reporter's Journey* (New York: Simon & Schuster, 2015), 164.
13. The story of Saddam Hussein's nuclear-weapons program is an entangled one. It begins in the aftermath of the First Gulf War with the discovery that he was much further along in developing a nuclear weapon than had been imagined. When evidence emerged that he had been so engaged, it also became clear that many American high-tech companies had been helping him in his endeavors. At the time, the 1980s, Hussein had been fighting a desperate war with Iran for nearly a decade and was seen by Washington as an ally in Middle Eastern geopolitics. The best summary of what preceded the First Gulf War and Hussein's likely ability to reinstitute his program afterward is Gary Milhollin, "Building Saddam Hussein's Bomb," *New York Times Magazine*, March 8, 1992, https://www.nytimes.com/1992/03/08/magazine/building-saddam-hussein-s-bomb.html.
14. Miller, *The Story*, 165–67.

15. Michael Isikoff and David Corn, *Hubris: The Inside Story of Spin, Scandal, and the Selling of the Iraq War* (New York: Broadway, 2007), 35.

16. Michael R. Gordon and Judith Miller, "Threats and Responses: The Iraqis; U.S. Says Hussein Intensifies Quest for A-Bomb Parts," *New York Times*, September 8, 2002, https://www.nytimes.com/2002/09/08/world/threats-responses-iraqis-us-says-hussein -intensifies-quest-for-bomb-parts.html.

17. *Meet the Press*, NBC, September 8, 2002.

18. David Barstow, William J. Broad, and Jeff Gerth, "The Nuclear Card: The Aluminum Tube Story—A Special Report; How White House Embraced Suspect Iraq Arms Intel- ligence," *New York Times*, October 3, 2004, https://www.nytimes.com/2004/10/03 /washington/us/the-nuclear-card-the-aluminum-tube-story-a-special-report-how.html.

19. See, for example, Jane Mayer, "The Manipulator," *New Yorker*, June 7, 2004, https://www .newyorker.com/magazine/2004/06/07/the-manipulator.

20. Risen, "My Life as a *New York Times* Reporter."

21. Risen, "My Life as a *New York Times* Reporter."

22. Hayden, *Playing to the Edge*, 94–95.

23. Gardner, *The War on Leakers*, 100–2.

24. David Folkenflik, "*New York Times* Editor: Losing Snowden Scoop 'Really Painful,'" NPR, June 5, 2014, https://www.npr.org/2014/06/05/319233332/new-york-times-editor -losing-snowden-scoop-really-painful.

25. Hayden, *Playing to the Edge*, 101.

26. Peter Baker, *Days of Fire: Bush and Cheney in the White House* (New York: Doubleday, 2013), 434. There were several things to debate here, besides specific questions of press freedom. For example, the question of purely domestic monitoring versus "foreign" com- munications, which few would argue would be outside the mandate of the agency. Hayden had claimed that was the case with Stellar Wind. But even if that were so, it appeared that no one was monitoring NSA practices very carefully. There was little oversight—as was true about several government programs in the post-9/11 era, such as the CIA rendition and interrogation sites. The real issue thus was not the number of Americans being monitored by mistake (or design!) but the erosion of privacy guaran- teed under the Fourth Amendment and the use of emergency powers to substitute for congressional action and approval.

27. Risen, "My Life as a *New York Times* Reporter."

28. "NSA Whistleblowers Testify in Bundestag Inquiry, Disclose 'Totalitarian' Surveil- lance," *rt.com*, July 3, 2014, http:/rt.com/news/170276-germany-nsa-bundestag-inquiry/. For more on Drake and Binney as well as others caught up in the effort to find the anony- mous informants, see Gardner, *The War on Leakers*.

29. Joseph Wilson, "What I Didn't Find in Africa," *New York Times*, July 6, 2003, https:// www.nytimes.com/2003/76/06/opinion/what-i-ddn-t-find-in-africa.html.

30. "Statement by George J. Tenet Director of Central Intelligence," July 11, 2003, https:// www.cia.gov/news-information/press-releases . . . /press . . . /pr07112003.html.

31. Isikoff and Corn, *Hubris*, 258.
32. Isikoff and Corn, *Hubris*, 291.
33. Isikoff and Corn, *Hubris*, 290.
34. Isikoff and Corn, *Hubris*, 277.
35. James Comey, *A Higher Loyalty: Truth, Lies, and Leadership* (New York: Flatiron, 2018), 68–75.
36. Gardner, *The War on Leakers*, 249–54; Keynote Roundtable, "Freedom of the Press and National Security in the Trump Era: Reconciling Competing Values in Democratic Governance," National Constitution Center, Philadelphia, PA, November 9, 2017.
37. *Frontline Interviews: Judith Miller*, PBS, February 13, 2007, https://www.pbs.org/wgbh/pages/frontline/newswar/interviews/miller.html.
38. Editorial, "Judith Miller Goes to Jail," *New York Times*, July 7, 2005, https://www.nytimes.com/2005/07/07/opinion/judith-miller-goes-to-jail.html.
39. It is impossible here to go into this question in the detail required to understand what happened and who was involved. One can start with Isikoff and Corn, *Hubris*, chap. 15, "A Cover Blown," and continue with Miller, *The Story*. Miller's "story" has become an indelible part of the debate over the Iraq War and all that followed.
40. R. Jeffrey Smith, "Cheney's Suspected Role in Security Breach Drove Fitzgerald," *Washington Post*, March 7, 2007.
41. The debate goes on and on as history moves to the present. Matthew Cooper, then a *Time* reporter, was involved along with Judith Miller in the Libby case; like Miller he accepted a waiver from Libby—but earlier, before going to jail. His reactions to Trump's pardon were dramatic and accusatory. See Matthew Cooper, "Donald Trump Pardoned Scooter Libby to Save Himself. Nothing Else Makes Sense," *USA Today*, April 17, 2018.
42. See Gardner, *The War on Leakers*, 189–225.
43. Gardner, *The War on Leakers*, 251.
44. President George W. Bush's Address to Congress and the Nation on Terrorism, September 20, 2001, http://www.johnstonsarchive.net/terrorism/bush911c.html.
45. For a contrary argument that journalists like Risen have traded in leaks for personal ambition and that the upshot of the leaks they publish actually drives presidents to find a narrower and narrower circle of advisers, see Rahul Sagar, *Secrets and Leaks: The Dilemma of State Secrecy* (Princeton, NJ: Princeton University Press, 2013), 158–62, 202–4.
46. James Risen, "If Donald Trump Targets Journalists, Thank Obama," *New York Times*, December 30, 2016.
47. My emphasis. The whole episode is put in context by David A. Graham, "Trump's Call for Russian Hacking Makes Even Less Sense After Mueller," *Atlantic*, March 27, 2019, https://www.theatlantic.com/politcs/archive/2019/03/reviewing-trumps-call-russian-hackjing-after-mueller/585838.
48. Charlie Savage, Adam Goldman, and Eileen Sullivan, "Julian Assange Arrested in London as U.S. Unseals Hacking Conspiracy Indictment," *New York Times*, April 11, 2019, https://www.nytimes.com/2019/04/11/world/europe/julian-assange-wikileaks-ecuador-embassy.html.

49. "WikiLeaks Founder Indicted on Espionage Act Charges, Raising Issues of Press Freedoms," CNN, May 22, 2019, https://www.cnn.com/2019/05/23politics/julian-assange-espionage-act-charges/index.html.

50. "WikiLeaks Founder Indicted."

51. James Risen, "The Indictment of Julian Assange Under the Espionage Act Is a Threat to the Press and the American People," *Intercept*, May 24, 2019, https://portside.org/node/20111/printable/print.

52. Marc Thiessen, "Julian Assange Is a Spy—WikiLeaks Is Not Journalism," *Fox News*, May 29, 2019, https://www.foxnews.com/opinion/marc-thiessen-jusice-department-assange.

CODA

Edward Snowden, National Security Whistleblowing, and Civil Disobedience

DAVID E. POZEN

N ATIONAL SECURITY WHISTLEBLOWERS are complicated characters. On the one hand, as the chapters in this volume reflect, they may appear disloyal, self-centered, overconfident in their own views, threatening to the general good. On the other hand, as the chapters also reflect, they may appear heroic, selfless, zealous for truth, essential to democratic accountability. The best-known whistleblowers are depicted as all of these things at the same time. As Hannah Gurman and Kaeten Mistry observe, national security whistleblowers are increasingly "included in the tradition of civil disobedience" even as they are increasingly indicted as public enemies.[1] Their cultural celebrity and legal precarity, their legitimation and persecution, have developed in dialectical relation since at least the Vietnam War.

No recent U.S. whistleblower has been more lionized or more vilified than Edward Snowden. He has been nominated for the Nobel Peace Prize and denounced as a "total traitor" deserving of the death penalty.[2] Although none of the essays in this volume focuses on Snowden, he is everywhere in its pages. His case "encapsulates," in Mistry and Gurman's words, the "ambiguous and paradoxical" attitudes toward national security whistleblowing that the volume highlights and historicizes.[3]

Perhaps we might look to Snowden to help theorize these attitudes as well. If defenders of whistleblowers are apt to include them in the tradition of civil disobedience, and if Snowden is the emblematic whistleblower of our age, what does civil disobedience theory have to tell us about Snowden's case? Conversely, what does Snowden's case have to tell us about civil disobedience theory as it relates to the national security state? Resolving the question whether Snowden is a civil disobedient (as he has suggested)[4] will not resolve the question whether his actions were justified. But unlike the label "whistleblower," the label "civil disobedient" comes with a substantial scholarly pedigree, affording an opportunity to place the Snowden debate within a larger philosophical context.

On most accounts, civil disobedience "involves a conscientious and communicative breach of law designed to demonstrate condemnation of a law or policy and to contribute to a change in that law or policy."[5] Theorists of civil disobedience disagree on a lot, but this is the core of virtually every definition: a morally serious violation of law that conveys a protest message and aspires to motivate reform. Isn't that Snowden? What's so difficult about his case?

The difficulty, I will suggest, is that most definitions of civil disobedience include additional elements, additional criteria for distinguishing civil disobedience from other presumptively less favored forms of lawbreaking, and Snowden does not clearly satisfy any of these. Yet Snowden does not clearly fail any of them either, at least not without a plausible justification or excuse. His case is therefore an awkward fit for civil disobedience theory, and this awkwardness may help explain some of the "ambiguous and paradoxical" attitudes that swirl around it.

Without purporting to be exhaustive, let us consider some of the ways in which Snowden, along with many other national security whistleblowers, puts pressure on traditional models of civil disobedience.

First, some prominent theories of civil disobedience require that the lawbreaking be a tactic of last resort, preceded by an earnest attempt at persuasion and an exhaustion of lawful alternatives. In *A Theory of Justice*, for instance, John Rawls writes that a "further condition for civil disobedience is the following. We may suppose that the normal appeals to the political majority have already been made in good faith and that they have failed."[6] Martin Luther King Jr.'s "Letter from Birmingham City Jail" cites "negotiation" as one of the "four basic steps" that must be taken before moving to "direct action."[7] There is some dispute about the facts of Snowden's case, but according to the National Security Agency (NSA), he did not appeal to his superiors, follow the normal whistleblower protocols, or otherwise attempt to change the surveillance system from within before divulging its details to the outside world. He did not satisfy Rawls's condition of fair notice.[8]

Against this charge, however, Snowden might respond that doing so would have been self-defeating. To be effective, disclosures of classified information generally need concealment before the fact. The NSA may well have shut down Snowden if it had gotten any wind of what he was contemplating.[9] Moreover, the legal regime for national security whistleblowing, to the extent it facilitates whistleblowing at all, is oriented toward allegations of discrete abuses by particular bad actors—abuses that can be quietly and surgically remedied once identified. The whistleblower regime is not well equipped to handle allegations, such as Snowden's, of formally authorized yet immoral and unconstitutional behavior on a sweeping scale. Indeed, there is something faintly ridiculous about the image of Snowden bringing his allegations to the NSA inspector general or a congressional committee under these circumstances. Both the nature of Snowden's methods (a media leak) and the nature of his protest (a comprehensive critique of agency practice) are hard to square with a commitment to advance notice and negotiation.

Second, many theories of civil disobedience require that the civil disobedient seek to minimize the extent of his or her lawbreaking and the collateral damage it causes. This is often discussed under the rubric of nonviolence, which Hannah Arendt believed to be a "generally accepted necessary characteristic of civil disobedience."[10] But the point is not necessarily limited to physical violence, as the gravamen of these discussions is that civil disobedience should be as civil—as uncoercive and undisruptive—as

possible.[11] Snowden may seem suspect on this ground. He reportedly pur-
loined tens of thousands of sensitive documents, and the NSA claims that
the harm to U.S. national security interests has been severe.[12]

Has it, though? Six years after Snowden fled the country, it remains
extremely unclear how many classified documents he took with him, which
tranches he has shared with whom, and what the effects have been.[13] As a
descriptive matter, outside observers cannot say with any confidence just
how reckless or judicious Snowden's lawbreaking has been. The public consequences of that lawbreaking, furthermore, have been mediated by the
media, as Snowden vested select journalists with the power to decide what
to publish. The breadth of Snowden's critique of the NSA complicates analysis of this criterion as well. Insofar as he intended to communicate the
message that the basic architecture of NSA surveillance had become
unmoored from democratic and constitutional constraints, his defenders
might insist that only a massive leak could illuminate the massive scope of
the problem. Whether one believes Snowden to have caused undue harm
depends not only on unknown facts, in other words, but also on what one
takes him to have been protesting and with what degree of warrant.

Third, Snowden's status as a government contractor arguably strains the
civil disobedience paradigm. The canonical examples in the literature, from
Dr. King to Rosa Parks to Mahatma Gandhi, were not working for the state
at the time they broke the law. There is something especially discomfiting,
some may maintain, about a government worker turning to civil disobedience and violating not only the generally applicable laws that everyone is
supposed to follow but also the employment contract—and in particular
the nondisclosure clause—that he or she signed. Such disobedience raises
concerns about the norm of promise keeping as well as more familiar concerns about public order and authority.

In Snowden's case, however, it was precisely his status as a government
insider that enabled him to identify an otherwise obscure policy problem
and respond to it. National security whistleblowing is like this. The protagonists serve in a position of trust at a public institution while occupying
"another, equally important position in the constitutional structure—that
of potential checks on abuses or mistakes to which they alone may be

privy."[14] When it comes to the hypersecretive activities of an agency such as the NSA, only an insider will have the prerequisite knowledge to be able to mount a meaningful challenge. If civil disobedience relies on a reasonably detailed grasp of the laws or policies that are being protested, we may have to acknowledge the possibility of governmental civil disobedience or else accept that there can be none at all in the intelligence field.

Fourth, some accounts of civil disobedience portray it as a collective practice. Arendt, for instance, writes that the civil disobedient "never exists as an individual; he can function and survive only as a member of a group."[15] Civil disobedients, in her telling, are not lone wolves but "organized minorities, bound together by common opinion."[16] Similarly, Michael Walzer writes that the "duty" of civil disobedience "arises when obligations incurred in some small group come into conflict with obligations incurred in a larger, more inclusive group, generally the state."[17] In contrast with these portraits, Snowden seems to have taken matters into his own hands. His famous predecessor Daniel Ellsberg at least collaborated with a former colleague (Anthony Russo) and reached out to individual members of Congress. As far as I am aware, Snowden did not attempt to recruit any allies in his plan to leak information about the NSA. This might suggest a troubling amount of independence from others who could have challenged his beliefs and thus a troubling amount of epistemic hubris.[18] What if Snowden had been mistaken about some key point of fact or law? What if his views on NSA surveillance had been ill-informed or idiosyncratic? A collective protest against the agency's operations, involving not just Snowden but a group of like-minded colleagues, might have abated these concerns.

Yet how could Snowden have pulled that off? How, that is, could he have formed such a group under the constraints of NSA classification and compartmentalization? National security whistleblowing typically demands a great deal of individual secrecy, during the planning and execution stages, to survive within the larger atmosphere of institutional secrecy. Banding together with fellow dissidents along the lines envisioned by Arendt and Walzer is infeasible in a setting like the NSA. In addition, while Snowden may have started out as a lone wolf, he did not end as one. He appears to have formulated and launched his protest plan by himself, but as already

FIGURE 12.1

Signs thanking Edward Snowden held by protesters during a rally against mass surveillance in Washington, DC, October 26, 2013.

Source: Photo by Rena Schild/Shutterstock.

mentioned, he enlisted the aid of journalists and deferred to their professional judgment in determining which documents to publish. The news media and, later, the civil-libertarian NGO community became the site of Snowden's collective praxis.

Fifth, certain commentators have taken the position that a civil disobedient, properly so called, must violate the same law that he or she means to challenge, as when a pacifist refuses to report for duty under a military-conscription statute. "The disobedience of laws which are not themselves the target of the protest," Supreme Court Justice Abe Fortas declared in 1968, "constitutes an act of rebellion, not merely of dissent."[19] Fortas plainly would not recognize Snowden's "act of rebellion" as civil disobedience. Snowden was indicted for violating laws, in particular the U.S. Code's prohibitions on unauthorized communication of national defense and intelligence information, that he may have found objectionable in various respects but that were not the target of his protest.[20]

Most theorists of civil disobedience, however, have not followed Fortas in ruling out the possibility of indirect civil disobedience,[21] and in Snowden's case it is hard to imagine what direct civil disobedience would have looked like. (Spying on Americans beyond what even the NSA's rules permitted?) Only by violating the laws limiting disclosure of classified information, it seems, could Snowden communicate his condemnation of the laws and policies governing NSA surveillance. Either Fortas's condition must be jettisoned, or national security whistleblowers will almost never be eligible to qualify as civil disobedients.

Finally, classic discussions of civil disobedience suggest that it must be undertaken with a willingness to submit to punishment. Dr. King's "Letter from Birmingham City Jail" focuses on this feature. "One who breaks an unjust law," according to King, "must do it openly, lovingly . . . and with a willingness to accept the penalty."[22] As Jessica Bulman-Pozen and I have written: "The civil disobedient's willingness to accept legal consequences evinces her commitment to the *polis* and humility before fellow citizens, notwithstanding her momentary turn away from the law. It is thus, for many theorists, a critical way of negotiating the paradox of law-breaking that is nonetheless law-respecting"[23]—a paradox that inheres in the pairing of "civil" with "disobedience" and that any satisfying account of civil disobedience must resolve. In line with these arguments, critics of Snowden have repeatedly insisted that his flight from the United States and from criminal prosecution, not to mention his residence in Russia, disqualifies him from civil disobedience status.[24] Secretary of State John Kerry, for example, told a television interviewer in 2014 that if Snowden "has a complaint about what's wrong with American surveillance" and seeks to cast himself as a civil disobedient, he "should man up," "come back here," and "stand in our system of justice and make his case."[25]

Once again, though, matters are more complicated than conventional accounts of civil disobedience might imply. Shortly after his disclosures were first reported, Snowden came forward to acknowledge his identity as their source, and in this sense he was not evasive at all. He has also been subject to a range of serious legal consequences, including possible "permanent displacement from his family and friends."[26] Thus far, it is true, Snowden has refused to come back and make his case to a jury of his peers in the Eastern District of Virginia (the jurisdiction in which he was charged), in a proceeding that would be partly closed to the public. After initially expressing an intention to "ask the courts and people of Hong Kong to decide [his] fate,"[27] Snowden appealed to "the international community" to judge his actions.[28] Such lofty language struck some observers as cagey and self-serving. But it starts to sound more felicitous when one considers the mismatch between the territorial limits and cultural biases of the Eastern District of Virginia and the global reach of the surveillance programs that Snowden exposed—programs that might be of concern to anyone in the world at risk of being sucked into the NSA's panoptic vortex.[29]

A deep question lurks in the background here: what is the moral and political community within which a putative civil disobedient ought to be judged? Theorists of civil disobedience have tended to ignore this question, presumably on the assumption that the relevant moral and political community lines up reasonably well with the legal jurisdiction in which the lawbreaking occurred. Snowden's intimation of a more cosmopolitan stance, a global ethics of resistance, complicates this assumption. It forces us to ask whether a willingness to submit to punishment, in the spirit of Dr. King, necessarily requires a willingness to submit to localized forms of punishment. This question will only grow increasingly acute as technological developments allow more and more whistleblowers to reach an international audience.

On numerous levels, then, Snowden's case does not map neatly onto traditional theories of civil disobedience. The same holds true for most cases of national security whistleblowing. One possible takeaway is that the ambivalent attitudes noted by Gurman and Mistry are not simply the product of polarized politics or insufficient consideration; rather, they reflect the genuine difficulties of locating such whistleblowers within our main ethical framework for assessing conscientious and communicative lawbreaking. Another possible takeaway points in a revisionist direction. Maybe certain aspects of the framework itself ought to be revisited and revised, or put aside altogether, in light of these difficulties.[30] Just as the chapters in this splendid volume urge us to move "beyond the reductive characterization of whistleblowers as heroes or traitors,"[31] we may need to move beyond the standard models of civil disobedience to gain greater normative purchase on what whistleblowers do.

NOTES

1. Hannah Gurman and Kaeten Mistry, "The Paradox of National Security Whistleblowing: Locating and Framing a History of the Phenomenon," chapter 1 in this volume.
2. Ryan Goodman, "Five (Overlooked) Decision Points for the Trump Administration in National Security," *Just Security*, January 4, 2017, https://www.justsecurity.org/35958/overlooked-decision-points-trump-administration-national-security, quoting a 2015 remark by then-presidential candidate Donald Trump.
3. Kaeten Mistry and Hannah Gurman, introduction, this volume.
4. See, for example, Melissa Chan, "Edward Snowden Invokes Martin Luther King to Defend Whistleblowing," *Time*, May 12, 2016, http://time.com/4327930/edward-snowden-martin-luther-king-whistleblowing; and Terrence McCoy, "Edward Snowden: 'I'd Like to Go Home,'" *Washington Post*, May 29, 2014, https://www.washingtonpost.com/news/morning-mix/wp/2014/05/29/edward-snowden-says-he-would-like-to-return-home-but-not-to-a-jail-cell.
5. Kimberley Brownlee, "Civil Disobedience," *Stanford Encyclopedia of Philosophy*, December 20, 2013, https://plato.stanford.edu/entries/civil-disobedience. See also, for example, Joseph Raz, *The Authority of Law: Essays on Law and Morality* (New York: Oxford University Press, 1979), 263: "*Civil Disobedience* is a politically motivated breach of law designed either to contribute directly to a change of a law or of a public policy or to express one's protest against . . . a law or a public policy."
6. John Rawls, *A Theory of Justice* (Cambridge, MA: Harvard University Press, 1971), 373.
7. Martin Luther King Jr., "Letter from Birmingham City Jail," in *A Testament of Hope: The Essential Writings and Speeches of Martin Luther King, Jr.*, ed. James Melvin Washington (New York: HarperCollins, 1986), 290.
8. See Kimberley Brownlee, "The Civil Disobedience of Edward Snowden: A Reply to William Scheuerman," *Philosophy and Social Criticism* 42 (2016): 966, explaining that Snowden fails Rawls's "fair-notice publicity" condition as well as his condition of willingness to accept legal consequences but arguing that Snowden qualifies as a civil disobedient under "more modest and more plausible" conceptions than Rawls's.

9. See Gurman and Mistry, "The Paradox of National Security Whistleblowing," contending that "the experiences of individuals who used [the official national security whistleblowing] channels," before Snowden, "highlighted the hollowness of their promises"; and Candice Delmas, "The Ethics of Government Whistleblowing," *Social Theory and Practice* 41 (2015): 99, suggesting, with reference to Snowden, that the requirement of breaking the law only as a last resort "is not violated if there are reasons to think that lawful attempts would be useless or counterproductive." See also Jessica Bulman-Pozen and David E. Pozen, "Uncivil Obedience," *Columbia Law Review* 115 (2015): 815–16: "In some cases . . . [advance] publicity would furnish legal enforcers the opportunity to thwart the endeavor. In these cases, subsequent acknowledgement and explanation of the act may fulfill the requirement of communicativeness, along with many of the social values this requirement is thought to serve."

10. Hannah Arendt, "Civil Disobedience," in *Crises of the Republic* (New York: Harcourt Brace Jovanovich, 1969), 76–77.

11. See Bulman-Pozen and Pozen, "Uncivil Obedience," 816–17, reviewing relevant literature.

12. See, for example, Deb Riechmann, "Costs of Snowden Leak Still Mounting 5 Years Later," AP News, June 4, 2018, https://apnews.com/797f390ee28b4bfbb0e1b13cfedf0593.

13. See Riechmann, "Costs of Snowden Leak Still Mounting 5 Years Later," describing rebuttals of the NSA's claims by Snowden supporters.

14. Heidi Kitrosser, "Free Speech Aboard the Leaky Ship of State: Calibrating First Amendment Protections for Leakers of Classified Information," *Journal of National Security Law and Policy* 6 (2013): 440.

15. Arendt, "Civil Disobedience," 55.

16. Arendt, "Civil Disobedience," 56.

17. Michael Walzer, *Obligations: Essays on Disobedience, War, and Citizenship* (Cambridge, MA: Harvard University Press, 1970), 10.

18. Cf. Rahul Sagar, "Is Edward Snowden Engaged in Civil Disobedience?—A Response to Glennon," *Just Security*, June 5, 2014, https://www.justsecurity.org/11267/edward-snowden-engaged-civil-disobedience-a-response-glennon: "[Snowden] acted unilaterally, leaving fellow citizens with no choice over whether and what kinds of classified information ought to be disclosed. He didn't appeal to them; he decided for them."

19. Abe Fortas, *Concerning Dissent and Civil Disobedience* (New York: Signet, 1968), 63.

20. See William E. Scheuerman, "Whistleblowing as Civil Disobedience: The Case of Edward Snowden," *Philosophy and Social Criticism* 40 (2014): 612, noting that Snowden "violated prohibitions on whistleblowing" as a means "to bring the injustices of U.S. surveillance policies to public attention, not because he necessarily aspire[d] to discredit either government non-disclosure rules or the Espionage Act."

21. See Bulman-Pozen and Pozen, "Uncivil Obedience," 813.

22. King, "Letter from Birmingham City Jail," 294 (emphasis omitted).

23. Bulman-Pozen and Pozen, "Uncivil Obedience," 817. See also, for example, H. A. Bedau, "Civil Disobedience and Personal Responsibility for Injustice," in *Civil Disobedience in*

Focus, ed. Hugo Adam Bedau (New York: Routledge, 1991), 51, stating that civil disobedience's occurrence within the framework of the rule of law necessitates "a willingness on the part of the disobedient to accept the legal consequences of his act"; and Bernard E. Harcourt, "Political Disobedience," in *Occupy: Three Inquiries in Disobedience* (Chicago: University of Chicago Press, 2013), 46–47: "[Civil disobedience] respects the legal norm at the very moment of resistance, and places itself under the sanction of that norm. If it resists the legal sanction that it brings upon itself, in truth it is no longer engaged in civil disobedience."

24. See Michael J. Glennon, "Is Snowden Obliged to Accept Punishment?" *Just Security*, June 3, 2014, https://www.justsecurity.org/11068/guest-post-snowden-obliged-accept -punishment, cataloging and disputing such arguments.

25. Glennon, "Is Snowden Obliged to Accept Punishment?"

26. Piero Moraro, "On (Not) Accepting the Punishment for Civil Disobedience," *Philosophical Quarterly* 68 (2018): 508. See also David Pozen, "What Happens When We Actually Catch Edward Snowden?" *Lawfare*, July 15, 2013, https://www.lawfareblog.com/what -happens-when-we-actually-catch-edward-snowden: "A long prison term is a terrible fate. But even a short prison term would scare any rational person, and exile is a profound punishment as well. Indeed, it is an ancient response to offenses that are viewed as betraying one's community."

27. Lana Lan, "Whistleblower Edward Snowden Tells SCMP: 'Let Hong Kong People Decide My Fate,'" *South China Morning Post*, June 15, 2013, https://www.scmp.com/news /hong-kong/article/1259422/edward-snowden-let-hong-kong-people-decide-my-fate.

28. Edward Snowden, "Snowden's Letter of Appeal to Washington," October 31, 2013, https://archive.nytimes.com/www.nytimes.com/interactive/2013/11/01/world/europe /02snowden-letter.html.

29. Cf. Scheuerman, "Whistleblowing as Civil Disobedience," 621–23, discussing the global implications of Snowden's disclosures and the "lack of a sufficiently independent global legal system in which Snowden . . . could freely and openly defend" his actions under international or domestic law.

30. In this spirit, see, for example, Erin Pineda, "Civil Disobedience and Punishment: (Mis) reading Justification and Strategy from SNCC to Snowden," *History of the Present* 5 (2015): 4, using "the discourse surrounding Snowden's exile as a space within which to reconsider the place of punishment in theories of civil disobedience and to question the perennial power of a certain version of civil rights history to set the terms of judgment for contemporary protest"; and Candice Delmas, "That Lonesome Whistle," *Boston Review*, June 14, 2016, http://bostonreview.net/editors-picks-world-us/candice-delmas -lonesome-whistle, arguing that Snowden's actions, like national security whistleblowing generally, does not qualify as civil disobedience but can be justified "on its own terms."

31. Mistry and Gurman, introduction.

CONCLUSION

KAETEN MISTRY AND HANNAH GURMAN

W HISTLEBLOWING IS NOT something that needs to be disincentivized any more," said Edward Snowden in early 2019. Speaking from Moscow, where he has lived in exile for six years, he explained: "The deck is already stacked against them."[1]

The Snowden episode encapsulates the polarizing nature of current debates about national security whistleblowing. Snowden is widely regarded as a principled whistleblower, having passed his revelations to established news organizations to report. In the aftermath of his disclosures, the USA Freedom Act of 2015 was signed into law, imposing new limits on the bulk collection of metadata of U.S. citizens by intelligence agencies. He often speaks via video link to journalists, advocates, and at conferences to defend freedom of speech and freedom of the press. Snowden has emerged as a cultural icon and has been the subject of a major Hollywood movie.[2] Meanwhile, he remains a bête noire in the U.S. political and national security realms. In 2016, the House Permanent Select Committee on Intelligence published its "comprehensive review of the unauthorized disclosures" by Snowden, concluding that he "caused tremendous damage to national security" by revealing countless documents unrelated to individual privacy matters but "of great interest to America's adversaries." "Snowden was not a whistleblower," it insisted,

FIGURE 13.1

Edward Snowden speaks via video link at the South by Southwest
festival, Austin, Texas, March 10, 2014.

Source: Photo by Michael Buckber/Getty Images.

because he did not disclose "fraud, waste, abuse, or other illegal activity to
the appropriate law enforcement or oversight personnel—including to
congress." Instead, he "was, and remains, a serial exaggerator and fabrica-
tor." In addition to charging Snowden under the Espionage Act, in September 2019 the Justice Department filed a civil lawsuit against him for
publication of his memoir. The charge, echoing the case of Frank Snepp,
seeks to seize profits for violation of nondisclosure agreements and failure
to submit the manuscript for prepublication review.[3]

The contrasting narratives surrounding Snowden are not new, but neither are they eternal. They are products of political, legal, social, and cultural developments of the last century. The Obama administration's
response to Snowden was simply an escalation of the war that's been waged
against whistleblowing for decades. The scale was unprecedented, but the
tools have been used by successive U.S. governments since World War I.

On the other side, the heroization of Snowden has a lineage that begins in the 1970s, when the idea and act of the principled whistleblower crystallized in American political culture.

This war has continued under Donald Trump, whose Department of Justice has aggressively pursued prosecutions against those who disclose information related to national security in the public interest. In August 2018, Reality Winner was sentenced to five years in prison for revealing the NSA's analysis of Russia's efforts to interfere in the 2016 elections. Two months later, Terry Albury, an FBI field agent, received a four-year sentence for disclosing the discriminatory surveillance of Muslim communities in Minnesota. In May 2019, Daniel Hale, a former Air Force and NSA analyst and National Geospatial Intelligence Agency contractor, was arrested and faced up to fifty years in prison for exposing the extent of civilian deaths under the drone program in Afghanistan. All three were prosecuted under the Espionage Act. At the same time, Chelsea Manning was again imprisoned after refusing to testify against Julian Assange for WikiLeaks' publication of the Iraq and Afghanistan War Logs. There have also been important legislative changes. In July 2019, the U.S. Congress passed a bill that widened the definition of "covert agent" in the 1982 Intelligence Identities Protection Act. Press freedom and transparency activists widely criticized this change, which expands the government's ability to prosecute whistleblowers, journalists, and activists who seek to uncover wrongdoing, abuse, and crime in the national security sphere.[4]

For all the idiosyncrasies and extreme tendencies of the Trump administration, its response to national security whistleblowers follows the well-worn pattern of past governments: an individual reveals privileged information in the name of the public interest; the state retaliates against them; the public, the press, and the courts struggle over the legitimacy and significance of the disclosures; and soon public debate settles around the personality and character of the whistleblower rather than the contents of the disclosure. This pattern is almost certain to continue no matter who the next president is.

That is because this paradigm is rooted deeper than any presidential administration. It is entrenched in the modern national security state and its culture of secrecy, in which any revelation is associated with espionage.

Examining the history helps us reckon with the broader phenomenon that has brought us here.

Whistleblowers fall into a binary: hero or traitor. Critics tar them with accusations of treachery, while supporters idealize them as saviors of democracy. Because of this, the public tends to examine the personalities and politics of individual whistleblowers. While this is understandable and not entirely without merit, it flattens complex human beings into one-dimensional caricatures. As Contragate exemplified, whistleblowers are not necessarily paragons of virtue or even upstanding citizens. Focusing on moral character continues a well-established process of shifting the terms of the debate away from the contents of a disclosure. Just as it was not possible to be sure about Yardley, Nickerson, Ellsberg, or Snepp, we don't definitively know the personalities or the politics of Snowden, Winner, Albury, or Hale. Speculation becomes dangerous when it overshadows public debate around secret surveillance, systemic discrimination, the reality of foreign wars and their casualties, and foreign interference in democratic elections. On the other side, the celebrification and heroization of whistleblowers reflects a political culture preoccupied with the revelation of secrets as a substitute for real political struggle.

Total state transparency is of course impractical, even dangerous. However, since the creation of the official secrecy regime, the executive branch has refused to acknowledge the possibility of a national security disclosure in the public interest. The legal and bureaucratic mechanisms designed to protect state secrets over the last century were improvised and often haphazard, resulting in inconsistencies, ambiguity, mismanagement, and overreach. Commentators, scholars, and legislators have sought an appropriate balance between security and liberty, but that discussion cannot occur without acknowledging how historical developments have circumscribed the very possibility of whistleblowing in the realm of national security. Debates about whether Snowden, Winner, or Hale are whistleblowers are products of this history, in which national security employees are bound to a secrecy regime for the rest of their lives. The idea of public-interest disclosures or the First Amendment rights of national security personnel are impossible.

The emergence of whistleblower-protection mechanisms is a reflection of the state's dogmatic approach to disclosures and efforts to define the phenomenon narrowly. The current whistleblowing-protection laws emerged in the context of indiscriminate state backlash against federal employees, but from the outset they excluded officials in the defense and intelligence establishment. The measures brought in to protect national security personnel over the past twenty years are not fully rooted in statute. Instead, they insist disgruntled officials use in-house reporting channels that "determine whether the complaint or information appears credible." Inspectors general in the national security agencies adjudicate whether the revelations should be relayed up the bureaucratic chain and eventually to Congress. Often they are not. These channels define "authorized disclosures" in narrow terms, focused on a "flagrant problem, abuse, [or] violation of law."[5] They are designed to enhance the functioning of national security, not to promote whistleblowing in the public interest.

The 2019 Ukraine whistleblowers who filed complaints about Trump's dealings with that country used the in-house channels, and it was largely because of congressional Democrat insistence that the revelations reached intelligence oversight committees and the public sphere. This unprecedented move was rooted in partisan wrangling around impeachment and the polarized politics of the Trump era. Nonetheless, debates in the immediate aftermath were marked by familiar tropes around whistleblowing, including the hero-traitor binary and doubts over whether the individuals were legitimate whistleblowers.[6]

The national security whistleblowing-protection mechanisms fail to acknowledge how the press—rather than the state—could be an appropriate arbitrator of what information is in the public interest. These internal channels have also perpetuated the very problem they were supposed to address: they have been used to retaliate against whistleblowers. In early 2018, congressional leaders expressed their dissatisfaction with the intelligence community's whistleblowing channels. The Intelligence and Judiciary Committees did not look to the executive branch to conduct a far-reaching review and instead conscripted the most prominent whistleblower NGO, the Government Accountability Project.[7]

Of course, what is or is not in the "public interest" will always be highly contested and conditioned by politics, ideology, and historical context. But definitions of the "public interest" cannot be left to the sole discretion of the government or politicians of the day to dictate what pertains to "national security." Moreover, unless national security whistleblowing is brought into closer conversation with other types of whistleblowing—social services, corporate, employment—it will remain exceptional, and its debates will remain ghettoized in the shadow of the national security state.

We cannot understand the national security whistleblowing phenomenon so long as we draw neat distinctions between whistleblowers and the press. The compromise struck over the first half of the twentieth century—the state could keep secrets, the national security employee could not disclose those secrets, but the press could publish them—was haphazard and imperfect. It was also contingent on a customary intimacy between the press and the executive branch, a bond that began to break down in the 1960s. While the Nixon administration tried unsuccessfully to attack newspapers, recent attacks on journalists and publishers who collaborate with whistleblowers pose clear dangers to press freedom. Despite the widespread dislike of Julian Assange, defenders of press freedom have highlighted the stakes of prosecuting someone under the Espionage Act who publishes or reports on information but does not have direct access to it. In the era of digital communication and surveillance, the bedrock principle of journalistic source protection is more and more embattled.[8]

To approach whistleblowing exclusively through political, security, or legal lenses ignores how the phenomenon reaches deep into civil society, social movements, and popular culture. Cultural representations of Ellsberg, Snowden, and Manning in particular have profoundly influenced popular consciousness. Simply put, the public is more likely to understand whistleblowing via popular culture than by reading the Espionage Act.

The last fifty years have seen the forging of a tradition of national security whistleblowing. It connects individual whistleblowers to one another as well as to civil society. While motives and ideologies differ, as Snowden once said, "If there had been no Thomas Drake, there would be no Edward Snowden." In 2013, Daniel Ellsberg declared, "I was Bradley Manning," and, two years later, he visited Snowden in Moscow. At age eighty-nine, Ellsberg continues to be one of the most outspoken defenders of national security whistleblowers.[9] The networks of activists, lawyers, and journalists that collaborate with whistleblowers have reflected and shaped professional and political cultures. GAP has become the pivotal whistleblower-advocacy group, bridging civil society and the state for over forty years. Activists have both inspired and been inspired by whistleblowers. This history has shaped the current work of filmmakers like Sonia Kennebeck, whose documentary film *National Bird* first brought Daniel Hale to public attention; lawyers like Jesselyn Radack, who represented Tom Drake and John Kiriakou and now represents Hale; and peace groups like Code Pink, who protested for many years on behalf of Chelsea Manning before Obama commuted her sentence in 2016. Despite the ongoing war on whistleblowing,

FIGURE 13.2

Protesters demonstrate in support of Chelsea (then Bradley) Manning in front of the White House, August 21, 2013.

Source: Photo by T. J. Kirkpatrick/Getty Images.Fig.

civil society and support networks have shaped a popular recognition of the phenomenon that pushes against the official state and legal frameworks.[10]

Recognizing the tradition of national security whistleblowing is not to valorize disclosure for its own sake nor to idealize the whistleblowers but instead to recognize a simple truth: The fates of national security whistleblowing and democracy are linked.

NOTES

1. "Exposing Secrets: The Past, Present, and Future of U.S. National Security Whistleblowing and Government Secrecy," London, January 17–18, 2019, https://wp.nyu.edu/whistleblowing/conference/.

2. At the time of writing, Snowden is president of the Freedom of the Press Foundation and recently authored a memoir, *Permanent Record* (New York: Metropolitan, 2019).

3. U.S. House Permanent Select Committee on Intelligence, "Review of the Unauthorized Disclosures of Former National Security Agency Contractor Edward Snowden," September 5, 2016, https://publicintelligence.net/us-hpsci-snowden-report/, 1–2, 4; Charlie Savage, "U.S. Tries to Seize Proceeds from Snowden's New Memoir," *New York Times*, September 17, 2019.

4. Dave Philipps, "Reality Winner, Former N.S.A. Translator, Gets More Than Five Years in Leak of Russian Hacking Report," *New York Times*, August 23, 2018, https://www.nytimes.com/2018/08/23/us/reality-winner-nsa-sentence.html; Rachel Weiner and Ellen Nakashima, "Former FBI Agent Gets Four Years in Prison for Leaking Classified Documents," *Washington Post*, October 18, 2018, https://www.washingtonpost.com/local/public-safety/former-fbi-agent-gets-four-years-in-prison-for-leaking-classified-documents/2018/10/18/be6eab54-d2ed-11e8-b2d2-f397227b43f0_story.html; Adam Goldman, "Ex-Intelligence Analyst Charged with Leaking Information to a Reporter," *New York Times*, May 9, 2019, https://www.nytimes.com/2019/05/09/us/politics/daniel-hale-leak-intercept.html; Jacy Fortin, "Chelsea Manning Ordered Back to Jail for Refusal to Testify in WikiLeaks Inquiry," *New York Times,* May 16, 2019, https://www.nytimes.com/2019/05/16/us/chelsea-manning-jail.html; Julian Barnes, "House Passes Intelligence Bill That Would Expand Secrecy Around Operatives," *New York Times*, July 17, 2019, https://www.nytimes.com/2019/07/17/us/politics/house-intelligence-authorization-act.html; Linda Moon, "Expanding the Covert Agent Secrecy Law Threatens to Chill Reporting," *Just Security*, July 25, 2019, https://www.justsecurity.org/65053/expanding-the-covert-agent-secrecy-law-threatens-to-chill-reporting/.

5. Intelligence Community Whistleblower Protection Act of 1998, https://www.congress.gov/bill/105th-congress/house-bill/3829/text.

6. Hannah Gurman and Kaeten Mistry, "The Ukraine Whistleblowers and the Breakdown of the Bipartisan War on Public Interest Whistleblowing," *Foreign Policy in Focus*, October 17, 2019, https://fpif.org/the-ukraine-whistleblowers-and-the-rise-of-partisan-whistleblowing/.

7. Jenna McLaughlin, "Lawmakers Demand Investigation Into Lack of Whistleblower Protections for Spies," *Foreign Policy*, January 18, 2018, https:/foreignpolicy.com/2018/01/18/lawmakers-demand-investigation-into-lack-of-whistleblower-protections-for-spies/.

8. Charlie Savage, "Julian Assange Charge Raises Fears About Press Freedom," *New York Times*, November 16, 2018, https://www.nytimes.com/2018/11/16/us/politics/julian-assange-indictment.html; Brian Barrett, "The Latest Julian Assange Indictment Is an Assault on Press Freedom," *Wired*, May 23, 2019, https://www.wired.com/story/julian-assange-espionage-act-threaten-press-freedom/; Alan Dershowitz, "Julian Assange Indictment Endangers Press Freedom," *The Hill*, May 24, 2019, https://thehill.com/opinion/judiciary/445447-julian-assange-indictment-endangers-press-freedom. Julian Assange is not an American citizen and has worked predominantly outside the United States. His prosecution thus poses dangers to press freedom both inside and outside the United States.

9. AJ+, "Edward Snowden on the Man Who Inspired His Work," *Al Jazeera America*, August 5, 2015, http://america.aljazeera.com/articles/2015/8/5/exclusive-edward-snowden-on-the-man-who-inspired-his-work.html; Daniel Ellsberg, "A Salute to Bradley Manning, Whistleblower, as We Hear His Words for the First Time," *Huffington Post*, May 12, 2013, https://www.huffpost.com/entry/bradley-manning-military-court-speech_b_2859353; Arundhati Roy and John Cusack, *Things That Can and Cannot Be Said: Essays and Conversations* (Chicago: Haymarket, 2016).

10. Government Accountability Project, "National Security," https://www.whistleblower.org/national-security/; *National Bird* (dir. Sonia Kennebeck, Ten Forward Films, 2016); Jesselyn Radack, "Whistleblowers Deserve Protection Not Prison," *New York Times*, December 18, 2013, https://www.nytimes.com/roomfordebate/2013/06/11/in-nsa-leak-case-a-whistle-blower-or-a-criminal/whistle-blowers-deserve-protection-not-prison; Jesselyn Radack, *Traitor: The Whistleblower and the "American Taliban"* (Whistleblower Press, 2012); Rachel Streitfeld, "Activists Rally to Free Bradley Manning in WikiLeaks Case," CNN, August 9, 2010, http://www.cnn.com/2010/CRIME/08/08/virginia.manning.rally/index.html.

FURTHER READING

Adams, Sam. *War of Numbers: An Intelligence Memoir.* 1966. Hanover, NH: Steerforth, 2012.

Agee, Philip. *Inside the Company: CIA Diary.* London: Penguin, 1975.

——. *On the Run.* Secaucus, NJ: Lyle Stuart, 1987.

Agee, Philip, Karl van Meter, and Louis Wolf, eds., *Dirty Work: The CIA in Western Europe.* New York: Dorset, 1978.

Ahmed, Sara. *The Cultural Politics of Emotion.* New York: Routledge, 2013.

Alford, C. Fred. *Whistleblowers: Broken Lives and Organizational Power.* Ithaca, NY: Cornell University Press, 2001.

Arendt, Hannah. "Lying in Politics." In *Crises of the Republic.* New York: Houghton Mifflin Harcourt, 1972.

——. "Truth and Politics." In *Between Past and Future.* New York: Penguin, 1969.

Baker, Peter. *Days of Fire: Bush and Cheney in the White House.* New York: Doubleday, 2013.

Bamford, James. *The Puzzle Palace: A Report on America's Most Secret Agency.* Boston: Houghton Mifflin, 1982.

Berlant, Lauren. *The Anatomy of National Fantasy: Hawthorne, Utopia, and Everyday Life.* Chicago: University of Chicago Press, 1991.

——. *The Queen of America Goes to Washington City: Essays on Sex and Citizenship.* Durham, NC: Duke University Press, 1997.

Brands, Hal. *Making the Unipolar Moment: U.S. Foreign Policy and the Rise of the Post–Cold War Order.* Ithaca, NY: Cornell University Press, 2016.

Braudy, Leo. *The Frenzy of Renown.* New York: Oxford University Press, 1986.

Braudy, Susan. *Family Circle: The Boudins and the Aristocracy of the Left.* New York: Knopf, 2003.

Brownlee, Kimberley. "The Civil Disobedience of Edward Snowden: A Reply to William Scheuerman." *Philosophy and Social Criticism* 42 (2016): 965–70.

Bulman-Pozen, Jessica, and David E. Pozen. "Uncivil Obedience." *Columbia Law Review* 115 (2015): 809–72.

Byrne, Malcolm. *Iran-Contra: Reagan's Scandal and the Unchecked Abuse of Presidential Power.* Lawrence: University Press of Kansas, 2014.

Capozzola, Christopher. *Uncle Sam Wants You: World War I and the Making of the Modern American Citizen.* New York: Oxford University Press, 2008.

Carle, Glenn L. *The Interrogator: An Education.* New York: Nation Books, 2011.

Carlson, Elliott. *Stanley Johnston's Blunder: The Reporter Who Spilled the Secret Behind the U.S. Navy's Victory at Midway.* Annapolis, MD: Naval Institute Press, 2017.

Castillo, Celerino. *Powderburns: Cocaine, Contras, and the Drug War.* Oakville, ONT: Mosaic, 1994.

Chen Mills, Amy. *CIA Off Campus: Building the Movement Against Agency Recruitment and Research.* Boston: South End, 1991.

Citizenfour. Directed by Laura Poitras. 2014.

Cockburn, Alexander, and Jeffrey St. Clair. *Whiteout: The CIA, Drugs, and the Press.* New York: Verso, 1997.

Colaresi, Michael. *Democracy Declassified: The Secrecy Dilemma in National Security.* New York: Oxford University Press, 2014.

Comey, James. *A Higher Loyalty: Truth, Lies, and Leadership.* New York: Flatiron, 2018.

Cullather, Nick. "Security and Liberty: The Imaginary Balance." In *The Snowden Reader*, ed. David P. Fiddler, 19–25. Bloomington: Indiana University Press, 2015.

Carruthers, Susan. *The Media at War.* 2nd ed. New York: Palgrave, 2011.

Davies, David R. *The Postwar Decline of American Newspapers.* Westport, CT: Praeger, 2006.

Dean, Michelle. "Contracts of Silence: How the Non-Disclosure Agreement Became a Tool for Powerful People to Stymie Journalists from Informing the Public." *Columbia Journalism Review*, Winter 2018. https://www.cjr.org/special_report/nda-agreement.php/.

Dean, Robert. *Imperial Brotherhood: Gender and the Making of Cold War Foreign Policy.* Amherst: University of Massachusetts Press, 2003.

Delmas, Candice. *The Duty to Resist: When Disobedience Should Be Uncivil.* New York: Oxford University Press, 2018.

——. "The Ethics of Government Whistleblowing." *Social Theory and Practice* 41 (2015): 77–105.

Devine, Tom, and Tarek F. Maassarani. *The Corporate Whistleblower's Survival Guide.* San Francisco: Berrett-Koehler, 2011.

Dewey, John. *The Public and Its Problems.* New York: Holt, 1927.

Draper, Theodore. *A Very Thin Line: The Iran-Contra Affairs.* New York: Hill & Wang, 1991.

Duffy, Peter. *Double Agent: The First Hero of World War II and How the FBI Outwitted and Destroyed a Nazi Spy Ring.* New York: Scribner, 2014.

Edgar, Harold, and Benno C. Schmidt Jr. "The Espionage Statutes and Publication of Defense Information." *Columbia Law Review* 73, no. 5 (May 1973): 930–1087.

Ellsberg, Daniel. "Secrecy and National Security Whistleblowing." *Social Research* 77 (2010): 773–804.

——. *Secrets: A Memoir of Vietnam and the Pentagon Papers.* New York: Viking Penguin Putnam, 2002.

Epstein, Edward Jay. *How America Lost Its Secrets: Edward Snowden, the Man and the Theft.* New York: Knopf, 2017.

Fallon, Mark. *Unjustifiable Means: The Inside Story of How the CIA, Pentagon, and U.S. Government Conspired to Torture.* New York: Reagan Arts, 2017.

Feaver, Peter. "Too Many Leaks." In "The Secret Sharers: Leaking and Whistle-Blowing in the Trump Era," *Foreign Affairs* 97, no. 6 (November/December 2018): 199–206.

Fenster, Mark. *Conspiracy Theories: Secrecy and Power in American Culture.* Minneapolis: University of Minnesota Press, 1999.

Fitzgerald, A. Ernest. *The High Priests of Waste.* New York: Norton, 1972.

Fortas, Abe. *Concerning Dissent and Civil Disobedience.* New York: Signet, 1968.

Franck, Thomas M., and Edward Weisband, eds. *Secrecy and Foreign Policy.* New York: Oxford University Press, 1974.

Frankfurt, Harry. *On Bullshit.* Princeton, NJ: Princeton University Press, 2005.

Friedman, Andrew. *Covert Capital: Landscapes of Denial and the Making of U.S. Empire in the Suburbs of Northern Virginia.* Berkeley: University of California Press, 2013.

Friedrich, Carl J. *The Public Interest.* New York: Atherton, 1962.

Gamson, Josh. *Claims to Fame: Celebrity in Contemporary America.* Berkeley: University of California Press, 1994.

Gardner, Lloyd C. *The War on Leakers: National Security and American Democracy, from Eugene V. Debs to Edward Snowden.* New York: New Press, 2016.

Glazer, Myron, and Penina Glazer. *The Whistleblowers.* New York: Basic Books, 1991.

Goodale, James. *Fighting for the Press: The Inside Story of the Pentagon Papers and Other Battles.* New York: CUNY Journalism Press, 2013.

Goren, Dina. "Communication Intelligence and the Freedom of the Press: The *Chicago Tribune*'s Battle of Midway Dispatch and the Breaking of the Japanese Naval Code." *Journal of Contemporary History* 16 (1981): 663–90.

Greenberg, David. *Nixon's Shadow: The History of an Image.* New York: Norton, 2004.

Greenwald, Glenn. *No Place to Hide: Edward Snowden, the NSA, and the Surveillance State.* New York: Metropolitan, 2014.

Gurman, Hannah. *The Dissent Papers: The Voices of Diplomats in the Cold War and Beyond.* New York: Columbia University Press, 2012.

H., Rebecca. "The 'Right to Write' in the Information Age: A Look at Prepublication Review Board." *Studies in Intelligence* 60, no. 4 (September 2016): 15–23, https://www.cia.gov/library /center-for-the-study-of-intelligence/csi-publications/csi-studies/studies/vol-60-no-4/the -right-to-write.html.

Harcourt, Bernard E. *Exposed: Desire and Disobedience in the Digital Age.* Cambridge, MA: Harvard University Press, 2015.

Harding, Luke. *The Snowden Files: The Inside Story of the World's Most Wanted Man.* London: Vintage, 2014.

Herken, Gregg. *The Georgetown Set: Friends and Rivals in Cold War Washington*. New York: Knopf, 2014.

Hertsgaard, Mark. *On Bended Knee: The Press and the Reagan Presidency*. New York: Schocken, 1998.

———. *Bravehearts: Whistleblowing in the Age of Snowden*. New York: Skyhorse, 2016.

Hess, Stephen. *The Government/Press Connection: Press Officers and Their Offices*. Washington, DC: Brookings Institution, 1984.

Hiam, Michael. *Who the Hell Are We Fighting: The Story of Sam Adams and U.S. Intelligence Wars*. Hanover, NH: Steerforth, 2006.

Hickman, Joseph. *Murder at Camp Delta: A Staff Sergeant's Pursuit of the Truth About Guantanamo Bay*. New York: Simon and Schuster, 2014.

Hickman, Joseph, and John Kiriakou. *The Convenient Terrorist: Two Whistleblowers' Stories of Torture, Terror, Secret Wars, and CIA Lies*. New York: Skyhorse, 2017.

Hogan, Michael J. *A Cross of Iron: Harry S. Truman and the Origins of the National Security State, 1945–1954*. New York: Cambridge University Press, 1998.

Holland, Max. *Leak: Why Mark Felt Became Deep Throat*. Lawrence: University Press of Kansas, 2012.

Hollister Hedley, John. "Secrets, Free Speech, and Fig Leaves: Reviewing the Work of CIA Authors." *Studies in Intelligence*, Spring 1998, https://www.cia.gov/library/center-for-the-study-of-intelligence/csi-publications/csi-studies/studies/spring98/Secret.html.

Holzer, Harold. *Lincoln and the Power of the Press: The War for Public Opinion*. New York: Simon and Schuster, 2014.

Hunt, Geoffrey, ed. *Whistleblowing in the Social Services: Public Accountability and Professional Practice*. London: Arnold, 1998.

Isikoff, Michael, and David Corn, *Hubris: The Inside Story of Spin, Scandal, and the Selling of the Iraq War*. New York: Broadway, 2007.

Jeffreys-Jones, Rhodri. *We Know All About You: The Story of Surveillance in Britain and America*. Oxford: Oxford University Press, 2017.

Johnson, Loch K. *A Season of Inquiry: The Senate Intelligence Investigation*. Lexington: University Press of Kentucky, 1985.

Johnson, Roberta Ann. *Whistleblowing: When It Works—and Why*. Boulder, CO: Lynne Rienner, 2003.

"Keeping Secrets: Congress, the Courts, and National Security Information." *Harvard Law Review* 103, no. 4 (February 1990): 906–25.

Kiriakou, John. *The Reluctant Spy: My Secret Life in the CIA's War on Terror*. New York: Bantam, 2009.

Kirkendall, Richard S., ed. *Civil Liberties and the Legacy of Harry S. Truman*. Kirksville, MO: Truman State University Press, 2013.

Kitrosser, Heidi. "Free Speech Aboard the Leaky Ship of State: Calibrating First Amendment Protections for Leakers of Classified Information." *Journal of National Security Law and Policy* 6 (2013): 409–46.

Knight, Peter. *Conspiracy Culture: From Kennedy to the X-Files*. London: Routledge, 2000.

Kohn, Stephen Martin. *The Whistleblower's Handbook: A Step-by-Step Guide to Doing What's Right and Protecting Yourself.* Guildford, CT: Lyons, 2011.

Kramer, Paul. "Power and Connection: Imperial Histories of the United States in the World." *American Historical Review* 116 (2011): 1348–91.

Kutler, Stanley, L. ed., *Abuse of Power: The New Nixon Tapes.* New York: Free Press, 1997.

Lebovic, Sam. *Free Speech and Unfree News: The Paradox of Press Freedom in America.* Cambridge, MA: Harvard University Press, 2016.

Leffler, Melvyn P. *Safeguarding Democratic Capitalism: U.S. Foreign Policy and National Security, 1920–2015.* Princeton, NJ: Princeton University Press, 2017.

Lester, Genevieve. *When Should State Secrets Stay Secret? Accountability, Democratic Governance, and Intelligence.* New York: Cambridge University Press, 2015.

Lewis, Carol W. "In Pursuit of the Public Interest." *Public Administration Review* 66, no. 5 (September/October 2006): 694–701.

Lichtblau, Eric. "The Untold Story of the Pentagon Papers Co-Conspirators." *New Yorker,* January 29, 2018. https://www.newyorker.com/news/news-desk/the-untold-story-of-the-pentagon-papers-co-conspirators.

Lipman, Frederick D. *Whistleblowers: Incentives, Disincentives, and Protection Strategies.* Hoboken, NJ: John Wiley, 2011.

Lowenthal, Mark M. *Intelligence: From Secrets to Policy.* Los Angeles: Sage, 2012.

Mackenzie, Angus. *Secrets: The CIA's War at Home.* Berkeley: University of California Press, 1997.

Madar, Chase. *The Passion of Bradley Manning: The Story of the Suspect Behind the Largest Breach in U.S. History.* New York: OR, 2012.

Marchetti, Victor. *Rope Dancer.* New York: Grosset & Dunlap, 1971.

Marks, John, and Victor Marchetti. *The CIA and the Cult of Intelligence.* New York: Knopf, 1974.

Maxwell, Lida. *Insurgent Truth: Chelsea Manning and the Politics of Outsider Truth-Telling.* New York: Oxford University Press, 2019.

Mayer, Jane. *The Dark Side: The Inside Story of How the War on Terror Turned Into a War on American Ideals.* New York: Anchor, 2008.

Mazzetti, Mark. *The Way of the Knife: The CIA, A Secret Army, and a War at the Ends of the Earth.* New York: Penguin, 2013.

McCarthy, David S. *Selling the CIA: Public Relations and the Culture of Secrecy.* Lawrence: University Press of Kansas, 2018.

McCoy, Alfred W. *The Politics of Heroin: CIA Complicity in the Global Drug Trade.* New York: Harper & Row, 1977.

——. *A Question of Torture: CIA Interrogation from the Cold War to the War on Terror.* New York: Metropolitan, 2006.

McGarvey, J. Patrick. *The CIA: The Myth and the Madness.* New York: Penguin, 1972.

McGehee, Ralph W. *Deadly Deceits: My 25 Years in the CIA.* New York: Sheridan Square, 1983.

McMillian, John. *Smoking Typewriters: The Sixties Underground Press and the Rise of Alternative Media in America.* New York: Oxford University Press, 2011.

Melley, Timothy. *The Covert Sphere: Secrecy, Fiction, and the National Security State.* Ithaca, NY: Cornell University Press, 2012.

——. *Empire of Conspiracy: The Culture of Paranoia in Postwar America*. Ithaca, NY: Cornell University Press, 2000.

Miceli, Marcia P., Janet P. Near, and Terry Morehard Dworkin, eds. *Whistle-Blowing in Organizations*. New York: Routledge, 2008.

Miller, Judith. *The Story: A Reporter's Journey*. New York: Simon & Schuster, 2015.

Mistry, Kaeten. "Embarrassing Indiscretions: The Origins and Culture of U.S. National Security Whistleblowing." In *The Culture of Intelligence: Germany, Britain, France, and the USA*, ed. Andreas Gestrich et al. Oxford: Oxford University Press, forthcoming.

——. "A Transnational Protest Against the National Security State: Whistleblowing, Philip Agee, and Networks of Dissent." *Journal of American History* 106, no. 2 (September 2019): 362–89.

Moran, Christopher. *Company Confessions: Secrets, Memoirs, and the CIA*. London: Biteback, 2015.

The Most Dangerous Man in America: Daniel Ellsberg and the Pentagon Papers. Directed by Judith Ehrlich and Rick Goldsmith. 2009.

Moynihan, Daniel Patrick. *Secrecy: The American Experience*. New Haven, CT: Yale University Press, 1998.

Mueller, Tom. *Crisis of Conscience: Whistleblowing in an Age of Fraud*. New York: Random House, 2019.

Murphy, Paul L. *World War I and the Origin of Civil Liberties in the United States*. New York: Norton, 1979.

Nader, Ralph, Peter Petkas, and Kate Blackwell, eds. *Whistle Blowing: The Report of the Conference on Professional Responsibility*. New York: Grossman, 1972.

Napoli, Russell P. *Intelligence Identities Protection Act and Its Interpretation*. New York: Nova Science, 2006.

Offe, Claus. "Whose Good Is the Common Good?" *Philosophy and Social Criticism* 38, no. 7 (September 2012): 665–84.

Olmsted, Kathryn S. *Challenging the Secret Government: The Post-Watergate Investigations of the CIA and FBI*. Chapel Hill: University of North Carolina Press, 1996.

——. *Real Enemies: Conspiracy Theories and American Democracy, WWI to 9/11*. New York: Oxford University Press, 2009.

On Company Business. Directed by Allan Francovich. 1980.

Oppenheim, Felix E. "Self-Interest and Public Interest." *Political Theory* 3, no. 3 (August 1975): 259–76.

Orentlicher, Diane F. "Snepp v. United States: The CIA Secrecy Agreement and the First Amendment." *Columbia Law Review* 81 (April 1981): 662–706.

Papandrea, Mary-Rose. "Leaker Traitor Whistleblower Spy: National Security Leaks and the First Amendment." *Boston University Law Review* 94 (2014): 449–544.

Parry, Robert. *Lost History: Contras, Cocaine, the Press, and Project Truth*. Arlington, VA: Medium Consortium, 1999.

Peters, Charles, and Taylor Branch. *Blowing the Whistle: Dissent in the Public Interest*. New York: Praeger, 1972.

Pineda, Erin. "Civil Disobedience and Punishment: (Mis)reading Justification and Strategy from SNCC to Snowden." *History of the Present* 5, no. 1 (2015): 1–30.

Pozen, David E. "Freedom of Information Beyond the Freedom of Information Act." *University of Pennsylvania Law Review* 165 (2017): 1097–1158.

——. "The Leaky Leviathan: Why the Government Condemns and Condones Unlawful Disclosures of Information." *Harvard Law Review* 127 (2013): 513–635.

Prados, John. *The Family Jewels: The CIA, Secrecy, and Presidential Power*. Austin: University of Texas Press, 2013.

——. *The Ghosts of Langley: Into the CIA's Heart of Darkness*. New York: New Press, 2017.

——. "Secrecy and Leaks: When the U.S. Government Prosecuted the *Chicago Tribune*." National Security Archive Briefing Book, October 25, 2017. https://nsarchive.gwu.edu /briefing-book/intelligence/2017-10-25/secrecy-leaks-when-us-government-prosecuted -chicago-tribune.

Preston, Andrew. "Monsters Everywhere: A Genealogy of National Security." *Diplomatic History* 38, no. 3 (June 2014): 477–500.

Rabban, David M. *Free Speech in its Forgotten Years*. Cambridge: Cambridge University Press, 1997.

Rabinowitz, Victor. *Unrepentant Leftist: A Lawyer's Memoir*. Chicago: University of Illinois Press, 1996.

Radack, Jesselyn. *Traitor: The Whistleblower and the "American Taliban."* Whistleblower Press, 2012.

Raskin, Marcus. *The Common Good: Its Politics, Policies, and Philosophy*. New York: Routledge, 1986.

Rawls, John. *A Theory of Justice*. Cambridge, MA: Harvard University Press, 1971.

Richardson, Peter. *A Bomb in Every Issue: How the Short, Unruly Life of* Ramparts *Magazine Changed America*. New York: New Press, 2009.

Roberts, Alasdair. *Blacked Out: Government Secrecy in the Information Age*. Cambridge: Cambridge University Press, 2006.

Rosenzweig, Paul, Timothy J. McNulty, and Ellen Shearer, eds. *Whistleblowers, Leaks, and the Media: The First Amendment and National Security*. Chicago: American Bar Association, 2015.

Ross Arnold, Jason. *Secrecy in the Sunshine Era: The Promises and Failures of U.S. Open Government Laws*. Lawrence: University Press of Kansas, 2014.

Rozell, Mark. J. *Executive Privilege: Presidential Power, Secrecy and Accountability*. 3rd ed. Lawrence: University Press of Kansas, 2010.

Rudenstine, David. *The Day the Presses Stopped: A History of the Pentagon Papers Case*. Berkeley: University of California Press, 1996.

Sagar, Rahul. *Secrets and Leaks: The Dilemma of State Secrecy*. Princeton, NJ: Princeton University Press, 2013.

Salter, Kenneth W. *The Pentagon Papers Trial*. Berkeley: Editorial Justa Publications, 1975.

Sargent, Daniel J. *A Superpower Transformed: The Remaking of American Foreign Relations in the 1970s*. New York: Oxford University Press, 2015.

Schenck Koffler, Judith, and Bennett L. Gershman. "The New Seditious Libel," *Cornell Law Review* 69, no. 4 (April 1984): 816–82.

Scheuermann, William. "Whistleblowing as Civil Disobedience: The Case of Edward Snowden." *Philosophy and Social Criticism* 40, no. 7 (2014): 609–28.

Schickel, Richard. *Intimate Strangers: The Culture of Celebrity.* New York: Doubleday, 1985.

Schoenfeld, Gabriel. *Necessary Secrets: National Security, the Media, and the Rule of Law.* New York: Norton, 2010.

Schrag, Peter. *Test of Loyalty: Daniel Ellsberg and the Rituals of Secret Government.* New York: Simon and Schuster, 1974.

Schudson, Michael. *The Rise of the Right to Know: Politics and the Culture of Transparency, 1945– 1975.* Cambridge, MA: Harvard University Press, 2015.

Schudson, Michael, and David Pozen, eds. *Troubling Transparency: The History and Future of Freedom of Information.* New York: Columbia University Press, 2018.

Schwartz, Tim. *A Public Service: Whistleblowing, Disclosure, and Anonymity.* New York: OR, 2019.

Secrets of the CIA. Directed by James Otis. 1998. https://www.youtube.com/watch?v=ut3UF9TIJ_E.

Sheinkin, Steve. *Most Dangerous: Daniel Ellsberg and the Secret History of the Vietnam War.* New York: Roaring Brook, 2015.

Smith, Jeffrey A. *Printers and Press Freedom: The Ideology of Early American Journalism.* New York: Oxford University Press, 1988.

Snepp, Frank. *Decent Interval: The American Debacle in Vietnam and the Fall of Saigon.* New York: Random House, 1977.

——. *Irreparable Harm: A Firsthand Account of How One Agent Took On the CIA in an Epic Battle Over Secrecy and Free Speech.* New York: Random House, 1999.

Snowden. Directed by Oliver Stone. 2016.

Snowden, Edward. *Permanent Record.* New York: Metropolitan, 2019.

Stanger, Allison. "No Ordinary Times." In "The Secret Sharers: Leaking and Whistle-Blowing in the Trump Era," *Foreign Affairs* 97, no. 6 (November/December 2018): 199–206.

——. *Whistleblowers: Honesty in America from Washington to Trump.* New Haven, CT: Yale University Press, 2019.

Stockwell, John. *In Search of Enemies: A CIA Story.* New York: Norton, 1978.

Stone, Geoffrey R. *Perilous Times: Free Speech in Wartime: From the Sedition Act of 1798 to the War on Terrorism.* New York: Norton, 2004.

——. *Top Secret: When Our Government Keeps Us in the Dark.* Lanham, MD: Rowman & Littlefield, 2007.

Sweeney, Michael S. *Secrets of Victory: The Office of Censorship and the American Press and Radio in World War II.* Chapel Hill: University of North Carolina Press, 2001.

Szilagyi, Andrew M. "Blowing Its Cover: How the Intelligence Identities Protection Act Has Masqueraded as an Effective Law and Why It Must Be Amended." *William & Mary Law Review* 51 (2010): 2269–312.

Taussig, Michael. *Defacement: Public Secrecy and the Labor of the Negative.* Stanford, CA: Stanford University Press, 1999.

Terrell, Jack. *Disposable Patriot: Revelations of a Soldier in America's Secret Wars.* Bethesda, MD: National Press Books, 1992.

Tyrrell, Ian, and Jay Sexton, eds. *Empire's Twin: U.S. Anti-Imperialism from the Founding Fathers to the Age of Terrorism.* Ithaca, NY: Cornell University Press, 2015.

Vladeck, Stephen I. "The Espionage Act and National Security Whistleblowing After Garcetti." *American University Law Review* 57 (2008): 1531–46.

——. "Inchoate Liability and the Espionage Act: The Statutory Framework and the Freedom of the Press." *Harvard Law and Policy Review* 1 (2007): 219–37.

——. "Is 'National Security Law' Inherently Paradoxical?" *American University National Security Law Brief* 1, no. 1 (2011): 11–17.

——. "Prosecuting Leaks Under U.S. Law." In *Whistleblowers, Leaks, and the Media: The First Amendment and National Security,* ed. Paul Rosenzweig et al., 29–42. Chicago: American Bar Association, 2015.

Walsh, Lawrence E. *Firewall: The Iran-Contra Conspiracy and Cover-Up.* New York: Norton, 1997.

Walzer, Michael. "Just and Unjust Leaks: When to Spill Secrets." *Foreign Affairs* 97, no. 2 (March/April 2018): 48–59.

——. *Obligations: Essays on Disobedience, War, and Citizenship.* Cambridge, MA: Harvard University Press, 1970.

War on Whistleblowers: Free Press and the National Security State. Directed by Robert Greenwald. 2013.

Wells, Christine. "National Security Information and the Freedom of Information Act." *Administrative Law Review* 56, no. 4 (Fall 2004): 1195–1221.

Wells, Tom. *Wild Man: The Life and Times of Daniel Ellsberg.* New York: Palgrave Macmillan, 2001.

Werth, Barry. *31 Days: The Crisis That Gave Us the Government We Have Today.* New York: Nan A. Talese, 2006.

White, Laura. "The Need for Governmental Secrecy: Why the U.S. Government Must Be Able to Withhold Information in the Interest of National Security." *Virginia Journal of International Law* 43 (2002): 1071–1110.

Wilford, Hugh. *The Mighty Wurlitzer: How the CIA Played America.* Cambridge, MA: Harvard University Press, 2008.

Winks, Robin W. *Cloak and Gown: Scholars in the Secret War, 1939–1961.* London: Harvill, 1987.

Wise, David, and Thomas B. Ross. *The Invisible Government.* New York: Random House, 1964.

Wright, Ann, and Susan Dixon. *Dissent—Voices of Conscience: Government Insiders Speak Out Against the War in Iraq.* Kihei, HI: Koa, 2008.

Young, Mark D. "National Insecurity: The Impacts of Illegal Disclosures of National Security Information." *I/S: A Journal of Law and Policy for the Informational Society* 10 (2014): 367–406.

CONTRIBUTORS

LLOYD C. GARDNER is the Charles Beard Professor of History at Rutgers University, emeritus, and a past president of the Society for Historians of American Foreign Relations. He is the author of nearly twenty books on American foreign relations. His most recent book is *The War on Leakers: National Security and American Democracy from Eugene V. Debs to Edward Snowden* (2016).

HANNAH GURMAN is clinical associate professor at New York University's Gallatin School of Individualized Study. She is the author of *The Dissent Papers: The Voices of Diplomats in the Cold War and Beyond* (2012) and editor of *Hearts and Minds: A People's History of Counterinsurgency* (2013).

RICHARD H. IMMERMAN is recently retired from Temple University, where he was professor of history, director of the Center for the Study of Force and Diplomacy, and distinguished faculty fellow. The recipient of multiple honors for his teaching and scholarship, Immerman was an assistant deputy director of national intelligence from 2007 to 2009, held the Francis W. De Serio Chair in Strategic Intelligence at the United States Army War College from 2013 to 2016, and has chaired the Historical Advisory Committee to the Department of State since 2010.

MATTHEW L. JONES is James R. Barker Professor of Contemporary Civilization at Columbia University. He is the author of *The Good Life in the Scientific Revolution* (2006) and *Reckoning with Matter: Calculating Machines, Innovation, and Thinking About Thinking from Pascal to Babbage* (2016) and is currently working on the history of data mining and surveillance.

JULIA ROSE KRAUT is a lawyer and a historian who writes about immigration and the First Amendment. She is the author of *Threat of Dissent: A History of Ideological Exclusion and Deportation in the United States* (forthcoming, 2020) and became the inaugural Judith S. Kaye Fellow for the Historical Society of the New York Courts in 2016.

SAM LEBOVIC is associate professor of history at George Mason University. He is the author of *Free Speech and Unfree News: The Paradox of Press Freedom in America* (2016), which was awarded the Ellis W. Hawley Prize, and is associate editor of the *Journal of Social History*.

LIDA MAXWELL is associate professor of political science and women's, gender, and sexuality studies at Boston University. She is the author of *Public Trials: Burke, Zola, Arendt, and the Politics of Lost Causes* (2014) and *Insurgent Truth: Chelsea Manning and the Politics of Outsider Truth-Telling* (2019).

TIMOTHY MELLEY is professor of English and director of the Humanities Center at Miami University. He is the author of *The Covert Sphere: Secrecy, Fiction, and the National Security State* (2012) and *Empire of Conspiracy: The Culture of Paranoia in Postwar America* (2000).

KAETEN MISTRY is senior lecturer in American history at the University of East Anglia. He is the author of *The United States, Italy, and the Origins of Cold War: Waging Political Warfare* (2016) and editor of *Reforms, Reflections, and Reappraisals: The CIA and U.S. Foreign Policy Since 1947* (2011).

DAVID E. POZEN is a professor of law at Columbia Law School, where he teaches and writes on constitutional law and information law, among other topics. In 2019, the American Law Institute named Pozen the recipient of its Early Career Scholars Medal.

JEREMY VARON is a professor of history at the New School. He is author of *Bringing the War Home: The Weather Underground, the Red Army Faction, and Revolutionary Violence in the Sixties and Seventies* (2004) and cofounder and editor of *The Sixties: A Journal of History, Politics, and Culture.*

INDEX

Naming Names column, 134. *See also* Marks
methodology
Nation (magazine), 137, 313
National Bird (2016), 345
national defense information, 4, 10, 34.
See also classified information; national
security information
national fantasy, 96, 109, 110, 114
National Geospatial Intelligence Agency,
341
National Lawyers Guild, 72, 75, 85
national security, 29–30, 34, 259, 310, 344;
affairs, 300; apparatus of, 31, 125;
disclosure, 342; dissenters, 174, 175;
employees, 195; establishment, 2, 21,
261; heroism and, 230; national security
law, 33; national security state, 4, 126,
130, 161, 246, 273, 341; officials, 144, 145;
Pentagon Papers and, 78; personnel,
129; public discussions of, 135; theory
and practice of, 124; underlying
purpose of, 21; widespread use of term,
15
National Security Agency (NSA), 1, 2, 26,
131, 180, 194; classification and, 331;
foreign intelligence and, 248; Fourth
Amendment and, 310; hacking of,
263–264; Hayden and, 307;
hypersecretive activities of, 331; Inman
and, 243; Iranian nuclear program and,
311; metadata collected by, 221;
Presidential Policy Directive 20, 223;
review authority for, 197; Snowden and,
329–330; terrorists and, 300;
unconstitutional surveillance practices
of, 88; warrantless surveillance by, 34;
wiretapping and, 306
National Security Alumni Association,
164
National Security Archive, 55, 205
National Security Council (NSC), 132, 139,
187, 243, 244, 254, 257, 271

National Security Decision Directive 84, 145
national security information, 18, 126, 130,
132. *See also* classified information;
national defense information
national security whistleblowing, 5, 36n1,
147, 189, 272, 327, 330; central paradox to,
9; concept of, 95, 96; definitions of, 30;
democracy and, 346; D. Ellsberg and,
124; genealogy of, 2; history of, 11;
interdisciplinary history of, 34; invoked
as existential threat, 9; key
characteristics of, 4, 28; motives behind,
31; new age of, 1; retaliation against, 23;
state retaliation and, 32; Trump and, 341;
unresolved questions for, 124
Navy, 45, 56
Navy Reserve, 24
NDA. *See* nondisclosure agreements
Nesson, Charles, 78, 86
Neutrality Act, 284, 285
New Left, 14, 15, 132
Newsweek (magazine), 105
New Yorker (magazine), 99
New York Review of Books (journal), 97
New York Times (newspaper), 3, 15, 28, 29, 34,
69, 78, 112, 228, 289, 318; ad in, 105; on
aluminum tubes, 304; Castillo and, 290;
credentials of, 315; Garin and, 87;
Manning and, 117; Miller at, 301, 316,
317; newspapers falling in line with
G. W. Bush, 305; not publishing
wiretapping story, 308; Schlesinger and,
99; Snowden and, 308; on wiretapping,
309
New York Times Co. v. United States
(1971), 78
New York Times Magazine, 100
Nicaragua, 271, 278
Nicaragua v. the United States, 164
Nickerson, John, 19, 45–46, 60, 62, 127, 342
Niger, 304, 312
Nimitz, Chester, 55

Vorenberg, James, 77
VVAW. *See* Vietnam Veterans Against the
War

Wallace, Mike, 227, 228
Wall Street Journal (newspaper), 227
Walzer, Michael, 331
War Department, 52
War on Drugs, 256
War on Leakers (Gardner), 33
War Production Board, 58
War Stories with Oliver North (television
show), 290
Washington Monthly (magazine), 13, 15, 128
Washington Post (newspaper), 15, 61, 78, 139,
243, 254, 275, 277, 308; Castillo and, 287,
290; Downie and, 319; Inman and, 266;
newspapers falling in line with G. W.
Bush, 305; Novak column in, 313
Washington Star-News (newspaper), 83
Washington Times (newspaper), 279, 280
Watergate, 21, 29, 124, 162, 195, 298; official
lies about, 213; Senate committee, 86;
special prosecutors investigating, 139
Watkins, Sherron, 222
weapons of mass destruction (WMD), 175,
234–235, 302, 303, 312
Weathermen Underground, 75, 85
Webb, Gary, 287–290
Weber, Max, 16, 46
Weinglass, Leonard, 79, 81, 91n48
Welch, Richard, 132, 141, 155
Wenner, Jann, 103–104, 106
West 57th (television show), 271, 279, 280
WHISPeR. *See* Whistleblower and Source
Protection Program
whistle, metaphor of, 11–12
Whistleblower Aid, 88
Whistleblower and Source Protection
Program (WHISPeR), 88
whistleblower-press relations, 291
Whistleblower Protection Act of 1989, 23

whistleblower-protection mechanisms,
22–26, 343
Whistle Blowing (book), 13, 14, 128
whistleblowing/whistleblower *vs.* leak/
leaker/leaking, 4–5, 10, 15, 26, 28, 30,
301
White House, 292, 299, 302, 309, 314; aides,
313; Contras and, 271, 273, 278, 283;
deceptions from, 95; haplessness of, 254;
Kiriakou and, 177; leaking from, 87;
Marchetti principle and, 139; officials,
136, 271, 283; "plumbers" from, 3, 102,
123–124; Stellar Wind and, 306;
J. Wilson and, 312
White House Correspondents Association,
53
Whyte, William H., 14
Wiebe, J. Kirk, 223
Wigand, Jeffrey, 227, 228
WikiLeaks, 25, 88, 245, 246, 261, 262, 292,
341; Assange and, 319; Manning and,
263; Pompeo on, 321
Wilkerson, Cathy, 75
Wilkerson, Lawrence, 174
Wilkes, Paul, 69, 86
willful communication, 17
Williams, Jake, 264, 265
Wilson, Charles, 45
Wilson, Joseph, 312, 314; campaign to
discredit, 313; Novak and, 315; "What I
Didn't Find in Africa," 312
Wilson, Sloan, 14
Wilson, Woodrow, 16, 48, 59
Winner, Reality, 1, 27, 209n8, 258, 259, 264,
341, 342
Winter Soldier Investigation, 162
wiretapping, 83, 306, 308, 309
Wise, David, 131
Wisner, Frank, 276
Witness (Chambers, W.), 217
Wizner, Ben, 88
WMD. *See* weapons of mass destruction

INDEX

GPSR Authorized Representative: Easy Access System Europe, Mustamäe tee
50, 10621 Tallinn, Estonia, gpsr.requests@easproject.com

www.ingramcontent.com/pod-product-compliance
Lightning Source LLC
Chambersburg PA
CBHW022132020426
42334CB00015B/857